WITHDRAW

Abridged
DEWEY
Decimal Classification ®

Contents

Abridged

DEWEY

Decimal Classification
and
Relative Index

Devised by

MELVIL DEWEY *1851-1931*

Edition 10

FOREST PRESS, INC.
OF
LAKE PLACID CLUB EDUCATION FOUNDATION

LAKE PLACID CLUB
NEW YORK 12946 U.S.A.
1971

Library of Congress Cataloging Data

Dewey, Melvil, 1851–1931.
  Abridged Dewey decimal classification and relative index.
Ed. 10.
  First–6th ed. published under title: Abridged decimal classifi-
cation and relativ index. 7th–9th ed. published under title:
Dewey decimal classification and relative index.

  1. Classification, Dewey decimal. I. Title.

Z696.D5192 1971   025.4'3   70–164427
ISBN 0–910608–13–X

THIS BOOK WAS COMPOSED, PRINTED AND BOUND
IN THE UNITED STATES OF AMERICA
AT KINGSPORT PRESS, INC., KINGSPORT, TENNESSEE

Contents

Publisher's Foreword

The first edition of the Decimal Classification, devised by Melvil Dewey in 1873 while still a student at Amherst College, was published in 1876, with a total of only 42 pages, of which 12 were tables, 18 index. By 1894 the Classification was in its 5th edition and had grown to 467 pages, with 235 of them tables, 191 index.

In 1894 the 1st abridged edition of the Decimal Classification appeared. Consisting of 194 pages (50 devoted to tables and 118 to index), it was about two fifths the size of the full edition. The tables contained approximately 1,100 numbers and constituted little more than a third summary: few numbers extended beyond three digits and those that did were mostly for geographical areas. It is interesting to note that each of the last three abridged editions (8–10) contains more pages than the 1894 full edition, but this is due primarily to the larger type and more open page format of the later editions.

Over the period since 1894 the connection between the abridged and the full editions has become closer; at first it was not felt necessary to follow each full edition with an abridged edition, but this has been the case beginning with the 4th abridged edition. The present Abridged edition 10 follows close on the heels of the three-volume Edition 18, on which it is based.

The purpose of the abridgments has been to provide a short form of the Classification adapted to the needs of small and slowly growing libraries. It has also come to serve well as an instrument for teaching the theory and application of the Dewey Decimal Classification and of classification in general.

Because of recurring complaints that the abridged editions were becoming too detailed and complex for the small collections for which they are intended, special attention has been given to Abridged edition 10 in an earnest effort to make it more suitable for the majority of its users. The present abridged edition is designed primarily for small general libraries, especially elementary and secondary school and small public libraries, in English-speaking countries, libraries with up to 20,000 titles *that do not expect to grow much larger*. This last criterion, new with this edition, has made simplifications possible, but with the result that the edition in some respects is not a true abridgment of the full edition. In fact, as well as having shorter numbers, the present abridged edition in some places presents different classification policies and slightly different numbers from those in Edition 18. The special characteristics and features of this edition are set forth in detail in the Preface, Introduction, and other explanatory matter that follows this Foreword.

To aid in achieving the desired goals two consultants, knowledgable as to the needs of small libraries, have studied the draft text for Abridged edition 10. The two consultants were Mary Louise Mann, formerly Coordinator of Secondary School Libraries, Washington Township, Indianapolis, Indiana, and presently a member of the Decimal Classification Editorial Policy Committee, and Mrs. Mary Seely Dodendorf, formerly Librarian in Charge, Catalog Department, Board of Education Library Section, Los Angeles, California. These consultants offered many valuable suggestions, and many of their recommendations have been incorporated. Some of the more far-reaching ones will have to await consideration for a future edition.

The editorial work on Abridged edition 10 was carried out by the Library of Congress under contract for Forest Press, Inc., as was that for Edition 18, with the policy advice of the Decimal Classification Editorial Policy Committee.

Forest Press, Inc. is a nonprofit subsidiary of Lake Placid Club Education Foundation. Its office has always been in Lake Placid, New York. On August 5, 1970, however, it opened a new office in Albany, New York, at the same time retaining its principal office in Lake Placid.

August 20, 1971

Preface

The Decimal Classification Editorial Policy Committee hopes that this 10th abridged edition will fill an unmet need of long standing. The Committee has recommended and Forest Press approved certain modifications in the editorial rules for this edition that should make it fit more nearly than the 7th, 8th, and 9th editions the requirements of the small general school and public libraries that are expected to be its chief users.

1 Relation to full edition Recent abridged editions have been developed from the respective full editions upon which each was based on the premise that all libraries will grow in size indefinitely, and that, therefore, even the smallest library using the abridged Dewey should be able, as it grows, to expand and deepen its classification simply by lengthening the class numbers used. Since in some sections the structure of the full system is very irregular, this has meant that many provisions had to be included that went far beyond the present needs of those very institutions for which they were intended. The present edition abandons that position, and is addressed to the thousands of general libraries that have no expectation of ever growing very big. It is not, therefore, in the strictest sense an *abridgment* of the full 18th edition, but a close *adaptation* of it.

Like those of Edition 18, the schedules of Abridged 10 are based on the principle of subject integrity. Both the subject matter and the notation are hierarchical, so that what is true of a given whole is true of all its parts. The schedules are developed according to logical principles, so that the classifier is guided to make correct decisions. The terminology of the classification scheme reflects the terminology used by the literature being classified.

For ease of use, this edition includes more example notes, more detailed and precise instructions, and freer use of laymen's terminology than did its immediate predecessor.

2 Degree of expansion For the reasons set forth in section 1 this edition provides not only fewer numbers than Edition 9, but also fewer opportunities to build numbers.

A comparative table of the number of entries in Editions 9 and 10 follows. This does not include centered headings, which are duplicated by the numbers that follow them, or entries for which the numbers are printed in brackets.

Class	Edition 9		Edition 10		Change	
	Total entries	Entries with built-in expansion	Total entries	Entries with built-in expansion	Total entries	Entries with built-in expansion
0	125	3	128	6	+3	+3
1	140	0	134	0	−6	0
2	192	15	175	10	−17	−5
3	458	32	436	30	−22	−2
4	137	20	103	10	−34	−10
5	276	16	223	15	−53	−1
6	409	6	311	1	−98	−5
7	377	13	317	10	−60	−3
8	156	6	127	12	−29	+6
9	260	73	257	73	−3	0
Total schedules	2,530	184	2,211	167	−319	−17
Tables	308	1	331	1	+23	0
Grand total	2,838	185	2,542	168	−296	−17

"Entries with built-in expansion" are those entries included in the total that may be expanded into additional entries by the application of instructions that appear in the schedules and tables.

3 **Notable new features**   This edition contains many new features, some of which are so notable as to justify special mention.

3.1 Tables   The utility of the Area Table and Table of Standard Subdivisions in Edition 9 proved itself so well that two more auxiliary tables have been added in Edition 10. The four tables, which appear following the introductory matter, are numbered for precise identification as follows:

1. *Standard Subdivisions*
2. *Areas*
3. *Subdivisions of Individual Literatures*   Used thruout 810–899, this table
   eliminates the back-and-forth page turning required by the number-building
   instructions in the 800 schedule of Edition 9.
4. *Subdivisions of Individual Languages*   Used thruout 420–499.

The auxiliary tables are now called "tables," while the main classification schedules, in earlier editions usually referred to as "tables" or "general tables," are now officially called "schedules."

3.2 Add instructions   The former instructions to expand a number or span of numbers by dividing like another span of numbers have been replaced by instructions that specify exactly what digits should be added to what base number.

3.3 DISCONTINUED NUMBERS For the first time, the schedules include discontinued numbers, i.e., numbers from the immediately preceding edition vacated because their content has been moved back to more general numbers. A note will indicate where the topics formerly in the dropped numbers are now to be classed. There are 188 of these discontinued numbers in this edition. The Committee hopes that this measure will eliminate some uncertainties that classifiers working with earlier editions have experienced. The information on discontinued numbers and relocations (see section 4) is also consolidated in a separate list following the tables, where it can be surveyed by classifiers planning how best to adjust their records to this new edition. As an additional aid, the few reused numbers are listed in section 4 of this preface.

3.4 CONCEPTS IN CENTERED HEADINGS Each of the 145 centered headings, which are used where a single concept is represented by a span of numbers, is accompanied by a note telling the classifier where to class comprehensive works on that concept.

3.5 PHOENIX SCHEDULES Completely remodeled schedules have been prepared for two disciplines, 340 Law and 510 Mathematics. Each is built on the same base number as the schedule it supersedes, but any other resemblance is likely to be coincidental. Such schedules are approved by the Committee only when the provisions of earlier editions are deemed entirely inadequate for classification of modern concepts. The obsolescent schedules and tables of concordance between the old and new schedules are included in this edition following the index to aid libraries in any reclassifying of their law and mathematics collections.

3.6 EXTRATERRESTRIAL WORLDS Looking toward the future, the DDC is beginning to become slightly less earth-oriented. By adjusting "Areas" notation 98 so as to accommodate Antarctica, Edition 10 makes "Areas" notation 99 available for extraterrestrial worlds, thus enabling the system to provide for anticipated literature on petrology of the moon, and later, no doubt, on the mineral resources of Mars, and even on conditions in the planetary system of Arcturus.

3.7 INDEX The index to Edition 10 contains entries for the terms named in the schedules and tables. Many entries are in the form of cross references, so that information is not duplicated repeatedly. The classifier may have to consult several entries to obtain all the information available, but at each step he will find at least one additional number, and will in all cases find either full and exact numbers or all the blocks needed to build a full and exact number.

This index does not indicate relocations as did the indexes of Editions 8 and 9. Relocations can be found and identified thruout the schedules and tables, and also in a special list.

4 Relocations There are 141 relocations, as compared with 281 in Edition 9 and 146 in Edition 8. A fair number of these are the result of the changes from abridgment to adaptation described in section 1, e.g., specific kinds of birds from 598.3–.9 to 598.2. The count and distribution are as follows:

Class	Number of relocations
0	4
1	1
2	1
3	41
4	4
5	14
6	36
7	25
8	3
9	0
Tables	12

Twelve numbers or spans are reused with new meanings: 230.1–.9, 252.01–.09, 264.01–.09, 331.702, 604, 614.5, 684.08–.09, 690.5–.8, 774, "Standard Subdivisions" notation 04, "Areas" notations 564 and 99. These numbers appeared in Edition 9 or earlier editions with different meanings.

The figures for both relocations and reused numbers exclude the numbers in the two completely new schedules, 340 Law and 510 Mathematics.

5 Spelling The founder of DDC (who was christened Melville Dewey, and for a time styled himself Melvil Dui) was deeply devoted to the cause of simplified spelling. This edition, in observance of tradition, continues the following practices: (1) it uses such forms as *catalog, program, tho, thoro,* and *thru;* and (2) it follows, to the extent that the editors found them, the shortest and most phonetic spellings recognized by Webster's *Seventh New Collegiate Dictionary,* e.g., *alinement.*

Members of the Decimal Classification Editorial Policy Committee during the preparation of this edition have been Margaret E. Cockshutt, Edwin B. Colburn, Betty M. E. Croft, Joel C. Downing (special representative from the (United Kingdom) Library Association), Virginia Drewry, Carlyle J. Frarey, Doralyn J. Hickey, Frances Hinton, John A. Humphry, Mary Louise Mann, Clare E. Ryan, Pauline A. Seely, Mrs. Marietta D. Shepard, and William J. Welsh. We hope not only that this edition may be better than its predecessors, but that future editions will be even better.

Frances Hinton
CHAIRMAN, DECIMAL CLASSIFICATION
EDITORIAL POLICY COMMITTEE

The Free Library of Philadelphia
Philadelphia, Pennsylvania 19103
August 1, 1971

Introduction

Comments on Structure and Use

1. Book classification

"Every reader his book." In these words S. R. Ranganathan described one of the major functions of libraries: to see that readers and students are led as directly as possible to the material they need. A number of devices are used for this purpose, one of which is classification.

Virtually any given set of objects may be classified, since to classify is simply to place together objects having certain characteristics in common, and to separate them from objects not having those characteristics. Textile fabrics, for example, can be classified by material (silk, cotton, wool), or form (knitted, crocheted, woven), or purpose (clothing, carpeting, bedclothing), or even color.

Classification of library materials (books, films, sound recordings, and other media) means their arrangement in such a manner as to bring together works dealing with the same subject. A classification scheme, such as the present one, is a listing of subjects covering the world of knowledge (or part of it) in some systematic order, together with a notation, or set of symbols, which can be affixed to books for their easy arrangement.

Although reader-interest groupings or other homemade arrangements are sometimes used, most librarians have found it preferable to follow one of the major existing book classification systems. The principal ones in use in the English-speaking world are the Dewey Decimal Classification and the Library of Congress Classification. The advantages of using one of these are that their notations are widely known and understood by other librarians and laymen, and that centralized cataloging services such as those of the Library of Congress, the H. W. Wilson Company, and the *British National Bibliography* use one or more of them for classification of specific books, thus making highly professional decisions available to subscribing libraries.

2. Dewey Decimal Classification

2.1 Basic plan and application The most widely used of all book classification systems, as well as the oldest, is the Dewey Decimal Classification, which is a hierarchical, or graduated, system using the decimal principle for subdivision; that is, each group in the successive division of knowledge is arrayed on a base of ten.

The first division is into ten main classes, covering the whole of human knowledge, and numbered 0, 1, 2, 3, 4, 5, 6, 7, 8, 9. Main class 0 is used for general works on many subjects from many points of view, such as general newspapers and encyclopedias, and also for certain specialized disciplines that deal with knowledge generally, such as information and communication, library science, and journalism. Main classes 1–9 consist each of a major discipline or group of related disciplines. Following are the ten main classes with their assigned meanings:

0	Generalities	5	Pure sciences
1	Philosophy and related	6	Technology (Applied sciences)
	disciplines	7	The arts
2	Religion	8	Literature (Belles-lettres)
3	The social sciences	9	General geography and history and
4	Language		their auxiliaries

In practice the notation always consists of at least three digits, with zero being used with its normal arithmetical value where required to fill out a number to three digits. Thus the full DDC notation for main class 6 is 600. The notation used to designate the complete span of each main class consists of one hundred three-digit numbers, e.g., 000–099 for generalities, 300–399 for social sciences, 600–699 for applied sciences.

Each main class has ten divisions, likewise numbered 0–9. These division numbers occupy the second position in the notation. Division 0 is used for general works on the entire main class, 1–9 for subclasses of the main class. Thus, 60 is devoted to general works on the applied sciences, 61 to medical sciences, 62 to engineering and allied operations, 63 to agriculture and related technologies, etc. The full DDC notations for these divisions, each filled out by the addition of a zero, are 600 for general works on main class 6, 610 for medical sciences, 620 for engineering, 630 for agriculture.

Again, each division has ten sections, also numbered 0–9. The section numbers occupy the third position in the notation. Thus, the full span of section numbers for each division listed above is 600–609, 610–619, 620–629, 630–639. In the sections, the 0 in the third position in the number is applied to general works on the entire division, and 1–9 are used for subsubclasses. Thus, 630 is assigned to agriculture and related technologies in general, 631 to agricultural techniques and apparatus, 632 to plant injuries, diseases, pests, and their control, 633 to production of field crops, 636 to animal husbandry. The system permits further subdivision to any degree desired, with a continued decimal notation, which consists of the addition, following any set of three digits from 000 to 999, of a decimal point and as many more digits as may be required. Thus, 631 for techniques and apparatus is divided into 631.2 for agricultural structures, 631.3 for agricultural tools, machinery, equipment, 631.5 for cultivation and harvesting, and other topics.

8

Preceding the full classification schedules are three summaries, showing in full notation the ten main classes, the one hundred divisions, and the almost one thousand sections.

Individual numbers in Dewey are not necessarily limited each to a specific or single subject. Altho many subjects have their own numbers, e.g., Swedish language 439.7, many other specific subjects are grouped together in a single notation, e.g., Danish and Norwegian languages both 439.8, all the African languages 496.

2.11 APPLICATION Each work acquired by a library may be assigned to one of the main classes, divisions, sections, or subsections to the degree of detail provided by the schedules of the DDC, and may be identified as belonging to its specific class by use of the appropriate notation. (The word class is used to refer to a main class or a subdivision of any degree, be it 600 or 620 or 621 or 621.3848.) The notation, or number, designates the work's class; when written on the work and on the catalog and other cards that describe the work, it provides a shorthand identification of the work's subject and determines its relative position within the library's entire collection and within the appropriate discipline.

To distinguish further the works in a class and to expedite identification, shelving, and physical retrieval, many large libraries and some smaller ones combine with the class number a book number; these together constitute the call number. The book number is usually based on authorship, but may, as in biography, be based on alphabetical subarrangement of individual subjects within the class notation. For the use and construction of book numbers the reader should consult Bertha R. Barden's *Book Numbers* (Chicago, American Library Association, 1937). Many libraries select author numbers from the Cutter or Cutter-Sanborn *Author Tables* (Chicopee, Mass., H. R. Huntting Co., 1969), or follow the system of *Author Numbers* used by the Library of Congress (Washington, D.C., 1966). Other systems sometimes used for arrangement within classes are by authors' surnames spelled out, by one or more letters of authors' surnames, and by dates of publication.

2.12 DISCIPLINE The concept of discipline, or branch of learning, is fundamental to an understanding of the Dewey system. The primary basis for DDC arrangement and development of subjects is by discipline, as defined by the main and subordinate classes, while subject, strictly speaking, is secondary. There is no one place for any subject in itself; a subject may appear in any or all of the disciplines. No class can be said to cover the scope of marriage, or water, or copper, or Brazil; in other words, there is no single number for any of these concepts or subjects. A work on marriage belongs in 301 if it deals with the sociological aspects of the subject, in 155 if the psychological, in 173 if the ethical, in 390 if it deals with customs, in 613 if it deals with hygiene. Similarly, a work on water may be classed with many disciplines, such as metaphysics, religion, economics, commerce, physics, chemistry, geology, oceanography, meteorology, and history.

No other feature of the DDC is more basic than this: that it scatters subjects by discipline. The index illustrates this quite clearly. Here, under each subject, will be found the numbers in which it may be classed according to its aspects, that is, the disciplines under which it may fall. For example:

Metals	669
arts	
engraving *see* Metal engraving	
handicrafts	745.56
sculpture *see* Metals sculpture	
chemistry	
inorganic	546
organic	547
technology	661
construction	
architecture	721
building	693.7
materials	
building	691
engineering	620.1
shipbuilding	623.82
metallography	669
metallurgy	669
mineral aspects	
economic geology	553
mineralogy	549
mining	622
pharmacology	615
products	
arts *see* Metals arts	
manufacturing	671–673
sculpture	
decorative arts	739
fine arts	731
toxicology	615.9

2.13 HIERARCHY The DDC is basically hierarchical in notation, and also in disciplinary and subject relationships.

2.131 *In notation* Hierarchy in notation means that each successive division of the discipline or subject is represented by a corresponding lengthening of the significant notation by one digit. To show this clearly in the schedules, the heading for each successive subdivision is indented to show explicitly its subordination to a broader concept, with depth of indention ordinarily depending on length of number. (For convenience in printing, indention is not used to show the subordination of a division to its main class.)

600	Technology (Applied sciences)	[Significant notation is 6]
620	Engineering and allied operations	[Significant notation is 62]
621	Applied physics	
621.3	Electrical, electronic, electromagnetic engineering	
621.38	Electronic and communication engineering	
621.388	Television	
621.388 8	Manufacturing and servicing of receiving sets	

The space between the sixth and seventh digits of the last number is not a basic part of the notation, but, for ease in reading, is left after each successive set of three digits beyond the decimal point in all numbers enumerated in the classification schedules and index.

Sometimes it will be found that there is a step in the successive divisions of the discipline or subject for which a unique position in the lengthening digital notation is not available. Such steps are shown in the schedules by spans of numbers; these are called centered headings. For example, under 380 Commerce, trade is covered in 381–382, communication services in 383–384, transportation services in 385–388. There is no possibility for digital expression of any of these major subdivisions of 380, and each is shown in the schedules, therefore, by a centered heading, e.g.,

▶ 385–388 Transportation services

385   Railroad transportation

For the classification of comprehensive works on the concept expressed in the heading, see section 3.43.

The subdivisions of a discipline or topic are not always to be found in notations subordinate to (and therefore longer than) the notation for the discipline or topic itself; these situations reflect the desire of Melvil Dewey and his successors to keep the notation as short as possible. For example, altho biology is denoted by 574, its branches the botanical and zoological sciences are classed in 580 and 590 respectively, rather than in 574.+.

The digit 0 when not in a terminal position is generally used to indicate a different basis for division of the discipline or subject represented by the digits preceding the 0, e.g.,

200	Religion
220	Bible
220.1	Origins and authenticity
220.6	Interpretation and criticism
221	Old Testament
225	New Testament
229	Apocrypha and other deuterocanonical works

In this sequence 220.1–.9 are used for general works dealing with the whole Bible in a particular way, whereas 221–229 are used for specific parts of the Bible.

2.132 *In discipline and subject* Hierarchy in disciplinary and subject relationships means that every concept in a notation more specific than that of a main class is subordinate to all the broader concepts of which it is a part, and whatever is true of each whole is true of all its parts. For example, whatever is stated to be true of 600 is likewise true of all its subdivisions, what is true of 620 is true of all *its* subdivisions, what is true of 621 is true of all its subdivisions, and so on down to the finest subdivision. Hence the note under 500 Pure sciences, "Class here comprehensive works on pure and applied sciences," applies to each subdivision: to 530, where are classed works dealing with both pure and applied physics, to 540, where are classed works dealing with both pure and applied chemistry, and to all the others. Similarly, the instruction under 631 General agricultural techniques, "Class applications to specific crops [and] products . . . in 633–638" applies to every part of 631; consequently, harvesting corn should be classed not in 631.5 for harvesting but in 633 for field crops including corn.

2.2 **Memory aids** The DDC notation lends itself readily to combining subjects, with the benefit of numerous memory aids. The auxiliary tables form the basis for much of the number building that results in uniform meanings of numbers in various contexts.

2.21 Areas The most notable memory aid is the constant repetition of a standard pattern of area arrangement. In nearly all developments by place, the digits 44, for instance, stand for France, 45 for Italy, 46 for Spain, 52 for Japan, 73 for United States. Consequently, since 9 is the significant notation for general history, 944 denotes history of France, 945 of Italy, 946 of Spain, 952 of Japan, 973 of United States. Likewise, since 91 is the significant notation for general geography, 914.4 designates geography of France, 914.5 of Italy, 917.3 of United States. These area numbers appear in Table 2, "Areas."

2.22 Languages Another common repetition is that of the numbers for languages. In this pattern 2 is used for the English language, 3 for German, 4 for French, etc. In most cases the language numbers for linguistics in main class 400 and literature in main class 800 are the same, e.g., 420 English linguistics, 820 English literature, 430 German linguistics, 830 German literature. In other subjects where the basis of subdivision is linguistic, the language sequence is closely parallel to that of 400 and 800. Under 030 Encyclopedias, for example, 031 is used for United States and Canadian English-language encyclopedias, 032 for other English-language encyclopedias, 033 for those in the Germanic languages, etc.

2.23 Other Various other patterns appear as a result of parallel subject developments, a full development at one place being repeated by analogy at other places. For example, botany at 581 and zoology at 591 are given the same development as biology at 574 (by means of the instruction "add . . . the numbers following 574"); the major languages are given the same development ("add . . . 'Subdivisions of Individual Languages' notation . . . from Table 4");

the Old and New Testaments at 221 and 225 respectively are developed like the Bible as a whole in 220. In fact, bibliographies and catalogs of specific subjects in 016 are given the same development as the whole classification, e.g., bibliography of applied sciences 016.6, of agriculture and related technologies 016.63, of harvesting 016.6315.

2.24 STANDARD SUBDIVISIONS A special kind of patterned repetition is that of the standard subdivisions, listed in Table 1. Virtually any subject or discipline may be presented in various forms: in a synopsis or outline, in a periodical, in a collection of writings, in tables, in illustrations. Similarly, most subjects may have certain modes of treatment in common: theory, technique, study and teaching, history. These common forms and modes are designated collectively as standard subdivisions, and they may be applied wherever they are appropriate. Their notation consists of two or more digits, of which the first is 0, e.g., 05 Serial publications. These digits may be added to any significant notation taken or derived from the schedules, e.g., serials on the applied sciences 605 (main class 6 plus standard subdivision 05), serials on agriculture and related technologies 630.5 (division 63 plus 05, with a decimal point following the third digit), serials on general agricultural techniques 631.05, on cultivation and harvesting 631.505. (See also section 3.353.)

2.3 The abridged edition A valuable feature of the Dewey notation, not shared by some of the other commonly used classification systems, is its adaptability to the needs of libraries of different sizes and natures. The DDC can be used equally as well for broad classification as for close. For example, a small library, or a large one with only a few titles on the subject, can class the production of any and all field crops in 633 without subdivision. A somewhat larger library, using the 18th unabridged edition, can class general works in 633, works on production of cereal crops in 633.1, of forage crops in 633.2, and so on. A library with a still larger collection can divide its books into such detail as it requires, e.g., wheat 633.11, millet 633.171, rubber plants 633.8952. As any library's collection increases in size, its books can be distinguished in finer and finer detail simply by the addition of further digits to the notation. A work on irrigation by furrow system can be placed in 631, 631.5, 631.58, 631.587, or 631.5872, depending on the degree of closeness in classification required. The full edition of the DDC may be used by general libraries of any size, from the largest, which may follow it in full detail for most subjects, to the smallest, which may reduce any or all schedules to the degree considered desirable. This abridged edition supplies reduction on a ready-made basis and is convenient for small libraries to use on that account.

Recent editions of the Abridged DDC have been so designed that any user could, at any time, for any part of its collections, divide its classes in more detail and expand into the accompanying unabridged edition simply by adding more digits to the class numbers already in use. Because of the DDC's historical irregularities, this made it necessary to give some of the abridged provisions in more detail than was appropriate for a small library. This edition discontinues that practice, and, as a result, expansion from its provisions into those of the full edition will require in many cases the *changing of existing digits*, not merely the adding of digits. For example, this edition provides for the biology of birds in 598.2; so does Edition 18, for general works, but for specific kinds of birds it provides the irregular development 598.3–.9 rather than 598.21–.29. A library using this abridged edition and suddenly falling heir to a large collection on ornithology requiring more detailed treatment than is afforded by the single number 598.2 must, to grow into the provisions of Edition 18, change 598.2 on many books and records to 598.3+, 598.4+, and so on thru 598.99.

In general, this 10th edition of the Abridged Dewey is intended for the classification of library materials in general elementary and secondary school and small public libraries in English-speaking countries, that have no particular specialization requiring detailed classification, and that do not expect to grow a great deal larger. Those that expect to grow much beyond 20,000 titles or that have fields of substantial specialization should use the full edition from the outset, reducing the provisions of individual schedules as current needs require.

Other kinds of libraries may also use this edition with profit, e.g., special libraries for works outside their fields of specialization, church libraries, private and personal libraries. It may also be used to organize personal information files, whatever their physical form.

3. How to use Dewey

3.1 Preliminaries Before the classifier tries to use the Dewey Decimal Classification, he should acquaint himself with the system as a whole. In particular, he should study the three main summaries preceding the schedules and learn the first summary of the ten main classes; he should then leaf thru the schedules. Knowledge of the pattern will come rapidly with use, and especially so if, in classifying, he consults the schedules first rather than the index. He should notice the effect of the principle of hierarchy: each entry is a part of and governed by every entry superior to it. To understand the full meaning and force of 621.3888, he must view it as a part of 621.388, which, in turn, is a part of 621.38, which is a part of 621.3, which is a part of 621, which is a part of 620, which is a part of 600.

He should not fail to look thru the four auxiliary tables.

He should also observe carefully the special nature of main classes 8 and 0. In class 8, subject is disregarded for works of pure literature, e.g., a play about Julius Caesar and Roman history, whether by Shakespeare or a novice, is a piece of imaginative literature, and belongs in the appropriate part of 800 instead of under history or biography. Arrangement of literature is first by the discipline belles-lettres, then by original language, then by literary form, e.g., literature (800), English (820), drama (822). In class 0, general encyclopedias (030), serials (050), newspapers (071–079), collections (080), and general publications of general organizations (061–068) have no specific subject, and are part of no one discipline; the most significant thing about them, after their generality, is their form. Arrangement of such generalities is first by form, then by language or place as the schedules provide, e.g., general serial publications (050), English (052), general organizations (060), in England (062). In all other classes (including 000–029, 069, 070.1–.9, 090) arrangement is first by most specific discipline and most specific subject under it, then by place, then by time if the schedules permit, then by form of presentation, e.g., social sciences (300), political science (320), legislature (328), United States (328.73), pictorial works (328.73022).

3.2 Analysis of a work   Before he can fit a work into the system, or class it, the classifier must know exactly what its subject is, and from what point of view and in what form that subject is treated. To discover this is not always easy: (1) Sometimes the *title* indicates what the work is about; however, this is often misleading, and some further investigation should always be made as a check. (2) For a book, *the table of contents* is usually an excellent guide to the subject matter. (3) If there is no table of contents, *chapter headings* and *marginal notes* are likely to give a good indication of the contents. Clues may also be provided by *bibliographies* and *lists of sources* used by the author. (4) It is always wise to scan the *preface* for the author's point of view, and the *blurb* for a general description of the work, tho the latter may be misleading. (5) If such sources prove unsatisfactory, a careful examination of the *text* may be necessary. (6) If the subject is complex or unfamiliar to the classifier, he may have to go to external sources. Information regarding the subject of the work may often be obtained from bibliographies, catalogs, biographical dictionaries, histories of literature, encyclopedias, reviews, and other *reference works.* (7) Subject *experts* should be consulted when all other methods fail, and sometimes for verification of a tentative decision. However, subject experts should not be encouraged to suggest improvements in the classification schedules; what is needed from them is assistance in placing, within the existing scheme, given works dealing with unfamiliar subjects.

The classifier should note that many works cover two or three or many subjects, considered separately or in their interrelationships; and that many works deal with two or more aspects of one or more subjects, that is, with a subject or subjects within two or several disciplines. Examples are works treating of both the economics and the technology of the textile manufacturing industry; of both nuclear physics and nuclear engineering; of both architectural design and construction principles of dwelling houses; and of the sociological, ethical, and religious aspects of divorce. The classifier should note, too, the current trend toward interdisciplinary studies in depth, particularly in the social sciences. To become a good practitioner of classification, it is most important that he analyze each work carefully, not only to ascertain its subject or subjects but also to determine to what extent it crosses traditional disciplinary lines of study.

3.3 Basic rules for selection of class number   Before considering the problems involved in the application of the schedules to such compound and complex subjects as those just mentioned, it is desirable to delineate the procedures for classing a work on one subject in one discipline.

3.31 APPROACH   Having determined the subject of the work, and the point of view from which that subject is treated, the classifier is ready to class it. There are two basic approaches to the classification schedules: direct, and thru the index. Beginners will usually find the latter approach speedier, but it is not recommended because it delays the process of becoming fully acquainted with the system. The classifier should note that, whether he is a beginner or an expert, he should *never* class solely from the index. The index provides leads to the schedules but is not exhaustive and can never reproduce the wealth of information available in them.

If the classifier's approach in a given situation is thru the index, he should first locate the entry for the subject, then examine the subheads under it for the proper aspect. If, for example, his work is on metals, he will find under "Metals" various aspects, subaspects, and subsubaspects. Finding the most specific one that characterizes his work, he can then turn to the correct part of the schedules and analyze the specific number that appears to fit. However, the more reliable approach is to go direct to the schedules, using the index if necessary to locate the proper discipline; only when he is uncertain about the relevance of a particular part of the schedules is it recommended that the classifier turn to the index. For more detailed information on use of the index, see section 3.6.

If his approach is direct, the classifier will first determine into which of the ten main classes the work falls. If the subject is metals, he must decide whether it relates to the science of metals (class 5), the technology of metals (class 6), the economics of the metals industry (class 3), artistic work in metals (class 7), or even metals in the Bible (class 2). Having chosen the proper main class, then, as if there were no other, he determines into which of its divisions the book falls. If the subject is metals technology, it may be metals as engineering materials (division 62), mining of metals (also 62), metallurgy (66), fabrication of articles in metals (67), metals in hardware (68), in building (69). Then in the same way he determines the proper section, subsection, and subsubsection, until he has come to the most specific heading, used by or appropriate to the library, that fully covers the subject of the work. (See also section 3.5 on reduction.) Even if that heading is less specific than the subject of the work, he has found the right number; for example, a work on education of the blind belongs under 371.9, even tho the heading encompasses other topics as well. At each step on the way the classifier should look carefully at the notes and directions, making certain that he has not followed a false trail, perhaps even chosen the wrong main class. He should not depend solely on the three main summaries; they exist only to speed him to tentative decisions and lack the fine distinctions that must be considered before any decision is final.

If he knows the schedules well or if he comes to them by way of the index, the classifier may start at once with a specific number. In that case it is most important that he go up the hierarchical ladder, testing at each level to see if the particular subject of his book belongs within the concept named and described. Whether he goes up or down he should analyze every step, including centered headings (which are readily identified by the inch-long lines preceding them and the indicators adjacent to them). He should read carefully every heading and note.

A description of the important features of the headings and notes follows in sections 3.32–3.36.

3.32 HEADINGS Each heading consists of a word or phrase so inclusive that it covers all subordinate topics and entries. The actual wording may be incomplete, because (from the principle of hierarchy) the heading must be read as part of the larger group that includes it, e.g., in 469 "Portuguese" means the Portuguese language, but in 869 the same heading means Portuguese literature.

Two terms in a heading separated by "and," and similarly three or more terms separated by commas, are usually coordinate and mutually exclusive, e.g., 196 [Philosophy of] Spain and Portugal, 070 Journalism, publishing, newspapers; however, "and" may at times join two terms into a compound concept, e.g., 021 The library and society. If two terms in a heading are separated by a space, the first includes but is broader than the second, and the number is used for both or either, e.g., 430 Germanic languages   German, where all of 431–439 comprises the Germanic languages, but only 431–438 comprises the German language. A term in parentheses is completely or nearly synonymous with the term preceding it, e.g., in Table 2, "Areas," —492 Netherlands (Holland).

A heading includes the totality expressed by it, even if some parts of the total are explicitly provided for in numbers that are not subdivisions of the number assigned to the heading. (See third paragraph of section 2.131.) Class elsewhere notes and cross references (sections 3.357 and 3.358) lead to component parts of the subject that are not in the number led from or any of its subdivisions. Examples: (1) 575 Organic evolution and genetics: "Class organic evolution and genetics of man in 573.2, of plants in 581, of animals in 591." This means that comprehensive works on organic evolution and genetics belong in 575. (2) 820 Literatures of English and Anglo-Saxon languages: *"For American literature in English, see* 810." This means that comprehensive works on English-language literature, British and American together, are to be classed in 820. (See also section 3.3511 on comprehensive works.)

3.33 DEFINITIONS, SCOPE NOTES, EXAMPLE NOTES In some instances a heading requires, for complete understanding, the qualifications stated in the note following it, e.g., 735 Modern sculpture: "Not limited by country or locality." Others are followed by definitions, e.g., 330 Economics: "The science of human behavior as it relates to utilization of wealth for satisfaction of needs and desires thru production, distribution, consumption." (This definition, and the one at 300 The social sciences, "The sciences that deal with social activities and institutions," rule out home economics as a subdivision of 330. The latter is, in fact, an applied science, is defined as "Care of household, family, person," and belongs in 640.) When no definition is given, the term is understood to be used as delimited by its subdivisions, or as defined in Webster's *Seventh New Collegiate Dictionary* or in other general college-level desk dictionaries of the English language.

Other headings are followed by scope notes enumerating specific qualifications applicable to the subject and/or its subdivisions, e.g., 631.2 Agricultural structures: "Description, maintenance, use and place in agriculture" of farmhouses, of barns, and of other structures. These aspects of agricultural buildings are thus differentiated from the architectural aspects; classification of farmhouses in 728.6 when considered architecturally is governed by part of the scope note under 725–728: "interdisciplinary works on design and construction." Still other headings are followed by notes giving examples that explain the heading by indicating the kinds of entities that the heading names or describes. When the heading bears little resemblance to the heading used for the same concept in the previous edition of the Classification, a note appears indicating the former heading, e.g., at 631, where the present heading is "General agricultural techniques, apparatus, equipment, materials," whereas the heading in Edition 9 was "Farming."

All such notes have hierarchical force, and govern all subordinate entries and topics. See section 2.132.

3.34 INCLUSION NOTES   Notes beginning "Including" do not have hierarchical force. They are enumerations of subordinate topics, not obviously part of the heading, on which there is not sufficient literature to justify separate provision. For example, 254 Parish government and administration is a subject with several named subtopics: some, such as public relations, have their own numbers, while others, such as membership, remain in the general number.

3.35 INSTRUCTION NOTES   Notes of instruction are of various kinds, as enumerated below.

3.351 *Class here notes*   An instruction to class a certain topic or concept "here" has hierarchical force; it means, class the specified topic or concept in "this" number and/or appropriate subdivisions. The note is used to make provision for concepts that overlap the heading, e.g., "Areas" notation 78 Western United States: "Class here . . . Rocky Mountains." Rocky Mountains and Western United States overlap like two intersecting circles, because the concept Rocky Mountains is both narrower and broader than the heading to which it is assigned, being located in only four of the eight states enumerated under —78 but also in other areas outside —78, such as Arizona and Alberta.

The class here note is used also to indicate subordinate qualifications, not obviously part of the heading, that are of a general nature and have applicability to the subject and its subdivisions; for example, 725–728 [Architecture of] specific types of structures: "Class here specific structures," which means class architecture of a specific government building in 725, of a specific synagogue in 726, of a specific castle in 728.8.

3.3511 *Comprehensive and interdisciplinary works*   One kind of concept that overlaps the heading is that of comprehensive works, e.g., 260: "Class here comprehensive works on Christian church"; 264: "Class here comprehensive works on worship." By its nature, such a note is always followed by a class elsewhere note or a cross reference (sections 3.357 and 3.358) leading to those component parts of the topic treated comprehensively at this point that will be found in other numbers.

A special kind of comprehensive work is the interdisciplinary work, which deals with the topic from the point of view of more than one discipline, e.g., 669: "Class here interdisciplinary works on metals," which is to say, class here works dealing with metals (or a metal) from such diverse aspects as prospecting, mining, physics, chemistry, geology, metallurgy, industrial fabricating, art work, economics. For more detail, see section 3.42.

3.352 *Optional provision*   Because there may be legitimate reasons for placing works in numbers other than those provided in the schedules, a few alternatives are provided, with the editors' preference clearly shown. For example, 913–919 General geography of specific places: "If preferred [i.e., if the classifier prefers], class in 930–990"; 930–990: "(It is optional to class here general geography . . . [the editors] prefer 913–919)." The preferred number will always be used on Library of Congress cataloging records. More detail on options is given in section 4.21.

3.353 *Use of more than one 0 in standard subdivisions*   As stated in section 2.24, standard subdivisions, which generally consist of two or more digits of which the first is 0, may be used with any number at any level whenever they are appropriate. But in some classes, for various reasons, notation beginning with 0 is used for another purpose, in which case the classifier is instructed to use notation with an additional 0, e.g., "Use 620.01–620.09 for standard subdivisions." This instruction does not have hierarchical force, but applies only exactly as stated, *except under the circumstances described below in section 3.3544.*

3.354 *Number building*   Frequently the opportunity is offered to expand a given number or series of numbers even tho the subdivisions are not specifically enumerated in the schedules. The following instructions describe the procedures to be followed:

3.3541 *Add from auxiliary tables*   Tables 2–4 supply digits which the classifier may add to certain numbers in the schedules to make them more specific. The numbers in the auxiliary tables are not class numbers and should never be used by themselves. Each instruction indicates exactly what may be added, from which table to what base. For example, under 027.4 Public libraries there appears the instruction, "Add 'Areas' notation 3–9 from Table 2 to base number 027.4." This means that for a work on public libraries in Japan, for example, the number 52 for Japan from Table 2 is to be placed following 027.4, which results in the full class number 027.452.

It may be seen that the base number to which table digits are added (e.g., 336) is not necessarily exactly the same as the number appearing in the number column for the heading (336.4–.9); however, the base number is always explicitly stated in the accompanying note.

Occasionally the base number is less than three digits. In this case, if the combined number consists of four or more digits a decimal point must be inserted after the third digit. For example, to obtain numbers for geography of a specific location, area notations are added to 91. The number for geography of Japan will be 915.2, that is 91 (geography) followed by 52 (Japan) with a decimal point inserted after the third digit.

3.3542 *Add from schedules* Similarly, the base number is always stated in the instruction to create a sequence by adding digits from another sequence in the schedules. For example, under 581.1–.9 General principles [of botany]: "Add to 581 the numbers following 574 in 574.1–574.9, e.g., plant ecology 581.5." The procedure to be followed here is: (1) in the sequence 574.1–.9 (biology in general) the number for ecology is 574.5; (2) in this number the digit following 574 is 5; (3) the classifier adds the digit 5 to the base number 581 to obtain 581.5.

The base numbers in the two sequences are not necessarily of the same length, e.g., 572.8 Specific races: "Add to 572.8 the numbers following 4 in 420–490, e.g., African races 572.896." Here the number for African in the sequence 420–490 is 496; the classifier adds the 96 that follows 4 to 572.8 and obtains 572.896.

At 016, Bibliographies and catalogs of specific subjects, complete class numbers may be added to the base number: "Add 001–999 to base number 016, e.g., bibliographies of astronomy 016.52" (520 being the complete number for astronomy).

(Users of earlier editions of the DDC will observe that the instructions just described replace the former "divide-like" instructions.)

3.3543 *General suggestions* The classifier is more likely to construct correct numbers if he ignores the decimal point until the final sequence of digits is obtained, after which he should insert a point following the third digit. Also, he should never terminate a number in 0 anywhere to the right of a decimal point.

The classifier should combine numbers only when specifically instructed to do so; otherwise he will soon find that he has derived combinations which block the orderly use of other official numbers.

3.3544 *Hierarchical force* Add notes do not have hierarchical force unless this is specifically so stated, e.g., 420–490 Specific languages: "Under each language identified by *, add to the designated base number the 'Subdivisions of Individual Languages' notation 01–86 from Table 4"; following this appear numerous languages preceded by asterisks, e.g., 469 *Portuguese, 420 *English (for which the base number is 42). (A similar example at 930–990 combines with the add instruction an instruction to use two 0s for standard subdivisions, a type of note that otherwise does not have hierarchical force; see section 3.353 above.) Since in such cases the instructions are applicable to various subdivisions, they do have hierarchical force.

3.355 *Citation order* As noted earlier, many subjects may be subdivided according to more than one kind of division, or characteristic, e.g., textiles by material, form, purpose, color. When a given work considers its subject simultaneously according to two or more characteristics the classifier is faced with a question of priority in cross classification. In some situations he will find instructions on priority of choice in the schedules themselves; in others he must rely on a few general principles, and occasionally simply on his judgment. The following rules may serve as guidance in determination of the correct number for a specific work and in maintenance of consistency:

(1) Follow stated instructions at the point of application or anywhere above that point in the hierarchy. Instructions are most commonly given in the schedules when the numbers for the different characteristics of division have no 0s or have the same number of 0s (see (2) and (3) below). They may be in the form of a table of precedence or a regular instruction note. An example of a table of precedence appears at centered heading 331.3–331.6, which tells the classifier who has a work on labor performed by aged women that he should place it in 331.3 (for aged persons) rather than in 331.4 (for women). An example of a regular instruction note appears at 331.2, "Class conditions of employment of special classes of workers in 331.3–331.6," which tells the classifier with a work on the wages of women that he should place it in 331.4 rather than in 331.2 (for wages). If the classifier happens to arrive first at 331.4, he will find in the first note under 331.3–331.6 that conditions of employment of special classes of workers are to be classed there; thus, whether he starts at 331.2 or at 331.4, he will (by checking up the hierarchical ladder) find that the correct number is 331.4.

(2) Give precedence to subdivisions without 0 notation before those with 0 notation (those without 0 usually being more specific), to one 0 before two, to two 0s before three. Example: Class diagnosis of liver diseases in 616.3 (not 616.07).

(3) If there are neither stated instructions nor a difference in the number of 0s (two or more characteristics of division are sometimes provided for in notation with the same number of 0s as well as in notation with no 0s), cite by most specific subject, then by place, then by time, then by form. Examples: Class weather in Europe in 551.6094 (551.6 weather, 094 Europe), not in 554 (geology of Europe); periodicals on science education in 507 (study and teaching of science) not in 505 (serial publications on science).

3.3551 *General special* This discussion introduces the principle of general special concepts, i.e., subdivision of a topic according to a characteristic which has general applicability to other subdivisions of the topic which are based on different characteristics. For example, commentaries (220.7) is a special approach to the general concept of Bible (220), i.e., the Bible as a whole may be presented in this way, or a single part of the Bible may be so presented, e.g., historical books 222. Sometimes the notation provides for the general special concept not only at the general level, as with Bible, but also at specific levels, e.g., 410 Linguistics, 415 Grammar in general, 469 Portuguese language, 469.5 Portuguese grammar.

3.356 *Relocations* A relocation is an adjustment in the schedules resulting in the shifting of a topic between successive editions from one number to another that differs in respects other than length, e.g., the shift of parochial welfare work from 258 in Edition 9 to 361.7 in Edition 10, or the shift of space propulsion systems from 629.42 to 629.47, whereby the original number is neither lengthened nor shortened, but is changed completely or in part. If the relocation is total, i.e., if the entire number formerly used is to be vacated, that number is enclosed in square brackets, and there is an instruction showing where the subject formerly in that number is now placed, e.g., [258] Parochial welfare work: "Class in 361.7." If the relocation is only partial, it is indicated in an instruction note, e.g., 301.2 Culture and cultural processes: "Class social conflict [*formerly* 301.2] in 301.6."

Total relocations are not to be confused with other, similar types of entries in square brackets and their instructions. One of these is entries showing that concepts normally belonging in standard subdivision notations are to be placed instead in other numbers, e.g., [610.23] Medicine as a profession: "Do not use; class in 610.69." Another is entries and instructions showing schedule reduction, e.g., [613.97] Hygiene for specific age groups: "Number discontinued; class in 613"; this is *not* a relocation, but a mere shortening of the number that was assigned to this topic in the previous edition. (However, the effect of all these, like that of the class elsewhere notes described in section 3.357, is the same: the classifier is instructed to class elsewhere a topic that he may have reason to think he should class at the point of instruction.)

Relocation notes are hierarchical in force at the point of instruction, and usually also at the point led to. For example, the note under 390, "Class cultural anthropology [*formerly* 390] in 301.2," tells the classifier that, while cultural anthropology was formerly in 390 and appropriate subdivisions, it is now to be classed in 301.2 and in appropriate subdivisions of 301.2 if its treatment at that number warrants it. Since at 301.2 the topic is shown in a class here note (see section 3.351), subdivisions of the subject may be classed also in the subdivisions of 301.2; if it had been shown in an inclusion note (see section 3.34), the subject would have been classed in 301.2 only and not in its subdivisions.

3.357 *Class elsewhere notes*   Class elsewhere notes (not to be confused with the class here notes described in section 3.351) are used for a variety of purposes, but in effect all of them instruct the classifier to class in a different number topics in some way related to one or more of the topics covered by the entry in which the note appears. The chief purposes are the following: (1) To avoid inconsistent classification by specifying citation order, as already mentioned in section 3.355, e.g., 331.2 Conditions of employment: "Class conditions of employment of special classes of workers in 331.3–331.6." (2) To show in which single number to class comprehensive works on a concept covered by a centered heading (compare section 3.43), e.g., 385–388 Transportation services: "Class comprehensive works in 380.5." (3) To scatter the subdivisions of a subject, e.g., 361 Social welfare work: "Class a specific application of social welfare work with the subject, e.g., social welfare services to prison inmates 365." (4) To indicate related numbers when potential confusion exists, e.g., 022, in which is included planning of library buildings based on functions: "Class architecture of libraries in 727." Except for occasional notes like the one in the last example, the schedules make no effort to lead from the subject in one discipline or aspect to the same subject in other disciplines; this is the function of the index (see sections 2.12 and 3.6). See also section 3.358.

These notes all have hierarchical force.

3.358 *Cross references* The third paragraph of section 2.131 stated that not all subdivisions of a concept are necessarily to be found in notations subordinate to that used for the concept as a whole. Cross references are a special kind of instruction note leading the classifier from the stated or implied totality of a given subject to component parts of that subject that are provided for elsewhere than in the number referred from or numbers directly subordinate to it, e.g., 660 Chemical and related technologies: *"For pharmaceutical chemistry, see* 615"; 351 Central governments: *"For specific national, state, provincial governments, see* 353–354." The totality from which component parts are separated need not appear in a heading, but may be in a note, e.g., 410 Linguistics, Class here comprehensive works on Indo-European languages: *"For specific Indo-European languages, see* 420–480." Like class elsewhere notes, cross references are not used to lead from one aspect of a subject to another aspect that belongs in a different discipline; they lead only from the whole subject within its discipline to parts of the subject within the same discipline located elsewhere. Only the index shows dispersion of a subject by disciplines.

Cross references have hierarchical force. For example, the cross reference from 500, in which are classed comprehensive works on pure and applied sciences, to 600, means that any subdivision of 500, in its applied aspect, belongs in 600, e.g., applied physics in 621, applied chemistry in 660.

3.36 SUMMARY OF HIERARCHICAL FORCE OF ENTRIES In section 2.132 it was indicated that the heading and notes applying to a given class apply also to all its subdivisions, but analysis of the different types of notes in sections 3.31–3.358 has shown that there are certain exceptions. These exceptions are here summarized. The following parts of an entry *do not have hierarchical force:* (1) Inclusion notes (section 3.34); these mention topics not yet requiring their own numbers. (2) Instruction notes about (a) the use of more than one 0 for standard subdivisions (section 3.353), and (b) number building (section 3.354): such instructions have hierarchical force only when specifically so designated, in which case the subdivisions to which they are applicable are identified by asterisks and repeated instructions in footnotes.

All other parts of an entry have hierarchical force.

3.37 STANDARD SUBDIVISIONS Having analyzed the number chosen for the work in hand thru all the steps of its hierarchical ladder, and having decided that it is the best and most specific number, the classifier is ready to consider what, if any, further specification may be desirable, i.e., whether any of the standard subdivisions are applicable. (See also section 2.24.) If, for example, the work deals with techniques, apparatus, equipment, or materials of the subject, he may add 028; if it consists of a collection of articles on the subject, he may add 08; if the work deals with the subject in the United States only (or in

Morocco), he may add 0973 (or 0964). The complete list of standard subdivisions appears in Table 1.

The classifier should not add standard subdivisions when they are redundant, e.g., if the number already means technique, it is unnecessary to add standard subdivision 028 Techniques, apparatus, equipment, materials.

The classifier should not add one standard subdivision to another standard subdivision unless there are specific instructions to do so. Attempts to do this will soon engender frustration and confusion.

Altho it is their standard meanings that make these subdivisions "standard," sometimes a particular standard subdivision when applied to a given subject may logically be assigned one or more meanings that are extensions of and compatible with the basic meaning, and the classifier will then find in the schedules an entry specifying the extension. For example, in 701 a note specifies that under the arts philosophy and theory includes esthetics, composition, perspective, and other topics peculiarly attributable to this discipline.

Sometimes a concept ordinarily placed in a standard subdivision number is found instead with an irregular notation; most such instances date from earlier editions of the DDC, prepared before the table of standard subdivisions became a feature. These instances are noted under the numbers where the classifier would normally expect to find them. Examples:

[610.23]   Medicine as a profession
             Do not use; class in 610.69

373.09   Historical and geographical treatment
             Class treatment by continent, country, locality in 373.3–373.9
             (not 373.093–373.099)
(That is, use 373.091–373.092 if needed, but instead of 373.093–373.099 use 373.3–373.9.)

602   Miscellany
             Class patents . . . in 608
(That is, use 602 and all its subdivisions with their regular meanings, except for patents, for which use 608.)

It is obvious that the classifier should not use a standard subdivision until he has made sure from the schedules that it has not been assigned an irregular notation or meaning.

When a standard subdivision or span of standard subdivisions is specifically named in the schedules, it is understood that, unless there are contrary instructions, the usual subsubdivisions may be used, e.g., 509 Historical and geographical treatment is to have "Areas" notation 1–9 from Table 2 added to it the same as any standard subdivision 09.

Many small libraries will not wish to use standard subdivisions at all, and there is no necessity for them to do so. In fact, most libraries using the abridged edition will probably use no more than two digits (01, 02, 07, etc.) except under 09, where they may prefer to add notations for places (e.g., 0973).

3.371 *General special* One standard subdivision requires special mention: 04 General special. As the note in Table 1 points out: "This subdivision is reserved for special concepts that have general application thruout the regular subdivisions of certain specific subjects; it is to be used only when specifically set forth in the schedules." This device is introduced for general special concepts at those places where no other kind of notation is feasible, and it follows the rules for citation order in section 3.355. Example: 604 General technologies.

3.38 SUBJECT NOT PROVIDED FOR   The fields of knowledge grow so fast that any edition of the DDC is outdated before it appears. There is little doubt that the classifier will have works on subjects for which the schedules and index have provided no place either explicitly or implicitly. He should *not* make up his own number for such a subject; the next edition could easily place the subject in a different number and use the number he devised for something else. The classifier's guiding principle should be to follow exactly the procedure outlined above to determine first the correct main class, then the correct division, then the correct section, continuing until he has arrived at the most specific heading that will contain the subject of his work. If he does this carefully, he will rarely be proved wrong. He should always stop at the most specific number possible in the schedules, even tho it may be only a three-digit number. Then, if the editors supply a detailed number later, he may use it simply by adding digits to the number originally chosen. An example from the past may be illustrative. Abridged 8 provided no place for transportation by overland air-cushion vehicles, but an alert classifier following the principles outlined here would have used 388.3, and found his decision confirmed by the appearance of 388.35 in Abridged edition 9.

3.4 **Complexities in selection of class number**   The foregoing rules and principles provide a basis for classing a work on one subject in one discipline. However, as noted in section 3.2, analysis of a work may show that it deals with two or three or many subjects, considered separately or in their interrelationships; or with two or more aspects of one or more subjects. In using the DDC as a shelf classification, obviously the classifier must choose one place and class the work there. Since most libraries employ other types of subject control in addition to shelf classification, such as a subject catalog, it is likely that other leads will be provided thru such tools. Specific instructions for classing a whole variety of compound and complex subjects are provided in such sources as W. S. Merrill's *Code for Classifiers*, 2d edition (Chicago, American Library Association, 1939) and *Guide to Use of [16th edition of] Dewey Decimal Classification, Based on the Practice of the Decimal Classification Office at the Library of Congress* (Lake Placid Club, N.Y., Forest Press, 1962). Because it is impossible to anticipate all combinations, or even a considerable percentage of them, a few basic principles, from which all the specific rules stem, are here set forth for guidance.

3.41 MORE THAN ONE SUBJECT   (1) The classifier should class a work dealing with two or more interrelated subjects with the one that receives the chief emphasis. This emphasis may be a reflection of the relative amount of space devoted to each subject, or of the author's purpose, or of both. For example, as a general rule the classifier should class with Keats an analytical work dealing with

Shakespeare's influence on Keats. The author's purpose in this imagined book may be said to be an exposition of Keats's work. Even tho the treatment of Shakespeare may actually occupy more space, if the author's purpose is pervasive thruout, then greater weight should be given to purpose, which would place the work with other works on Keats. But if the treatment of Keats occupies only a small portion of the work, say less than a third, and does not permeate the portion that deals specifically with Shakespeare, then the preponderance of space devoted to Shakespeare should carry more weight than the author's purpose of explaining Keats, and the work should be placed with other works on Shakespeare. Such decisions are sometimes very difficult to make. For other examples, astronomy for surveyors should be classed with astronomy, psychology applied to typewriting with typewriting. (2) The classifier should class a work dealing with two or more subjects that are not particularly interrelated, e.g., a description of the beliefs and practices of Judaism, Christianity, and Islam, with the one that preponderates. (3) If no emphasis or preponderance is apparent, he should class a work on *three or more* subjects that are all subdivisions of a broader subject with the broader one, e.g., a work dealing approximately equally with Hinduism (294.5), Judaism (296), and Islam (297) in 290. (4) If no emphasis or preponderance is apparent, he should class a work on *two* subjects with the one coming first in the schedules, e.g., a work dealing equally with Judaism and Islam in 296; however, if those two subjects are both subdivisions of a broader subject and together constitute the major portion of the broader subject, he should class the work with that broader subject. Some classifiers prefer to class any work on two subjects that are both part of a broader one with the broader, and some prefer to class such a work with the one treated first in the work, but these procedures are not recommended.

3.42 MORE THAN ONE ASPECT   (1) The classifier should class an interdisciplinary work, dealing with a subject within two or more disciplines, i.e., from two or more points of view or aspects, with the aspect that receives the most emphasis. For example, a work dealing with both the scientific and the engineering principles of electrodynamics is classed in 537.6 if the engineering aspects are introduced primarily for illustrative purposes, but in 621.31 if the basic scientific theories are introduced primarily as a preliminary to the author's development of an exposition of engineering principles and practices. (See also section 3.44.) (2) He should class a work dealing with a subject from two or more aspects, but having no apparent emphasis, with the aspect that preponderates. (3) He should class a work dealing with a subject from two or more aspects, but having no apparent emphasis or preponderance, in accordance with instructions on treatment of interdisciplinary works given in the schedules, when such notes occur (compare section 3.3511), e.g., interdisciplinary works on coal in 553. (However, this instruction is not valid and should not be followed unless one of the aspects dealt with in the work is the one that normally belongs in the number designated for interdisciplinary use, e.g., 553 is not a valid number for an interdisciplinary work on coal unless economic geology (the subject of 553) is one of the aspects considered in the work.) (4) Lacking apparent emphasis or preponderance, and lacking specific valid instructions on treatment of interdisciplinary works— relatively few such notes appear—the classifier should class a work dealing with a subject from two or more aspects with the underlying, broader, or purposive discipline, e.g., science underlies technology so he should prefer 500s to 600s, art is broader than literature so he should prefer 700s to 800s, economic utilization is the purpose of fabrication so he should prefer 330s to 670s or 680s. (5) Lacking any other principle, he should class in the discipline that comes first in the schedules.

To class a work on two or more interrelated subjects considered from two or more aspects, the classifier may have to apply a combination of the foregoing rules, and he should not overlook the possibilities of main class 0, e.g., 001.3– 001.6, 080.

3.43 COMPREHENSIVE WORKS ON CONCEPTS IN CENTERED HEADINGS As seen in section 2.131, there are steps in the successive divisions of a discipline or subject for which positions in the lengthening digital notation are not available. These are represented by spans of numbers in centered headings. Since a given book can have but one class number, every centered heading is followed by a note stating what single number the classifier should use for comprehensive works on the concept expressed in the heading. (See also section 3.357.) The basis for the editors' choice of number varies, since each case is dependent on the schedule structure for the particular subject. The comprehensive number specified may be (1) the next higher number, e.g., England ("Areas" notation 421– 428) in notation 42; (2) a general special subdivision of the next higher number, e.g., transportation services (385–388) in 380.5; (3) a preceding specific number, e.g., Old Testament (specific parts 222–224) in 221; (4) the first or one of the other numbers subordinate to the centered heading, e.g., Christian church (250– 280) in 260.

3.44 APPLICATIONS The classifier should class the application of a principle, concept, science, procedure, or technique to another principle, concept, science, procedure, or technique with the application. For example, general principles of radio communication engineering, including the circuitry and instruments used in space communication, are classed in 621.3841; but the application of space communication to (i.e., its use in) astronautics is classed in 629.43 and 629.45; and the use of astronautics in weather forecasting is classed in 551.6.

3.45 WORKS RELATED TO OTHER WORKS The classifier should ordinarily place with the original work translations, abridgments, criticisms, and reviews of it, indexes and concordances to it. Since an adaptation modifies the original work in form, scope, presentation, and possibly language, it may or may not be classed with it, depending upon the amount and kind of modification. It is normally the function of the book number, referred to in section 2.11, to distinguish among such related works.

3.5 Reduction As noted in section 2.3, a valuable feature of the DDC notation is its adaptability to both close and broad classification. How close or how broad the classification of a specific library should be is a matter of administrative determination. It is unlikely that any library, no matter how large or specialized, will in its shelf classification follow the unabridged edition to its fullest expanded detail in every section. The detail in this Abridged DDC is intended to be approximately as much as the libraries for which it is designed will require, but even this edition may be too detailed in some classes for some libraries, so that at times reduction will be advisable, either from the provisions of the schedules themselves, or from the numbers recommended by central classification services for specific titles.

3.51 How to reduce notation   The classifier should never reduce the notation to less than the most specific three-digit number, no matter how small his collection may be.

The classifier should cut at a reasonable point, i.e., one that will bring about a useful grouping. This requires special care when applied to numbers that have been built. For example, if the library has a large collection on the subject of economic conditions, the classifier may find it desirable to place a work on economic conditions in Cambridgeshire in 330.9425, but many librarians consider geographical breakdown below the level of country unnecessarily detailed except in 930–990 for general history and 913.3–919 for geography. Indeed, with a quite small collection the classifier may consider 330.94 satisfactory for works on economic conditions in all or any part of Europe.

A number should never be reduced so that it ends in a 0 anywhere to the right of the decimal point, since such a 0 is meaningless.

The classifier should record in the schedules all decisions for reduction, but not try to record decisions of this nature in the index.

3.52 Segmentation on printed cards   To assist classifiers who have neither the time nor the inclination to make cuts, Dewey Decimal numbers recorded since 1967 on Library of Congress catalog cards, printed catalogs, and MARC tapes, which are given in their fullest unabridged form (see section 3.7), have been presented in from one to three segments. This service enables those libraries that find full DDC notations excessively long for their purposes to cut the numbers meaningfully. Places are designated in the notation at which libraries of various sizes may terminate the number. (1) Many numbers are printed in one segment; it is recommended that libraries of all sizes consider using such numbers without reduction. (2) Other numbers are printed in two or three segments; it is recommended that libraries using the Abridged DDC as their basic classification tool consider using only the first segment of such numbers.

Segmenting is shown by prime marks; it must be emphasized that these marks are not part of the notation. For example, with 301.29′56′073, libraries making cuts at the recommended places in the notation will mark their cards and books 301.29 or 301.2956; 301.2956073 will be used if no reduction is desired.

Segments on LC cards, with a few exceptions, have consisted of the abridged and unabridged base numbers and the various synthetic elements that together make up a complete DDC number. This basis has been followed on the assumption that small libraries generally consider five-digit numbers to be of maximum desirable length. Some recommendations provide numbers longer than this, but they occur relatively infrequently. However, with the advent of this 10th abridged edition, which, as was shown in section 2.3, no longer necessarily provides numbers that differ only in length from those in the corresponding full edition, the first and other segments may not be identical with the numbers given in the Abridged DC, and librarians using the abridged edition should take numbers from LC cards only after careful comparison with their abridged schedules. Examples: (1) for zoology of penguins, the printed card gives 598.4'41, but this edition gives 598.2; (2) for laws on price fixing, the printed card gives 343.07'25, but this edition gives 343.7. A list follows the tables giving the numbers in the 18th edition for which the corresponding numbers in this 10th abridged edition vary in respects other than length.

3.6 Index In order to make the best use of the index the classifier should know what he may expect to find in it, how it is organized, and how to use it.

3.61 BASIC CONTENT The index contains an entry for each of the major significant terms named in the schedules and tables, with leads to various aspects. Class numbers are given for most subjects that have their own numbers in the schedules and for many subjects whose numbers are obtained thru number building. However, it is not feasible to include in the index every topic likely to be written about, or every possible aspect even for those topics that are included, and still keep it within a reasonable size. The index does *not* include all names of persons, cities, organizations, minerals, plants, animals, chemical compounds, drugs, manufactured articles, and similar enumerations.

3.62 RELATIVITY The index is considered relative because, whereas in the schedules the different aspects of a subject are scattered according to discipline, in the index they are brought together under the name of the subject, with their various locations in the schedules indicated. For example, if the classifier has a work on metals and looks under that term, he will find, as shown in section 2.12, many aspects and subaspects, including arts, chemistry, materials, metallurgy, mining, and products, each leading to one or more specific precise numbers in the schedules. Some index entries and numbers are set in boldface, e.g., Metals products **manufacturing 671–673**; this means that the topic and the number are divided in the schedules, either by stated subdivisions or by a provision for number building.

3.63 CROSS REFERENCES In order to conserve space but still provide a maximum amount of information, the index utilizes many cross references, both direct and generalized. Direct references are of two kinds, those that refer to a different term of the same level, and those that refer up to a term on a broader level. Those in the first category usually refer to a synonym or a variant spelling, e.g., Teutonic *see* Germanic, Keramic *see* Ceramic. Refer up references are supplied to help the classifier find the proper location for specific topics that do not have their own numbers in the schedules and to alert him to additional aspects that cannot be repeated in the index under countless specific headings because of space limitations, e.g., Copper *see* Metals. This type of reference is possible in the index because of the hierarchical principle on which the schedules are based, whatever is true of a whole being also true of its parts. Generalized (or scatter) references are used to lead to applications, aspects, kinds, uses, occurrences, etc. of the topic.

Often a subject has its own number(s) for one or more aspects, but in other aspects shares a number or numbers with a broader concept (unlike the concept Copper, which in *all* aspects shares the numbers used for the broader concept Metals). In such a case, the specific numbers that apply are given under the name of the subject, and the other aspects are covered by generalized references, which tell the classifier: for *"other aspects see"* the term for the broader concept. Turning to the broader concept the classifier will find new numbers. For example, under Handwear he will find 685 for commercial manufacture, and the reference *"other aspects see* Clothing." Under Clothing he will find additional aspects where handwear and clothing share the same numbers, e.g., domestic manufacture, social customs.

Since no space would be saved by a reference leading to a heading with only one line of information (which can just as easily be repeated at the point referred from), a reference is made only when it leads to at least two lines of information.

3.64 SUBJECTS OR ASPECTS NOT FOUND IN INDEX   In many cases, however, the index does not spell out the other possible aspects, and the classifier must always be on the alert to remember that the basic arrangement of Dewey is by discipline. For example, Cats is indexed only to the aspects domestic animals and experimental animals, yet may be written about as agricultural pests, as subjects of conservation, as subjects of drawing, as subjects of commercial or sportive hunting, as zoological or paleozoological phenomena, as well as from still other aspects. None of these aspects are indexed, because in none of them is cats given a separate number. The classifier can find the correct numbers in one of two ways:

(1) He can look for the various aspects under their own names, e.g., Pests, Conservation, Drawing, Hunting, Zoology, which will bring him close to the number he needs, but then he must examine the schedule for the exact number. For instance, he will find the exact numbers under Pests (632), Conservation (639), and Hunting (639 for commercial and 799.2 for sportive); but Drawing will lead him to 740, where he must scan the schedule to find that 743 is the number for drawing specific subjects; and Zoology will lead him to 591, where he will be told that specific animals are classed in 592–599, and he will then, upon examination of 592–599, find mammals in 599.

(2) He can look under a broader concept of which cats form a part, in this case Mammals. In fact, he should be alert, at all times when he cannot find in

the index the precise term he wants, to look under a broader or more general term. Examples are legion:

Not finding:	He should try:
Adopted children	Children
Declension	Grammar
Dinners	Meals
Electron microscopes	Microscopes
Factory ships	Vessels (nautical)
Kings (chessmen)	Chess
Microclimatology	Climatology
Retinas	Eyes
Rummy	Card games
Vinyls	Plastics

It may be that the classifier will think of Ships rather than of Vessels; if so, under that term he will find a reference to Vessels. Or perhaps he will think of Language or Linguistics instead of Grammar, in which cases he would have to examine the 400 schedule and Table 4 to find the exact numbers for grammar.

3.65 COORDINATION WITH SCHEDULES   It is obvious that the index entries, because they are closely coordinated with each other and with the schedules, must be used with care and thought; and further that it is not advisable to use a number printed in the index under the topic sought without first following up the various references. It is equally not advisable to classify from the index alone without reference to the schedules, which is the only place where, on the various steps of the hierarchical ladder, may be found all the information about coverage and correct use of the various numbers.

3.66 ARRANGEMENT AND OTHER GENERAL INFORMATION   Except where sense or syntax requires otherwise, nouns are entered in the index in plural form.

Unless relativity requires inversion, adjective + noun phrases are entered in direct form only, e.g., Mechanical engineering, not Engineering mechanical. However, if the classifier cannot find such a phrase under the adjective he should look under the noun alone, e.g., not finding Anglican bishops he should look under Bishops (which would lead to Clergy).

Index entries are arranged alphabetically word by word. Terms indented below the main headings are alphabeted in one group even tho they may be a mixture of topical subheadings and words that, when combined with the main heading, form phrases or inverted subjects. Indention in the index has the same hierarchical force that it has in the schedules. Terms followed by explanatory words in parentheses are alphabeted separately. Hyphenated words are considered to be single words. Hyphens are often used to make distinctions in relationships, e.g., Washing clothing, Washing-machines, and the classifier should check all such possibilities. Abbreviations are filed as if spelled in full. A list of abbreviations used precedes the index. Initialisms are filed as if each letter were a separate word, e.g., ADP is arranged as A D P preceding Abacuses. Names beginning with Mc and M' are arranged as if spelled Mac. Modified vowels, such as ä, ö, ü, are arranged as a, o, u.

Numbers preceded by a dash and a term in italics are from the auxiliary tables. For example, numbers preceded by "*s.s.–*" will be found in Table 1 Standard Subdivisions, while "*area–*" refers to Table 2 Areas. Numbers supplied by the tables are never used alone, but are added as appropriate to schedule numbers.

Digits to the right of the decimal point, and digits in numbers from tables, are printed in groups of three. This device is purely for ease is reading and copying. The spaces are not part of the numbers, and the groups are not related to those shown in DDC numbers on Library of Congress cataloging records.

3.7 General suggestions It will usually be to the classifier's benefit to check to determine whether one of the centralized classification services has already assigned a number for the work he is classing. Even if his own library does not follow the same edition of DDC or the same policies as the central service, or has made local adaptations of its own, the decisions of experts are helpful. Among the more important sources for Dewey numbers from the latest unabridged edition are Library of Congress catalog cards and book catalogs, the *ALA Booklist, Publishers' Weekly,* and *American Book Publishing Record.* Since 1967 numbers in all of these have been segmented to show in most cases abridged edition provisions, as described in section 3.52. Numbers from the latest abridged edition appear on H. W. Wilson Company catalog cards and in *Book Review Digest* and the various parts of the *Standard Catalog Series.* Since 1969 the *British National Bibliography,* which formerly applied a combination of the latest and earlier unabridged editions, with numerous special detailed subdivisions (using letter notation) not officially authorized by the DDC editors, has followed the latest edition without change, also segmenting to show in most cases abridged edition provisions. Numbers assigned by such services should always be verified against the schedules used by the classifier, for the reasons given in section 3.52.

To promote consistency and future efficiency, the classifier should make a local record of all decisions. Most libraries maintain a shelflist or similar record which records all works in classified order, thus showing how the different class numbers have been used. Decisions on specific problems may be written at the pertinent point in the classification schedules or kept in a separate record, or a combination of methods may be employed.

4. Variations from recommended practice

4.1 Principle of usefulness Altho an important feature of the DDC is that its notation provides a universal language that can be understood in all libraries and even in all countries, nevertheless a classifier, in serving the special needs of a library's users, may sometimes find it desirable to modify specific printed provisions in ways other than reduction (for which see section 3.5). This is permissible if there is a *real* and *permanent* local need. By "real" is meant that each variation should have a demonstrable reason that can be recorded and defended. By "permanent" is meant that a specific need of a temporary or short-term nature should not be met by adjustment of class numbers. In any event variations should be adopted only with caution; see section 4.4.

The classifier should record in the schedules every decision for variation, but, as with reductions, he should not try to record such decisions in the index.

4.2 Officially recognized variations A number of important variations appear in the printed schedules or are otherwise officially recognized. They are available, and recommended for use by libraries whose needs they will serve, but are not reflected in the practices of the Decimal Classification Division as recorded on Library of Congress cataloging records.

4.21 OPTIONAL PROVISION Certain topics are given two (or more) specific placements. One of these is always preferred by the editors, and in each case an instructional note appears under both the preferred and the optional numbers (see section 3.352). Several examples follow.

Instead of the traditional DDC arrangement of pure literature by form, which separates the works of an author who writes in different forms, e.g., poetry and drama, some libraries prefer to have all of the literary works of an author together. Under each language they may then arrange all of the works written in that language in one alphabetical author sequence regardless of the literary form of the works. The DDC recognizes this method of arranging literary works by a note in Table 3 Subdivisions of Individual Literatures, under centered heading —1–8 Specific forms: "Class description, critical appraisal, collected works of an individual author with the form with which he is chiefly identified; or, if preferred, class these and also single works regardless of form all in —8." (In the preferred arrangement, even when description, criticism, collected works, etc. of an author are classed with the form with which he is chiefly identified, single works should still be classed by form, e.g., Galsworthy as a whole, and his novels, in 823, but his plays in 822.) Under —8 the classifier will find: "(It is optional to class here description, critical appraisal, single and collected works of individual authors regardless of form: prefer —1–8)."

Treatment of biography varies greatly from one library to another. Many libraries prefer it arranged with pertinent subjects, e.g., biography of engineers with engineering, of statesmen with general history of appropriate countries, of artists with art. On the other hand, most popular libraries prefer all or most biography together, either subarranged by subject or (for individual biography) in one alphabet by biographee. Accordingly, while use of standard subdivision 092 with each subject is the editors' recommended treatment of biography for libraries using the full edition, a note appears under 920 in this edition indicating a preference for arrangement in one alphabet by libraries using the abridged edition. (Library of Congress cataloging records identify biographies by giving [B] as an optional classification in addition to the preferred subject number.)

Traditionally, Dewey has placed the various branches of geography under the specific topics that are considered by area, e.g., economic geography 330.9, plant geography 581.9. However, with a growing academic and research interest in geography, numerous libraries have in recent years come to prefer an arrangement that brings all geography together. Such an arrangement is supplied optionally at 910.1, which is then subdivided by subject, e.g., economic geography 910.133, plant geography 910.158.

General geography of specific continents, countries, localities is placed by editors' preference in 913–919, but, optionally, may be placed in 930–990 with general history of these areas.

4.22 TYPES OF WORKS NOT CLASSIFIED   Many popular libraries follow the policy of not classifying certain categories of works, but, instead, of arranging them alphabetically. Most frequently this kind of treatment is given to individual works of fiction published in English, no matter what the country of origin or language of composition. These are merely arranged by author, e.g., Dickens, Hemingway, Proust, Zweig. In a similar manner, some libraries arrange all their bound periodical sets, no matter what the subject, in a single sequence by title.

4.3 Unofficial variations   Other variations may prove to be useful in specific situations even tho not officially recognized.

4.31 ATTRACTION   Because of special local interest or special collections of books, it may on occasion be desirable to bring together all works on a given subject in only one of the several possible disciplines, e.g., *all* works on Jews in 296, *all* works on automobiles in 629.2.

4.32 STANDARD SUBDIVISIONS   Some libraries will prefer to keep their employment of standard subdivisions consistent, always using regular notations instead of the irregular notations described in section 3.37. This is not likely to create future difficulty, and may be effected by canceling the special instructions to use irregular notation under specific subjects.

4.4 Caution   Altho it is possible to adopt variations from recommended practice when such will prove useful, many such adoptions are short-sighted, and variations should be held to the barest minimum. Every modification of the established schedule means additional work for the catalogers of the future, since these modifications prevent a library from taking full advantage of centralized classification services. Modifications may later have to be undone and books redistributed. Tampering with the Dewey schedule is rarely worthwhile.

5. Changes between editions

Several kinds of changes occur between editions that require special methods for adjustment within established library collections: (1) expansions and reductions, which result in topics being assigned longer or shorter numbers than in earlier editions; (2) relocations (see section 3.356); (3) reused numbers; and (4) phoenix schedules, which are totally new developments on established bases.

Ideally, for maximum utilization of the Classification, all such changes should be adopted promptly, not only for materials currently received but also for materials classed earlier. However, this is not usually practical, and the following compromises may be considered:

5.1 Expansions and reductions Because of its different emphasis and approach (as described in section 2.3), this edition has very few expansions but a good many reductions as compared with its predecessor, Abridged 9.

Most libraries adopt each new expansion that is expected to serve a special need, and assign the lengthened number to works received after the date of adoption. Not often, however, do they reclassify older materials into a more specific number. There is no great loss in this omission, because the older works in the shorter number will remain either adjacent to or near the new works in the longer number and will be grouped with works on the broader subject of which their specific topics form a part. A typical expansion in this edition is 155.67 Psychology of the aged, which was formerly included in 155.6.

Libraries are somewhat less likely to adopt a new reduction, tho in cases where there are no numbers intervening between the longer and shorter numbers, there is little reason for not doing so. A typical reduction in this edition is the discontinuance of 599.1–.9 for the zoology of various kinds of mammals, all of which are now brought together in 599.

5.2 Relocations It is a good policy for a library to adopt each relocation as soon as it can, and in any event to use the new number for classification of new materials. Failure to adopt it for future use means loss of the benefits of centralized classification service and the courting of future conflict. Failure to reclassify older materials means separation of works on a given subject. However, local circumstances, such as an active weeding program and the shelving of older material in closed stacks, may make this tolerable. Suggested methods of reducing the inconvenience are to place cross references in the shelflist and appropriate labels or wooden-block dummies on the shelves. A list of relocations in this edition, together with discontinued numbers, appears between the tables and the schedules.

5.3 Reused numbers Assignment of new topics to vacated numbers is held by the editors to an absolute minimum (except for phoenix schedules, for which see section 5.4), because such reuse is a potential source of very great confusion. Unlike relocations, which may separate like materials, reuse of numbers results in unlike materials sharing the same number. For example, the 6th and earlier abridged editions used 774 for photomechanical processes of photography, the 7th–9th editions did not use it at all, and the present edition uses it for holography. Other reused numbers in this edition, exclusive of those in phoenix schedules, are listed in the preface. It is strongly recommended that old material be removed from them and placed in appropriate new locations when each number is first used with its new meaning.

5.4 Phoenix schedules The 9th abridged edition provided a completely new development of the schedule for psychology, a discipline for which the older development was totally inadequate to meet the requirements of modern literature. Law and mathematics are treated likewise in this edition. The superseded, or obsolescent, schedules for 340 Law and 510 Mathematics are reprinted following the index, together with tables of concordance for important topics. The editors realize that introduction into an existing book collection of the provisions of these new schedules is difficult and expensive, but recommend nevertheless that they be adopted. Failure to do so will mean continued use of schedules incapable of dealing with literature of the 1970s. In order to avoid chaos in the collections, reclassification, with the aid of the concordances, of works previously classed according to the older schedules should proceed as rapidly as possible.

6. Acknowledgments

It is my pleasant duty once again to give public thanks to those who have contributed materially to such success as this 10th abridged edition may merit.

Thanks, first, to DDC's users. To the hundreds of librarians who studied and criticized or reviewed Edition 17 and Abridged 9, some in print, some in correspondence, some face to face, and to the reviewers and critics of draft schedules of Edition 18, and Abridged 10 both at home and abroad, especially to the many critics of 340 and 510. To interested groups in formal organizations, notably the Classification Committee and the Policy and Research Committee of the Cataloging and Classification Section of the Resources and Technical Services Division of the American Library Association, and the Dewey Decimal Classification Sub-Committee of the Research and Development Committee of the (United Kingdom) Library Association. To A. J. Wells and J. C. Downing, and their staff at the British National Bibliography, who have supplied significant new insights into classification theory and practice.

Thanks, second, to all those officially connected with the Dewey Decimal Classification, to whose statesmanship, foresight, and imaginative understanding of libraries' needs may be credited the basic principles, enduring and new, which underlie this edition. This includes the directors of Forest Press, Inc., its executive director and assistant executive director, all members of the Decimal Classification Editorial Policy Committee, and my superiors in the Library of Congress.

Thanks, third, to the staff of the Decimal Classification Division, who did the hard work, most notably to Mrs. Helen L. Branch, Mrs. Elaine H. Canlas, Winton E. Matthews, Mrs. Emily K. Spears, and Assistant Editor Margaret J. Warren.

7. Conclusion

The foreword to the 15th full edition "earnestly" requested "all users to give us the benefit of their criticism in order that sometime our successors may actually bring out 'the perfect book.'" It appears unlikely that this or any other general classification will ever be "perfect"; nevertheless, improvement is always possible and devoutly to be pursued. So, once again, we urge all who use the DDC, whether students, teachers, or classifiers, to continue to give us the "benefit of their criticism."

Benjamin A. Custer
EDITOR

Decimal Classification Division
Processing Department
The Library of Congress
Washington, D.C. 20540
July 15, 1971

Glossary

References to futher information on each term defined may be found in the Index to Preface, Introduction, and Glossary, which follows.

Add note. An instruction directing the addition to a designated base number of digits derived either from a number sequence in the schedules or from a table. Replaces the former instruction to "divide like."

Application. A principle, concept, procedure, or technique basic to a specific discipline, used in another discipline. Example: application of psychology to management.

"Areas". Table 2. A table of notations designating geographical areas. Applied to other notations in the schedules and tables thru add notes.

Aspect. That part of a single subject which belongs to a specific discipline. Examples: the technical and economic aspects of automobile manufacture.

Attraction. Classification of a specific aspect of a subject in a discipline not devoted to that aspect, usually because the correct discipline contains no specific provision for the subject in question.

Author number. A combination of letters and/or figures representing the name of an author.

Auxiliary table. *See* **Table.**

Base number. (1) In a sequence of numbers, that portion which does not vary but remains the same in each member of the sequence. To this number digits from the tables or from another sequence in the schedules may be added as instructed. (2) The unvarying portion of a sequence from which digits are taken to form another sequence may also be referred to as a base number.

Bibliographic classification. *See* **Close classification.**

Book number. That portion of a call number which designates a specific individual work within its class. May consist of author number and/or other elements, e.g., subject of a biography.

Broad classification. (1) Use of only the more inclusive classes of a classification scheme, omitting detailed subdivision. Also called reduction of numbers. (2) A classification scheme which does not provide for minute subdivision of topics. *See also* **Reduction of numbers.**

Call number. A set of letters, numerals, and/or other symbols providing complete identification of an individual work and its relative location, consisting of class and book number and sometimes of such other data as date, volume number, copy number, location symbol.

Centered heading. A heading representing a concept for which there is no specific number in the hierarchy of notation, and which, therefore, covers a span of numbers.

Characteristic of division. Any of the various ways in which a given subject may be divided. Example: division of textiles by material, process used in manufacture, color, destined usage, etc.

Citation order. The order in which the classifier should select the subdivisions of a subject that is divided by more than one characteristic. Example: diagnosis of liver diseases is classed by liver diseases rather than by diagnosis. May be specified by an instruction note or a table of precedence (*q.v.*).

Class. (*noun*) (1) A group of objects exhibiting one or more common characteristics, usually identified by a specific notation. (2) One of the ten major groups numbered 0–9 of the DDC. Also known as main class. (3) A subdivision of the DDC of any degree of specificity. (*verb*) To assign a class number to an individual work. *See also* **Classify.**

Class elsewhere note. An instruction under a heading directing that certain specific portions of the topic, or related topics, be classed in another number.

Class here note. An instruction under a heading directing that topics broader than the heading, or otherwise not obviously part of the heading be classed in the given number *and,* by implication, *its subdivisions.*

Class number. That portion of a call number which designates the class of a given work.

Classification. (1) An arrangement in some logical order of the whole field of knowledge, or of some specified portion thereof. (2) The art of arranging books or other objects in conformity with such a scheme.

Classify. To arrange a collection of works according to the provisions of a classification scheme. *See also* **Class** (*verb*).

Close classification. (1) A classification providing for minute subdivision of topics. Also called bibliographic classification. (2) Arrangement of works in conformity with the provisions of such a scheme.

Comprehensive work. A work on a given subject *within one discipline* covering all, or most, of the subdivisions of the subject. *See also* **Interdisciplinary work.**

Cross classification. A situation in which a given work deals with two or more subdivisions of a subject, with each subdivision representing a different characteristic of division. Such a situation creates the possibility of inconsistent classification. Example: a work on diagnosis of liver diseases deals with two subdivisions of diseases, liver diseases (kind of disease) and diagnosis (procedure), and may be classed with either. *See also* **Citation order.**

Cross reference. An instruction note leading from the point at which comprehensive works on a subject are classed (whether stated or implied) to subdivisions of the topic located in numbers other than those subordinate to the number used for comprehensive works.

DDC. Dewey Decimal Classification.

Discipline. An organized field of study or branch of learning dealing with specific kinds of subjects and/or subjects considered from specific points of view.

Discontinued number. A number from the immediately preceding edition vacated because its content has been moved back to a more general number.

Divide-like. (*Obsolete*) An instruction to develop a span of numbers like another sequence by using the same pattern of terminal digits. Superseded by **Add note** (*q.v.*).

Division of DDC. The second degree of subdivision in the Classification (the first degree of subdivision of one of the ten main classes), represented by the second digit in the notation, e.g., the 2 in 620. There are 100 of these.

Entry. (1) In schedules and tables a self-contained unit of the text consisting of a number or span of numbers, a heading, and often one or more notes. (2) In index a term or phrase followed by information in the form either of a number or of a reference to another term or phrase.

Expansion. The development of a concept or series of concepts in the schedules or tables to provide for more minute subdivision.

General special concept. A subdivision of a topic according to a characteristic which has general applicability to other subdivisions that are based on different characteristics. Example: division of diseases by the process of diagnosis, which applies to kinds of diseases, such as liver diseases.

Heading. A word or phrase used as the title or rubric of a given class.

Hierarchical force. The property by which headings and certain notes apply to all subdivisions of the topic described and defined.

Hierarchy. The arrangement of disciplines and subjects in an order ranging from the most general to the most specific. In DDC degree of specificity is indicated by length of notation and by depth of indention.

Inclusion note. An enumeration of subordinate topics under a heading, not obviously part of it, that have not yet been given separate provision. Such notes do *not* have hierarchical force.

Instruction note. A note directing the user to take some specific step which is not obvious from the heading and its context or from the general notes.

Interdisciplinary work. A work dealing with a specific subject from the point of view of more than one discipline.

Main class of DDC. One of the ten major subdivisions of the Classification, represented by the first digit in the notation, e.g., the 6 in 600.

Memory aid. Any of various methods of using the same combination of numbers to represent the same topic in various contexts.

Notation. Numerals, letters, and/or other symbols used to represent the main and subordinate divisions of a classification scheme.

Number building. The process of making a number more specific thru addition of segments taken from other parts of the classification.

Number column. The column of numbers printed at the left side of the entries in the schedules and tables, and at the right side of those in the index.

Optional provision. A variation from the preferred provision, offered to users in the printed schedules and tables of the DDC, but not used in centralized classification as supplied by the Library of Congress.

Phoenix schedule. A completely new development of the schedule for a specific discipline. Except by chance, only the basic number for the discipline remains the same as in previous editions, all other numbers being freely reused.

Precedence table. *See* **Table of precedence.**

Reduction of numbers. Dropping by the classifier of one or more digits at the end of a number given in the schedules or tables. Results in a shorter number with a more inclusive meaning, thus in broader classification. *See* **Broad classification** (1).

Reduction of schedules. Dropping by the editors of some or all of the previous subdivisions of a number with resultant classification of these concepts in a higher number. This results in a notation for the topic that is one or more digits shorter than it was in the immediately preceding edition. *See* **Discontinued number.**

Relativity. That property of the index which reverses the subordination of subject to discipline, thus bringing together from all disciplines the various aspects of individual subjects.

Relocation. An adjustment in the schedules resulting in the shifting of a topic between successive editions from one number to another that differs in respects other than length.

Reuse of numbers. A total change in the meaning of a given number from one edition to another. Rarely occurs in DDC unless the reused number has been vacant for at least 25 years.

Scatter note. A class elsewhere note that does not lead to a specific location, but indicates that the topic will be classed in a wide variety of applicable locations.

Scatter reference. A cross reference in the index not referring to a specific term but suggesting a variety of possibilities.

Schedules. The series of numbers constituting the notation for the ten main DDC classes and all their subdivisions. Formerly called general tables or tables.

Scope note. A note enumerating general special qualifications applicable to a subject and its subdivisions but not given a separate development.

Section of DDC. The third degree of subdivision in the Classification (the second degree of subdivision of one of the ten main classes, and the first degree of subdivision of one of the 100 divisions), represented by the third digit in the notation, e.g., the 9 in 629. There are 1000 of these.

Shelf classification. A classification designed for use in arranging books on shelves rather than for minute precision in designating subject areas and relationships.

"Standard Subdivisions". Table 1. A table of notations designating certain frequently occurring forms or methods of treatment applicable to any subject or discipline. May be added, as required, to any number in the schedules.

"Subdivisions of Individual Languages". Table 4. A table of notations designating regularly occurring topics applicable to any language. May be added, as directed, to individual languages in 420–490.

"Subdivisions of Individual Literatures". Table 3. A table of notations designating regularly occurring topics applicable to any literature. May be added, as directed, to individual literatures in 810–890.

Subject. A specific unit or object of study. May be a person, group of people, thing, place, process, activity, abstract concept. Usually exhibits aspects belonging to more than one discipline.

Summary. A listing of the chief subdivisions of a number (i.e., those one digit longer) set forth at the head of the full development of the topic. The first three summaries (of main classes, divisions, sections respectively) stand at the head of the whole classification.

Synthesis of notation. *See* **Number building.**

Table. A sequence of dependent notations indicating various special concepts used repeatedly with a variety of subjects and disciplines. Used in number building but never by itself. Also called auxiliary table. Formerly called supplementary tables. The term **Tables** was formerly used also for what are now called **Schedules** (*q.v.*).

Table of precedence. A table stating the correct citation order under a subject that the schedules subdivide according to several characteristics. *See also* **Citation order.**

Work. A unit or series of units of information having physical form and lending itself to bibliographic description. Examples: books, periodicals, phonorecords, films, microforms.

Index to Preface, Introduction, and Glossary

References otherwise unidentified are to the numbered sections of the Introduction. References identified as *pref.* are to the numbered sections of the Preface. References to *glossary* indicate that a definition may be found in the alphabetically arranged Glossary. Section numbers printed in boldface type are those where the most important information is supplied, e.g., under Add notes, **3.3541–3.3544.**

Tables

Use of the Tables

These are *auxiliary* tables, and are used only in conjunction with the classification schedules. In some instances, the numbers from one table may be added to those of another table, but in all cases the numbers from one or a combination of tables are to be used only with appropriate numbers from the schedules.

The dash preceding each number merely shows that the number never stands alone. The dash is omitted when the table number is added to a schedule number to make a complete class number.

Full instructions may be found in the Introduction, those for the use of Table 1 in section 3.37, and those for Tables 2–4 in sections 3.3541 and 3.3543–3.3544.

Specific directions as to applicability precede each table.

Table 1. Standard Subdivisions

The following notations are never used alone, but may be used as required with any number from the schedules, e.g., classification (—01 in this table) of African languages (496): 496.01. If the number thus constructed exceeds three digits in length, a decimal point is inserted following the third digit

—01   Philosophy and theory

    Including classification, value, languages and communication, scientific principles, indexes, methodology

    (It is optional to class here techniques of writing, prefer 808; professional and occupational ethics, prefer 174)

    For dictionaries, see —03

—016   Bibliographies and catalogs

    (Use of this number is optional; prefer 016)

—02   Miscellany

    Including synopses, outlines, manuals, handbooks, patents, indentification marks, humorous treatment, audiovisual treatment, commercial miscellany, works for specific types of users

—021   Tabulated and related materials

    Tables, formulas, specifications, statistics, lists, inventories, catalogs of articles

    For catalogs of museums and exhibits, see —074

—022   Illustrations and models

    Including charts, designs, plans, diagrams

—023   The subject as a profession, occupation, hobby

    If preferred, class the subject as a profession or occupation in 331.7

    Number discontinued; class in —02

—[024]   Works for specific types of users

    Number discontinued; class in —02

—025   Directories

—026   Law

    (Use of this number is optional; prefer 340)

—[027]   Patents and identification marks

    Number discontinued; class in —02

—028   Techniques, apparatus, equipment, materials

> Ways in which specific objectives of an art or skill are obtained ("how-to-do-it"); necessary tools and materials
>
> Class here laboratory manuals, data processing as applied to the subject
>
> Class data processing in research in —07

—03   Dictionaries, encyclopedias, concordances

—*04*   General special

> This subdivision is reserved for special concepts that have general application thruout the regular subdivisions of certain specific subjects; it is to be used only when specifically set forth in the schedules

—05   Serial publications

> Including periodicals
>
> Class administrative reports and proceedings of organizations in —06
>
> If preferred, class periodicals on all subjects in 050, journals in 070

—06   Organizations

> History, charters, regulations, membership lists, administrative reports and proceedings of permanent, temporary, business organizations

—[061–065]   Specific kinds of organizations

> Numbers discontinued; class in —06

—07   Study and teaching

> Including secondary, higher, adult schools and courses; research; students, learners, apprentices, novices; competitions and awards; programed teaching and learning, use of teaching machines
>
> Class here resources
>
> Class elementary schools in 372.1, elementary textbooks and courses in 372.3–372.8, textbooks at higher levels on a subject as treatises; do not use —07 for textbooks

—[071–072]   Schools, courses, research

> Numbers discontinued; class in —07

—074   Museums and exhibits

> Collections, guidebooks, catalogs

—075   Collecting and collections of objects

> *For museums and exhibits, see* —074

Table 1. Standard Subdivisions

—076   Review and exercise

> Workbooks with problems, questions, answers

> Including civil service examinations

—[077–
  079]   Other topics

> Numbers discontinued; class in —07

—08   Collections

> Not planned and written as complete wholes

> Class literary essays in 800

—09   Historical and geographical treatment

—091   Treatment by areas, regions, places in general

> History and description

> Add "Areas" notation 1 from Table 2 to base number —09, e.g., the subject in Torrid Zone —0913

> Class persons associated with the subject regardless of area, region, place in —092; treatment by specific continents, countries, localities in —093–099

—092   Persons regardless of area, region, place

> Description and critical appraisal of work

> (It is optional to class here biography, autobiography, diaries, reminiscences of persons associated with the subject; see treatment described at 920)

—093–099   Treatment by specific continents, countries, localities; extraterrestrial worlds

> History and description by place, by specific instance of the subject

> Add "Areas" notation 3–9 from Table 2 to base number —09, e.g., the subject in United States —0973

> Class treatment by areas, regions, places not limited by continent, country, locality in —091; persons associated with the subject regardless of area, region, place in —092

Table 2. Areas

The following notations are never used alone, but may be used as required (either directly when so noted or thru the interposition of "Standard Subdivisions" notation 09 from Table 1) with any number from the schedules, e.g., adult education (374.9) in Japan (—52 in this table) 374.952, history (9) of Japan 952, geography (91) of Japan 915.2. If the number thus constructed exceeds three digits in length, a decimal point is inserted following the third digit

SUMMARY

—1   Areas, regions, places in general
—2   Persons regardless of area, region, place
—3   The ancient world
        —4–9 The modern world
—4   Europe
—5   Asia   Orient   Far East
—6   Africa
—7   North America
—8   South America
—9   Other parts of world and extraterrestrial worlds   Pacific Ocean islands (Oceania)

—1   Areas, regions, places in general

Not limited by continent, country, locality

Class persons regardless of area, region, place as instructed at 920; specific continents, countries, localities in —3–9

▶   —11–13 Zonal regions

Class comprehensive works in —1

—11   Frigid Zones

—12   Temperate Zones (Middle Latitude Zones)

—13   Torrid Zone (Tropics)

▶   —14–16 Physiographic regions

Class comprehensive works in —1

—14   Land and land forms

Continents; islands; elevations, e.g., mountains; depressions and openings, e.g., valleys, caves; plane regions, e.g., prairies; coastal regions; soil

—15   Types of vegetation

Forests, grasslands, deserts

Table 2. Areas

—16 Air and water

  Including salt-water lagoons, inland seas, coastal pools; fresh and brackish surface and ground waters

—161 Atmosphere

  Troposphere, stratosphere, ionosphere

—162 Oceans and seas

  Class ocean and sea basins in —182

   For Atlantic Ocean, see —163; Pacific Ocean, —164; Indian Ocean, —165

—163 Atlantic Ocean

  Including Arctic Ocean, Baltic Sea, North Sea, Mediterranean Sea, Black Sea, Labrador Sea, Caribbean Sea, Gulf of Mexico

  Class Atlantic sector of Antarctic waters in —167

—164 Pacific Ocean

  Including Bering Sea, Sea of Okhotsk, Sea of Japan, East China Sea, South China Sea, Java Sea, Arafura Sea

  Class Pacific sector of Antarctic waters in —167

—165 Indian Ocean

  Including Red Sea, Persian Gulf, Andaman Sea, Timor Sea

  Class Indian Ocean sector of Antarctic waters in —167

—167 Antarctic waters

  Atlantic, Pacific, Indian Ocean sectors

—17 Socioeconomic regions

  Including regions where specific racial, ethnic, national groups predominate; where specific languages predominate; where specific religions predominate

—171 Political orientation

  Empires and political unions, blocs, nonself-governing territories

  Class Roman Empire in —37

—172 Degree of economic development

  Regions of high, medium, low development

—173 Concentration of population

  Urban, suburban, rural regions

—[174–176]   Regions where specific racial, ethnic, national groups, specific languages, specific religions predominate

Numbers discontinued; class in —17

—18   Other kinds of terrestrial regions

—181   Hemispheres

Eastern, Western, Northern, Southern

—182   Ocean and sea basins

Continents facing and islands in specific major bodies of water, e.g., Atlantic region

Class here the Occident

Class ocean and sea waters in —162–167

—19   Space

Class extraterrestrial worlds in —99

—2   Persons regardless of area, region, place

When instructed to add "Areas" notation 1–9 directly from Table 2 instead of adding "Standard Subdivisions" notation 091–099 from Table 1, class here description and critical appraisal of work, e.g., elementary educators 372.92

(It is optional to class here biography, autobiography, diaries, reminiscences of persons associated with the subject; see treatment described at 920)

—[22–24]   Collected and individual persons

Numbers discontinued; class in —2

▶   —3–9 Specific continents, countries, localities; extraterrestrial worlds

Class here specific instances of the subject

Class comprehensive works in "Standard Subdivisions" notation 09 from Table 1; areas, regions, places not limited by continent, country, locality in —1; persons regardless of area, region, place as provided at 920

—3   The ancient world

If preferred, class in —4–9

—31   China

Table 2. Areas

—32	Egypt
—33	Palestine
	Including Judea
—34	India
—35	Mesopotamia and Iranian Plateau
	Class central Asia in —39
—36	Europe north and west of Italian peninsula
—362	British Isles
—363	Germanic regions
	For British Isles, see —362
—364	Celtic regions
	Including Gaul
	For British Isles, see —362
—366	Iberian Peninsula
—37	Italian peninsula and adjacent territories
	Including Etruria, Sicily, Malta, Sardinia, Corsica
	Class here Roman Empire
—38	Greece
	Including Mycenae
	For Aegean Sea islands, see —391
—39	Other parts of ancient world
—391	Aegean Sea islands
	Including Crete
—392	Asia Minor and Cyprus

► ## —4–9 The modern world; extraterrestrial worlds

(It is optional to class here the ancient world; prefer —3)

Class comprehensive works on specific physiographic regions or features extending over more than one country, state or other unit and identified by * with the unit where noted in this table, e.g., Scottish Highlands —411, Appalachian Mountains —74. Class works on a part of such a region or feature with the specific unit where the part is located, e.g., Scottish Highlands in North Central Scotland —412, Blue Ridge —755; but, if preferred, class parts of such a region or feature with comprehensive works on the region or feature, e.g., Scottish Highlands in North Central Scotland —411, Blue Ridge —74

Class comprehensive works in "Standard Subdivisions" notation 09 from Table 1

—4   Europe

SUMMARY

—41	Scotland and Ireland	
—42	British Isles	England
—43	Central Europe	Germany
—44	France and Monaco	
—45	Italy and adjacent territories	
—46	Iberian Peninsula and adjacent islands	Spain
—47	Eastern Europe	Union of Soviet Socialist Republics (Soviet Union)
—48	Northern Europe	Scandinavia
—49	Other parts of Europe	

—41   Scotland and Ireland

► ## —411–414 Divisions of Scotland

Class comprehensive works in —41

—411   Northern Scotland

Shetland and Orkney Islands, Caithness, Sutherland, Ross and Cromarty

Class here *Scottish Highlands, *Hebrides

—412   North central Scotland

Inverness, Nairn, Moray, Banff, Aberdeen, Kincardine

* Class parts of this physiographic region or feature as instructed under —4–9

56

Table 2. Areas

—413   *Central Scottish Lowlands

     Angus, Perth, Fife, Kinross, Clackmannan, Stirling, Dunbarton, Argyll, Bute

     Class here *Forth River

—414   Southern Scotland

     Renfrew, Ayr, Lanark, the Lothians, Berwick, Peebles, Selkirk, Roxburgh, Dumfries, Kirkcudbright, Wigtown

     Class here *Clyde River

—415   Ireland

     For divisions of Ireland, see —416–419

▶   —416–419 Divisions of Ireland

     Class comprehensive works in —415

—416   Ulster   Northern Ireland

     Antrim, Londonderry, Tyrone, Down, Armagh, Fermanagh, Donegal, Monaghan, Cavan

---

▶   —417–419 Republic of Ireland

     Class comprehensive works in —415

     For Donegal, Monaghan, Cavan, see —416

—417   Connacht

     Leitrim, Sligo, Mayo, Galway, Roscommon

—418   Leinster

     Longford, Westmeath, Meath, Louth, Dublin, Wicklow, Kildare, Offaly, Laoighis, Carlow, Wexford, Kilkenny

—419   Munster

     Waterford, Tipperary, Clare, Limerick, Cork, Kerry

—42   British Isles   England

     Class here Great Britain, United Kingdom

     For Scotland and Ireland, see —41

▶   —421–428 England

     Class comprehensive works in —42

—421   Greater London

     Including boroughs created from Essex [*formerly* —426], from Kent and Surrey [*both formerly* —422]

* Class parts of this physiographic region or feature as instructed under —4–9

—422   Southeastern England

     Surrey, Kent, Sussex, Hampshire, Berkshire; Isle of Wight

     Class here *Thames River

     Class London boroughs created from Kent and Surrey [*both formerly* —422] in —421

     For Greater London, see —421

—423   Southwestern England and Channel Islands

     Including Wiltshire, Dorset, Devon, Cornwall, Somerset

—424   Midlands of England, and Monmouth

     Including Gloucester, Hereford, Shropshire, Stafford, Worcester, Warwick

     For East Midlands, see —425

—425   East Midlands of England

     Derby, Nottingham, Lincoln, Leicester, Rutland, Northampton, Huntingdon and Peterborough, Bedford, Oxford, Buckingham, Hertford, Cambridge, Isle of Ely

     Class here the *Fens

—426   Eastern England

     Norfolk, Suffolk, Essex

     Class London boroughs created from Essex [*formerly* —426] in —421

—427   North central England

     Cheshire, Lancashire, York

—428   Northern England and Isle of Man

     Including Durham, Northumberland, Cumberland, Westmorland

     Class here *Lake District

—429   Wales

     For Monmouth, see —424

—43   Central Europe   Germany

     For Switzerland, see —494

—436   Austria and Liechtenstein

—437   Czechoslovakia

—438   Poland

—439   Hungary

* Class parts of this physiographic region or feature as instructed under —4-9

Table 2. Areas

—44 France and Monaco

Class a specific overseas department of France with the subject, e.g., Martinique —729

For Corsica, see —459

—[443–449] Parts of France

Numbers discontinued; class in —44

—45 Italy and adjacent territories

Including independent states of San Marino, Vatican City

—[453–456] Parts of Italy, Vatican City

Numbers discontinued; class in —45

—458 Sicily and adjacent islands

Including Malta

—459 Sardinia and Corsica

—46 Iberian Peninsula and adjacent islands   Spain

Including Balearic Islands, Andorra, Gibraltar

For Canary Islands, see —64

—469 Portugal

Including Madeira, Azores

—47 Eastern Europe   Union of Soviet Socialist Republics (Soviet Union)

For Asiatic Russia, see —57; Soviet Republics of central Asia, —58; Balkan Peninsula, —496

—471 Finland

—[473–479] Parts of Soviet Union

Numbers discontinued; class in —47

—48 Northern Europe   Scandinavia

For Finland, see —471; Iceland and Faeroes, —491

—481 Norway

Including divisions of Norway [*formerly* —482–484]

—[482–484] Divisions of Norway

Class in —481

—485 Sweden

Including divisions of Sweden [*formerly* —486–488]

—[486–488]   Divisions of Sweden

> Class in —485

—489   Denmark

> *For Greenland, see —98*

—49   Other parts of Europe

—491   Iceland and Faeroes

—492   Netherlands (Holland)

> Class Netherlands Antilles in —729
>
> *For Surinam, see —88*

—493   Belgium and Luxembourg

—494   Switzerland

> Class here *Alps

—495   Greece

> Class here Byzantine Empire
>
> *For Aegean Sea islands, see —499*

—496   Balkan Peninsula

> Class here *Danube River, Ottoman Empire
>
> Class Turkey in Europe [*formerly* —496] in —561
>
> Class each specific country of Balkan Peninsula, of Ottoman Empire not provided for here with the subject, e.g., Greece —495

—496 5   Albania

—497   Central Balkans   Yugoslavia

—497 7   Bulgaria

—498   Romania

—499   Aegean Sea islands

> Class Euboea, Kythera in —495

—499 8   Crete

* Class parts of this physiographic region or feature as instructed under —4–9

Table 2. Areas

—5   Asia   Orient   Far East

Class here Eurasia

For Europe, see —4

SUMMARY

—51 China and adjacent areas
—52 Japan and adjacent islands
—53 Arabian Peninsula and adjacent areas
—54 South Asia   India
—55 Iran (Persia)
—56 Middle East (Near East)
—57 Siberia (Asiatic Russia)
—58 Central Asia
—59 Southeast Asia

▶

—51–52 Far East

Class comprehensive works in —5, Far Eastern Siberia in —57, southeast Asia in —59

—51   China and adjacent areas

Including Taiwan (Formosa), Hong Kong and Macao colonies, Tibet, Outer Mongolia (Mongolian People's Republic)

—[512–517] Taiwan, Hong Kong, Macao, Tibet, Outer Mongolia

Numbers discontinued; class in —51

—519   Korea

—52   Japan and adjacent islands

Including Ryukyu and Bonin Islands

—[521–528] Tokyo, Ryukyu and Bonin Islands

Numbers discontinued; class in —52

—53   Arabian Peninsula and adjacent areas

Including Yemen, Southern Yemen, Oman, Qatar, Bahrein, Kuwait, Saudi Arabia; Gaza Strip, Sinai Peninsula

—54   South Asia   India

Class here *Himalayas, *Indus River, *Brahmaputra River

For southeast Asia, see —59

—549   Pakistan and other jurisdictions

Including Maldive Islands, Sikkim, Bhutan, Ceylon, Nepal

—[549 3]   Ceylon

Number discontinued; class in —549

* Class parts of this physiographic region or feature as instructed under —4–9

—55	Iran (Persia)
—56	Middle East (Near East)

Class each specific country of Middle East not provided for here with the subject, e.g., Saudi Arabia —53

—561	Turkey

Class here divisions of Turkey [*formerly* 562–566]; Turkey in Europe [*formerly* —496]; Asia Minor

—[562–566]	Divisions of Turkey

Class in —561

—*564*	Cyprus
—[564 5]	Cyprus

Number discontinued; class in —564

—567	Iraq
—569	Eastern Mediterranean
—569 1	Syria
—569 2	Lebanon
—569 4	Palestine Israel

Class here *Jordan River, *Dead Sea

For Jordan, see —5695; *Gaza Strip,* —53

—569 5	Jordan
—57	Siberia (Asiatic Russia)

Class here Soviet Union in Asia

Class Soviet Republics of central Asia in —58

—58	Central Asia

Including Kirghiz, Kazakh, Turkmen, Tadzhik, Uzbek Soviet Socialist Republics

—581	Afghanistan
—59	Southeast Asia
—591	Burma
—593	Thailand (Siam)
—594	Laos

* Class parts of this physiographic region or feature as instructed under —4–9

Table 2. Areas

—595	Commonwealth of Nations territories

Malaysia (Malaya, Sabah, Sarawak), Brunei protectorate, independent republic of Singapore

Class here North Borneo [*formerly* —911], Malay Peninsula

For Burma, see —591; *Thailand,* —593

—596	Cambodia
—597	Vietnam

Class here *Mekong River

—598	Indonesia [*formerly* —91]

Class here Sunda Islands [*formerly* —92], Malay Archipelago, Borneo

For North Borneo, see —595; *Philippine Islands,* —599; *New Guinea,* —95

—599	Philippine Islands [*formerly* —914]
—6	Africa
—61	North Africa

Including Tunisia, Libya

Class here Barbary States

Class each specific part of North Africa not provided for here with the subject, e.g., Algeria —65

—62	Countries of the *Nile Egypt

Including Suez

For Sinai, see —53

—624	Sudan

Including provinces of Sudan [*formerly* —625–629]

—[625–629]	Provinces of Sudan

Class in —624

—63	Ethiopia (Abyssinia)
—64	Northwest African coast and offshore islands

Morocco, Spanish West Africa, Canary Islands

—65	Algeria

* Class parts of this physiographic region or feature as instructed under —4–9

—66   West Africa and offshore islands

> Including Mauritania, Mali, Upper Volta, Niger, Senegal, Sierra Leone, the Gambia, Guinea republic, Portuguese Guinea, Cape Verde Islands, Dahomey, Togo, islands of the Gulf of Guinea
>
> Class here *Sahara Desert

—666   Liberia and Ivory Coast

—667   Ghana

—669   Nigeria

—67   Central Africa and offshore islands   East Africa

> Including Cameroons, Rio Muni, Gabon, Republic of the Congo (former Middle Congo), Angola, Central African Republic, Chad, Equatorial Guinea, Spanish Guinea, Rwanda, Burundi, French Somaliland, Socotra, Somalia, Mozambique
>
> Class here Black Africa, Africa south of the Sahara
>
> Class each specific country of Black Africa, of Africa south of the Sahara, not provided for here, with the subject, e.g., Nigeria —669

—675   Congo Republic

> Former Belgian Congo

—676   Uganda and Kenya

—678   Tanzania

—68   South Africa   Republic of South Africa

> Including Botswana, Swaziland, Lesotho, South-West Africa (Namibia)

—689   Rhodesia, Zambia, Malawi

—69   South Indian Ocean islands

> Including Madagascar (Malagasy Republic), Seychelles, Réunion, Mauritius

—7   North America

> Class Western Hemisphere in —181

—701   North American Indians in North America

* Class parts of this physiographic region or feature as instructed under —4–9

Table 2. Areas

SUMMARY

—71	Canada	
—72	Middle America	Mexico
—73	United States	
—74	Northeastern United States (New England and Middle Atlantic states)	
—75	Southeastern United States (South Atlantic states)	
—76	South central United States	Gulf Coast states
—77	North central United States	Lake states
—78	Western United States	
—79	Great Basin and Pacific Slope region of United States	Pacific Coast states

—71 Canada

—711   British Columbia

    Class here *Rocky Mountains in Canada

—712   Northern territories and prairie provinces

    Including Yukon and Northwest Territories

    Class here Canadian Arctic

—712 3   Alberta

—712 4   Saskatchewan

—712 7   Manitoba

—713   Ontario

    Class here *Great Lakes in Canada

—714   Quebec

    Class here *Saint Lawrence River

—715   New Brunswick

    Class here Maritime Provinces, Atlantic Provinces

     For Nova Scotia, see —716; *Prince Edward Island,* —717

—716   Nova Scotia

—717   Prince Edward Island

—718   Newfoundland and adjacent islands

    Including Saint Pierre, Miquelon

     For Labrador, see —719

—719   Labrador

    Territory of province of Newfoundland

* Class parts of this physiographic region or feature as instructed under —4–9

—72	Middle America Mexico
—[725]	Valley of Mexico

Number discontinued; class in —72

—728	Central America

For Panama, see —862

—728 1	Guatemala
—728 2	British Honduras (Belize)
—728 3	Honduras
—728 4	El Salvador
—728 5	Nicaragua
—728 6	Costa Rica
—729	West Indies (Antilles) and Bermuda

Including Lesser Antilles (Caribbees), Bahama Islands

▶   —729 1–729 5 Greater Antilles

Class comprehensive works in —729

—729 1	Cuba and adjacent islands
—729 2	Jamaica and adjacent islands
—729 3	Dominican Republic

Class here comprehensive works on Hispaniola

For Haiti, see —7294

—729 4	Haiti
—729 5	Puerto Rico
—[729 6–729 8]	Lesser Antilles (Caribbees)

Numbers discontinued; class in —729

—729 9	Bermuda
—73	United States

For specific states, see —74–79

Table 2. Areas

▶ **—74–79 Specific states of United States**

Class comprehensive works in —73

For Hawaii, see —969

—74 **Northeastern United States (New England and Middle Atlantic states)**

Class here *Appalachian Mountains, *Connecticut River, United States east of Allegheny Mountains, United States east of Mississippi River

For southeastern United States, see —75; south central United States, —76; north central United States, —77

▶ **—741–746 New England**

Class comprehensive works in —74

—741 Maine

—742 New Hampshire

—743 Vermont

—744 Massachusetts

—745 Rhode Island

—746 Connecticut

▶ **—747–749 Middle Atlantic states**

Class comprehensive works in —74

—747 New York

Class here *Lake Ontario

—[747 1] New York City

Number discontinued; class in —747

—748 Pennsylvania

—749 New Jersey

—75 **Southeastern United states (South Atlantic states)**

Class here southern states, Piedmont, *Atlantic Coastal Plain

For south central United States, see —76

—751 Delaware

* Class parts of this physiographic region or feature as instructed under —4–9

—752	Maryland
	Class here *Potomac River
—753	District of Columbia (Washington)
—754	West Virginia
—755	Virginia
	Class here *Blue Ridge, *Chesapeake Bay
—756	North Carolina
—757	South Carolina
—758	Georgia
—759	Florida
—76	South central United States Gulf Coast states

▶   —761–764 Gulf Coast states

Class comprehensive works in —76

For Florida, see —759

—761	Alabama
—762	Mississippi
—763	Louisiana
—764	Texas
	Class here *Rio Grande
—766	Oklahoma
—767	Arkansas
—768	Tennessee
	Class here *Tennessee River and Valley
—769	Kentucky
	Class here *Ohio River, *Cumberland Mountains
	Class Ohio Valley in —77

* Class parts of this physiographic region or feature as instructed under —4–9

Table 2. Areas

—77	North central United States Lake states

Class here Middle West, *Mississippi River and Valley, *Ohio Valley, *Great Lakes

Class Ohio River in —769; each specific state of Middle West not provided for here with the subject, e.g., Kansas —781

▶ **—771–776 Lake states**

Class comprehensive works in —77

For New York, see —747; Pennsylvania, —748

—771   Ohio

Class here *Lake Erie

—772   Indiana

—773   Illinois

—774   Michigan

Class here Lakes *Huron, *Michigan, *Superior

—775   Wisconsin

—776   Minnesota

—777   Iowa

—778   Missouri

—78   Western United States

Class here the West, *Missouri River, *Rocky Mountains

For Great Basin and Pacific Slope region of United States, see —79

—781   Kansas

—782   Nebraska

—783   South Dakota

—784   North Dakota

▶ **—786–789 Rocky Mountains states**

Class comprehensive works in —78

For Idaho, see —796

—786   Montana

—787   Wyoming

—788   Colorado

* Class parts of this physiographic region or feature as instructed under —4–9

—789	New Mexico
—79	Great Basin and Pacific Slope region of United States Pacific Coast states
—791	Arizona

Class here *Colorado River

—792	Utah
—793	Nevada
—794	California
—795	Oregon

Class here Pacific Northwest, *Cascade and *Coast Ranges

For Idaho, see —796; *Washington,* —797; *British Columbia,* —711

—796	Idaho
—797	Washington
—798	Alaska
—8	South America

Class here Latin America, Spanish America, the *Andes

For Middle America, see —72

—801	South American Indians in South America
—81	Brazil
—82	Argentina
—83	Chile
—84	Bolivia
—85	Peru
—86	Northwestern South America and Panama
—861	Colombia
—862	Panama

For Panama Canal Zone, see —863

—863	Panama Canal Zone
—866	Ecuador
—87	Venezuela

* Class parts of this physiographic region or feature as instructed under —4–9

Table 2. Areas

—88   Guianas

> Guyana (British Guiana), Guyane (French Guiana), Surinam (Dutch Guiana)

—89   Other parts of South America

—892   Paraguay

—895   Uruguay

—9   Other parts of world and extraterrestrial worlds
Pacific Ocean islands (Oceania)

—[91]   Indonesia

> Class in —598

—[911]   North Borneo

> Class in —595

—[914]   Philippine Islands

> Class in —599

—[92]   Sunda Islands

> Class in 598

—93–96 Pacific Ocean islands (Oceania)

Class comprehensive works in —9; each specific island or group of islands not provided for here with the subject, e.g., Japan —52

—93   New Zealand and Melanesia

> Including New Caledonia territory, New Hebrides, Bismarck Archipelago; Loyalty, Solomon, Admiralty Islands
>
> *For Louisiade Archipelago, D'Entrecasteaux Islands, see —95; Fiji, —96*

—931   New Zealand

> Including Chatham, Pitt, Auckland, Antipodes islands

—931 2   North Island

—931 5   South Island and Stewart Island

—94   Australia

> Including Lord Howe and Norfolk Islands

—941   State of Western Australia

—942   Central Australia

>   Including state of South Australia, Northern Territory
>
>   Class here northern Australia
>
>>   *For state of Western Australia, see* —941; *Queensland,* —943

—943   Queensland

>   Including Great Barrier Reef

—944   New South Wales

>   Class here *Murray River

—945   Victoria

—946   Tasmania

—947   Australian Capital Territory

—95   New Guinea (Papua)

>   Including West Irian (province of Indonesia), Louisiade Archipelago, D'Entrecasteaux Islands

—96   Other parts of Pacific

>   Polynesia and Micronesia
>
>   Including Easter, Pitcairn, Henderson, Ducie, Oeno, Society, Tubuai (Austral), Gambier, Rapa, Cook, Manihiki, Marquesas, Tuamotu, Line, Caroline, Marianas (Ladrone), Gilbert, Ellice, Phoenix, Marshall Islands; Tonga, Samoa, Tokelau, Nauru, Palmyra, Midway, Fiji

—969   Hawaii

>   State of the United States of America

—97   Atlantic Ocean islands

>   Bouvet Island, Falklands, Saint Helena, their dependencies
>
>   Class each specific island or group of islands not provided for here with the subject, e.g., Azores —469

—98   Arctic islands and Antarctica [*formerly* —99]

>   Including Svalbard (Spitsbergen), Greenland, Jan Mayen Island, Franz Josef Land, Novaya Zemlya (New Land), Severnaya Zemlya (Northern Land)
>
>   Class each Arctic island or group of islands not provided for here with the subject, e.g., Northwest Territories of Canada —712

—99   Extraterrestrial worlds

>   Worlds other than man's Earth
>
>   Class Antarctica [*formerly* —99] in —98
>
>   Class space in —19

* Class parts of this physiographic region or feature as instructed under —4–9

Table 3. Subdivisions of Individual Literatures

The following notations are never used alone, but may be used as required with the base numbers for individual literatures identified by * under 810–890, e.g., English (base number 82) poetry (—1 in this table): 821. If the number thus constructed exceeds three digits in length, a decimal point is inserted following the third digit, e.g., Portuguese (base number 869) poetry 869.1

—01–07   Standard subdivisions

>   Notations from Table 1

—08   Collections

>   In more than one form by more than one author
>
>   Class here works giving equal attention to collections of literary texts and to history, description, critical appraisal of the specific literature
>
>   Class collections by individual authors in —1–8
>
>   *For history, description, critical appraisal, see* —09

—09   History, description, critical appraisal

>   Of more than one form by more than one author
>
>   Class description, critical appraisal of individual authors in —1–8

—1–8 Specific forms

>   Observe table of precedence under 800
>
>   Class description, critical appraisal, collected works of an individual author with the form with which he is chiefly identified; or, if preferred, class these and also single works regardless of form all in —8; class comprehensive works in the base number for the language (adding 0 when required to make a three-digit number)

—1   Poetry

>   Including description, critical appraisal, single and collected works of individual authors

—101–107   Standard subdivisions

>   Notations from Table 1

—108   Collections by more than one author

>   Class here works giving equal attention to collections of texts and to history, description, critical appraisal
>
>   *For history, description, critical appraisal, see* —109

—109   History, description, critical appraisal of more than one author

—2   Drama

Including description, critical appraisal, single and collected works of individual authors

—201–207   Standard subdivisions

Notations from Table 1

—208   Collections by more than one author

Class here works giving equal attention to collections of texts and to history, description, critical appraisal

For history, description, critical appraisal, see —209

—209   History, description, critical appraisal of more than one author

—3   Fiction

Including description, critical appraisal, single and collected works of individual authors

—301–307   Standard subdivisions

Notations from Table 1

—308   Collections by more than one author

Class here works giving equal attention to collections of texts and to history, description, critical appraisal

For history, description, critical appraisal, see —309

—309   History, description, critical appraisal of more than one author

—4   Essays

Including description, critical appraisal, single and collected works of individual authors

—401–407   Standard subdivisions

Notations from Table 1

—408   Collections by more than one author

Class here works giving equal attention to collections of texts and to history, description, critical appraisal

For history, description, critical appraisal, see —409

—409   History, description, critical appraisal of more than one author

Table 3. Subdivisions of Individual Literatures

—5   Speeches

> Including description, critical appraisal, single and collected works of individual authors

—501–507   Standard subdivisions

> Notations from Table 1

—508   Collections by more than one author

> Class here works giving equal attention to collections of texts and to history, description, critical appraisal
>
> *For history, description, critical appraisal, see* —509

—509   History, description, critical appraisal of more than one author

—6   Letters

> Including description, critical appraisal, single and collected works of individual authors

—601–607   Standard subdivisions

> Notations from Table 1

—608   Collections by more than one author

> Class here works giving equal attention to collections of texts and to history, description, critical appraisal
>
> *For history, description, critical appraisal, see* —609

—609   History, description, critical appraisal of more than one author

—7   Satire and humor

> Including description, critical appraisal, single and collected works of individual authors

—701–707   Standard subdivisions

> Notations from Table 1

—708   Collections by more than one author

> Class here works giving equal attention to collections of texts and to history, description, critical appraisal
>
> *For history, description, critical appraisal, see* —709

—709   History, description, critical appraisal of more than one author

—8   Miscellaneous writings

> Quotations, epigrams, diaries, journals, reminiscences, experimental and nonformalized works, prose literature
>
> Including description, critical appraisal, single and collected miscellaneous writings of individual authors; description, critical appraisal, collected works of individual authors not limited to or chiefly identified with one specific form
>
> (It is optional to class here description, critical appraisal, single and collected works of individual authors regardless of form; prefer —1–8)
>
> Class a specific identifiable form of literature with the form, e.g., essays —4

—801–807   Standard subdivisions

> Notations from Table 1

—808   Collections by more than one author

> Class here works giving equal attention to collections of texts and to history, description, critical appraisal
>
> *For history, description, critical appraisal, see* —809

—809   History, description, critical appraisal of more than one author

Table 4. Subdivisions of Individual Languages

The following notations are never used alone, but may be used as required with the base numbers for individual languages identified by * under 420–490, e.g., English (base number 42) reading (—84 in this table): 428.4. If the number thus constructed exceeds three digits in length, a decimal point is inserted following the third digit. Standard subdivisions are added to —1–8 as usual from Table 1, e.g., serial publications on grammar of the language —505

—01–02   Standard subdivisions

> Notations from Table 1

—03   Encyclopedias

> Class dictionaries of the standard form of the language in —3

—05–09   Standard subdivisions

> Notations from Table 1

▶   —1–6 Standard form of the language

Descriptive, analytical, historical works only

Class comprehensive works in the base number for the language (adding 0 when required to make a three-digit number), practical works on standard usage in —8

—1   Written and spoken codes of the standard form of the language

> Including abbreviations, acronyms, punctuation, notation (alphabet or ideographs), capitalization, spelling, pronunciation, intonation, paleography
>
> *For etymology, see —2; dictionaries, —3; structural system, —5*

—2   Etymology of the standard form of the language

> Phonetic, graphic, semantic development of words and morphemes
>
> Including foreign elements
>
> *For notation, spelling, pronunciation, intonation, see —1*

—3   Dictionaries of the standard form of the language

> Including bilingual dictionaries; dictionaries of abbreviations, acronyms, synonyms, antonyms, homonyms
>
> Class a bilingual dictionary with the language in which it will be the more useful, e.g., most libraries in English-speaking regions will find a dictionary of German and English most useful classed with German in 433. If classification with either language is equally useful, class with the language coming later in the sequence 420–490, e.g., a dictionary of German and French in 443

—[31–39] Specific kinds of dictionaries

> Numbers discontinued; class in —3

—5   Structural system (Grammar) of the standard form of the language

> Morphology and syntax

—6   Prosody of the standard form of the language

—7   Nonstandard forms of the language

> Description, analysis, usage of slang; dialects; regional, provincial, colonial, early variations

—[709]   Modern nonregional variations

> Number discontinued; class in —7

—8   Standard usage of the language (Applied linguistics)

> Practical works on general, formal, informal usage
>
> Including translating and interpreting to and from other languages
>
> Class here the language for foreigners
>
> For *dictionaries, see* —3; *composition,* 808

—81   Words

> Spelling, pronunciation, meaning

►   —82–83 Expression

> Class comprehensive works in —8

—82   Structural approach to expression

> Formal presentation of grammar, vocabulary, reading selections
>
> For *words, see* —81; *reading,* —84

—83   Audio-lingual approach to expression

> Informal presentation thru practice in correct usage
>
> For *pronunciation, see* —81

Table 4. Subdivisions of Individual Languages

—84 Reading

Remedial and developmental

For readers, see —86

—86 Readers

Graded selections with emphasis on structure and vocabulary as needed

Relocations and Discontinued Numbers

Here for the convenience of classifiers wishing to survey the changes between the past and present editions are brought together in one list all the relocations between Abridged editions 9 and 10, and all numbers discontinued since 9.

In a relocation one or more topics are shifted to a new number differing from the old in respects other than length. If the relocation is partial, the original number remains, but if it is total the original number is vacated and, therefore, meaningless; in a few instances a vacated number has been immediately reused with a new meaning. A discontinued number is the result of schedule reduction between editions, in which case one or more topics are shifted to another number shorter than the old but not otherwise differing from it. These features are described and explained in the Preface, sections 3.3 and 4, and in the Introduction, sections 3.356 and 5.

The column headed *Edition 9* indicates in numerical order each number in that edition from which a topic or group of topics has been shifted; the column headed *Edition 10* indicates each corresponding number in the present edition to which a topic or group of topics has been shifted. If two or more topics have been shifted from one number to two or more numbers, each separate shift is shown.

Numbers in the *Edition 9* column printed in square brackets are no longer in use (or, if in use, have completely new meanings, and are therefore also listed among the reused numbers in section 4 of the Preface): if followed by an asterisk, they have been discontinued as a result of schedule reduction; otherwise, they have lost their content as a result of total relocation. Numbers in the *Edition 9* column not printed in brackets have lost part of their meaning thru relocation, but still retain some of their original meaning. For example, part of what was in 026–027 has been relocated to 021.7; all that was in 164 has been relocated to 511; all that was in 311 has been relocated, some to 001.4 and some to 519.5; 028.8 has been discontinued and all its content moved up to the broader number 028.

Only numbers appear in this list; for details of the topics concerned the classifier should consult the appropriate parts of the schedules and tables.

The letters "s.s." mean standard subdivisions from Table 1; "area" means area subdivisions from Table 2; "lang. sub." means subdivisions of individual languages from Table 4.

Edition 9	Edition 10	Edition 9	Edition 10
[021.1–.4]*	021	[331.881–.889]*	331.88
[025.33–.37]*	025.3	332.2	332.1
026–027	021.7	332.5	332.4
[027.509 3–.509 9]	027.53–.59	[332.63–.67]*	332.6
[027.709 3–.709 9]	027.73–.79	332.7	332.1–.3
[027.809 3–.809 9]	027.82	[333.6]	333.5
[028.8]*	028	333.7–.9	333.1–.5
[131.3]*	131	335.42	329
[155.28]*	155.2	[335.44]	329
[155.41–.45]*	155.4	336.2	336.1
[164]	511	338.4	380.3
[220.4]*	220	338.4	380.5
[220.52–.59]*	220.5	[339.41–.49]*	339.4
[220.91–.95]*	220.9	351.8	379
[230.1–.9]*	230	[352.000 93–.000 99]	352.03–.09
[232.92–.97]*	232.9	[353.032–.036]*	353.03
[241.3–.4]*	241	355.02	301.6
[242.2–.8]*	242	[355.07]*	355
[248.2–.8]*	248	[355.47]*	355.4
[252.01–.09]*	252	[358.8]*	358
[258]	361.7	[359.32]*	359.3
[262.7]*	262	362.1–.4	651.5
[264.01–.09]*	264	362.6	362.5
[266.1–.9]*	266	362.6	362.7
301.18	322.4	[363.35]*	363.3
301.2	301.6	[364.13–.17]*	364.1
301.4	301.18	[364.35]	364.36
301.42	301.41	[364.37]*	364.3
301.44	301.45	[364.7]	365
[301.451–.453]*	301.45	[370.12]*	370.1
[301.47]	362.1–.4	[371.26–.27]*	371.2
[311]	001.4	[371.36–.38]*	371.3
[311]	519.5	371.39	370.19
[321.7]	321.8	[371.42–.48]*	371.4
323.1	322	[371.85–.89]*	371.8
323.1	323.3	[371.91–.95]*	371.9
[323.2]	322.4	[378.33–.34]*	378.3
[323.43]*	323.4	[383.2]*	383
[323.46–.48]*	323.4	[384.7–.9]*	384
[323.49]*	323.4	390	301.2
[325.1–.3]*	325	[394.26]*	394.2
[328.1]	060.4	[398.21–.24]*	398.2
[328.1]*	328	[398.3–.4]*	398
[328.3]*	328	399	394
329	301.15	419	001.54
330.1	338.5	[479.1]	440
[331.15]	331.89	[489.3]*	489
331.5	331.1	[491.1–.5]*	491
331.6	331.5	[491.79]*	491.7
[331.81]	331.2	[491.9]*	491
[331.86]	331.2	[492.41–.48]*	492.4

Edition 9	Edition 10	Edition 9	Edition 10
[492.49]	437	[613.94–.95]*	613.9
[492.7]*	492	[613.97]*	613
496	493	614.5	614.4
[499.9]*	499	[614.58]*	614.5
515	604.2	[614.83–.85]*	614.8
523.01	522	616.4	618.1
523.1	574.999	[616.85–.89]*	616.8
523.2	523.007 4	[618.3]	618.2
[523.39]*	523.3	[618.4]	618.2
[523.49]*	523.4	[618.5]	618.2
[523.69]*	523.6	[618.6]	618.2
[523.79]*	523.7	[618.7]	618.2
[523.89]*	523.8	[618.8]	618.2
[530.11–.16]*	530.1	[618.92–.97]*	618.9
[531.9]*	531	621.1	625.2
[532.9]*	532	621.1	629.22
[533.6]*	533	621.32	621.36
[533.9]*	533	[621.381 7]*	621.381
[534.9]*	534	[621.383]	621.382
[535.9]*	535	[621.384 19]*	621.384 1
[536.9]*	536	[621.384 3]	621.384 2
537.1	530.1	[621.384 6]	621.384 5
537.1	530.4	[621.386]	621.385
[537.9]*	537	[621.387]	621.385
[538.9]*	538	[621.388 1–.388 6]*	621.388
[539.75–.76]*	539.7	[621.55]*	621.5
[539.9]*	539	[621.97]*	621.9
[549.1–.7]*	549	[623.5]	623.4
[560.17]*	560	[623.84–.87]	623.82
572	301.2	624	690
[574.929]*	574.92	[629.282–.284]*	629.28
576	574.2	[629.42]	629.47
[576.1]*	576	630.1	301.34
577	574.2	630.1	901.9
577	574.3	630.2	631
578	502.8	[630.21–.29]	630.1
578	535	[635.1–.6]*	635
579	069	[635.93–.97]*	635.9
[582.1]*	582	[636.59]*	636.5
[595.76–.79]*	595.7	[636.72–.76]*	636.7
[597.2–.5]*	597	[636.9]*	636
[598.11–.14]*	598.1	641.3	641.2
[598.29]*	598.2	[641.59]*	641.5
[598.3–.9]	598.2	[649.1–.7]*	649
[599.1–.9]*	599	[652.8]*	652
[607.4–.9]*	607	[655]	686
[608.7]*	608	[655.1–.3]	686.2
610.69	617	[655.4–.5]	070.5
611	616.07	[655.7]	686.3
[612.6]*	612	[657.2–.8]*	657
613.1	613.5	[658.37]*	658.3
[613.4]*	613	658.38	658.31

Edition 9	Edition 10	Edition 9	Edition 10
[658.42–.43]*	658.4	[790.013]*	790.01
[658.83]*	658.8	[790.019]	790.19
[658.86–.87]*	658.8	[790.023]	790.13
[658.88]*	658.8	[792.82]*	792.8
[658.89]	658.85	[793.33–.34]*	793.3
[659.11]*	659.1	[794.12–.18]*	794.1
[659.15–.17]*	659.1	[796.357 2–.357 8]*	796.357
[669.1–.9]*	669	796.4	796.9
679	604.6	[796.56]*	796.5
[684.08–.09]*	684	[797.21–.24]*	797.2
[684.7]	688.6	[799.17]*	799.1
[690.5–.8]*	690	[799.24–.27]*	799.2
[694.2–.6]*	694	[799.29]*	799.2
[697.1–.8]*	697	[808.02–.06]*	808
[701.1–.9]*	701	[808.31]*	808.3
[701.8]	702.8	[808.51]*	808.5
[704.945–.947]*	704.94	[808.54–.55]*	808.5
708	069	[808.89]*	808.8
[708.1–.9]*	708	[809.8–.9]*	809
731	730.1	[879.9]	840
[731.5–.8]*	731	[891.1–.5]*	891
[737.49]*	737.4	[891.9]*	891
[740.1–.9]	741.01–.09	[892.49]	839
741	745.6	896	893
[741.4]	741.01	[899.9]*	899
[741.4]	741.2	[909.824–.826]*	909.82
[741.59]*	741.5	[910.02–.09]*	910
[744]	604.2	[912.1–.9]*	912
[744.4]	526.8	[913.02–.04]*	913
[744.4]	720.28	[920.02–.09]*	920
[747.2]*	747	[929.1–.3]*	929
[749.201–.204]*	749.2	[929.5]*	929
[749.21–.29]*	749.2	[940.531–.539]*	940.53
[770.282–.284]*	770.28	[940.541–.548]*	940.54
771	661	[950.4]*	950
772	686.4	[973.31–.38]*	973.3
[778.1]	686.4	[973.71–.78]*	973.7
778.3	621.36	[s.s.—024]*	s.s.—02
778.3	686.4	[s.s.—027]*	s.s.—02
[780.07]	350	[s.s.—061–065]*	s.s.—06
[780.07]*	780	[s.s.—071–072]*	s.s.—07
[780.15]*	780.1	[s.s.—077–079]*	s.s.—07
[781.1–.2]*	781	[area—174–176]*	area—17
[782.12–.15]*	782.1	[area—22–24]*	area—2
[784.1–.3]*	784	area—422	area—421
[784.8]*	784	area—426	area—421
[786.2]	786.1	[area—443–449]*	area—44
[786.3]	786.1	[area—453–456]*	area—45
[786.4]	786.1	[area—473–479]*	area—47
[786.6]	786.5	[area—482–484]	area—481
[786.7]	786.5	[area—486–488]	area—485
[786.8]	786.5	area—496	area—561

Edition 9	Edition 10	Edition 9	Edition 10
[area—512–517]*	area—51	[area—747 1]*	area—747
[area—521–528]*	area—52	[area—91]	area—598
[area—549 3]*	area—549	[area—911]	area—595
[area—562–566]	area—561	[area—914]	area—599
[area—564 5]*	area—564	[area—92]	area—598
[area—625–629]	area—624	[area—99]	area—98
[area—725]*	area—72	[lang. sub.—31–39]*	lang. sub.—3
[area—729 6–729 8]*	area—729	[lang. sub.—709]*	lang. sub.—7

Variations Between Abridged 10 and Edition 18

The following table is provided as a convenience for users of the 10th abridged edition who check the numbers assigned from the 18th full edition by centralized classification services, such as that of the Library of Congress. As explained in the Introduction, section 3.52, the first segment of a full Dewey number on an LC card is usually identical with the number provided by the abridged edition, but not always. Here are listed the Edition 18 numbers from which the corresponding Abridged edition 10 numbers vary in respects other than length. In some cases only part of the content of a number in the full edition is in a different number, with part in the same number; for example, that part of area notation 564 and its subdivisions in Edition 18 having to do with provinces of Turkey is in this edition covered by notation 561, but the part covering Cyprus remains in —564.

Edition 18	Abridged edition 10	Edition 18	Abridged edition 10
001.55–.56	001.54	346.07–.09	346.7
025.8	025.7	346.3–.9	346.093–.099
301.35–.36	301.34	347.01–.04	347.1
331.87	331.88	347.05–.08	347.5–.8
333.3 (part)	333.5	347.3–.9	347.093–.099
341.44–.46	341.42	348.3–.9	348.093–.099
342.02–.03	342.2	351.001–.009	351.04
342.04–.09	342.4–.9	351.01–.09	351.04
342.3–.9	342.093–.099	353.01–.09	353.03
343.01–.03	343.1–.3	364.35	364.36
343.04–.06	343.4	368.6–.7	368.5
343.07–.09	343.7–.9	368.81–.82	368.5
343.3–.9	343.093–.099	598.3–.9	598.2
344.01–.06	344.1–.6	614.5 (part)	614.4
344.07–.08	344.7	616.02–.04 (part)	616.07
344.09	344.9	618.3–.8	618.2
344.3–.9	344.093–.099	621.316	621.313
345.05–.08	345.5–.8	621.383	621.382
345.3–.9	345.093–.099	621.384 3	621.384 2
346.01–.04	346.1–.4	621.384 6	621.384 5
346.045–.046	346.44	621.386–.387	621.385
346.048	346.47	623.5	623.4
346.05–.06	346.5–.6	623.84–.87	623.82

Edition 18	Abridged edition 10	Edition 18	Abridged edition 10
624.3–.8	624.2	909.1–.4	909.07
625.3–.6	625.1–.2	909.4–.6	909.08
630.21–.29	630.1	area—393	area—392
646.1	646.2	area—482–484	area—481
658.89	658.85	area—486–488	area—485
707.4	708	area—562–563	area—561
741.92–.99 (part)	743	area—564 (part)	area—561
748.6–.8	748.2	area—565–566	area—561
786.2–.4	786.1	area—625–629	area—624
786.6–.8	786.5		

Standard subdivision variations: In addition to the specific schedule variations shown above there are numerous cases of standard subdivision variations between Edition 18 and Abridged edition 10, principally in the number of zeros. For example, the Abridged 10 number corresponding to 625.1003 in Edition 18 is 625.103. Because of this and a few other types of differences, all Dewey numbers ending in standard subdivisions should be compared with the abridged schedules.

Summaries

First Summary *
The 10 Main Classes

000   **Generalities**

100   **Philosophy & related disciplines**

200   **Religion**

300   **The social sciences**

400   **Language**

500   **Pure sciences**

600   **Technology (Applied sciences)**

700   **The arts**

800   **Literature (Belles-lettres)**

900   **General geography & history**

* Consult schedules for complete and exact headings

Second Summary *
The 100 Divisions

000 Generalities
- 010 Bibliographies & catalogs
- 020 Library & information sciences
- 030 General encyclopedic works
- 040
- 050 General serial publications
- 060 General organizations & museums
- 070 Journalism, publishing, newspapers
- 080 General collections
- 090 Manuscripts & book rarities

100 Philosophy & related disciplines
- 110 Metaphysics
- 120 Knowledge, cause, purpose, man
- 130 Popular & parapsychology, occultism
- 140 Specific philosophical viewpoints
- 150 Psychology
- 160 Logic
- 170 Ethics (Moral philosophy)
- 180 Ancient, medieval, Oriental
- 190 Modern Western philosophy

200 Religion
- 210 Natural religion
- 220 Bible
- 230 Christian doctrinal theology
- 240 Christian moral & devotional
- 250 Local church & religious orders
- 260 Social & ecclesiastical theology
- 270 History & geography of church
- 280 Christian denominations & sects
- 290 Other religions & comparative

300 The social sciences
- 310 Statistics
- 320 Political science
- 330 Economics
- 340 Law
- 350 Public administration
- 360 Social pathology & services
- 370 Education
- 380 Commerce
- 390 Customs & folklore

400 Language
- 410 Linguistics
- 420 English & Anglo-Saxon languages
- 430 Germanic languages   German
- 440 French, Provençal, Catalan
- 450 Italian, Romanian, Rhaeto-Romanic
- 460 Spanish & Portuguese languages
- 470 Italic languages   Latin
- 480 Helenic   Classical Greek
- 490 Other languages

500 Pure sciences
- 510 Mathematics
- 520 Astronomy & allied sciences
- 530 Physics
- 540 Chemistry & allied sciences
- 550 Sciences of earth & other worlds
- 560 Paleontology
- 570 Life sciences
- 580 Botanical sciences
- 590 Zoological sciences

600 Technology (Applied sciences)
- 610 Medical sciences
- 620 Engineering & allied operations
- 630 Agriculture & related
- 640 Home economics
- 650 Managerial services
- 660 Chemical & related technologies
- 670 Manufactures
- 680 Miscellaneous manufactures
- 690 Buildings

700 The arts
- 710 Civic & landscape art
- 720 Architecture
- 730 Plastic arts   Sculpture
- 740 Drawing, decorative & minor arts
- 750 Painting & paintings
- 760 Graphic arts   Prints
- 770 Photography & photographs
- 780 Music
- 790 Recreational & performing arts

800 Literature (Belles-lettres)
- 810 American literature in English
- 820 English & Anglo-Saxon literatures
- 830 Literatures of Germanic languages
- 840 French, Provençal, Catalan
- 850 Italian, Romanian, Rhaeto-Romanic
- 860 Spanish & Portuguese literatures
- 870 Italic languages literatures   Latin
- 880 Hellenic languages literatures
- 890 Literatures of other languages

900 General geography & history
- 910 General geography   Travel
- 920 Biography, genealogy, insignia
- 930 General history of ancient world
- 940 General history of Europe
- 950 General history of Asia
- 960 General history of Africa
- 970 General history of North America
- 980 General history of South America
- 990 General history of other areas

* Consult schedules for complete and exact headings

Third Summary *
The 1000 Sections

Generalities

000 Generalities
001   Knowledge & its extension
002
003   Systems
004
005
006
007
008
009

010 Bibliographies and catalogs
011   General bibliographies
012   Of individuals
013   Of works by specific classes of writers
014   Of anonymous & pseudonymous works
015   Of works from specific places
016   Of specific subjects
017   General subject catalogs
018   General author & date catalogs
019   General dictionary catalogs

020 Library & information sciences
021   The library & society
022   Physical plant of libraries
023   Personnel & positions
024   Regulations for use of libraries
025   Library operations
026   Libraries for specific subjects
027   General libraries
028   Reading & reading aids
029   Documentation

030 General encyclopedic works
031   American
032   Others in English
033   In other Germanic languages
034   In French, Provençal, Catalan
035   In Italian, Romanian, Rhaeto-Romanic
036   In Spanish & Portuguese
037   In Slavic languages
038   In Scandinavian languages
039   In other languages

040
041
042
043
044
045
046
047
048
049

050 General serial publications
051   American
052   Others in English
053   In other Germanic languages
054   In French, Provençal, Catalan
055   In Italian, Romanian, Rhaeto-Romanic
056   In Spanish & Portuguese
057   In Slavic languages
058   In Scandinavian languages
059   In other languages

060 General organizations & museums
061   In North America
062   In England & Wales
063   In central Europe
064   In France & Monaco
065   In Italy & adjacent territories
066   In Iberian Peninsula & adjacent islands
067   In eastern Europe
068   In other areas
069   Museum science

070 Journalism, publishing, newspapers
071   In North America
072   In England & Wales
073   In central Europe
074   In France & Monaco
075   In Italy & adjacent territories
076   In Iberian Peninsula & adjacent islands
077   In eastern Europe
078   In Scandinavia
079   In other areas

080 General collections
081   American
082   Others in English
083   In other Germanic languages
084   In French, Provençal, Catalan
085   In Italian, Romanian, Rhaeto-Romanic
086   In Spanish & Portuguese
087   In Slavic languages
088   In Scandinavian languages
089   In other languages

090 Manuscripts & book rarities
091   Manuscripts
092   Block books
093   Incunabula
094   Books notable for printing
095   Books notable for bindings
096   Notable illustrations & materials
097   Notable ownership or origin
098   Works notable for content
099   Books notable for format

* Consult schedules for complete and exact headings

Philosophy and related disciplines

100	**Philosophy & related disciplines**		150	**Psychology**
101	Theory of philosophy		151	
102	Miscellany of philosophy		152	Physiological & experimental
103	Dictionaries of philosophy		153	Intelligence & intellect
104			154	Subconscious states & processes
105	Serials on philosophy		155	Differential & genetic psychology
106	Organizations of philosophy		156	Comparative psychology
107	Study & teaching of philosophy		157	Abnormal & clinical psychologies
108	Collections of philosophy		158	Applied psychology
109	Historical treatment of philosophy		159	Other aspects
110	**Metaphysics**		160	**Logic**
111	Ontology		161	Induction
112	Classification of knowledge		162	Deduction
113	Cosmology		163	
114	Space		164	
115	Time, duration, eternity		165	Fallacies & sources of error
116	Motion, change, evolution		166	Syllogisms
117	Matter & form		167	Hypotheses
118	Force & energy		168	Argument & persuasion
119	Number & quantity		169	Analogy
120	**Knowledge, cause, purpose, man**		170	**Ethics (Moral philosophy)**
121	Epistemology		171	Systems & doctrines
122	Cause & effect		172	Ethics of political relationships
123	Freedom & necessity		173	Ethics of family relationships
124	Teleology		174	Professional & occupational ethics
125	Finite & infinite		175	Ethics of recreation
126	Consciousness & personality (The self)		176	Sexual ethics
127	The unconscious & the subconscious		177	Ethics of social relations
128	Man		178	Ethics of temperance & intemperance
129	Origin & destiny of individual souls		179	Other applications of ethics
130	**Popular & parapsychology, occultism**		180	**Ancient, medieval, Oriental philosophy**
131	Popular psychology		181	Oriental
132			182	Pre-Socratic Greek
133	Parapsychology & occultism		183	Sophistic, Socratic & related Greek
134			184	Platonic
135	Dreams & the mystic traditions		185	Aristotelian
136			186	Skeptic & Neoplatonic
137	Personality analysis & improvement		187	Epicurean
138	Physiognomy		188	Stoic
139	Phrenology		189	Medieval Western
140	**Specific philosophical viewpoints**		190	**Modern Western philosophy**
141	Idealism & related systems & doctrines		191	United States & Canada
142	Critical philosophy		192	British Isles
143	Intuitionism & Bergsonism		193	Germany & Austria
144	Humanism & related systems		194	France
145	Sensationalism & ideology		195	Italy
146	Naturalism & related systems		196	Spain & Portugal
147	Pantheism & related systems		197	Russia & Finland
148	Liberalism & other systems		198	Scandinavia
149	Other systems & doctrines		199	Other countries

Religion

200 **Religion**
201 Philosophy of Christianity
202 Miscellany of Christianity
203 Dictionaries of Christianity
204 Christian mythology
205 Serials on Christianity
206 Organizations of Christianity
207 Study & teaching of Christianity
208 Collections on Christianity
209 History & geography of Christianity

210 **Natural religion**
211 God
212 Nature of God
213 Creation
214 Theodicy
215 Science & religion
216 Good & evil
217 Worship & prayer
218 Man
219 Analogy

220 **Bible**
221 Old Testament
222 Historical books of Old Testament
223 Poetic books of Old Testament
224 Prophetic books of Old Testament
225 New Testament
226 Gospels & Acts
227 Epistles
228 Revelation (Apocalypse)
229 Apocrypha & pseudepigrapha

230 **Christian doctrinal theology**
231 God, Trinity, Godhead
232 Jesus Christ & his family
233 Man
234 Salvation (Soteriology)
235 Spiritual beings
236 Eschatology
237
238 Creeds & confessions of faith
239 Apologetics & polemics

240 **Christian moral & devotional theology**
241 Moral theology
242 Devotional literature
243 Evangelistic writings for individuals
244
245 Hymns without music
246 Art in Christianity
247 Church furnishings & related
248 Personal religion
249 Worship in family life

250 **Local church & religious orders**
251 Preaching (Homiletics)
252 Texts of sermons
253 Secular clergymen & duties
254 Parish government & administration
255 Religious congregations & orders
256
257
258
259 Parochial activities

260 **Social & ecclesiastical theology**
261 Social theology
262 Ecclesiology
263 Times & places of religious observance
264 Public worship
265 Other rites, ceremonies, ordinances
266 Missions
267 Associations for religious work
268 Religious training & instruction
269 Organized spiritual renewal

270 **History & geography of church**
271 Religious congregations & orders
272 Persecutions
273 Doctrinal controversies & heresies
274 Christian church in Europe
275 Christian church in Asia
276 Christian church in Africa
277 Christian church in North America
278 Christian church in South America
279 Christian church in other areas

280 **Christian denominations & sects**
281 Primitive & Oriental churches
282 Roman Catholic Church
283 Anglican churches
284 Protestants of Continental origin
285 Presbyterian & related churches
286 Baptist, Disciples, Adventist
287 Methodist churches
288 Unitarianism
289 Other denominations & sects

290 **Other religions & comparative**
291 Comparative religion & mythology
292 Classical religion & mythology
293 Germanic religion & mythology
294 Religions of Indic origin
295 Zoroastrianism
296 Judaism
297 Islam & religions derived from it
298
299 Other religions

The social sciences

300 **The social sciences**	350 **Public administration**
301 Sociology	351 Central governments
302	352 Local units of government
303	353 United States federal & states
304	354 Other central governments
305	355 Military art & science
306	356 Infantry
307	357 Cavalry
308	358 Armored, technical, air, space forces
309 Social situation & conditions	359 Sea (Naval) forces & warfare
310 **Statistics**	360 **Social pathology & services**
311	361 Social welfare work
312 Statistics of populations	362 Social pathology & its alleviation
313	363 Other social services
314 General statistics of Europe	364 Crime & its alleviation
315 General statistics of Asia	365 Penal institutions
316 General statistics of Africa	366 Association & associations
317 General statistics of North America	367 General clubs
318 General statistics of South America	368 Insurance
319 General statistics of other areas	369 Miscellaneous kinds of associations
320 **Political science**	370 **Education**
321 Forms of states	371 The school
322 Relation of state to social groups	372 Elementary education
323 Relation of state to its residents	373 Secondary education
324 Electoral process	374 Adult education
325 International migration	375 Curriculums
326 Slavery & emancipation	376 Education of women
327 International relations	377 Schools & religion
328 Legislation	378 Higher education
329 Practical politics	379 Education & the state
330 **Economics**	380 **Commerce**
331 Labor economics	381 Internal commerce
332 Financial economics	382 International commerce
333 Land economics	383 Postal communication
334 Cooperatives	384 Other systems of communication
335 Socialism & related systems	385 Railroad transportation
336 Public finance	386 Inland waterway transportation
337	387 Water, air, space transportation
338 Production	388 Ground transportation
339 Macroeconomics	389 Metrology & standardization
340 **Law**	390 **Customs & folklore**
341 International law	391 Costume & personal appearance
342 Constitutional & administrative law	392 Customs of life cycle & domestic life
343 Miscellaneous public law	393 Death customs
344 Social law	394 General customs
345 Criminal law	395 Etiquette
346 Private law	396
347 Civil procedure	397
348 Laws, regulations, cases	398 Folklore
349	399 Customs of war & diplomacy

Language

Pure sciences

500	**Pure sciences**	**550**	**Sciences of earth & other worlds**
501	Philosophy & theory	551	Physical & dynamic geology
502	Miscellany	552	Rocks (Petrology)
503	Dictionaries & encyclopedias	553	Economic geology
504		554	Geology of Europe
505	Serial publications	555	Geology of Asia
506	Organizations	556	Geology of Africa
507	Study & teaching	557	Geology of North America
508	Collections, travels, surveys	558	Geology of South America
509	Historical & geographical treatment	559	Geology of other areas & worlds
510	**Mathematics**	**560**	**Paleontology**
511	Generalities	561	Paleobotany
512	Algebra	562	Fossil invertebrates
513	Arithmetic	563	Fossil Protozoa, Parazoa, Metazoa
514	Topology	564	Fossil mollusks
515	Analysis	565	Other fossil invertebrates
516	Geometry	566	Fossil vertebrates
517		567	Fossil Anamnia
518		568	Fossil Sauropsida
519	Probabilities & applied mathematics	569	Fossil mammals
520	**Astronomy & allied sciences**	**570**	**Life sciences**
521	Theoretical astronomy	571	
522	Practical & spherical astronomy	572	Human races
523	Descriptive astronomy	573	Physical anthropology
524		574	Biology
525	Earth (Astronomical geography)	575	Organic evolution & genetics
526	Mathematical geography	576	Microbes
527	Celestial navigation	577	General nature of life
528	Nautical almanacs (Ephemerides)	578	Microscopy in biology
529	Time (Chronology)	579	Collection & preservation of specimens
530	**Physics**	**580**	**Botanical sciences**
531	Mechanics	581	Botany
532	Mechanics of fluids	582	Seed-bearing plants
533	Mechanics of gases	583	Dicotyledons
534	Sound & related vibrations	584	Monocotyledons
535	Visible light & paraphotic	585	Naked-seed plants
536	Heat	586	Seedless plants
537	Electricity & electronics	587	Vascular cryptogams
538	Magnetism	588	Bryophyta
539	Modern physics	589	Thallophyta
540	**Chemistry & allied sciences**	**590**	**Zoological sciences**
541	Physical & theoretical chemistry	591	Zoology
542	Laboratories, apparatus, equipment	592	Invertebrates
543	General analysis	593	Protozoa, Parazoa, Metazoa
544	Qualitative analysis	594	Mollusks
545	Quantitative analysis	595	Other invertebrates
546	Inorganic chemistry	596	Vertebrates
547	Organic chemistry	597	Anamnia
548	Crystallography	598	Reptiles & birds
549	Mineralogy	599	Mammals

Technology (Applied sciences)

600	**Technology (Applied sciences)**	**650**	**Managerial services**
601	Philosophy & theory	651	Office services
602	Miscellany	652	Written communication processes
603	Dictionaries & encyclopedias	653	Shorthand
604	General technologies	654	
605	Serial publications	655	
606	Organizations	656	
607	Study & teaching	657	Accounting
608	Collections, patents, inventions	658	General management
609	Historical & geographical treatment	659	Advertising & public relations
610	**Medical sciences**	**660**	**Chemical & related technologies**
611	Human anatomy, cytology, tissues	661	Industrial chemicals
612	Human physiology	662	Explosives, fuels, related products
613	General & personal hygiene	663	Beverage technology
614	Public health	664	Food technology
615	Pharmacology & therapeutics	665	Industrial oils, fats, waxes, gases
616	Diseases	666	Ceramic & allied technologies
617	Surgery & related topics	667	Cleaning, color & related
618	Other branches of medicine	668	Other organic products
619	Experimental medicine	669	Metallurgy
620	**Engineering & allied operations**	**670**	**Manufactures**
621	Applied physics	671	Metal manufactures
622	Mining engineering & related	672	Ferrous metals manufactures
623	Military & nautical engineering	673	Nonferrous metals manufactures
624	Civil engineering	674	Lumber, wood, cork technologies
625	Railroads & roads	675	Leather & fur technologies
626		676	Pulp & paper technology
627	Hydraulic engineering	677	Textiles
628	Sanitary & municipal engineering	678	Elastomers & their products
629	Other branches of engineering	679	Other products of specific materials
630	**Agriculture & related**	**680**	**Miscellaneous manufactures**
631	General techniques & apparatus	681	Precision instruments & related
632	Plant injuries, diseases, pests	682	Small forge work
633	Field crops	683	Hardware
634	Orchards, fruits, nuts, forestry	684	Furnishings & home workshops
635	Garden crops (Horticulture)	685	Leather & fur goods & related
636	Animal husbandry	686	Printing & related activities
637	Dairy & related technologies	687	Clothing
638	Insect culture	688	Other final products
639	Nondomestic animals & plants	689	
640	**Home economics**	**690**	**Buildings**
641	Food & drink	691	Building materials
642	Food & meal service	692	Auxiliary construction practices
643	The home & its equipment	693	Construction in specific materials
644	Household utilities	694	Wood construction Carpentry
645	Household furnishings	695	Roofing & auxiliary structures
646	Sewing, clothing, personal grooming	696	Utilities
647	Public households	697	Heating, ventilating, air conditioning
648	Household sanitation	698	Detail finishing
649	Child rearing & home nursing	699	

The arts

700 The arts	**750 Painting & paintings**
701 Philosophy & theory	751 Processes & forms
702 Miscellany	752 Color
703 Dictionaries & encyclopedias	753 Abstractions, symbolism, legend
704 General special aspects	754 Subjects of everyday life
705 Serial publications	755 Religion & religious symbolism
706 Organizations	756 Historical events
707 Study & teaching	757 Human figures & their parts
708 Galleries, museums, art collections	758 Other subjects
709 Historical & geographical treatment	759 Historical & geographical treatment
710 Civic & landscape art	**760 Graphic arts Prints**
711 Area planning (Civic art)	761 Relief processes
712 Landscape design	762
713 Landscape design of trafficways	763 Lithographic processes
714 Water features	764 Serigraphy & chromolithography
715 Woody plants	765 Metal engraving
716 Herbaceous plants	766 Mezzotinting & aquatinting processes
717 Structures	767 Etching & drypoint
718 Landscape design of cemeteries	768
719 Natural landscapes	769 Prints
720 Architecture	**770 Photography & photographs**
721 Architectural construction	771 Apparatus, equipment, materials
722 Ancient & Oriental architecture	772 Metallic salt processes
723 Medieval architecture	773 Pigment processes of printing
724 Modern architecture	774 Holography
725 Public structures	775
726 Buildings for religious purposes	776
727 Buildings for educational purposes	777
728 Residential buildings	778 Specific fields of photography
729 Design & decoration	779 Collections of photographs
730 Plastic arts Sculpture	**780 Music**
731 Processes & representations	781 General principles
732 Primitive, ancient, Oriental	782 Dramatic music
733 Greek & Roman sculpture	783 Sacred music
734 Medieval sculpture	784 Voice & vocal music
735 Modern sculpture	785 Instrumental ensembles & their music
736 Carving & carvings	786 Keyboard instruments & their music
737 Numismatics & sigillography	787 String instruments & their music
738 Ceramic arts	788 Wind instruments & their music
739 Art metalwork	789 Percussion, mechanical, electrical
740 Drawing, decorative & minor arts	**790 Recreational & performing arts**
741 Drawing & drawings	791 Public performances
742 Perspective	792 Theater (Stage presentations)
743 Drawing & drawings by subject	793 Indoor games & amusements
744	794 Indoor games of skill
745 Decorative & minor arts	795 Games of chance
746 Textile arts & handicrafts	796 Athletic & outdoor sports & games
747 Interior decoration	797 Aquatic & air sports
748 Glass	798 Equestrian sports & animal racing
749 Furniture & accessories	799 Fishing, hunting, shooting

Literature

800 **Literature (Belles-lettres)**	**850** **Italian, Romanian, Rhaeto-Romanic**
801 Philosophy & theory	851 Italian poetry
802 Miscellany about literature	852 Italian drama
803 Dictionaries & encyclopedias	853 Italian fiction
804	854 Italian essays
805 Serial publications	855 Italian speeches
806 Organizations	856 Italian letters
807 Study & teaching	857 Italian satire & humor
808 Rhetoric (Composition) & collections	858 Italian miscellaneous writings
809 History, description, critical appraisal	859 Romanian & Rhaeto-Romanic
810 **American literature in English**	**860** **Spanish & Portuguese literatures**
811 American poetry	861 Spanish poetry
812 American drama	862 Spanish drama
813 American fiction	863 Spanish fiction
814 American essays	864 Spanish essays
815 American speeches	865 Spanish speeches
816 American letters	866 Spanish letters
817 American satire & humor	867 Spanish satire & humor
818 American miscellaneous writings	868 Spanish miscellaneous writings
819	869 Portuguese
820 **English & Anglo-Saxon literatures**	**870** **Italic languages literature** **Latin**
821 English poetry	871 Latin poetry
822 English drama	872 Latin dramatic poetry & drama
823 English fiction	873 Latin epic poetry & fiction
824 English essays	874 Latin lyric poetry
825 English speeches	875 Latin speeches
826 English letters	876 Latin letters
827 English satire & humor	877 Latin satire & humor
828 English miscellaneous writings	878 Latin miscellaneous writings
829 Anglo-Saxon (Old English)	879 Other Italic languages
830 **Literatures of Germanic languages**	**880** **Hellenic languages literatures**
831 German poetry	881 Classical Greek poetry
832 German drama	882 Classical Greek drama
833 German fiction	883 Classical Greek epic poetry
834 German essays	884 Classical Greek lyric poetry
835 German speeches	885 Classical Greek speeches
836 German letters	886 Classical Greek letters
837 German satire & humor	887 Classical Greek satire & humor
838 German miscellaneous writings	888 Classical Greek miscellaneous writings
839 Other Germanic languages	889 Modern Greek
840 **French, Provençal, Catalan**	**890** **Literatures of other languages**
841 French poetry	891 East Indo-European & Celtic
842 French drama	892 Afro-Asiatic (Hamito-Semitic)
843 French fiction	893 Hamitic & Chad languages
844 French essays	894 Ural-Altaic, Paleosiberian, Dravidian
845 French speeches	895 Of East & Southeast Asia
846 French letters	896 African languages
847 French satire & humor	897 North American aboriginal
848 French miscellaneous writings	898 South American aboriginal
849 Provençal & Catalan	899 Other languages

General geography and history and their auxiliaries

900 **General geography & history**
901 Philosophy of general history
902 Miscellany of general history
903 Dictionaries of general history
904 Collected accounts of events
905 Serials on general history
906 Organizations of general history
907 Study & teaching of general history
908 Collections of general history
909 General world history

910 **General geography   Travel**
911 Historical geography
912 Graphic representations of earth
913 Geography of ancient world
914 Europe
915 Asia
916 Africa
917 North America
918 South America
919 Other areas & worlds

920 **Biography, genealogy, insignia**
921
922
923
924
925
926
927
928
929   Genealogy, names, insignia

930 **General history of ancient world**
931 China
932 Egypt
933 Palestine
934 India
935 Mesopotamia & Iranian Plateau
936 Northern & western Europe
937 Italian peninsula & adjacent areas
938 Greece
939 Other parts of ancient world

940 **General history of Europe**
941 Scotland & Ireland
942 British Isles   England
943 Central Europe   Germany
944 France
945 Italy
946 Iberian Peninsula   Spain
947 Eastern Europe   Soviet Union
948 Northern Europe   Scandinavia
949 Other parts of Europe

950 **General history of Asia**
951 China & adjacent areas
952 Japan & adjacent islands
953 Arabian Peninsula & adjacent areas
954 South Asia   India
955 Iran (Persia)
956 Middle East (Near East)
957 Siberia (Asiatic Russia)
958 Central Asia
959 Southeast Asia

960 **General history of Africa**
961 North Africa
962 Countries of the Nile   Egypt
963 Ethiopia (Abyssinia)
964 Northwest coast & offshore islands
965 Algeria
966 West Africa & offshore islands
967 Central Africa & offshore islands
968 South Africa
969 South Indian Ocean islands

970 **General history of North America**
971 Canada
972 Middle America   Mexico
973 United States
974 Northeastern United States
975 Southeastern United States
976 South central United States
977 North central United States
978 Western United States
979 Great Basin & Pacific Slope

980 **General history of South America**
981 Brazil
982 Argentina
983 Chile
984 Bolivia
985 Peru
986 Northwestern South America
987 Venezuela
988 Guianas
989 Other parts of South America

990 **General history of other areas**
991
992
993 New Zealand & Melanesia
994 Australia
995 New Guinea (Papua)
996 Other parts of Pacific   Polynesia
997 Atlantic Ocean islands
998 Arctic islands & Antarctica
999

Schedules

Use of the Schedules

Full instructions on use of the schedules may be found in the Introduction, section 3.

Coordination and subordination of subjects are shown by indention and length of number as described in the Introduction, section 2.131, and are shown also in part by the prominence of the typeface.

A number in square brackets [ ] is not in force, or is no longer in force with the meaning indicated.

A number in *italics* is a reused number, i.e., it has a different meaning from that which it had in one or more of the earlier editions 6–9 (1945–1965).

Asterisks (*) lead to footnotes, which, in turn, usually lead to detailed instructions at a point earlier in the schedule.

000   Generalities

001   Knowledge and its extension

.2   Scholarship and learning

.3   Humanities

.4   Methodology and research

> Including statistical method [*formerly* 311], operations research, resources, support of and incentives for research

> Class research in a specific subject with the subject, using "Standard Subdivisions" notation 07 from Table 1, e.g., research in linguistics 410.7; methodology of a specific subject with the subject, using "Standard Subdivisions" notation 01 from Table 1, e.g., methodology in linguistics 410.1; data processing and computerization in 001.6; mathematical methodology in 510

.5   Information and communication

> Class data processing in 001.6

.501   Philosophy and theory

> Class communication theory in 001.5

.53   Cybernetics

> Including bionics, artificial intelligence, information theory

> Class computers in 001.6, control in 003

.54   Communication

> Thru nonverbal language [*formerly* 419], spoken verbal language, written and other records

> Including audiovisual mediums

.6   Data processing

> Nonmechanized, automatic, electronic

> Including systems analysis, computer programing

> Class data processing in a specific subject with the subject, using "Standard Subdivisions" notation 028 from Table 1, e.g., data processing in banking 332.1028

.9   Controversial and spurious knowledge

> Curiosities, mysteries, deceptions and hoaxes, errors, delusions, superstitions

003 Systems

> Theory, analysis, design, testing, building, operation of regularly interacting or independent groups of elements
>
> Class systems analysis in data processing in 001.6, mathematics of programing in 519.7

010 **Bibliographies and catalogs**

> Of books, other printed and written records, audiovisual records
>
> (It is optional to class here bibliographies and catalogs of reading for children and young adults; prefer 028.52)
>
> If preferred, class bibliographies and catalogs of motion-picture films in 791.43

011 General bibliographies

> Lists of works not limited to a specific kind of coverage or place of publication, no matter how arranged

---

▶   012–016 Special bibliographies and catalogs

Class comprehensive works in 010

012 Bibliographies and catalogs of individuals

> Works by or about persons not clearly associated with any specific subject

013 Bibliographies and catalogs of works by specific classes of writers

> *For bibliographies and catalogs of individuals, see* 012

014 Bibliographies and catalogs of anonymous and pseudonymous works

015 Bibliographies and catalogs of works from specific places

> Works issued or printed in specific regions, continents, countries, localities, or by specific firms
>
> Add "Areas" notation 1–9 from Table 2 to base number 015

016 Bibliographies and catalogs of specific subjects

> If preferred, class with the specific subject, using "Standard Subdivisions" notation 016 from Table 1, e.g., bibliographies of astronomy 520.16
>
> Add 001–999 to base number 016, e.g., bibliographies of astronomy 016.52
>
> Class in 016.78 bibliographies, catalogs, thematic catalogs of music scores and parts; but, if preferred, class as in the first note above or in 781.9. Class in 016.7899 catalogs and lists of music recordings; but, if preferred, class as in the first note above or in 789.9

►   017–019 General catalogs

Lists of works held in a specific collection or group of collections and not limited to a specific kind of coverage or place of publication

Class comprehensive works in 010

017   General subject catalogs

Alphabetically arranged or classified

018   Author catalogs and catalogs arranged by date

019   Dictionary catalogs

020   **Library and information sciences**

The science and art utilized in identification, collection, organization, use of books, other printed and written records, audiovisual materials

For bibliographies and catalogs, see 010

.75   Book collecting

021   The library and society

Goals, promotion, government relations

Class here information organizations, comprehensive works on libraries

For regulations for use of libraries, see 024; *specific kinds of institutions,* 026–027

[.1–.4]   Purpose and relations of libraries

Numbers discontinued; class in 021

.6   Library development and cooperation

Including union catalogs, bibliographical centers, library networks

Class cooperation in a specific activity with the activity, e.g., cooperative cataloging 025.3; specific kinds of library networks in 026–027

.7   Promotion of libraries

Example: friends-of-the-library organizations [*formerly also* 026–027]

.8   Libraries and government

Library commissions and governing boards, financial support, gifts of books, copyright deposits, official exchange of publications, political pressures, censorship

Class library laws in 344.9

022 Physical plant of libraries and information centers

Location, planning based on function, equipment, facilities

Class here library quarters in buildings devoted primarily to other activities, e.g., physical plant of school libraries

Class architecture of libraries in 727

For maintenance of physical plant, see 025

023 Personnel and positions

Qualifications, titles, job descriptions, organization, training of administrative and staff personnel

Including staff manuals

024 Regulations for use of libraries

Including interlibrary loans

025 Library operations

Including maintenance of physical plant

Class here technical processes

For physical plant, see 022; personnel and positions, 023; documentation, 029

.1 Administration

As related to function

Including finance, printing, publishing, specific duplication processes

Class management in 658

.17 Treatment of special materials

Arrangement, care, use of manuscripts, archival materials, rarities, pamphlets, broadsides, clippings, serials, documents, maps, books in raised characters, microreproductions, recordings, music scores, other audiovisual materials

Class a special kind of treatment with the kind, e.g., cataloging 025.3

.2 Acquisitions

Selecting and acquiring materials by purchase, exchange, gift, deposit

Including physical preparation for storage

.3 Cataloging

Including cataloging of special materials, cooperative cataloging, recataloging, filing

[.33–.37] Subject cataloging and filing

Numbers discontinued; class in 025.3

.4   Classification

> Principles, systems, notations, schedules
>
> Including reclassification

.5   Services to patrons

> Reference, information, reader advisory services
>
> Class reference, reader, advisory services to special groups in 027.6, each specific service not provided for here with the subject, e.g., circulation services 025.6

.6   Circulation services

> Lending and renting materials, keeping records of loans and rentals
>
> Class regulations for interlibrary loans in 024

.7   Binding, repair, maintenance services

> Including arrangement, inventory, preservation

▶ 026–027 Specific kinds of institutions

> Class here specific institutions, specific kinds of systems and networks
>
> Class friends-of-the-library orgainzations [*formerly* 026–027] in 021.7
>
> Class comprehensive works in 021, a specific activity or service with the subject, e.g., information services 025.5

026   Libraries devoted to specific subjects

> Class here information organizations and library departments and collections in specific fields; comprehensive works on special libraries
>
> Class special libraries not devoted to specific subjects in 027.6

027   General libraries

> Not devoted to specific subjects
>
> Including private, family, proprietary, rental libraries
>
> Do not use standard subdivisions; class in 027

.4   Public libraries

> Institutions that serve free all residents of a community, district, or region, usually supported in whole or in part from public funds
>
> Class here branches, bookmobiles; reference, research, county, regional libraries
>
> Add "Areas" notation 3–9 from Table 2 to base number 027.4

.5   Government libraries

National, state, provincial

.509   Historical and geographical treatment

Class treatment by continent, country, locality [*all formerly*
027.5093–027.5099] in 027.53–027.59

.53–.59   Treatment by continent, country, locality [*all formerly*
027.5093–027.5099]

Add "Areas" notation 3–9 from Table 2 to base number 027.5

.6   Libraries for special groups and specific organizations

Including libraries of learned societies, for minority groups, welfare
institutions, religious organizations, old-age groups, business and
industrial organizations

Class here reference, reader, advisory services to special groups

For libraries for educational institutions, see 027.7

.62   Libraries for children and young adults

Including storytelling in libraries

027.7–027.8 Libraries for educational institutions

Class comprehensive works in 027.7

.7   College and university libraries

Class here comprehensive works on libraries for educational
institutions

For school libraries, see 027.8

.709   Historical and geographical treatment

Class treatment by continent, country, locality [*all formerly*
027.7093–027.7099] in 027.73–027.79

.73–79   Treatment by continent, country, locality [*all formerly*
027.7093–027.7099]

Add "Areas" notation 3–9 from Table 2 to base number 027.7

.8   School libraries

Libraries in public, private, church-supported elementary and
secondary schools

.809   Historical and geographical treatment

Class treatment by continent, country, locality [*all formerly*
027.8093–027.8099] in 027.82

.82	Treatment by continent, country, locality [*all formerly* 027.8093–027.8099]

Add "Areas" notation 3–9 from Table 2 to base number 027.82

028   Reading and reading aids

Including use of books and other records as sources of recreation and self-development

.1   Book reviews

Class technique of book reviewing in 808, critical appraisal of literature in 800, reviews on a specific subject with the subject

.5   Reading of children and young adults

.52   Bibliographies and catalogs

If preferred, class in 010

.7   Use of books and other records as sources of information

[.8]   Use of books and other records as sources of recreation and self-development

Number discontinued; class in 028

029   Documentation

Assembling, coding, providing accessibility to recorded knowledge

---

▶   029.4–029.7 Specific documentation procedures

Class comprehensive works in 029

For cataloging, see 025.3; *classification,* 025.4

.4   Abstracting

Manual and mechanized

Class composition of abstracts in 808

.5   Indexing

Manual and mechanized indexing of individual, serial, collected records

Including coordinate, chain, relative indexing

.7   Mechanized storage, search, retrieval of information

Use of computers and other equipment

Including machine translation

030   General encyclopedic works

▶   031–039 In specific languages

Class here specific encyclopedias and works about them

031   American

English-language encyclopedias originating in Western Hemisphere and Hawaii

032   In English

For American English-language encyclopedias, see 031

033   In other Germanic languages

Class Scandinavian-language encyclopedias in 038

034   In French, Provençal, Catalan

035   In Italian, Romanian, Rhaeto-Romanic

036   In Spanish and Portuguese

037   In Slavic languages

038   In Scandinavian languages

039   In other languages

050   General serial publications and their indexes

Class here periodicals

(It is optional to class here periodicals on all subjects; prefer specific subject, using "Standard Subdivisions" notation 05 from Table 1, e.g., periodicals on astronomy 520.5)

Class administrative reports and proceedings of general organizations in 060

▶   051–059 In specific languages

Class here specific serial publications and works about them

Class bilingual and polylingual publications with the preponderant language; if no language is preponderant, class in 050

If preferred, arrange general serial publications regardless of language alphabetically under 050

051   American

English-language serial publications of Western Hemisphere and Hawaii

052   In English

For American English-language serial publications, see 051

053 **In other Germanic languages**

Class Scandinavian-language serial publications in 058

054 **In French, Provençal, Catalan**

055 **In Italian, Romanian, Rhaeto-Romanic**

056 **In Spanish and Portuguese**

057 **In Slavic languages**

058 **In Scandinavian languages**

059 **In other languages**

060 **General organizations and museum science**

General organizations: history, charters, regulations, membership lists, administrative reports and proceedings of societies, academies, foundations, associations, conferences, congresses whose activity is not limited to a specific field

Including general international organizations

Class here interdisciplinary works on organizations

Class organizations devoted to a specific subject with the subject, using "Standard Subdivisions" notation 06 from Table 1, e.g., organizations devoted to library and information sciences 020.6

.4 General rules of order [*formerly* 328.1]

▶ **061–068 General organizations**

Class comprehensive works in 060

061 **General organizations in Canada and United States**

Class organizations in Hawaii in 068

062 **General organizations in England and Wales**

Class organizations in Scotland and Ireland in 068

063 **General organizations in Germany, Austria, Czechoslovakia, Poland, Hungary**

064 **General organizations in France and Monaco**

065 **General organizations in Italy and adjacent territories**

066 **General organizations in Spain, Portugal, adjacent territories**

067 **General organizations in Finland and Soviet Union**

068 **General organizations in other geographical areas**

069   Museum science

Class here art museum economy [*formerly* 708]

Including maintenance, display of biological specimens [*both formerly* 579]

Class museums as aids in study and teaching of a specific subject with the subject, using "Standard Subdivisions" notation 074 from Table 1, e.g., museums as aids in study and teaching of mineralogy 549.074

070   Journalism, publishing, newspapers

(It is optional to class here journals on all subjects; prefer specific subject, using "Standard Subdivisions" notation 05 from Table 1, e.g., science journals 505)

Use 070.01–070.08 for standard subdivisions of journalism and newspapers

---

▶   070.1–070.4 Journalism

Collecting, writing, editing information and opinion of current interest for presentation in newspapers, periodicals, newsreels, radio, television

Class comprehensive works in 070, general periodicals in 050, general newspapers in 071–079

.1   News media

Newpapers, periodicals, radio and television, newsreels and documentary films

Class specific journalistic activities and types of journalism regardless of medium in 070.4, sociology of mass media in 301.16

.4   Specific journalistic activities and types of journalism

News gathering and reporting, editing, interpretation and opinion, features and special topics; journalism for special groups

Including pictorial journalism

Class school journalism in 371.8

.5   Publishing [*formerly* 655.4–655.5]

Including governmental publishing

.9   Historical treatment of newspapers and journalism

Class historical treatment in specific areas in 071–079 (not 070.93–070.99)

▶   **071–079 Geographical treatment of newspapers and journalism**

> Class here specific general newspapers and works about them
>
> If preferred, arrange newspapers alphabetically under 070
>
> Class comprehensive works in 070

071   **In Canada and United States**

> Class newspapers and journalism in Hawaii in 079

072   **In England and Wales**

> Class newspapers and journalism in Scotland and Ireland in 079

073   **In Germany, Austria, Czechoslovakia, Poland, Hungary**

074   **In France and Monaco**

075   **In Italy and adjacent territories**

076   **In Spain, Portugal, adjacent territories**

077   **In Finland and Soviet Union**

078   **In Scandinavia**

079   **In other geographical areas**

080   **General collections**

> Class here essays, addresses, lectures, quotations

▶   **081–089 In specific languages**

> Class bilingual and polylingual collections with the preponderant language; if no language is preponderant, class in 080
>
> If preferred, arrange collections alphabetically under 080

081   **American**

> English-language collections of Western Hemisphere and Hawaii

082   **In English**

> *For American English-language collections, see* 081

083   **In other Germanic languages**

> Class Scandinavian-language collections and anthologies in 088

084   **In French, Provençal, Catalan**

085   **In Italian, Romanian, Rhaeto-Romanic**

086   **In Spanish and Portuguese**

087   In Slavic languages

088   In Scandinavian languages

089   In other languages

090   **Manuscripts and book rarities**

> Development, description, critical appraisal

091   Manuscripts

092   Block books

093   Incunabula

> Books printed before 1501

094   Books notable for printing

> First editions, limited editions, special editions, typographic masterpieces
>
> *For block books, see* 092; *incunabula,* 093

095   Books notable for bindings

096   Books notable for illustrations and materials

097   Books notable for ownership or origin

098   Works notable for content

> Prohibited works, literary forgeries and hoaxes

099   Books notable for format

> Miniature editions, unusual dimensions and shapes

100 Philosophy and related disciplines

Philosophy: a branch of learning that investigates and evaluates the ultimate nature of existences and relationships thru observation, speculation, reasoning, but not experimentation

Class the ultimate nature of existences and relationships within the context of revelation, deity, worship in 200; philosophy of a specific discipline or subject with the discipline or subject, using "Standard Subdivisions" notation 01 from Table 1, e.g., philosophy of history 901

101 Theory of philosophy

102 Miscellany of philosophy

103 Dictionaries, encyclopedias, concordances of philosophy

105 Serial publications of philosophy

106 Organizations of philosophy

107 Study and teaching of philosophy

108 Collections of philosophy

Class collected writings of individual philosophers in 180–190

109 Historical treatment of philosophy

Not limited by period or place

Class history, description, critical appraisal of philosophy of specific periods and places in 180–190

110 Metaphysics (Speculative philosophy)

For knowledge, cause, purpose, man, see 120

111 Ontology

Nature of relations and being

For cosmology, see 113

  .1 Existence and essence

  .8 Transcendental properties of being

Unity, truth, goodness, evil, beauty (esthetics)

112 Classification of knowledge

113 Cosmology

Origin of universe and life, cosmic harmony

Class specific topics of cosmology not provided for here in 114–119

114   Space

> Including relation of space and matter

115   Time, duration, eternity

> Including relation of time and motion, space-time, implications of theories of relativity

116   Motion, change, evolution

> Class relation of time and motion in 115

117   Matter and form

> Class relation of space and matter in 114

118   Force and energy

119   Number and quantity

120   Knowledge, cause, purpose, man

> *For psychology, see* 150

121   Epistemology

> Origin, sources, limits, validity of knowledge
>
> Including doubt, belief, faith, worth
>
> Class knowledge and its extension in 001, logic in 160

122   Cause and effect

> Including chance versus cause
>
> > *For final cause, see* 124

123   Freedom and necessity

> Determinism, indeterminism, chance
>
> Class chance versus cause in 122

124   Teleology

> Design, purpose, final cause

125   Finite and infinite

126   Consciousness and personality (The self)

127   The unconscious and the subconscious

128   Man

> His soul, mind, nature, life and death
>
> > *For consciousness and personality, see* 126; *the unconscious and the subconscious,* 127; *origin and destiny of individual souls,* 129

129   Origin and destiny of individual souls

> Incarnation, reincarnation, immortality

130   Popular psychology, parapsychology, occultism

131   Popular psychology

>   Including personal well-being, happiness, success
>
>   *For personality analysis and improvement, see* 137

[.3]   Personal well-being, happiness, success

>   Number discontinued; class in 131

133   Parapsychology and occultism

>   Including frauds
>
>   *For esoteric and cabalistic traditions, see* 135.4

.1   Apparitions

>   Including ghosts

.3   Divinatory arts

>   Including numerology, geomancy, fortunetelling by cards and tea leaves, crystal gazing, dowsing
>
>> *For horoscopes, see* 133.5; *palmistry,* 133.6; *dream books,* 135.3; *divinatory graphology,* 137

.4   Magic, witchcraft, demonology

>   Including voodooism; love, good-luck, therapeutic charms

.5   Mundane (Judicial) astrology

>   Zodiacal signs, planets, horoscopes, ephemerides

.6   Palmistry

.8   Extrasensory perception and psychokinesis

>   Psychokinesis: influence on motion without physical intervention
>
>   Including telepathy, clairvoyance, clairaudience, precognition

.9   Spiritualism

>   Communication with discarnate spirits
>
>   Including mediumship, physical and psychic phenomena

135   Dreams and the mystic traditions

.3   Dream books

.4   Esoteric and cabalistic traditions

>   Including mysteries of the ancient elements, Rosicrucian mysteries

137   Personality analysis and improvement

>   Including analytic and divinatory graphology (handwriting analysis)
>
>   Class personality analysis thru physiognomy in 138

138   Physiognomy

> Determination of character from analysis of features

139   Phrenology

> Determination of mental capacities from skull structure

140   **Specific philosophical viewpoints**

> Class a specific branch of philosophy with the subject, e.g., metaphysics 110; an application of a specific viewpoint with the subject, e.g., utilitarianism in ethics 171

141   Idealism and related systems and doctrines

> Including spiritualism, panpsychism, subjectivism, voluntarism, Platonism, Neoplatonism, transcendentalism, individualism, personalism, romanticism

142   Critical philosophy

> Existentialism, Kantianism, neo-Kantianism, phenomenalism, phenomenology
>
> > *For critical realism, see* 149

143   Intuitionism and Bergsonism

> > *For mysticism, see* 149

144   Humanism and related systems and doctrines

> Including pragmatism, instrumentalism, utilitarianism

145   Sensationalism and ideology

146   Naturalism and related systems and doctrines

> Including dynamism, energism, materialism, atomism, mechanism, evolutionism, logical positivism, empiricism

147   Pantheism and related systems and doctrines

> Including panentheism, animism, vitalism, parallelism, occasionalism, monism, pluralism, dualism

148   Liberalism, eclecticism, syncretism, traditionalism, dogmatism

149   Other philosophical systems and doctrines

> Including nominalism, conceptualism, realism, neorealism, critical realism, mysticism, anthroposophy, optimism, meliorism, pessimism, rationalism, intellectualism, innatism, nativism, agnosticism, skepticism, nihilism, fatalism, linguistic analysis
>
> > *For existentialism, see* 142

150   Psychology

Class psychological principles of a specific discipline or subject with the discipline or subject using "Standard Subdivisions" notation 01 from Table 1, e.g., psychological principles of advertising 659.01

.1   Philosophy and theory

.19   Systems, schools, viewpoints

Including speculative systems, e.g., faculty school; functionalism; reductionism, e.g., behaviorism; psychoanalytic systems, e.g., Freudian; Gestalt psychology; field theory

152   Physiological and experimental psychology

.1   Sensory perception

Visual, auditory, olfactory, gustatory, tactile, proprioceptive perceptions

.3   Movements and motor functions

Including reflexes, motor learning, handedness and laterality, locomotion, vocal and graphic expressions, coordination

.4   Emotions and feelings

.5   Motivation (Drives)

.8   Quantitative psychology

Threshold, discrimination, reaction-time studies based on psychophysical methods

Class a specific application with the subject, e.g., fatigue studies in industrial management 658.5

153   Intelligence, intellectual and conscious mental processes

.1   Memory and learning

.2   Ideation

Concepts and concept formation, abstraction, association of ideas, inspiration

.3   Imagination and imagery

Including creativity

.4   Knowledge (Cognition)

Including thought and thinking, reasoning, intuition, value, judgment

For ideation, see 153.2

.7   Perceptual apprehension and understanding

> Including attention, apperception, preperception, subliminal perception; errors; perception of space, time, rhythm, movement
>
> *For sensory perception, see 152.1; extrasensory perception, 133.8*

.8   Will (Volition)

> Including choice and decision, persuasion, brainwashing (menticide)

.9   Intelligence and aptitudes

> Including tests and testing

154   Subconscious states and processes (Depth psychology)

.2   The subconscious

.3   Secondary consciousness

> Daydreams, fantasies, reveries

.6   Sleep phenomena

> Sleep, dreams, somnambulism

.7   Hypnotism

155   Differential and genetic psychology

.2   Individual psychology

> Character, individual differences, personality traits and determinants, adaptability, personality development and modification; typology, e.g., classification scheme of Sheldon
>
> Including appraisals and tests

[.28]   Appraisals and tests

> Number discontinued; class in 155.2

.3   Sex psychology

> Erogeneity and libido, sex and personality, masculinity, femininity, bisexuality, sex relations

---

155.4–155.7 Developmental psychology

Class comprehensive works in 155

.4   Child psychology

> Motor, adaptive, personal-social behavior of children thru age eleven
>
> Including siblings, "only" children; adopted, foster, institutionalized, exceptional children

[.41–.45]   Topics in child psychology

> Numbers discontinued; class in 155.4

.5   Psychology of adolescents

Ages twelve to twenty

.6   Psychology of adults and aged

.67   Aged

Mental and physical impairments, adaptability problems

.7   Evolutional psychology

Influence of heredity on personal characteristics

.8   Ethnopsychology and national psychology

.9   Psychology of influence, pattern, example

Influence of physical and social environment, of housing, of clothing, of special environments and situations, e.g., prisons, disasters

156   Comparative psychology

Studies of behavior mechanisms in animals and plants

157   Abnormal and clinical psychologies

Abnormal psychology: study of behavior patterns of psychotic, psychoneurotic, mentally deficient individuals

Class psychology of exceptional children in 155.4

158   Applied psychology (Special developments)

Including successful living, interpersonal relations, interviewing, leadership, cooperation

Class a specific application with the subject, e.g., educational guidance and counseling 371.4

.6   Vocational interests

.7   Industrial psychology

159   Other aspects

160   **Logic**

Science of reasoning processes

161   Induction

For *hypotheses, see* 167; *analogy,* 169

162   Deduction

For *syllogisms, see* 166

[164]   Symbolic (Mathematical) logic

> Class in 511

▶   165–169 Specific topics

Class comprehensive works in 160

165   Fallacies and sources of error

> Contradictions, paradox, fictions

166   Syllogisms

167   Hypotheses

168   Argument and persuasion

169   Analogy

170   **Ethics (Moral philosophy)**

171   Systems and doctrines

> Perfectionism, hedonism, utilitarianism, altruism, egoism; systems based on authority, on intuition and moral sense, on conscience, on evolution and education

> Including natural law

> Class systems and doctrines applied to specific human qualities, relationships, activities in 172–179; morals and duties in comparative religion in 291.5; in a specific religion with the religion, e.g., Christian moral theology 241

▶   172–179 Applied ethics

Inherent rightness and wrongness of specific human qualities, relationships, activities

Class comprehensive works in 170

172   Ethics of political relationships

> Including citizenship, public office, international relations

173   Ethics of family relationships

> Including marriage, separation, divorce, responsibilities of parents for children and home life, of children to parents

174   Professional and occupational ethics

> If preferred, class with the specific profession or occupation, using "Standard Subdivisions" notation 01 from Table 1, e.g., medical ethics 610.1

175   Ethics of recreation

Sportsmanship, fair play, other ethical concepts concerning participation in, watching and listening to recreational activities

Including games of chance, betting, human and animal combat, racing, hunting

176   Sexual ethics

Including celibacy, chastity, continence, adultery, prostitution, homosexuality, birth control (contraception), artificial insemination, obscenity in art and literature

177   Ethics of social relations

Including courtship, friendship, courtesy, hospitality, conversation, gossip, slander, truthfulness, flattery, personal appearance, philanthropy, slavery and other discriminatory practices

Class etiquette in 395

178   Ethics of temperance and intemperance

Abstinence and moderation in use of alcoholic beverages, tobacco, narcotics, food

179   Other applications of ethics

Virtues, vices, faults, failings not otherwise provided for

Including genocide, homicide, suicide, abortion, capital punishment, dueling, cruelty to children and animals, profanity, blasphemy, obscenity in speech

---

► ## 180–190 Historical and geographical treatment of philosophy

Class here development, description, critical appraisal, collected writings of individual philosophers regardless of viewpoint

Class comprehensive works in 109

180   Ancient, medieval, Oriental philosophy

.1–.9   Standard subdivisions of ancient philosophy

Notations from Table 1

181   Oriental

        Ancient, medieval, modern

        Including philosophy based on specific religions, e.g., Judaism

---

▶   182–188 Ancient Western

                      Class comprehensive works in 180

▶   182–185 Ancient Greek

        Class comprehensive works in 180, Skeptic and Neoplatonic philosophy in 186

182   Pre-Socratic Greek

183   Sophistic, Socratic and related Greek philosophies

184   Platonic

185   Aristotelian

186   Skeptic and Neoplatonic

▶   187–188 Ancient Roman

        Class comprehensive works in 180, Skeptic and Neoplatonic philosophy in 186

187   Epicurean

188   Stoic

189   Medieval Western

        Including early Christian philosophy

190   **Modern Western philosophy**

        Class here comprehensive works on Christian philosophy, on modern philosophy, on Western philosophy, on European philosophy

        For ancient, medieval, Oriental philosophy, see 180

191   United States and Canada

192   British Isles

193   Germany and Austria

194   France

195   Italy

196   Spain and Portugal

200 Religion

Beliefs, attitudes, practices of individuals and groups with respect to ultimate nature of existences and relationships within context of revelation, deity, worship

Class here comprehensive works on Christianity

Class comparative religion in 291, devil worship in 133.4

.1 Philosophy and theory of religion

Including psychological aspects, e.g., religious experience based on use of psychedelic drugs

.2 Miscellany of religion

.3 Dictionaries, encyclopedias, concordances of religion

.4 Religious mythology

.5 Serial publications of religion

.6 Organizations of religion

.7 Study and teaching of religion

Class religious instruction and exercises in nonsectarian schools in 377 (not 200.7)

.8 Collections on religion

.9 Historical and geographical treatment of religion and religious thought

Religious situation and conditions

Class historical and geographical treatment of a specific religion with the subject, e.g., history of Judaism 296.09

201 Philosophy and theory of Christianity

Including Christian theology

202 Miscellany of Christianity

203 Dictionaries, encyclopedias, concordances of Christianity

204 Christian mythology

205 Serial publications on Christianity

206 Organizations of Christianity

Class Christian church in 260

207   Study and teaching of Christianity

> Class Christian training and instruction in Sunday schools, church
> schools, vacation Bible schools, under other church auspices in 268

[.4–.6]   Standard subdivisions

> Do not use; class in 207

208   Collections on Christianity

**209   Historical and geographical treatment of Christianity and
Christian thought**

> Class historical and geographical treatment of organized Christian
> church in 270

210   Natural religion

> Religious beliefs and attitudes attained thru observation and interpretation
> of evidence in nature, thru speculation, thru reasoning, but not thru
> revelation

211   God

> General concepts
>
> Including theism, deism, rationalism, humanism, secularism,
> humanitarianism, agnosticism, skepticism, atheism
>
> *For nature of God, see 212*

212   Nature of God

> Polytheism, dualism, monotheism, pantheism, theosophy,
> anthropomorphism
>
> Including anthroposophy

213   Creation

> By fiat, by evolutionary growth and change
>
> Including creation of life, of man

214   Theodicy

> Vindication of God's justice and goodness in permitting existence of
> evil and suffering
>
> Including Providence

215   Science and religion

> Antagonism and reconciliation
>
> Including technology and religion, cybernetics and religion
>
> Class scientific theories of creation in 213

216   Good and evil

> *For theodicy, see* 214

217   Worship and prayer

218   Man

> His nature and place in universe
>
> Including immortality

219   Analogy

> Religious belief based on correspondences
>
> Class religious belief on a specific subject with the subject, e.g., on immortality 218

220   Bible

> Holy Scriptures of Judaism and Christianity
>
> Including original texts and early versions
>
> Class Christian Biblical theology in 230–270, Jewish in 296.3; Biblical precepts in Christian codes of conduct in 241.5, in Jewish codes in 296.3

.01   Philosophy and theory

> Class indexes in 220.2

.02   Miscellany

[.03]   Dictionaries, encyclopedias, concordances

> Do not use; class dictionaries and encyclopedias in 220.3, concordances in 220.2

.05–.08   Standard subdivisions

> Notations from Table 1

.09   Historical and geographical treatment

> Class literary and external history in 220.6; geography, history, chronology, persons of Bible lands in Bible times in 220.9

.1   Origins and authenticity

> Canon, inspiration, authorship, prophetic message

.2   Concordances and indexes

.3   Dictionaries and encyclopedias

[.4]   Original texts and early versions

> Number discontinued; class in 220

.5   Modern versions

> Complete texts, selections from more than one part
>
> Including Authorized (King James), Douay versions
>
> Class commentaries with text in 220.7; selections compiled for a specific purpose with the purpose, e.g., for meditations 242

[.52–.59]   By language

> Numbers discontinued; class in 220.5

.6   Interpretation and criticism

> Literary and external history of Bible, symbolism and typology, harmony, exegesis (higher criticism), historical criticism
>
> *For commentaries, see* 220.7

.7   Commentaries

> Criticism and interpretation arranged in textual order with or without text

.8   Special subjects treated in Bible

> Examples: science, commerce, position of women

.9   Geography, history, chronology, persons of Bible lands in Bible times

[.91–.95]   Geography, biography, archeology, history

> Numbers discontinued; class in 220.9

▶   221–229 Specific parts of Bible

> Class comprehensive works in 220

221   Old Testament

> *For specific parts of Old Testament, see* 222–224

.1–.9   Generalities

> Add to 221 the numbers following 220 in 220.1–220.9, e.g., commentaries 221.7

▶   222–224 Specific parts of Old Testament

> Class comprehensive works in 221

222   Historical books of Old Testament

> Pentateuch (Torah: Genesis, Exodus, Leviticus, Numbers, Deuteronomy), Joshua (Josue), Judges, Ruth, Samuel, Kings, Chronicles (Paralipomena), Ezra (Esdras 1), Nehemiah (Esdras 2, Nehemias), Esther
>
> (It is optional to class here Tobit (Tobias), Judith, deuterocanonical part of Esther; prefer 229)

223   Poetic books of Old Testament

> Job, Psalms, Proverbs, Ecclesiastes, Song of Solomon (Canticle of Canticles)
>
> (It is optional to class here Wisdom of Solomon (Wisdom), Ecclesiasticus (Sirach); prefer 229)

224   Prophetic books of Old Testament

> Isaiah (Isaias), Jeremiah (Jeremias), Lamentations, Ezekiel (Ezechiel), Daniel, Hosea (Osee), Joel, Amos, Obadiah (Abdias), Jonah (Jonas), Micah (Micheas), Nahum, Habakkuk (Habacuc), Zephaniah (Sophonias), Haggai (Aggeus), Zechariah (Zacharias), Malachi (Malachias)
>
> (It is optional to class here Baruch, Song of the three children, Susanna, Bel and the dragon, Maccabees 1 and 2 (Machabees 1 and 2); prefer 229)

225   New Testament

> *For specific parts of New Testament, see 226–228*

.1–.9   Generalities

> Add to 225 the numbers following 220 in 220.1–220.9, e.g., commentaries 225.7
>
> Class biography of Jesus Christ, Mary, Joseph, Joachim, Anne, John the Baptist in 232

▶   226–228 Specific parts of New Testament
                   Class comprehensive works in 225

226   Gospels and Acts

> Gospels: Matthew, Mark, Luke, John

227   Epistles

> Epistles of Paul to Romans, Corinthians, Galatians, Ephesians, Philippians, Colossians, Thessalonians, Timothy, Titus, Philemon, Hebrews; Epistles of James, Peter, John, Jude

228   Revelation (Apocalypse)

229   Apocrypha, pseudepigrapha, deuterocanonical works

Esdras, Tobit (Tobias), Judith, Esther, Wisdom of Solomon (Wisdom),
Ecclesiasticus (Sirach), Baruch, Epistle of Jeremy, Song of the three
children, Susanna, Bel and the dragon, Prayer of Manasses, Maccabees
(Machabees), pseudo gospels, other Old and New Testament pseudepigrapha

Including pseudepigrapha in Dead Sea Scrolls

If preferred, class Tobit (Tobias), Judith, deuterocanonical part of Esther
in 222; Wisdom of Solomon (Wisdom), Ecclesiasticus (Sirach), in 223;
Baruch, Song of the three children, Susanna, Bel and the dragon,
Maccabees 1 and 2 (Machabees 1 and 2) in 224

▶   **230–280 Christianity**

Class comprehensive works in 200

For Bible, see 220

▶   **230–270 Specific elements of Christianity**

Class here Biblical theology, specific elements of specific denominations and sects

If preferred, class specific elements of specific denominations and
sects in 280

Class comprehensive works in 200

▶   **230–240 Christian theology**

Class comprehensive works in 201

For social and ecclesiastical theology, see 260

230   **Christian doctrinal theology (Christian dogma)**

Class moral theology in 241, doctrinal controversies in general church
history in 273

.1–.9   Standard subdivisions

Notations from Table 1

Use of these numbers for doctrines of specific denominations and
sects is discontinued; class in 230

▶   **231–236 Specific doctrines**

Class comprehensive works in 230, doctrines on church government, organization, nature in 262

231   **God, Trinity, Godhead**

Including miracles, revelation, theodicy

For Jesus Christ, see 232

232   **Jesus Christ and his family**

Including Christ as Logos (Word of God), prophet, priest, king; incarna-
tion, messiahship, sacrifice, atonement, resurrection, second coming,
judgment, divinity and humanity of Christ

Class here Christology

.9   **Doctrines on family and life of Jesus**

Including infancy, public life, teachings, passion and death, resurrection, appearances, ascension, character and personality, influence,
historicity of Jesus; Joseph, Joachim, Anne, John the Baptist

.91   **Mary, mother of Jesus (Mariology)**

Immaculate Conception, annunciation, virginity, assumption,
sanctity and virtues, spiritual powers

[.92–.97]   **Other aspects of family and life of Jesus**

Numbers discontinued; class in 232.9

233   **Man**

Creation and fall, sin, original sin, accountability, soul, freedom of
choice between good and evil

For salvation, see 234; eschatology, 236

234   **Salvation (Soteriology)**

Grace, faith, redemption, regeneration, repentance, forgiveness,
obedience, justification, sanctification, predestination and free will

Including sacraments as means of grace

235   **Spiritual beings**

Saints, angels, devils

Former heading: Invisible world

Class Mary, Joseph, Joachim, Anne, John the Baptist in 232.9

236   Eschatology

> Death, future state of man, millennium, resurrection of the dead, last judgment
>
> Including Antichrist

238   Creeds, confessions of faith, covenants, catechisms

> Class catechetics in 268, creeds and catechisms on a specific doctrine with the subject, e.g., attributes of God 231

239   Apologetics and polemics

> Exposition of Christian doctrines refuting alleged errors in other systems
>
> Class apologetics and polemics on a specific doctrine with the subject, e.g., nature of the church 262

240   **Christian moral and devotional theology**

241   Moral theology

> Including sins and vices, virtues, conscience, moral laws, specific moral problems
>
> *For guides to conduct of Christian life, see 248*

[.3–.4]   Sins and vices, virtues

> Numbers discontinued; class in 241

.5   Codes of conduct

> Ten Commandments, Golden Rule, precepts of church
>
> Class church law in 262.9

242   Devotional literature

> Texts of meditations, contemplations, prayers for individuals and families
>
> Class devotional sermons in 252
>
> *For evangelistic writings, see 243; hymns, 245*

[.2–.8]   Specific kinds of devotional literature

> Numbers discontinued; class in 242

243   Evangelistic writings for individuals and families

> Works designed to convert readers, promote repentance
>
> Class evangelistic sermons in 252

245   Hymns without music

> Texts for individuals and families
>
> Class musical scores and parts in 783.9, modern metrical versions of psalms in 223

246   **Art in Christianity**

Religious significance and purpose of architecture, icons, symbols, insignia, colors, lights; of musical, rhythmic, dramatic arts

Former heading: Symbolism and symbolic objects and places

Class creation, description, critical appraisal as art in 700

For church furnishings and related articles, see 247

247   **Church furnishings and related articles**

Furniture, plastic arts, paintings, textiles

248   **Practice of religion in personal and family life**   **Personal religion**

Including conversion, stewardship, witness bearing, guides to conduct of Christian life

Class prayers and other devotional literature in 242–245

For Christian worship in family life, see 249

[.2–.8]   **Specific aspects of personal religion**

Numbers discontinued; class in 248

249   **Christian worship in family life**

▶   **250–280 Christian church**

Class comprehensive works in 260

250   **Local Christian church and Christian religious orders**

Class public worship in 264, missions in 266, religious training and instruction in 268, comprehensive works on Christian church in 260

▶   **251–254 Local church**

Class comprehensive works in 250, special parochial activities in 259

251   **Preaching (Homiletics)**

Preparation and delivery of sermons

Including radio and television preaching

Class texts of sermons in 252, evangelism in 253.7

252   Texts of sermons

> Class sermons on a specific subject with the subject, e.g., God's Providence 231

.01–.09   Standard subdivisions

> Notations from Table 1
>
> Use of these numbers for texts of sermons by specific denominations and sects is discontinued; class in 252

253   Secular clergymen and pastoral duties

> Priests, ministers, pastors, rectors, vicars, curates, chaplains, elders, deacons, assistants
>
> Including life and person
>
> Class here pastoral duties of laymen
>
> Class education of clergymen in 207, personal Christianity for clergymen in 248, religious clergy in 255
>
> *For preaching, see 251; parish government and administration, 254*

.5   Counseling

.7   Evangelism

254   Parish government and administration

> As related to function
>
> Including membership, programs, buildings, equipment, grounds
>
> Class management in 658

.2   In specific kinds of communities

> Urban, suburban, rural

.3   Radio and television work

.4   Public relations and publicity

> *For radio and television work, see 254.3*

.8   Finance

> Budget, income, methods of raising money, expenditures

255   Religious congregations and orders (Monasticism)

> Government, organization, administration as related to function
>
> Class here comprehensive works on Christian religious congregations and orders
>
> Class special parochial activities in 259, management in 658
>
> *For religious congregations and orders in church organization, see 262; in church history, 271*

[258]   Parochial welfare work

> Class in 361.7

259   Parochial activities by parishes and religious orders

> Examples: camp programs, recreation; work with children, soldiers, students, foreigners
>
> *For parochial welfare work, see 361.7*

260   Christian social and ecclesiastical theology

> Institutions, services, observances, disciplines, work of Christianity and Christian church
>
> Class here comprehensive works on Christian church
>
> *For historical and geographical treatment, see 270; local church and religious orders, 250; denominations and sects, 280*

261   Social theology

> Attitude of Christianity toward and influence on secular matters and other religions

.1   Role of Christian church in society

> Examples: role in education, in social amelioration

.2   Christianity and other religions and irreligion

> Including Christian church and the apostate and indifferent

.5   Christianity and intellectual development

> Examples: attitude toward science, toward growth of knowledge

.7   Christianity and civil government

> Attitude toward and influence on political activities and ideologies
>
> Including religious freedom, theocracy

.8   Christianity and socioeconomic problems

> Attitude toward and influence on social problems, the economic order, international affairs
>
> *For Christianity and civil government, see 261.7; role of Christian church in society, 261.1*

262   Ecclesiology

> Church government, organization, nature
>
> Including governing leaders, parishes and religious orders in church organization, specific forms of organization, general councils, church and ministerial authority, ecumenicalism

[.7]   Nature of the church

> Number discontinued; class in 262

.9   Church law and discipline

Canon (ecclesiastical) law

263   Days, times, places of religious observance

Including Sunday, Sabbath (seventh-day observance), events of church year, specific saints' days, other feast and fast days

264   Public worship

Divine services, religious ceremonies, liturgies, their conduct and texts

Class here comprehensive works on worship

Class private worship for individuals and families in 240, Sunday-school services in 268, musical scores and parts in 783

For other rites, ceremonies, ordinances, see 265

.01–.09   Standard subdivisions

Notations from Table 1

Use of these numbers for public worship by specific denominations and sects is discontinued; class in 264

265   Other rites, ceremonies, ordinances

Preparation, instruction, performance

Including sacraments

266   Missions

Class here missionary societies

For mission schools, see 377

[.1–.9]   Of specific denominations and sects

Numbers discontinued; class in 266

267   Associations for religious work

Including Salvation Army, Young Men's and Young Women's Christian Associations

For missionary societies, see 266; *religious congregations and orders,* 255

268   Religious training and instruction

In Sunday schools, church schools, vacation Bible schools, under other church auspices

Including catechetics

Class religious instruction in nonsectarian schools in 377, religious training of child in home in 649

For catechisms, see 238

269 **Organized spiritual renewal**

    Revivals, camp meetings, retreats

270 **Historical and geographical treatment of organized Christian church (Church history)**

    Use 270.01–270.08 for standard subdivisions

    Class historical and geographical treatment of specific denominations and sects in 280

▶   **270.1–270.8 Historical periods**

      Class comprehensive works in 270

.1 Apostolic period to 325

.2 Period of ecumenical councils, 325–787

.3 Struggle between papacy and empire, 787–1054

    Including great schism

.4 Period of papal supremacy, 1054–1200

.5 Late Middle Ages to Renaissance, 1200–1517

.6 Reformation and Counter-Reformation, 1517–1648

.7 Peace of Westphalia to French Revolution, 1648–1789

.8 Modern church, 1789–

    Class here ecumenical movement

▶   **271–273 Specific topics of church history**

      Class comprehensive works in 270

271 Religious congregations and orders in church history

272 Persecutions in general church history

273 Doctrinal controversies and heresies in general church history

    Including Gnosticism, Manicheism, Sabellianism, Arianism, Donatism, Pelagianism, Albigensianism, Waldensianism, antinomianism, Molinism, Jansenism, Pietism

    Class persecutions of heretics in 272

▶ ## 274–279 Treatment by continent, country, locality

Class comprehensive works in 270; geographical treatment of a specific subject with the subject, e.g., persecutions in England 272

274 Christian church in Europe

Add "Areas" notation 41–49 from Table 2 to base number 27, e.g., Christian church in France 274.4

275 Christian church in Asia

Add "Areas" notation 51–59 from Table 2 to base number 27, e.g., Christian church in Japan 275.2

276 Christian church in Africa

Add "Areas" notation 61–69 from Table 2 to base number 27, e.g., Christian church in South Africa 276.8

277 Christian church in North America

Add "Areas" notation 71–79 from Table 2 to base number 27, e.g., Christian church in Pennsylvania 277.48

278 Christian church in South America

Add "Areas" notation 81–89 from Table 2 to base number 27, e.g., Christian church in Brazil 278.1

279 Christian church in other parts of world

Add "Areas" notation 93–98 from Table 2 to base number 27, e.g., Christian church in Australia 279.4

280 Denominations and sects of Christian church

Including Protestantism

Class here general historical and geographical treatment of, comprehensive works on specific denominations and sects and their individual local churches

(It is optional to class here specific elements of specific denominations and sects; prefer 230–270)

281 Primitive and Oriental churches

Including Apostolic, Monophysite, Coptic, Abyssinian, Nestorian churches

.9 Eastern Orthodox churches

Including Greek, Russian, Syrian, Ukrainian

Add "Areas" notation 4–9 from Table 2 to base number 281.9

282   Roman Catholic Church

> Class Oriental churches in communion with Rome in 281
>
> Add "Areas" notation 4–9 from Table 2 to base number 282

283   Anglican churches

284   Protestant denominations of Continental origin

> Lutheran churches, Calvinistic and Reformed churches in Europe; Hussite, Anabaptist, Albigensian, Waldensian, Huguenot, Moravian, Arminian, Remonstrant churches; modern schisms in Catholic Church
>
> *For Presbyterian churches, see 285; Baptist churches, 286; Church of the New Jerusalem, 289.4; Mennonites, 289.7*

285   Presbyterian, American Reformed, Congregational churches

> Including United Church of Christ
>
> Class United Church of Canada in 287
>
> *For Christian Church, see 286*

286   Baptist, Disciples of Christ, Adventist churches

> Including Christian Church

287   Methodist churches

> Including United Church of Canada

288   Unitarianism

> Unitarian Church, Unitarian Universalist Association
>
> *For Universalist Church, see 289.1*

289   Other denominations and sects

.1   Universalist Church

.2   [Permanently unassigned]

> If it is desired to give local emphasis and a shorter number to a specific denomination or sect not separately provided for, class it here

.3   Latter-Day Saints

> Including Mormons

.4   Church of the New Jerusalem (Swedenborgianism)

.5   Church of Christ, Scientist (Christian Science)

.6   Society of Friends (Quakers)

.7   Mennonite churches

> Including Amish, Church of God in Christ

.8   Shakers

      United Society of True Believers in Christ's Second Appearing

.9   Others

      Examples: Assemblies of God, Churches of God, Church of the Nazarene, Jehovah's Witnesses, Pentecostal Assemblies, New Thought, United Brethren, Unity School of Christianity

      If preferred, class a specific denomination or sect requiring local emphasis in 289.2

      For Salvation Army, see 267

290   Other religions and comparative religion

291   Comparative religion and religious mythology

      Including primitive religions

.06   Organizations

      Class religious organizations in 291.6

.1   Relationships and attitudes of religions

      Mythological foundations; social theologies: attitudes toward and influence on civil governments and other religions, attitudes toward science and other cultural manifestations

.2   Doctrinal theologies (Dogmas)

      Objects of worship and veneration, man and his soul, eschatology

.3   Forms of worship and other practices

      Rites and ceremonies; symbolism, symbolic objects, emblems; sacred times and places; divination, witchcraft

      For personal religion, see 291.4

.4   Personal religion

      Religious experience; private worship, prayer, meditation, contemplation; guides to conduct of life

.5   Moral theology

      Conscience, sins, vices, virtues, duties

      For guides to conduct of life, see 291.4

.6   Leaders and organization

.7   Activities inspired by religious motives

      Examples: religious wars, missions, religious training and instruction

.8   Sources

      Sacred books and scriptures, oral traditions, laws and decisions

.9   Sects and reform movements

> Class a specific aspect of a specific sect or reform movement with the subject, e.g., moral theology 291.5

▶   *292–299 Specific religions and their mythologies*

Class comprehensive works in 290

292   Classical (Greek and Roman) religion and religious mythology

293   Germanic religion and religious mythology

294   Religions of Indic origin

> Including the Vedas

.3   Buddhism

.4   Jainism

.5   Hinduism (Brahmanism)

.6   Sikhism

295   Zoroastrianism (Mazdaism, Parseeism)

296   Judaism

.06   Organizations

> Class religious organizations in 296.6

.1   Sources

> Talmudic literature, Midrash, Haggadah, Cabala, Maimonides, Responsa, Halakah, other laws and decisions
>
> *For Old Testament, see 221*

.3   Doctrinal, moral, social theology

> Including Biblical theology
>
> Class guides to conduct of life in 296.7

.4   Public services, rites, traditions

> Liturgy, hymns, prayer, music, responsive reading, symbolism, ceremonies, sermons, comprehensive works on public and private worship and prayer
>
> Including Sabbath, festivals, holy days, fasts, rites and customs for specific occasions, e.g., bar mitzvahs
>
> Class musical scores and parts in 783
>
> *For personal and family religion, see 296.7*

.6   Leaders, organization, activities

Class laws and decisions in 296.1

.7   Personal and family religion

Religious experience, daily devotions and worship, observance of
dietary laws, conduct of life

For moral theology, see 296.3

.8   Sects and movements

Examples: orthodox, conservative, reform Judaism

Class a specific aspect of a sect or movement with the subject, e.g.,
public services 296.4

297   Islam and religions derived from it

Including Islamic sects, religion of Black Muslims, Babism, Bahai faith

For Sikhism, see 294.6

298   [Permanently unassigned]

If it is desired to give local emphasis and a shorter number to a specific
religion, class it here

299   Other religions

Including Taoism, Confucianism, Shintoism

If preferred, class a specific religion requiring local emphasis in 298

300

---

300   The social sciences

> The sciences that deal with social activities and institutions
>
> Class here behavioral sciences
>
> Use 300.1–300.9 for standard subdivisions
>
> Class military, diplomatic, political, economic, social, welfare aspects of a war with history of the war; a specific behavioral science with the subject, e.g., psychology 150

301   Sociology

> The science that deals comprehensively with social activities and institutions
>
> Including theories of social causation, e.g., social physics; biological, geographical, sociological determinism
>
> Class customs and folklore in 390, social pathology in 362

   .09   Historical and geographical treatment

> Class historical and geographical treatment of social conditions in 309.1

SUMMARY

301.1	**Social psychology**
.2	**Culture and cultural processes**
.3	**Ecology and community**
.4	**Social structure**
.5	**Institutions**
.6	**Social conflict and accommodation**

   .1   Social psychology

> Study of collective responses and behavior of groups and other collectivities
>
> Class social influence on individuals in 155.9

   .11   Social interaction

> Person to person, person to group, group to group
>
> Including role theory

   .14   Communication

> *For mass communication, see 301.16*

.15   Social control and socialization

Social control thru coercion, indoctrination, authority, leadership; socialization of adults, of young people

Former heading: Group behavior

Including public opinion [*formerly also* 329], propaganda

.16   Mass communication

Mass media and their audiences

.18   Groups [*formerly also* 301.4]

Audiences, publics, crowds, mobs, voluntary associations, bureaucracies, small (primary) groups

Including sociometry

Class pressure groups [*formerly* 301.18] in 322.4

For the community, see 301.34

.2   Culture and cultural processes

Beliefs, knowledge, technology, folkways, mores, language

Including subcultures

Class here primitive races [*formerly* 572], cultural [*formerly* 390] and social anthropology, comprehensive works on anthropology

Class social conflict [*formerly* 301.2] in 301.6

Class criminal anthropology in 364.2, physical anthropology in 573

.209   Historical and geographical treatment of general, cultural, social anthropology as disciplines

Class historical and geographical treatment of culture in 900, of cultural processes in 301.29

.24   Social change

Changes in beliefs, values, norms, institutions, techniques, organizational patterns induced by contact between cultures, social innovation, reform, science and technology

For conflict, see 301.6; *planning,* 309.2

.29   Historical and geographical treatment of cultural processes

Add "Areas" notation 1–9 from Table 2 to base number 301.29

Class cultural situation in 901.9

.3   Ecology and community

.31   Ecology

Influence and effect of environment on human groups

Class here interdisciplinary works on pollution

Class a specific aspect of pollution with the subject, e.g., public health measures 614.7

For populations, see 301.32

.32   Populations

Density, increase, decrease, movement, characteristics

Including immigration, emigration, internal migration

Class migration to cities in 301.34, statistical tables of populations in 312

.34   The community

Urban and rural communities

Including agricultural sociology [*formerly also* 630.1]

Class local planning in 309.2

.4   Social structure

Former heading: Institutions and groups

Class here prejudice, discrimination, segregation

Class groups [*formerly* 301.4] in 301.18

Class industrial, religious, racial, class conflict in 301.6

.41   The sexes and their relations

Including marital sexual relations [*formerly* 301.42], extramarital and abnormal sexual relations, celibacy, courtship

.42   Marriage and family

Including monogamy, polygamy; family dissolution thru death, divorce, remarriage; interracial, intercultural, interreligious marriage

Class marital sexual relations [*formerly* 301.42] in 301.41

Class marriage counseling in 362.8, child care and training in 649

.43   Specific age levels

Children, adolescents, mature and middle-aged persons, aged persons

.44   Social classes

Classes determined by economic status, by ownership of property, by family and kinship ties, by location and duration of residence, by occupation, by possession of authority and power, by legal status, by education

Including alienated and excluded classes, e.g., hobos, tramps, untouchables, hippies

Class aggregates distinctive because of language, aggregates of specific racial origin in 301.45 [*both formerly* 301.44]

.45   Nondominant aggregates

Aggregates of specific racial [*formerly also* 301.44], ethnic, national origins; adherents to specific religious organizations

Including aggregates distinctive because of language [*formerly* 301.44], because of social practices

[.451–.453]   Aggregates of specific ethnic and national origin

Numbers discontinued; class in 301.45

[.47]   Illness and disability

Class in 362.1–362.4

.5   Institutions

Complex patterns governing behavior in certain fundamental and recurring situations

Former heading: Sociology of everyday activities and preoccupations

Including economic, educational, recreational, religious, political, military institutions

.6   Social conflict [*formerly* 301.2] and accommodation

Industrial, religious, racial, class conflict

Including sociology of wars [*formerly* 355.02], riots, revolutions

309   Social situation and conditions

Class social pathology and its alleviation in 362

.1   Historical and geographical treatment

Add "Areas" notation 1–9 from Table 2 to base number 309.1

.2   Planning and assistance

Formulation of objectives and procedures; provision of technical, economic, educational, other forms of assistance toward improvement of social conditions by governmental, private, international agencies

Including voluntary service groups, e.g., United States Peace Corps

Class planning and assistance in a single specific field with the subject, e.g., education 370.19

▶   **310–390 Specific social sciences**

The sciences that deal with specific social activities and institutions

Class comprehensive works in 300

310   Statistics

Collections of quantitative data

Class statistics of a specific subject other than population with the subject, using "Standard Subdivisions" notation 021 from Table 1, e.g., statistics on banking 332.1021

.9   Historical and geographical treatment

Class general statistics by continent, country, locality in modern world in 314–319 (not 310.94–310.99)

[311]   Statistical method

Class comprehensive works on statistical method in 001.4, statistical mathematics in 519.5

312   Statistics of populations (Demographic statistics)

Vital statistics, somatology, population destiny, movement, other characteristics

---

▶   314–319 General statistics by continent, country, locality in modern world

Class comprehensive works in 310

314   General statistics of Europe

Add "Areas" notation 41–49 from Table 2 to base number 31, e.g., general statistics of England 314.2

315   General statistics of Asia

Add "Areas" notation 51–59 from Table 2 to base number 31, e.g., general statistics of Japan 315.2

316   General statistics of Africa

Add "Areas" notation 61–69 from Table 2 to base number 31, e.g., general statistics of Tanzania 316.78

317 General statistics of North America

Add "Areas" notation 71–79 from Table 2 to base number 31, e.g., general statistics of British Columbia 317.11

318 General statistics of South America

Add "Areas" notation 81–89 from Table 2 to base number 31, e.g., general statistics of Argentina 318.2

319 General statistics of other parts of world

Add "Areas" notation 93–98 from Table 2 to base number 31, e.g., general statistics of Australia 319.4

320 Political science

Study of the formalized institutions and processes by which society as a whole is governed

For public administration, see 350; law, 340

.01 Philosophy and theory

Class political theories and ideologies in 320.5

.02–.08 Standard subdivisions

Notations from Table 1

.09 Historical and geographical treatment

Class political situation and conditions in 320.9

.1 The state

Origin, territory, population, sovereignty

Including emerging states, geopolitics

Class government in 320.3–320.4, specific forms of states in 321, relations of state to population in 322–324

.3 Comparative government

Structure, functions, activities

.4 Descriptive government (Civics)

Structure, functions, activities

Add "Areas" notation 1–9 from Table 2 to base number 320.4

Class legislative branch in 328, executive branch in 350, judicial branch in 347

For comparative government, see 320.3

.5   Political theories and ideologies

> Liberalism, conservatism, anarchism, Gandhism, theocracy, socialism, communism, fascism, other forms of collectivism
>
> Including nationalism, "pan" movements, racism
>
> Class here political aims of communism
>
> Class theories and ideologies on a specific subject with the subject, e.g., theories of the state 320.1

.9   Political situation and conditions

> Add "Areas" notation 1–9 from Table 2 to base number 320.9

321   Forms of states

> Including forms determined by geographical distribution of power, e.g., unitary states, federal states; forms determined by extent of territory governed, e.g., empires, supranational states, national states, city states; ideal states, e.g., anarchy, utopias; semisovereign and dependent states

.1   Primitive and despotic states

.3   Feudal system

.4   Pure democracies

.5   Elitist systems

> Former heading: States controlled by select few
>
> Autocracies, theocracies, oligarchies, plutocracies

.6   Absolute monarchies

[.7]   Modern constitutionalism

> Class in 321.8

.8   Democratic forms

> Presidential and cabinet systems, republics, limited monarchies
>
> Including modern constitutionalism [*formerly* 321.7]
>
> > *For pure democracies, see* 321.4

.9   Authoritarian forms

> Including communist and fascist states
>
> > *For despotic states, see* 321.1; *elitist systems,* 321.5; *absolute monarchies,* 321.6

▶   322–324 Internal relations of state

Class comprehensive works in 323

322   Relation of state to social groups and their members

Including religious bodies [*formerly also* 323.1], military organizations
(armed forces), labor movements and groups, business and industry

Class relation of states to political parties in 329, comprehensive works
on internal relations of state in 323

.4   Political action groups

Including revolutionary and subversive groups [*both formerly* 323.2],
pressure groups [*formerly* 301.18], protest and reform movements

Class role of pressure groups in practical politics in 329, legislative
lobbying in 328

323   Relation of state to its residents

Class here comprehensive works on internal relations of state

For relation of state to social groups and their members, see 322;
electoral process, 324

▶   323.1–323.3 Relation of state to social aggregates

Class comprehensive works in 323.1

.1   Nondominant aggregates

Racial, national, ethnic groups

Class here comprehensive works on relation of state to social
aggregates

Class socioeconomic aggregates in 323.3, religious bodies in 322
[*both formerly* 323.1]

For social classes, see 323.3

[.2]   Revolutionary and subversive groups

Class in 322.4

.3   Social classes

Including socioeconomic aggregates [*formerly also* 323.1]

▶   323.4–323.6 Relation of state to individuals

Class comprehensive works in 323

.4   Civil rights

Including rights to personal security (life), economic rights (property rights), rights of assembly and association, right of petition, limitation and suspension of individual rights and guarantees

.42   Equal protection of the laws

Including procedural rights, e.g., trial by jury, rights of nondominant aggregates, e.g., blacks

[.43]   Personal security (Life)

Number discontinued; class in 323.4

.44   Freedom of action (Liberty)

Including freedom of conscience and religion, of speech, of press

[.46–.48]   Other individual rights

Numbers discontinued; class in 323.4

[.49]   Limitation and suspension of individual rights and guarantees

Number discontinued; class in 323.4

.5   Political rights

Right to be represented, right to hold office

Class electoral process in 324

.6   Citizenship and related topics

Acquisition of citizenship, duties and obligations of citizens, relation of state to aliens and stateless persons

Including passports and visas, expatriation and repatriation

324   Electoral processes

Local, regional, state, national elections; election procedures, e.g., registration, voting; qualifications for voting

Including ballot systems, corruption and irregularities, recall

Add "Areas" notation 4–9 from Table 2 to base number 324

For primary elections, see 329

325   International migration

> Immigration, emigration, colonization
>
> Including political refugees

[.1–.3]   Immigration, emigration, colonization

> Numbers discontinued; class in 325

.4–.9   International migration to and colonization in specific continents, countries, localities in modern world

> Add "Areas" notation 4–9 from Table 2 to base number 325

326   Slavery and emancipation

327   International relations

> Affairs of the world political community
>
> Including power politics, espionage, subversion, conduct of propaganda and psychological warfare, promotion of peace, disarmament, diplomacy
>
> Class international organizations in 341.22–341.24, military art and science in 355

.3–.9   Foreign policies of specific nations

> Attitudes, courses of action, objectives adopted by governments of states in their relations with other states and regions
>
> Add "Areas" notation 3–9 from Table 2 to base number 327

328   Legislation

> Legislative function; legislative branch of government; basis of representation, powers, sessions, internal organization and discipline of legislative bodies; enactment of legislation; personal privileges and immunities of legislators
>
> Including lobbying, ombudsman system, initiative and referendum, parliamentary rules and procedures

[.1]   Parliamentary rules and procedures

> Class general rules of order [*formerly* 328.1] in 060.4, parliamentary rules and procedures of legislative bodies in 328

[.3]   Legislative branch of government

> Number discontinued; class in 328

.4–.9   Legislative branch of specific jurisdictions in modern world

> Add "Areas" notation 4–9 from Table 2 to base number 328

329   Practical politics   Political parties

Campaign techniques and literature; nomination of candidates for office, e.g., primary elections, nominating conventions; election history; relation of state to political parties; party finance

Including Marxist organizations and their activities, e.g., First, Second, Vienna Internationals [*all formerly* 335.42], other communist international organizations [*formerly* 335.44]; pressure and other interest groups

Class public opinion [*formerly* 329] in 301.15

Class electoral process in 324, legislative lobbying in 328

▶   329.3–329.6 Specific political parties of United States

If preferred, class in 329.973

Class comprehensive works, specific parties not provided for here in 329

.3   Democratic Party

.6   Republican Party

.9   Political parties of other countries

Add "Areas" notation 3–9 from Table 2 to base number 329.9

(It is optional to class in 329.973 specific political parties of United States; prefer 329.3–329.6)

330   **Economics**

The science of human behavior as it relates to utilization of wealth for satisfaction of needs and desires thru production, distribution, consumption

For commerce, see 380

.01   Philosophy and theory

Class theories in 330.1

.02–.08   Standard subdivisions

Notations from Table 1

.09   Historical and geographical treatment

Class economic situation and conditions in 330.9

.1   Systems and theories

Class theories of value [*formerly* 330.1] in 338.5

.12   Systems

Free-enterprise, mixed, planned economies

Class socialism and related systems in 335

.15 Schools of economic thought

> Examples: mercantilism, physiocracy, classical economics, historical and mathematical schools, Keynesianism, marginal utility ("Austrian") school

> Including theories of wealth and property

> (It is optional to class here socialist and related schools; prefer 335)

.9 Economic situation and conditions (Economic history and geography)

> If preferred, class economic geography in 910.1

> Add "Areas" notation 1–9 from Table 2 to base number 330.9

331 Labor economics

> Class here industrial relations

> Class personnel management in 658.3

.1 Labor force and market

> Composition, size, quality of labor force; types of employment, e.g., wage and salary earners, self-employed; systems of labor, e.g., drafted workers, slave labor [*both formerly* 331.5], free labor; labor productivity; labor supply and demand; labor mobility; obtaining employment; maladjustments in labor market, e.g., unemployment, labor shortages, discrimination

> Class here comprehensive works on special classes of workers

> Class labor force and market with respect to special classes of workers in 331.3–331.6

[.15] Conciliation measures

> Class in 331.89

.2 Conditions of employment

> Wages, hours (occurrence and duration of work periods [*formerly* 331.81]), training [*formerly* 331.86], worker security, worker discipline

> Including conditions of employment in specific industries and occupations, pensions, other fringe benefits

> Class conditions of employment of special classes of workers in 331.3–331.6

▶   331.3–331.6 Labor force by personal characteristics

Class here labor force and market, conditions of employment, specific industries and occupations, labor unions, labor-management bargaining with respect to special classes of workers

Observe the following table of precedence, e.g., aged Chinese women 331.3

> Workers of specific age groups
> Women workers
> Special categories of workers
> Categories of workers by racial, ethnic, national origin

Class comprehensive works in 331.1

.3   Workers of specific age groups

Children, young adults, middle-aged, aged

.4   Women workers

.5   Special categories of workers

Migrant workers [*formerly* 331.6], contract workers, apprentices, prisoners, workers suffering physical and mental handicaps

Class drafted workers, slave labor [*both formerly* 331.5] in 331.1

For categories of workers by racial, ethnic, national origin, see 331.6

.6   Categories of workers by racial, ethnic, national origin

Immigrants; native-born nonindigenous ethnic groups, e.g., blacks in United States; indigenous ethnic groups, e.g., North American Indians in North America

Class migrant workers [*formerly* 331.6] in 331.5

.7   Labor by industry and occupation

Professional, managerial, service, clerical, agricultural, industrial, unskilled occupations

Including government employment, choice of vocation

(It is optional to class here specific subjects as professions or occupations; prefer specific subject using "Standard Subdivisions" notation 023 from Table 1, e.g., architecture as a profession 720.23)

Class a specific element of labor with the subject, e.g., wages 331.2

.702   Miscellany

Use of this number for choice of vocation is discontinued; class in 331.7

.8   Labor unions (Trade unions) and labor-management bargaining

> Class labor unions and labor-management bargaining in relation to special classes of workers in 331.3–331.6

[.81]   Occurrence and duration of work periods

> Class in 331.2

[.86]   Training

> Class in 331.2

.88   Labor unions (Trade unions)

> Kinds of unions, e.g., craft, industrial, company unions; union security arrangements, e.g., closed, open, union shop; labor union organization, e.g., union elections, union financial policies

> Including unions in specific industries and occupations

> Class general management of unions in 658

[.881–.889]   Unions in specific occupations; open, closed, union shop

> Numbers discontinued; class in 331.88

.89   Labor-management (Collective) bargaining and disputes

> Conciliation measures [*formerly* 331.15], e.g., arbitration, mediation; negotiations; strikes; other labor and management measures, e.g., boycotts, injunctions, lockouts

> Including strikes in specific industries and occupations, right-to-work policy

332   Financial economics

> Former heading: Lucrative capital

> Including capital (that portion of the stock of economic goods which is expected to produce a return), capital formation

> *For land, see* 333

.02   Miscellany

.024   Personal finance

> Including estate planning

> Class investment guides in 332.6

.06   Organizations

> Class financial institutions in 332.1–332.3

▶ 332.1–332.3 Financial institutions and their functions

Class here clearinghouses [*formerly* 332.7]

Class comprehensive works in 332.1

.1 Banks and banking

Central, commercial, international

Including savings departments [*formerly* 332.2] and trust services of commercial banks

Class here comprehensive works on money and banking, on financial institutions and their functions

Class management of financial institutions in 658

For specialized banking institutions, see 332.2; *credit and loan institutions,* 332.3; *money,* 332.4; *credit,* 332.7

.2 Specialized banking institutions

Savings banks, trust companies

Including postal savings banks

Class savings departments [*formerly* 332.2], trust services, of commercial banks in 332.1

For agricultural institutions, see 332.3; *investment banking,* 332.6; *cooperative banking,* 334

.3 Credit and loan institutions

Agricultural institutions, e.g., land banks; savings and loan associations; loan brokers, e.g., pawnbrokers; consumer and sales finance institutions; industrial banks; credit and loan functions of insurance companies

Class credit unions in 334

.4 Money

Forms of money, e.g., paper [*formerly* 332.5], gold and silver coins; inflation, deflation; monetary standards, e.g., fiat money [*formerly* 332.5], gold standard; foreign exchange; monetary policy

Class other mediums of exchange, managed currency in 332.5, use of monetary policy for economic stabilization in 339.5, relation of central banks to monetary policy in 332.1

.5 Other mediums of exchange

Barter instruments, commercial paper, managed currency, social credit money

Class paper and fiat money [*both formerly* 332.5] in 332.4

.6 Investment finance

Stocks, bonds, real estate, mutual funds, commodities and commodity futures; exchange of securities and commodities; investment banking

Including government securities, brokerage firms, securities and commodities markets, speculation, international exchange of securities, investment guides

[.63–.67] Securities, investment, investments

Numbers discontinued; class in 332.6

.7 Credit

Agricultural, real-estate, commercial, mercantile, industrial, personal loans; consumer credit; credit restrictions and collapse (bankruptcy); credit instruments, e.g., checks, money orders; commercial paper, e.g., promissory notes, drafts

Class clearinghouses [*formerly* 332.7], credit functions of specific financial institutions in 332.1–332.3

For interest and discount, see 332.8

.8 Interest and discount

Including rediscount, usury

Class interest and discount tables in 513

.9 Counterfeiting, forgery, alteration

Class counterfeit coins in 737.4, counterfeit paper money, counterfeit stamps in 769

333 Land economics

Land: the sum total of natural and man-made resources over which possession of the earth gives control

.01 Philosophy and theory

Including theory of economic rent

333.1–333.5 Control of land

Right to possession and use of land; right to transfer of possession and use

Class here control of specific kinds of land, of specific kinds of natural resources [*both formerly* 333.7–333.9]

Class comprehensive works in 333

.1 Public control of land

Acquisition, control, sale, grant of land by society as a whole thru its official representatives

Including tribal and community control, eminent domain, nationalization

.2   **Control of land by non-governmental collectivities**

Including open-field system

.3   **Individual control of land**

Forms of tenure, real estate

For absentee ownership, see 333.4

.4   **Absentee ownership**

.5   **Rental and leasing arrangements**

Tenancy; landlord-tenant relations; cash, share, percentage rental

Including rental of urban lands [*formerly* 333.6]

Class legal aspects in 346.43

[.6]   **Rental of urban lands**

Class in 333.5

►   **333.7–333.9 Utilization of specific natural resources**

Class here pollution

Class control of specific kinds of land, of specific kinds of natural resources [*both formerly* 333.7–333.9] in 333.1–333.5

Class comprehensive works in 333.7

.7   **Land utilization**

Conservation and use of forest, agricultural, urban, recreational lands

Class here comprehensive works on utilization of specific natural resources, on power resources

For utilization of mineral resources, see 333.8; utilization of other natural resources, 333.9

.8   **Utilization of subsurface (mineral) resources**

Conservation and use of fuels, e.g., coal, oil, gas, and other minerals

.9   **Utilization of other natural resources**

Conservation and use of water, shorelands, submerged lands and tidelands, air, space, biological resources

Including wildlife refuges and habitats

334   **Cooperatives**

Voluntary organizations established by groups of individuals to engage in production and distribution of economic goods with distribution of earnings on the basis of patronage or participation

Including consumers', producers', housing, banking cooperatives

335   Socialism and related systems

> Including utopian, Fabian, guild, Christian socialism; syndicalism; anarchism; voluntary socialist and anarchist communities
>
> Class here interdisciplinary works on political and economic aspects of socialism and related systems
>
> If preferred, class in 330.15
>
> Class political aspects of socialism and related systems in 320

.4   Marxian systems (Marxism)

> Including dialectical materialism, historical materialism, theory of class struggle, labor theory of value, social ownership of means of production

[.41]   Basic concepts

> Number discontinued; class in 335.4

.42   Scientific socialism

> Marxian doctrines and systems characteristic of period before 1917
>
> Including early communism (1848–1875)
>
> Class First, Second, Vienna Internationals [*all formerly* 335.42] in 329
>
> > For democratic socialism, see 335.5

.43   Communism (Marxism-Leninism)

> Communism of post-1917 period
>
> Including Russian, Yugoslav, Chinese, Cuban communism; Trotskyite doctrines; comparison with capitalism, cooperation, other forms of collectivism

[.44]   Communist international organizations

> Class in 329

.5   State socialism and democratic socialism

.6   National socialism

> Including fascism, Falangism

336   Public finance

> Financial transactions of national, state, local governments and their units
>
> Class financial administration of central governments in 351.7, of local governments in 352

.09   Historical and geographical treatment

> Class treatment by continent, country, locality in modern world in 336.4–336.9 (not 336.094–336.099)

.1   Revenues

> Including public income from fees, licenses [*both formerly* 336.2], rents, franchises, public lands, mineral rights, deposits, investments, loans, lotteries, public industries and services, reparations, interest on war loans; grants and technical assistance funds from other governmental units; payments in lieu of taxes
>
> *For taxes, see 336.2; public borrowing, 336.3*

.2   Taxes and taxation

> Class licenses, fees [*both formerly* 336.2] in 336.1
>
> Class economic effects of taxation in 339.5

.3   Fiscal policy

> Public securities, borrowing, debt, expenditure
>
> Class investment in public securities in 332.6; use of fiscal policy in economic stabilization, economic effects of public expenditure in 339.5
>
> *For taxation, see 336.2*

.4–.9   Public finance by continent, country, locality in modern world

> Add "Areas" notation 4–9 from Table 2 to base number 336

338   Production

> Making economic goods and services available for satisfaction of human wants thru extraction, manufacture, transportation, storage, exchange
>
> Class here factors of production, entrepreneurship; production efficiency, e.g., automation, machines in production, cost-output ratio
>
> Class specific factors of production in 331–333, marketing in 380

▶   338.1–338.4 Specific kinds of industries

> Capital formation, costs, prices, income, surpluses, shortages, government policies
>
> Class here specific products
>
> Class comprehensive works in 338, organization of production in specific kinds of industries in 338.6

▶   338.1–338.3 Primary (Extractive) industries

> Class comprehensive works in 338

.1   Agriculture

> Including food supply

.2   Mineral industries

.3   Other extractive industries

> Fishing, whaling, hunting, trapping, culture of invertebrates and cold-blooded vertebrates

.4   Secondary industries

> Manufacturing, construction, service, professional

> Class communication industries in 380.3, transportation industries in 380.5 [*both formerly* 338.4]

.5   General production economics

> Costs, prices, economic fluctuations (business cycles); laws of supply and demand, factoral proportions, diminishing marginal returns

> Including theories of value [*formerly* 330.1], government regulation of prices, business forecasting

> Class production economics of specific kinds of industries in 338.1–338.4, effect of money on prices in 332.4, economic stabilization in 339.5

> *For organization of production, see 338.6*

.6   Organization of production

> Big business; small business; systems of production, e.g., guild system, domestic (cottage) system, factory system; location of industry; specialization; competition and restraint

> Including organization of production in specific kinds of industries

> Class monopoly and monopolies in 338.8

> *For organizations and their structure, see 338.7*

.7   Organizations and their structure

> Individual proprietorships, partnerships, corporations, organizations in specific industries

> Class financial institutions in 332.1–332.3, organizations engaged in communication and transportation in 383–388, insurance companies in 368, government corporations in 350

> *For cooperatives, see 334; combinations, 338.8*

.8   Combinations

> Horizontal, vertical, conglomerate combinations; trusts, holding companies, interlocking directorates, pools, cartels; mergers, amalgamations; monopoly and monopolies; international organizations

> Including combinations in specific industries

.9   Production programs and policies

Examples: control, subsidies, grants by government; nationalization

Class production programs and policies with respect to specific kinds of industries in 338.1–338.4

.909   Historical and geographical treatment

Class treatment by country and locality in 338.93–338.99 (not 338.9093–338.9099)

.91   International

Foreign economic policies, relations, assistance

.93–.99   National, state, provincial, local

Add "Areas" notation 3–9 from Table 2 to base number 338.9

339   Macroeconomics

Behavior and functioning of the economy as a totality; national income, saving, investment, consumption

Former heading: Distribution of capital goods and consumption of consumer goods

Class money and banking in 332.1–332.4

For economic fluctuations, see 338.5

.2   Income distribution and accounting

Functional distribution of income (wages, proprietor's income, rent, corporate profits, interest), input-output accounts (interindustry accounts), flow-of-funds accounts

Including national, regional, local distribution and accounting

For measures of national income, see 339.3

.3   Measures of national income

Gross national product (GNP), net national product (NNP), national income (NI), personal income (PI), disposable personal income (DPI)

.309   Historical and geographical treatment

Class income accounts of specific countries and localities in 339.33–339.39 (not 339.3093–339.3099)

.33–.39   Income accounts of specific countries and localities

Add "Areas" notation 3–9 from Table 2 to base number 339.3

.4   Factors affecting national income

> Income-consumption relations, costs, prices, saving, investment, economic causes and effects of poverty, consumption, standard of living, conservation of national resources

> Former heading: Consumption and conservation of income and wealth

> Class conservation policies for natural resources in 333.7–333.9, economic stabilization in 339.5

[.41–.49]   Miscellaneous aspects of national income

> Numbers discontinued; class in 339.4

.5   Economic stabilization and growth

> Use of fiscal policy (taxation, spending, public debt), of monetary policy (changes in bank reserves, rediscount rates, sale and purchase of government securities)

> Including economic effects of taxation, of expenditure

340   Law

> This schedule is completely new, prepared with little or no reference to earlier editions and assigning new meanings to most numbers. Such numbers are italicized

> Including comparative law, law reform

> If preferred, class law of a specific subject with the subject using "Standard Subdivisions" notation 026 from Table 1, e.g., law of education 370.26

[.01]   Philosophy and theory

> Do not use; class in 340.1

.02   Miscellany

.03   Dictionaries

> Class encyclopedias in 348

.05–.09   Standard subdivisions

> Notations from Table 1

.1   Philosophy and theory

> Including jurisprudence; origin, nature, sources, limits of law; rule of law; legal reasoning; justice; law and ethics; law and society

.5 Systems of law

Primitive, ancient, Roman, medieval Roman, Byzantine, Roman-Dutch, medieval European, feudal, Oriental, Islamic law; civil law systems (systems derived from Roman law); common law systems

Including equity

Class religious laws of a specific religious body with the body, e.g., Christian canon law 262.9; law of specific countries in 340.09

.9 Private international law (Conflict of laws)

Class domestic conflict of laws in 342.4

341 International law

Including relation of international and domestic law

Class here treaties

.1 Sources of international law

Treaties, judicial decisions, custom, general principles of law, works of publicists

Class texts of treaties on a specific subject with the subject in international law, e.g., on air transportation 341.42, general treaties in 341

.2 The world community

Including world government; semisovereign and dependent states, e.g., mandates, satellites; nonself-governing territories; areas having special status in international law, e.g., Berlin

▶

341.22–341.24 Corporate bodies

Class comprehensive works in 341.2, specialized world agencies with the subject in international law, e.g., World Health Organization 341.7

.22 League of Nations

.23 United Nations

.24 Regional associations and organizations

Examples: Organization of American States, Arab League

.26 States

Sovereignty, origin, succession, termination, liability

Including recognition of states and governments

For relations between states, see 341.3; jurisdiction of states, 341.4

.3   Relations between states

Diplomatic procedures, personnel, agencies; negotiation, ratification, validity, binding force, termination, interpretation of treaties

Including consular officials and functions, officials and representatives of international organizations

Class texts of treaties on a specific subject with the subject in international law, e.g., genocide convention 341.77; general treaties in 341

For jurisdictional relations of states, see 341.4; disputes and conflicts, 341.5; cooperation, 341.7

.4   Jurisdiction and jurisdictional relations of states

Including extraterrestrial space, moon, planetary bodies

.42   Jurisdiction over physical space

Territory and its acquisition, boundaries, bodies of water, airspace

Including maritime law, water and air transportation

Class fisheries, pollution control, conservation of sea resources in 341.7

.48   Jurisdiction over persons

Criminal and civil jurisdiction over citizens, aliens, stateless persons, refugees; nationality; citizenship; immigration; passports; visas; basic human rights; extraterritoriality; extradition; right of asylum

Including jurisdiction of state over its nationals in other areas

Class private international law in 340.9, international crimes in 341.77, liability of states for aliens in 341.26

.5   Disputes and conflicts between states

Negotiation, mediation, conciliation, arbitration, adjudication; coercive methods of settlement short of war, e.g., boycott, sanctions, peaceful blockade

Including international courts and court procedure, role of international organizations

Class disputes on a specific subject with the subject in international law, e.g., jurisdictional disputes 341.4

For law of war, see 341.6

.6   Law of war

Conduct of war, e.g., weapons, espionage; neutrality and neutral nations; treatment of sick, wounded, prisoners; termination of war, e.g., treaties, laws of occupation; status of individuals, e.g., enemy aliens, noncombatants

Including international law and civil war, war crimes

.7   International cooperation

Including international judicial cooperation; international economic law, e.g., monetary law, investments, tariffs, transportation, postal regulations, communication, copyright, patents, trademarks, economic and technical assistance; international social law and cultural relations, e.g., conservation, labor, public health, fisheries and fishing, pollution control

Class laws of specific countries with respect to foreign investments in 346, international law of water and air transportation in 341.42

For extradition, see 341.48

.72   Defense and mutual security

Peaceful (friendly) occupation, status of forces, bases and other military installations, military assistance, international security forces

Including civil defense

.73   Peace and disarmament

Including suspension of weapons testing

.77   International criminal law

Genocide, piracy, slave trade, white slave traffic, drug traffic, traffic in obscene publications, counterfeiting

For war crimes, see 341.6

▶
342–348 Internal law

Law of individual states and nations, often called municipal law

Class in 342–346 laws, regulations, cases, procedure, courts relating to specific topics in law, e.g., tax laws 343.4

If preferred, class laws, regulations, cases on specific subjects in law in 348, courts and procedure in specific fields in 347

Class comprehensive works in 340

▶
342–345 Public law

Class comprehensive works in 342

342   Constitutional and administrative law

Class here comprehensive works on public law

*For miscellaneous public law, see 343; social law, 344;
criminal law, 345*

.2   Constitutions and other basic instruments of government

Texts, sources, history

Including municipal charters, revision and amendment of constitutions

Class amendments dealing with a specific subject with the subject in constitutional law, e.g., selection of chief executive 342.6

.4   Structure of government

Levels and branches of government, their functions, powers, relations

Including domestic conflict of laws

Class government corporations in 346.6

*For legislative branch, see 342.5; executive branch, 342.6;
judicial branch, 347*

.5   Legislative branch of government

Powers, functions, duties; privileges and immunities of legislators; basis of representation; legislative procedure

.6 Executive branch of government

Powers, functions, duties, terms of office, modes of selection of chief and deputy chief executives; executive departments and ministries; government officials and employees (civil service)

Including administrative law and procedure, regulatory agencies, ombudsmen, martial law

Class regulatory agencies dealing with a specific subject with the subject in law, e.g., Civil Aeronautics Board of United States 343.9

.7 Election law

Including right to vote

Class mode of selection of chief executives in 342.6

.8 Jurisdiction of governmental units over persons

Immigration, emigration, passports, visas, citizenship, nationality, status of aliens; individual rights; status of religious, racial, political parties and groups; government liability

Class liability of schools, school officials, school districts in 344.7, right to vote in 342.7

.9 Local government

343 Miscellaneous public law

.1 Military and defense law

Draft, conscription, selective service, recruitment; organization, training, pay, leave, allowances, living conditions, discipline and conduct of military services

Including conscientious objectors, reserves, military courts and court procedure, military penology; veterans' law

For martial law, see 342.6

.2 Law of public property

Acquisition, disposal, regulation, control of personal and real property

Including eminent domain, nationalization

Class government regulation of private and public real property in 346.44

.3 Law of public finance

Monetary, budgetary, revenue law; public borrowing and debt

Class international law of monetary exchange in 341.7, government securities in 346.7

For tax law, see 343.4

.4 Tax law

National, state, local taxes

Including estate and tax planning

.7 Regulation of industry

Unfair practices, e.g., restraint of trade, price fixing and discrimination; economic assistance, e.g., price supports, subsidies; quantity and quality controls; weights and measures; packaging

Including rationing, consumer protection, antitrust law, comprehensive works on regulation of industry and trade

Class public health and safety measures in 344.4; regulation of real-estate business in 346.43; of banks, insurance companies and agencies, organizations engaged in marketing securities in 346.7

For regulation of organization, see 346.6; of trade, 343.8; of public utilities, 343.9

.8 Regulation of foreign and domestic trade

Including prices, advertising and labeling, marketing, commodity exchanges and exchange transactions

.9 Control of public utilities

Rates, rate making, operations, facilities, services

Including water and power supply, e.g., electric power; transportation, communication, pipelines, pedestrian traffic, postal service

Class here maritime and admiralty law

Class transportation safety in 344.4; traffic accidents in 346.3; police traffic services in 344.5; traffic offenses in 345; property laws relating to motor vehicles in 346.47, to rights-of-way in 346.43; international maritime law in 341.42; a specific subject of maritime or admiralty law with the subject in law, e.g., maritime contracts 346.2; libel in 346.3; freedom of press in 342.8; censorship in 344.5

344 Social law

.1 Labor

.2 Social insurance

Workmen's compensation; accident and health, old-age and survivors', unemployment insurance

.3 Welfare

Welfare work and services, penal institutions

Class adoption of children in 346.1

.4 **Public health and safety**

Medical personnel and practice, quarantine, immunization, control of disease carriers, public sanitation, waste disposal, pollution and noise control, disposal of dead, product purity and safety, industrial hygiene and safety

Including mental public health, birth control, veterinary public health

For public safety, see 344.5

.5 **Public order, safety, morals**

Police services; crime prevention; control of public gatherings; control of explosives and firearms; disaster and emergency planning and relief; civil defense; control of gambling, prostitution, drug and liquor traffic

Including censorship and control of information

.6 **Public works**

Including housing

.7 **Education and schools**

Public and private

Including segregation and discrimination; educational and cultural exchanges; liability of schools, school officials, school districts

.9 **Culture and religion**

Including libraries, archives, museums, galleries, historical buildings and monuments, science, arts, amusements

Class cultural exchanges in 344.7

345 **Criminal law**

Including criminal courts, offenses, offenders, liability, responsibility, guilt, legal aid

.5 **Criminal procedure**

Criminal investigation and law enforcement, e.g., wiretapping, warrants, search and seizure, arrests; rights of suspects, e.g., jury trial, habeas corpus

Including interstate rendition (extradition), crime and the press

Class comprehensive works on civil and criminal procedure in 347

For evidence, see 345.6; trials, 345.7; juvenile procedure, 345.8

.6   Evidence

Admissibility; kinds, e.g., documentary, circumstantial, scientific, testimony of witnesses, expert testimony

Including confessions

.7   Trials

Including preliminary hearings, pretrial release, grand jury proceedings

Class appellate procedure in criminal cases in 347.8

.8   Juvenile procedure

Including juvenile courts

346   Private law

Including names, domiciles, births, deaths, status, capacity of persons

.1   Domestic relations

Marriage, husband and wife, divorce, separation, annulment, alimony, parent and child, guardian and ward

Including adoption of children

Class marital property relations in 346.4

.2   Contracts

Including quasi-contract, agency, liability, public (government) contracts

Class extracontractual liability in 346.3; criminal liability in 345; government liability in 342.8; liability of schools, school officials, school districts in 344.7; specific contracts in 346.7; contracts dealing with a specific subject with the subject in law, e.g., contracts of partnership 346.6

.3   Torts

Negligence, accidents, assault and battery; malpractice; abuse of legal process, false arrest, false imprisonment; libel, slander, invasion of privacy; torts involving property, e.g., trespass, nuisance

Including extracontractual liability; strict liability (liability without fault), e.g., product liability, liability for damage caused by children or animals

.4 Property

Including marital property relations, future interests (expectancies)

For public property, see 343.2

.43 Real property

Land, permanent fixtures, natural resources

Including sale, real-estate business, real-estate mortgages, land titles, title investigations, easements, servitudes, tenancy, rent, rent control, horizontal property (condominiums), cooperative owner-ship

Class organization of real-estate businesses in 346.6, transfer of real property by inheritance in 346.5

For government control and regulation, see 346.44

.44 Government control and regulation of real property

Public and private property

Including conservation, land reform, regional and city planning, zoning

For rent control, see 346.43

.47 Personal property

Including intangible property: copyright, design protection, patents, trademarks, business names, licenses, goodwill

Class transfer of personal property by inheritance in 346.5

For sale, negotiable instruments, see 346.7

.5 Inheritance, succession, fiduciary trusts, trustees

Including probate law and practice

.6 Associations (Organizations)

Organization, ownership, management of nonprofit organizations, business enterprises, corporations, unincorporated enterprises, e.g., partnerships

Including government corporations; organization of associations en-gaged in specific types of enterprises, e.g., organization of railroad companies

Class municipal corporations in 342.9

.7   Commercial law

Sale; loan; secured transactions, e.g., chattel mortgages; installment sales (hire-purchase); debtor-creditor relationships; bankruptcy; banks and banking; insurance; securities, e.g., stocks, bonds; negotiable instruments, e.g., checks, drafts, trade acceptances

Including agricultural and consumer credit, government securities

Class regulation of industry and trade in 343.7–343.9; sales of real property in 346.43; regulation of organization of banks, insurance companies and agencies, organizations engaged in marketing securities in 346.6

347   Civil procedure

Including arbitration

Class here judicial branch of government, comprehensive works on civil and criminal procedure

(It is optional to class here courts and procedure in specific fields of law; prefer specific subject, e.g., tax procedure 343.4)

For administrative procedure, see 342.6; criminal procedure, 345.5

.1   Courts

Powers, functions, jurisdiction, organization, officials of courts of general, original, specialized, appellate jurisdiction

.5   General procedure

Including motions, limitation of actions, parties to trial, jury trial, forms and form books

For evidence, see 347.6; trials, 347.7; appellate procedure, 347.8

.6   Evidence

Admissibility; kinds, e.g., documentary, circumstantial, scientific; testimony of witnesses, expert testimony

Including privileges and immunities of witnesses, privileged communications, compulsion of attendance

.7   Trials

Including pretrial procedure, e.g., publication of notice, service of process; juries and jury selection; judgments, e.g., attachment and garnishment

.8   Appellate procedure

348   Laws (Statutes), regulations, cases

Including digests, citators, checklists, tables, indexes, encyclopedias

(It is optional to class here laws, regulations, cases covering specific subjects in law; prefer specific subject, e.g., tax codes 343.4)

350   Public administration   Executive branch   Military art and science

> Public administration: structure, internal management, activities of government agencies charged with execution of law and public policy
>
> Including official support and regulation of music [*formerly also* 780.07]
>
> Class administrative aspects of legislative branch of government in 328, of judicial branch in 347

351   Central governments

> Governments of nations, states, provinces
>
> *For specific national, state, provincial governments, see* 353–354

.04   Executive branch of government

> Chief executive; executive departments and ministries; special commissions, corporations, agencies, quasi-administrative bodies

.1   Personnel management

> Personnel planning and policy; job classification, analysis, description; recruitment and selection; placement; training; supervision; motivation; promotion and demotion; wage and salary administration; hours of work; leave; working conditions; personnel services, e.g., health programs; grievances and appeals; collective bargaining; separation from service
>
> Including loyalty oaths
>
> *For civil service examinations, see* 351.3; *pensions,* 351.5

.3   Civil service examinations

> Class examinations on a specific subject with the subject, using "Standard Subdivisions" notation 076 from Table 1, e.g., accounting 657.076

.5   Pensions

.7   Specific administrative activities

> Including internal administration, e.g., procurement, records management; financial administration, e.g., fiscal policy, budget, tax administration; maintenance of social order, e.g., police organization and management, civil defense, control of alcoholic beverages, of drugs, of gambling, of prostitution; regulation of public health; fire and accident protection
>
> Class comprehensive works on a specific technique or operation and its public administration with the subject, e.g., police services 363.2; regulation and control of water supply in 351.8
>
> *For personnel management, see* 351.1; *other administrative activities,* 351.8

.8   Other administrative activities

Assemblage and dissemination of information, e.g., census taking;
authorization of standards, e.g., weights and measures; issuance and
regulation of money; regulation of industry and trade; regulation of
public utilities, e.g., communication and transportation; provision of
postal service; regulation of labor; provision of welfare services, of
housing, of other public works; cultural services, e.g., libraries; regulation of sports; scientific research; foreign affairs; defense

Class education and the state [*formerly* 351.8] in 379

Class administration of fiscal policy in 351.7, comprehensive works on
a specific technique or operation and its public administration with
the subject, e.g., banking 332.1

.9   Malfunctioning of government

Grievances and claims against the state, abuse of administrative
responsibility and authority, embezzlement, misappropriation of funds,
bribery, influence peddling, conflict of interest, investigation of public
officials, impeachment

Former heading: Governmental accountability

Including ombudsman system

352   Local units of government

Urban and rural municipalities, counties, parishes, special-purpose
authorities and districts

Class school boards and districts in 379

[.000 93–.000 99]   Treatment by continent, country, locality

Class in 352.03–352.09

.001–.008   Standard subdivisions

Notations from Table 1

.009   Historical and geographical treatment

Class treatment by continent, country, locality in 352.03–353.09
(not 352.0093–352.0099)

.03–.09   Treatment by continent, country, locality [*formerly also*
352.00093–352.00099]

Add "Areas" notation 3–9 from Table 2 to base number 352.0, e.g.,
administration of local governments, of a specific local government,
in New York State 352.0747

> ### 353–354 Specific national, state, provincial governments

Class comprehensive works in 351

353   United States federal and state governments

(If it is desired to give local emphasis and a shorter number to central governments of a specific country, it is optional to class them here; in that case class United States federal and state governments in 354.73–354.79, 354.969)

Do not use standard subdivisions

Class specific state governments in 353.97–353.99

.001–.009   Government service, specific administrative activities, governmental malfunctioning in federal government

Add to 353.00 the numbers following 351 in 351.1–351.9, e.g., civil service examinations 353.003

.03   Executive branch of federal government

Chief executive; executive departments; special commissions, corporations, agencies, quasi-administrative bodies

Class specific executive departments in 353.1–353.8

[.032–.036]   Specific aspects of executive branch

Numbers discontinued; class in 353.03

> ### 353.1–353.8 Specific executive departments in federal government

Class comprehensive works in 353.03

.1   Department of State

.2   Department of the Treasury

.3   Department of the Interior

.4   Post Office Department

.5   Department of Justice

.6   Department of Defense

Including Departments of the Air Force and the Army

For Department of the Navy, see 353.7

.7   Department of the Navy

.8   Other departments

.81   Department of Agriculture

.82	Department of Commerce
.83	Department of Labor
.84	Department of Health, Education, and Welfare
.85	Department of Housing and Urban Development
.86	Department of Transportation
.9	State governments

> Add "Areas" notation 7–9 from Table 2 to base number 353.9, e.g., administration of Hawaii 353.9969

354 Other central governments

> Including international governments
>
> Add "Areas" notation 3–9 from Table 2 to base number 354

355 Military art and science

> Conduct of warfare and defense
>
> Including military research and development
>
> Class here land forces and operations, combined forces and operations
>
> Class relation of state to military organizations in *322*, civilian administration and control of military activities in *351.8*, adminstraton of defense departments in *351.04*
>
> *For specific kinds of military forces and warfare, see 356–359*

.001–.008	Standard subdivisions

> Notations from Table 1

.009	Historical and geographical treatment

> Class military aspects of history of specific wars in *900* (not *355.0093–355.0099*)

.02	War and warfare

> Limited, total, nuclear, conventional, international, insurgent, revolutionary, resistance warfare; causes, economics, results of war
>
> Class sociology of wars [*formerly* 355.02] in *301.6*
>
> Class sociology of military institutions in *301.5*

.03	Military situation and policy

> Including mutual security pacts, military missions and assistance
>
> Class combat strategy in *355.4*

[.07]	Military research and development

> Number discontinued; class in *355*

.1   **Military life and postmilitary benefits**

Length of service, leaves, furloughs, reserve status, termination of service, promotion, demotion, morale, living conditions, customs, conduct, discipline, etiquette, rewards, pay, allowances, uniforms, colors, standards, ceremonials

Including veterans' rights and benefits

Class issue and use of uniforms in 355.8

.2   **Military resources**

Mobilization and demobilization of manpower, raw materials, industrial resources, transportation and communication facilities

Including civilian manpower, universal training and service, conscientious objectors

.3   **Organization and personnel of military forces**

Combat units, e.g., armies, divisions, companies; ranks, e.g., staff and high command, commissioned and warrant officers, noncommissioned officers, enlisted personnel; special services, e.g., administrative and supply services, intelligence and counterintelligence units, health and chaplain services

Including foreign legions; home guards, e.g., United States National Guard; frontier troops; colonial, expeditionary, allied, coalition, international forces; reserves

.4   **Military operations**

Logistics, tactics, strategy

Including encampment, reconnaissance, communication, guerrilla warfare, street fighting, riot suppression, siege warfare, frontier and coastal defense, tactical and strategic geography, occupation of conquered territory, military government

[.47]   **Tactical and strategic geography**

Number discontinued; class in 355.4

.5   **Training maneuvers, exercises, drills**

Basic training, drills, small arms and bayonet practice, self-defense, officers' maneuvers and exercises, tactical exercises, camp and fortification operations, grand maneuvers, maneuvers involving civil population

.6 Central administration

> Personnel management, supply and financial administration
>
> Including housing administration, graves registration
>
> *For organization of military forces, see 355.3*

.7 Military installations and land reservations

> Including quarters for personnel; artillery, engineering, medical installations; supply depots

.8 Military equipment and supplies (Materiel)

> Food; clothing; camp equipment; ordnance; transportation equipment, e.g., trucks, trains; communication equipment; medical supplies

---

▶ 356–359 Specific kinds of military forces and warfare

Units and services

Class here history of specific military organizations not limited to any one war

Class comprehensive works in 355, history of specific military organizations in specific wars in 900

▶ 356–357 Land forces and warfare

Operations; training maneuvers, exercises, drills; installations; equipment and supplies (materiel)

Class comprehensive works in 355

For armored and technical land forces and warfare, see 358

356 Infantry

> Including ski and mountain troops, paratroops, commandos, rangers, guerrillas

357 Cavalry

> Horse and mechanized
>
> Including bicycle and motorcycle troops

358 **Armored and technical land forces and warfare, air and space forces**

> Including coast, field, antiaircraft artillery; guided (strategic) land missile forces and warfare; engineer forces; chemical, biological, nuclear forces; space forces
>
> Class here comprehensive works on missile forces, warfare, defense
>
> Class naval missile forces in 359.9

.4 **Air forces and warfare**

> Military life and resources; organization and personnel; operations; training maneuvers, exercises, drills; central administration; installations; equipment and supplies (materiel)
>
> Including bombing, pursuit and fighting, transportation, reconnaissance, communications forces and operations

[.41] **Functions and organization**

> Number discontinued; class in 358.4

[.8] **Space forces**

> Number discontinued; class in 358

359 **Sea (Naval) forces and warfare**

.1–.2 **Naval life and resources**

> Add to 359 the numbers following 355 in 355.1–355.2, e.g., customs 359.1

.3 **Organization and personnel of naval forces**

> Combat units, e.g., fleets, task forces, divisions, squadrons, flotillas; types of ships; ranks, e.g., staff and high command, commissioned and warrant officers, petty officers, enlisted personnel; special services, e.g., administrative and supply services, health and chaplain services
>
> Including reserves

[.32] **Types of ships**

> Number discontinued; class in 359.3

.4 **Naval operations**

> Logistics, tactics, strategy
>
> Including coastal defense, tactical and strategic geography

.5–.8 **Other elements**

> Add to 359 the numbers following 355 in 355.5–355.8, e.g., naval bases 359.7

.9   Specialist forces

> Marines, coast guard; construction and engineering forces, e.g., United States Seabees; frogmen, guided missile forces, other technical forces

360   Social pathology, social services, association

361   Social welfare work

> General methods of alleviation of social problems

> Class here counseling and related services, material relief, free and paid assistance

> Class a specific application of social welfare work with the subject, e.g., social welfare services to prison inmates 365

> *For insurance, see* 368

[.09]   Historical and geographical treatment

> Do not use; class in 361

.2   Planning

.3   Casework

> Including casework for specific types of counselors, e.g., legal and ministerial counseling

.4   Group work

.5   Disaster relief

> Including relief of displaced persons, refugees, prisoners of war

.6   Public welfare work

> By central and local governments

.7   Private welfare work

> Including parochial welfare work [*formerly* 258], fund raising

.8   Community organization

> Coordination thru social service exchanges, community chests, united charities

362   Social pathology and its alleviation

> Causes, nature, extent, social effects, prevention, alleviation of social problems and disorders

> Class general methods of alleviation in 361

> *For disaster relief, see* 361.5; *crime and its alleviation,* 364

[.09]   Historical and geographical treatment

> Do not use; class in 362

▶   362.1–362.4 Illness and disability [*formerly also* 301.47]

Class here services of general and special hospitals, clinics, sanitariums, dispensaries, nursing and custodial homes; medical and pychiatric social work

Class medical records management [*formerly* 362.1–362.4] in 651.5

Class comprehensive works in 362.1, illnesses and disabilities of specific groups in 362.6–362.8, medical science in 610

.1   Physical illness

Class here comprehensive works on illness and disability

For mental illness, see 362.2; mental retardation, 362.3; physical handicaps and disablements, 362.4

.2   Mental illness

Including alcoholism, narcotics addiction, services to the addicted

For institutions for the criminally insane, see 365

.3   Mental retardation

.4   Physical handicaps and disablements

Blindness, partial blindness, deafness, deaf-mutism, partial deafness, crippled conditions

.5   Poverty

Temporary or chronic financial disadvantage

Including services to financially disadvantaged survivors and dependents not of specific groups [*formerly also* 362.6], budget counseling, employment services, legal aid

Class poverty connected with a specific group or condition with the subject, e.g., poverty of the aged 362.6

▶   362.6–362.8 Social pathology of specific groups and its alleviation

Institutional and noninstitutional services; services to those suffering illnesses and handicaps

Class comprehensive works in 362

.6   Problems of aged people and their alleviation

Including services to aged survivors and dependents

Class services to young survivors and dependents in 362.7, to financially disadvantaged survivors and dependents not of specific groups in 362.5 [*both formerly* 362.6]

.7   Problems of young people and their alleviation

Infants, children, adolescents

Including services to young survivors and dependents [*formerly also* 362.6], aid to dependent children, day care, foster home care, adoption

.8   Problems of other groups and their alleviation

Families, unmarried mothers, minority groups, laboring classes, victims of crimes of violence

363   Other social services

.2   Police services

Personnel and operations

Including patrol; surveillance; pursuit and apprehension; traffic control; enforcement of sanitation, building, licensing laws and ordinances; location of missing persons; records and communications, e.g., photograph and fingerprint files; laboratories

Class police services in maintenance of public safety in 363.3, in control of factors affecting public morals in 363.4

For criminal investigation, see 364.12; prevention of crime and delinquency, 364.4

.3   Maintenance of public safety

Censorship; control of information, of public gatherings, of explosives, of firearms; civil defense and other disaster and emergency planning; fire prevention and control

[.35]   Civil defense

Number discontinued; class in 363.3

.4   Control of factors affecting public morals

Drugs, alcoholic beverages, prostitution, gambling

.5   Public works

Including public housing

Class communication and transportation facilities in 380

.6   Public utilities

Water supply, electric power, gas

Class communication and transportation services in 380

364   Crime and its alleviation (Criminology)

> Class here comprehensive works on criminology and criminal law
>
> *For criminal law, see* 345

[.09]   Historical and geographical treatment

> Do not use; class in 364

.1   Offenses

> Including individual offenders, organized crime, union racketeering

.12   Criminal investigation (Detection)

> Evidence; methods of accumulating, preserving, presenting evidence tending toward identification, apprehension, conviction of criminals
>
> Including wiretapping, lie detection

[.13–.17]   Specific types of offenses

> Numbers discontinued; class in 364.1

.2   Causes of crime and delinquency

> Influence of natural and social environments, characteristics of the individual, economic factors
>
> Including criminal anthropology

.3   Offenders

> Criminal types, e.g., habitual, professional, occasional, one-time offenders; criminally insane; specific ages and sexes, e.g., female offenders
>
> Including criminal psychology
>
> Class individual offenders in 364.1, causes of crime and delinquency in 364.2, prevention in 364.4, correction in 364.6

[.35]   Predelinquents

> Class in 364.36

.36   Juvenile delinquents

> Including predelinquents [*formerly* 364.35]

[.37]   Adults

> Number discontinued; class in 364.3

.4   Prevention of crime and delinquency

> Eugenic practices; control of population, economic conditions, social factors; welfare services; law enforcement; preventive police work

.6   Correction of crime and delinquency

Imprisonment and detention; capital and corporal punishment;
economic, civil, political penalties, e.g., deportation,
loss of citizenship, fines

Including probation, parole, suspended and indeterminate sentence,
pardon, amnesty, welfare services to offenders

*For treatment of discharged offenders, see 364.8; penal
institutions, welfare services to prisoners, 365*

[.7]   Correctional institutions

Class in 365

.8   Treatment of discharged offenders

Rehabilitation, other welfare services

365   Penal institutions

Kinds, e.g., jails, detention homes, reformatories, penitentiaries, prisons,
penal colonies, pre-release guidance centers; prison systems, e.g., con-
gregate, silent, progressive; prison plant; prison security measures;
reception, classification, treatment, discipline, release and
discharge of prisoners

Including correctional institutions [*formerly* 364.7], institutions for
specific classes of persons, e.g., juveniles, women, political offenders,
criminally insane; convict labor; welfare services to prisoners; prison
reform

[.09]   Historical and geographical treatment

Do not use; class in 365

366   Association and associations

Organizations formed for common purposes of a fraternal nature
or for mutual assistance

Examples: Freemasonry, Order of the Eastern Star, Knights of Pythias,
Independent Order of Odd Fellows, Daughters of Rebekah,
Rosicrucians, Benevolent and Protective Order of Elks

Class organizations devoted to a specific subject with the subject, using
"Standard Subdivisions" notation 06 from Table 1, e.g., agricultural
organizations 630.6

*For general clubs, see 367; miscellaneous kinds of associations, 369;
orders of knighthood, 929.7; Greek-letter societies in education, 371.8*

367   General clubs

Examples: social clubs, study clubs

[.09]   Historical and geographical treatment

Do not use; class in 367

185

368   Insurance

> Including conventional sales groupings, e.g., automobile, aviation, real property insurance
>
> Class here actuarial science, rates, rate making, underwriting, claims, finance, lapsation, persistence, termination; comprehensive works on insurance companies
>
> Class credit and loan functions of insurance companies in 332.3

[.09]   Historical and geographical treatment

> Do not use; class in 368

.1   Insurance against damage to and loss of property

> Fire, disaster, riot, civil commotion, extended coverage, war risk insurance
>
> *For transportation insurance, see 368.2; casualty insurance, 368.5; miscellaneous forms of insurance, 368.8*

.2   Transportation insurance

> Insurance against damage to and loss of property in transit, insurance against damage to and loss of instrumentalities of transportation
>
> Including postal insurance; ocean and inland marine insurance; automobile, truck, bus, railroad, air transportation insurance

.3   Insurance against death, old age, illness, injury

> Life insurance, annuities, accident and health insurance, disability income insurance
>
> Including group insurance, dental and hospital insurance
>
> *For government-sponsored insurance, see 368.4*

.4   Government-sponsored insurance

> Workmen's compensation, accident and health, maternity, old-age and survivors, unemployment insurance; insurance against crimes of violence
>
> Including social security

.5   Casualty insurance

> Including liability insurance, e.g., automobile liability; insurance against glass breakage; insurance against industrial casualties, e.g., boiler accidents, power interruption; burglary, robbery, theft insurance; business interruption and strike insurance

.8   Miscellaneous forms of insurance

> Fidelity and surety bonds; credit, title, bank deposit, mortgage insurance; investment guarantees

369   Miscellaneous kinds of associations

      Including hereditary, military, patriotic societies

.4   Young people's societies

.42   Boys'

      For Boy Scouts, see 369.43

.43   Boy Scouts

.46   Girls'

      For Camp Fire Girls, see 369.47

.463   Girl Scouts and Girl Guides

.47   Camp Fire Girls

.5   Service clubs

      Including Rotary, Kiwanis, Lions

370   Education

Class study and teaching of a specific subject at the elementary level in 372.3–372.8; higher levels with the subject, using "Standard Subdivisions" notation 07 from Table 1, e.g., study of agriculture 630.7

.1   Philosophy, theories, principles

      Including philosophic foundations, e.g., idealism, realism, pragmatism; classification

.11   Aims, objectives, values

      Liberal, moral, ethical, character education; education for vocational effectiveness, for social responsibility, for creativity, for effective use of leisure

[.12]   Classification and philosophic foundations

      Number discontinued; class in 370.1

.15   Educational psychology

      Investigation of psychological problems involved in education, together with practical application of psychological principles to education

      Including psychological effects of education, psychology of learning specific subjects

.19 Education and society

> Influence of community on education, role of school in fostering society, economic and cultural situation of students; segregation and integration
>
> Including intercultural education, e.g., exchange of students [*formerly* 371.39], of teachers; comparative education; fundamental education, e.g., "head start"; parent-teacher associations
>
> Class education of exceptional children in 371.9

.7 Study and teaching of education

> Class in-service training of teachers in 371.1

371 The school

> Public and private
>
> Class schools of specific levels in 372–374, relation of state to school in 379

.1 Teaching and teaching personnel

> Classroom management and control; teacher relations, e.g., teacher-parent relations; personal and professional qualifications of teachers; organization of teaching force in the school; evaluation of teachers; in-service training
>
> Including academic freedom, team teaching, use of teacher aids, nonteaching activities of teaching personnel
>
> Class parent-teacher associations in 370.19, examination and certification of teachers in 379, personnel management in schools in 658.3
>
> *For methods of instruction, see 371.3*

.2 Educational administration

> Standards and accreditation; admission methods and standards; tuition; school year; school day; class schedules and periods; grouping of pupils for instruction, e.g., homogeneous grouping, non-graded schools; educational tests and measurements; marking systems; promotion and failure of students; dropouts, graduation
>
> Including supervisory and other nonteaching personnel, e.g., school psychologists; standardized and other mass examinations

[.26–.27] Educational tests and measurements

> Numbers discontinued; class in 371.2

.3   **Methods of instruction and study**

Lecture, recitation and discussion, project (unit), laboratory methods; work-study programs; field trips; independent study plans; individualized instruction; programed learning; honors work; private tutoring; teaching aids, materials, devices; lesson plans and planning

Including techniques of study

Class methods used in teaching exceptional students in 371.9; methods used in teaching specific subjects at elementary level in 372.3–372.8, at higher levels with the subject, using "Standard Subdivisions" notation 07 from Table 1, e.g., methods used in teaching mathematics 510.7

.32   **Textbooks and other printed media**

Methods, use, value

.33   **Audio and visual materials for teaching**

Methods, use, value of radio, sound recordings, pictures, slides, filmstrips, motion pictures, bulletin boards, television

Including classroom creation and design of audio and visual materials

[.36–.38]   **Specific methods of teaching**

Numbers discontinued; class in 371.3

.39   **Teaching machines**

Class student exchanges [*formerly* 371.39] in 370.19

.4   **Guidance and counseling**

Educational, vocational, personal guidance

Including group guidance

Class student mental health in 371.7; choice of vocation in 331.7; characteristics of a specific occupation with the subject, using "Standard Subdivisions" notation 023 from Table 1, e.g., librarianship as a profession 020.23

For guidance of exceptional students, see 371.9

[.42–.48]   **Specific kinds of guidance**

Numbers discontinued; class in 371.4

.5   **School discipline**

General regulations for student conduct; incentives; punishments; student participation in maintenance of discipline, e.g., prefectorial systems, student government

For classroom control, see 371.1

.6 Physical plant

Locations, sites, grounds, buildings; instructional spaces, e.g., class-rooms, laboratories, workshops, physical education facilities; nonin-structional facilities, e.g., dormitories, infirmaries, student unions; furnishings; apparatus, equipment, supplies

Class architecture of buildings for educational purposes in 727, environmental engineering in 690, facilities for exceptional students in 371.9

.7 School health and safety

Physical and mental health of students, safety programs, medical care, lunch and milk programs

.8 The student

Attitudes and behavior, organizations, housing and transportation, activities

Including Greek-letter societies, school journalism

Class school discipline in 371.5, guidance and counseling in 371.4

[.806] Organizations

Do not use; class in 371.8

[.85–.89] Greek-letter societies and other activities

Numbers discontinued; class in 371.8

.9 Special education

Education employing special curriculums, methods, facilities, tech-niques, apparatus, equipment, materials for exceptional students, e.g., gifted, blind, deaf, crippled, retarded, delinquent, emotionally dis-turbed students; students belonging to disadvantaged segments of society, e.g., slum students

Class here guidance of exceptional students, study and teaching of specific subjects

Class fundamental education in 370.19

[.91–.95] Specific kinds of exceptional students

Numbers discontinued; class in 371.9

▶ 372–374 Levels of education and schools

Class comprehensive works on education in 370, on schools in 371

For higher education, see 378

372   Elementary education

Class special education at elementary levels in 371.9

[.09]   Historical and geographical treatment

Do not use; class in 372.9

.1   The elementary school

Teaching and teaching personnel, educational administration, methods of instruction and study, guidance and counseling, discipline, physical plant, health and safety, the student, curriculums

Class specific levels in 372.2, curriculums in specific subjects in 372.3–372.8

[.109]   Historical and geographical treatment

Do not use; class in 372.9

.2   Levels of elementary schools

Public and private

.21   Preschool institutions

Nursery schools, kindergartens

.24   Elementary schools

Primary grades, infant schools (Great Britain), intermediate grades, middle schools, junior schools (Great Britain)

Including elementary sections of all-age schools

Class post-elementary, advanced elementary sections, upper sections of all-age schools in 373.2

372.3–372.8 Specific elementary school subjects

Class here curriculums in specific subjects; methods of instruction and study; textbooks; specific subjects for specific levels of instruction, e.g., music for primary grades

Class comprehensive works in 372.1

.3   Science and health

Including hygiene, nature study

.4   Reading

Methods of instruction, e.g., whole word methods, phonics; readers

Including remedial reading

Class readers on a specific subject with the subject in elementary education, e.g., science readers 372.3

.5 Creative and manual arts

> Drawing, painting, design, modeling, sculpturing, sewing, handicrafts; paper work, e.g., cutting, pasting, origami

.6 Language arts (Communication skills)

> Spelling, handwriting (penmanship), oral expression, grammar and word study, composition, literature (including storytelling, drama), foreign languages (including English as a foreign language)

> Including listening

> *For reading, see 372.4*

.7 Mathematics

.8 Other studies

> Examples: social studies (including history and geography), physical education, music

.9 Historical and geographical treatment of elementary education and schools

> Add "Areas" notation 1–9 from Table 2 to base number 372.9

373 Secondary education

> Class special education at secondary level at 371.9

.09 Historical and geographical treatment

> Class treatment by continent, country, locality in 373.3–373.9 (not 373.093–373.099)

.1 The secondary school

> Teaching and teaching personnel, educational administration, methods of instruction and study, guidance and counseling, discipline, physical plant, health and safety, the student, curriculums

> Class specific kinds and levels of secondary schools in 373.2, curriculums in a specific subject in 375

.109 Historical and geographical treatment

> Class treatment by continent, country, locality in 373.3–373.9 (not 373.1093–373.1099)

.2 Types and levels of secondary education and schools

> Public and private; specific levels, e.g., junior and senior high schools, sixth forms (Great Britain); schools offering specific types of curriculums, e.g., academic, vocational, comprehensive (multilateral), general

> Including upper sections of all-age schools, advanced and post-elementary classes of elementary schools; apprenticeship programs conducted by educational system

> Class continuation schools in 374.8, labor aspects of apprenticeship training in 331.2, management programs in 658.31

>> *For schools supported by religious groups, see 377; elementary sections of all-age schools, 372.24*

.3–.9 Secondary education and schools by continent, country, locality

> Add "Areas" notation 3–9 from Table 2 to base number 373

374 Adult education

> *Voluntary, purposeful efforts toward self-development of adults*

> Including correspondence schools and instruction

> Class special education of adults in 371.9

[.09] Historical and geographical treatment

> Do not use; class in 374.9

.1 Self-education

.2 Group education

> Special interest groups; reading and discussion groups; use of mass media; community centers; other private and governmental institutions and agencies

> Class libraries and library services in 020

>> *For schools, see 374.8*

.8 Schools

> Continuation schools, night schools

>> *For college extension departments, see 378.1*

.9 Historical and geographical treatment

> Add "Areas" notation 1–9 from Table 2 to base number 374.9

375   Curriculums

     Programs of study offered, proposed, suggested

     Do not use standard subdivisions; class in 375

     Class comprehensive works on curriculums at a specific level with the level, e.g., secondary 373.1

376   Education of women

     Secondary and higher education

     Including coeducation versus separate education for women, convent education, women's colleges

     Class elementary education of girls in 372, specific secondary schools in 373.3–373.9, specific topics in higher education in 378.1–378.3, specific colleges for women in 378.4–378.9

[.09]   Historical and geographical treatment

     Do not use; class in 376

377   Schools and religion

     Religious instruction and exercises in nonsectarian schools, monastic and mission schools, other schools supported by religious groups

     Class schools for women supported by religious groups in 376; a specific school with its level, e.g., a specific secondary school in Ohio 373.771

378   Higher education

     Public and private institutions

     Including aims and objectives, finance, academic degrees

     Class special education at higher levels in 371.9

.025   Directories

     Class directories of institutions by continent, country, locality in modern world in 378.4–378.9

.09   Historical and geographical treatment

     Class treatment by continent, country, locality in modern world in 378.4–378.9 (not 378.094–378.099)

.1   **Institutions of higher education**

Teaching, faculty, educational administration, methods of instruction and study, guidance and counseling, discipline, physical plant, health and safety, the student, curriculums in junior colleges, four-year colleges, higher-level institutions (universities), evening colleges, extension departments

Class institutions for the study and teaching of a specific occupation or subject with the subject, using "Standard Subdivisions" notation 07 from Table 1, e.g., Christian theological seminaries 207; institutions supported by religious groups in 377, specific institutions in 378.4–378.9, financial management in 658.1, courses of study in specific subjects in 375, exchange of college and university teachers in 370.19

.109   **Historical and geographical treatment**

Class treatment by continent, country, locality in modern world in 378.4–378.9 (not 378.1094–378.1099)

.3   **Student finances**

Fellowships, scholarships, loans, employment, costs, expenditures

Including educational exchanges as a means of student finance

Class comprehensive works on educational exchanges in 370.19, veterans' benefits in 355.1

[.33–.34]   **Fellowships and scholarships**

Numbers discontinued; class in 378.3

.4–.9   **Higher education and institutions by continent, country, locality in modern world**

Class here directories, specific colleges for women

Add "Areas" notation 4–9 from Table 2 to base number 378

If preferred, arrange specific colleges and universities alphabetically under each continent, and under specific countries requiring local emphasis

(It is optional to class here publications of specific colleges and universities; prefer specific subject)

379   **Education and the state [*formerly also* 351.8]**

National, state, local financial support, control, supervision of public and private education

Including school boards and districts; examination, certification, registration, appointment of teachers

.09   **Historical and geographical treatment**

Class public education by continent, country, locality in modern world in 379.4–379.9 (not 379.094–379.099)

.4–.9   Public education by continent, country, locality in modern world

> Add "Areas" notation 4–9 from Table 2 to base number 379

380   **Commerce, communications, transportation**

> Class here marketing
>
> Do not use standard subdivisions
>
> Class public regulation and control in 350

.1   Exchange of goods and services (Trade)

> Commercial policy, specific commodities and services
>
> Class domestic trade in 381, foreign trade in 382

.3   Communication services [*formerly also* 338.4]

> Activities, facilities
>
> Class specific kinds in 383–384

.5   Transportation services [*formerly also* 338.4]

> Activities, facilities
>
> Including mergers and consolidations of systems, comparative studies of kinds of transportation
>
> Class specific kinds in 385–388

▶   381–382 General internal and international commerce (trade)

> Class comprehensive works in 380.1

381   Internal commerce (Domestic trade)

> Commercial policy, specific commodities and services

382   International commerce (Foreign trade)

> Commercial policy, specific commodities and services, imports, exports; trade agreements, e.g., European Common Market, European Free Trade Association, East European Economic Organization
>
> Including import quotas and embargoes, licensing of exports and imports, export subsidies
>
> Class here trade between nations and their colonies, protectorates, trusts

.1   General international economic relations

> Including balance of payments, balance of trade
>
> Class international banks and banking in 332.1, international monetary exchange in 332.4, international investment in 332.6, international loans in 336.3, international organization of business in 338.8, production programs and policies in 338.9

.7   Tariff policy

Free trade, tariff for revenue, protective and prohibitive tariff, subsidies, drawbacks, exemptions

Class customs taxes in 336.2, tariff policy with respect to specific commodities in 382

383–384 Communication services

Services, operations, facilities, apparatus, equipment, rates, costs, efficiency of operation, mechanization, automation, income, finance, systems of ownership, organization

Class comprehensive works in 380.3

383   Postal communication

Including international systems and conventions

Class philately in 769

.09   Historical and geographical treatment

Class national systems in 383

[.2]   Use of postage stamps

Number discontinued; class in 383

384   Telecommunication and other systems of communication

Including recordings, motion pictures, visual signaling, alarms, warning systems

.1   Telegraphy

Morse and other code telegraphy, printing telegraphy

Including facsimile transmission

Class postal facsimile transmission in 383

For radiotelegraphy, see 384.5; submarine cable telegraphy, 384.4

.4   Submarine cable telegraphy

.5   Wireless communication

Including radiotelegraphy, radiotelephony

.54   Radiobroadcasting

Class here comprehensive works on radio and television broadcasting

Class radio journalism in 070.1, public entertainment in 791.4

For television broadcasting, see 384.55

.55   Television broadcasting

Including pay (subscription) television, closed circuit
communication, videotapes

.6   Telephony

Class here comprehensive works on wire and cable communication

For telegraphy, see 384.1; radiotelephony, 384.5

[.7–.9]   Other systems of communication

Numbers discontinued; class in 384

385–388 Transportation services

Transportation of passengers and freight, services in passenger and
freight terminals, costs, rates, income, finance, efficiency, systems
of ownership, facilities, apparatus, equipment

Class comprehensive works in 380.5, postal transportation in 383

385   Railroad transportation

Tracks, roadways, bridges, tunnels, stations, yards, roundhouses,
train sheds, shop buildings, signals, locomotives, cars

Including narrow-gage, industrial, interurban, inclined, mountain railway
systems; monorailways; railroad combined with other transportation
systems, e.g., piggyback services, ship railway systems

For local rail transit systems, see 388.4

386   Inland waterway transportation

River, canal, lake transportation

Including ferry transportation, ports, ships

Class comprehensive works on water transportation in 387

387   Water, air, space transportation

Class here comprehensive works on water transportation

For inland waterway transportation, see 386

387.1–387.5 Ocean (Marine) transportation

Class comprehensive works in 387

.1   Seaports

Activities, facilities

.2   Ships

Description, history, rating, tonnage, classification

Including air-cushion ships

.5   Maritime transport (Merchant marine services)

Including routes, salvage operations

.7   Air transportation

Airports and landing fields, aircraft, routes

.8   Space transportation

388   Ground transportation

Other than nonlocal rail transportation

.1   Roads and highways

For urban roads and streets, see 388.4

.3   Vehicular transportation

Traffic flow and maintenance, vehicular services (by bus, truck, private passenger automobile), terminals and stops

Including early forms of vehicular transportation, e.g., stagecoach services

Class urban vehicular transportation in 388.4

.34   Vehicles

Description, history, classification

For air-cushion vehicles, see 388.35

.35   Air-cushion vehicles

Description, history, classification

Class here comprehensive works on air-cushion vehicles

Class air-cushion ships for inland waterways in 386, for ocean in 387.2

.4   Urban transportation

Vehicular and pedestrian traffic, urban roads and streets, local rail transit systems (surface, elevated, underground), terminals and parking facilities

Former heading: Local rail and trolley transit systems

Class here comprehensive works on parking

Class vehicles in 388.34, a specific aspects of parking with the subject, e.g., city planning 711

.5   Pipeline transportation

389   Metrology and standardization

Metrology: weights and measures used in commerce and daily life

Including imperial (British) and metric systems

For horology, see 529

390   **Customs and folklore**

> Class cultural anthropology [*formerly* 390] in 301.2

391–395 Customs

> Rites, ceremonies, other external and formalized patterns of social behavior accompanying social functions; ways and means of carrying out social functions
>
> Class comprehensive works in 390
>
> *For customs of war and diplomacy, see* 399

391   **Costume and personal appearance**

> Garments, jewelry, hair styles, body contours, use of cosmetics and perfume, personal cleanliness and hygiene, tattooing, mutilation
>
> Including fashion

392   **Customs of life cycle and domestic life**

> Customs connected with birth, child rearing, attainment of puberty and majority, the home and domestic arts, courtship, betrothal, weddings, marriage, relations between sexes, treatment of aged
>
> *For death customs, see* 393

393   **Death customs**

> Burial, cremation, embalming, exposure, mourning

394   **General customs**

> Former heading: Public and social customs
>
> Including cannibalism [*formerly* 399], games, toys, dances, official ceremonies and observances, pageants, processions, parades, fairs, customs of chivalry, dueling, suicide

   .1   **Eating, drinking, using tobacco and narcotics**

> Use situations, methods of use, prohibited uses

   .2   **Special occasions**

> Holidays, carnivals, fast days

   [.26]   **Holidays**

> Number and its subdivisions discontinued; class in 394.2

395   **Etiquette**

> Prescriptive and practical works on social relations
>
> Including hospitality and entertainment, table decor, social correspondence
>
> *For military etiquette, see* 355.1; *protocol of diplomacy,* 341.3

398   Folklore

           Including sociology of folklore, of superstitions

           Class belles-lettres in 800

.08   Collections

           Class collections of folk literature in 398.208

.09   Historical and geographical treatment

           Class historical and geographical treatment of folk literature in 398.209

.2   Folk literature

           Texts, literary appraisal and criticism

           Including fairy tales; stories of ghosts, heroes, the supernatural

           For religious mythology, see 200.4; minor forms of folk literature, 398.5–398.9

[.21–.24]   Specific kinds

           Numbers discontinued; class in 398.2

[.3–.4]   Sociology of specific subjects of folklore

           Numbers discontinued; class in 398

           398.5–398.9 Minor forms of folk literature

           Class comprehensive works in 398.2

.5   Chapbooks

.6   Riddles

.8   Rimes and games

           Nursery rimes, counting-out rimes, street cries and songs

.9   Proverbs

399   Customs of war and diplomacy

           Examples: dances, peace pipe, treatment of captives, e.g., scalping

           Class cannibalism [*formerly* 399] in 394

400   Language

Expression and comprehension of ideas thru systematic symbolism

Class nonverbal language in 001.54; language of a specific subject with the subject, using "Standard Subdivisions" notation 01 from Table 1, e.g., language of science 501

401   Philosophy and theory

> Including universal languages, psycholinguistics

402   Miscellany

403   Dictionaries, encyclopedias, concordances

405   Serial publications

406   Organizations

407   Study and teaching

408   Collections

409   Historical and geographical treatment

> Add "Areas" notation 1–9 from Table 2 to base number 409, e.g., languages of Canada 409.71

> Class historical and geographical treatment of specific languages and groups of languages in 420–490 (not 409.3–409.9)

410   Linguistics

Science and structure of spoken and written language

Class here comprehensive works on Indo-European languages

Class linguistics of specific languages in 420–490

> For specific Indo-European languages, see 420–480

411   Notations (Alphabets and ideographs)

412   Etymology

> Phonetic, graphic, semantic development of words and morphemes

> For notations, see 411; phonology, 414

413   Polyglot dictionaries and lexicography

414   Phonology

415   Structural systems (Grammar)

Morphology and syntax

416   Prosody

417   Dialectology and paleography

Class specific elements, e.g., grammar, in 411–416

418   Usage (Applied linguistics)

Including translation, interpretation

For polyglot dictionaries, see 413

419   Verbal language other than spoken and written

Example: manual alphabet (deaf mute) language

Class nonverbal language [*formerly* 419] in 001.54

420–490 Specific languages

Class here comprehensive works on specific languages and their literatures

Under each language identified by *, add to the designated base number the "Subdivisions of Individual Languages" notation 01–86 from Table 4

Class comprehensive works in 410

For literatures of specific languages, see 810–890

420–480 Specific Indo-European languages

Class comprehensive works in 410

For East Indo-European and Celtic languages, see 491

420   *English and Anglo-Saxon languages

Base number for English: 42

Special interpretations of the provisions of Table 4, "Subdivisions of Individual Languages," for use with English appear below under 427–428

421   Written and spoken codes of standard English

422   Etymology of standard English

423   Dictionaries of standard English

425   Structural system (Grammar) of standard English

426   Prosody of standard English

* Add to base number as instructed under 420–490

427   Nonstandard English

Including Middle English

For Old English, see 429

428   Standard English usage (Applied linguistics)

Class here Basic English

429   Anglo-Saxon (Old English)

430   Germanic (Teutonic) languages   *German

Base number for German: 43

A special interpretation of the provisions of Table 4, "Subdivisions of Individual Languages," for use with German appears below under 437

For English and Anglo-Saxon languages, see 420

431   Written and spoken codes of standard German

432   Etymology of standard German

433   Dictionaries of standard German

435   Structural system (Grammar) of standard German

436   Prosody of standard German

437   Nonstandard German

Including Yiddish [*formerly* 492.49]

438   Standard German usage (Applied linguistics)

439   Other Germanic (Teutonic) languages

   .3   Dutch, Flemish, Afrikaans

   .7   Swedish

   .8   Danish and Norwegian

440   *French, Provençal, Catalan languages

Base number for French: 44

Class here comprehensive works on Romance languages [*formerly* 479.1]

For Italian, Romanian, Rhaeto-Romanic languages, see 450; *Spanish and Portuguese languages,* 460

441   Written and spoken codes of standard French

442   Etymology of standard French

443   Dictionaries of standard French

* Add to base number as instructed under 420–490

445	Structural system (Grammar) of standard French
446	Prosody of standard French
447	Nonstandard French
448	Standard French usage (Applied linguistics)
449	Provençal and Catalan
450	***Italian, Romanian, Rhaeto-Romanic languages**
	Base number for Italian: 45
451	Written and spoken codes of standard Italian
452	Etymology of standard Italian
453	Dictionaries of standard Italian
455	Structural system (Grammar) of standard Italian
456	Prosody of standard Italian
457	Nonstandard Italian
458	Standard Italian usage (Applied linguistics)
459	Romanian and Rhaeto-Romanic
460	***Spanish and Portuguese languages**
	Base number for Spanish: 46
461	Written and spoken codes of standard Spanish
462	Etymology of standard Spanish
463	Dictionaries of standard Spanish
465	Structural system (Grammar) of standard Spanish
466	Prosody of standard Spanish
467	Nonstandard Spanish
468	Standard Spanish usage (Applied linguistics)
469	*Portuguese

* Add to base number as instructed under 420–490

470   Italic languages   *Latin

Base number for Latin: 47

Special interpretations of the provisions of Table 4, "Subdivisions of Individual Languages," for use with Latin appear below under 471–478

For Romance languages, see 440

▶   471–476 Classical Latin

Class here classical revival (medieval and modern) Latin

471   Written and spoken codes of classical Latin

472   Etymology of classical Latin

473   Dictionaries of classical Latin

475   Structural system (Grammar) of classical Latin

476   Prosody of classical Latin

477   Old (Preclassical), Postclassical, Vulgar Latin

478   Classical Latin usage (Applied linguistics)

Class here classical revival (medieval and modern) Latin usage

479   Other Italic languages

Including Osco-Umbrian languages

For Etruscan, see 499

[.1]   Romance languages

Class in 440

480   Hellenic languages   *Classical Greek

Class here classical languages

Base number for classical Greek: 48

Special interpretations of the provisions of Table 4, "Subdivisions of Individual Languages," for use with Greek appear below under 487

For Latin, see 470

481   Written and spoken codes of classical Greek

482   Etymology of classical Greek

483   Dictionaries of classical Greek

485   Structural system (Grammar) of classical Greek

486   Prosody of classical Greek

* Add to base number as instructed under 420–490

487 **Postclassical Greek**

> Hellenistic and Byzantine Greek
>
> Including Biblical Greek (Koine)

488 **Classical Greek usage (Applied linguistics)**

489 **Other Hellenic languages**

> Including modern Greek (Katharevusa and Demotic)

[.3] **Modern Greek**

> Number discontinued; class in 489

490 **Other languages**

491 **East Indo-European and Celtic languages**

> Including Indic languages, e.g., Sanskrit, Panjabi, Hindi, Urdu, Bengali, Sinhalese, Romany (Gipsy); Iranian languages, e.g., Persian; Baltic languages, e.g., Lithuanian, Latvian (Lettish); Albanian, Armenian

[.1–.5] **Specific languages**

> Numbers discontinued; class in 491

.6 **Celtic languages**

> Including Irish and Scottish Gaelic, Manx, Welsh (Cymric), Breton

.7 **East Slavic languages   *Russian**

> Including Ukrainian, Belorussian
>
> Base number for Russian: 491.7
>
> Class comprehensive works on Slavic languages in 491.8

[.79] **Ukrainian and Belorussian**

> Number discontinued; class in 491.7

.8 **Slavic languages**

> Including Common Slavic, Bulgarian, Macedonian, Serbo-Croatian, Slovenian, Polish, Czech, Slovak, Wendish, Polabian
>
> Class here Balto-Slavic languages
>
> Class East Slavic languages in 491.7, Baltic languages in 491

[.9] **Baltic and other East Indo-European languages**

> Number discontinued; class in 491

* Add to base number as instructed under 420–490

492   Afro-Asiatic (Hamito-Semitic) languages

Including Akkadian, Aramaic, Ethiopic, Samaritan, Arabic, Canaanite-Phoenician languages

For Hamitic and Chad languages, see 493

.4   Hebrew

[.41–.48]   Hebrew

Numbers discontinued; class in 492.4

[.49]   Yiddish

Class in 437

[.7]   Arabic

Number discontinued; class in 492

493   Hamitic and Chad languages

Including Hausa [*formerly* 496], Old Egyptian, Coptic, Berber, Cushitic languages

494   Ural-Altaic, Paleosiberian, Dravidian languages

Altaic languages, e.g., Manchu, Mongolian, Turkish; Uralic languages, e.g., Samoyed, Hungarian, Finnish, Estonian, Lapp; Paleosiberian languages; Dravidian languages, e.g., Tamil, Malayalam, Kanarese, Telugu

495   Languages of East and Southeast Asia   Sino-Tibetan languages

Including Tibeto-Burman, Burmese, Cambodian languages

.1   Chinese

.6   Japanese

.7   Korean

.9   Thai and Vietnamese (Annamese)

496   African languages

Including Bantu, e.g., Swahili; Hottentot, Bushman, Ibo, Yoruba languages

Class Hausa [*formerly* 496] in 493

For Afro-Asiatic languages, see 492

497   North American aboriginal languages

Class here comprehensive works on American aboriginal languages

For South American aboriginal languages, see 498

498   South American aboriginal languages

499   Other languages

Including Negrito, Papuan, Malayan, Philippine, Polynesian, Melanesian, Micronesian, Australian, Basque, Elamitic, Etruscan, Sumerian, Caucasian languages; artificial languages, e.g., Esperanto

[.9]   Artificial languages

Number discontinued; class in 499

500   Pure sciences

Class here comprehensive works on pure and applied sciences

Class scientific principles of a specific subject with the subject, using "Standard Subdivisions" notation 01 from Table 1, e.g., scientific principles of photography 770.1

For applied sciences, see 600

.1   Natural sciences

.2   Physical sciences

.5   Space sciences

.9   Natural history

Comprehensive description of phenomena in nature

Add "Areas" notation 1–9 from Table 2 to base number 500.9

501   Philosophy and theory

502   Miscellany

.8   Techniques, apparatus, equipment, materials

Including microscopy [*formerly* 578]

503   Dictionaries, encyclopedias, concordances

505   Serial publications

506   Organizations

507   Study and teaching

508   Collections, travels, surveys

.3   Travels and surveys

For geographical treatment of travels and surveys, see 508.4–508.9

.4–.9   Geographical treatment of travels and surveys

Add "Areas" notation 4–9 from Table 2 to base number 508

509   Historical and geographical treatment

510   Mathematics

This schedule is completely new, prepared with little or no reference to earlier editions and assigning new meanings to many numbers. Such numbers are italicized

Class here finite mathematics

.1   Philosophy and theory

Class mathematical logic in 511

511   Generalities

Including symbolic (mathematical) logic [*formerly* 164], sets, Boolean algebra, approximations, expansions, graph theory, numerical analysis (numerical solutions), mathematical models (mathematical simulation), algorithms

Class generalities applied to a specific branch of mathematics with the branch, e.g., arithmetic approximation 513

For calculus of finite differences, see 515

512   Algebra

Including algebra combined with other branches of mathematics; groups, fields, rings, number theory, lattices, precalculus; linear, multilinear, multidimensional algebras, e.g., topological, vector, tensor algebras

Class here universal, modern, abstract algebra

Class algebra combined with arithmetic in 513, linear algebra combined with analysis in 515

For arithmetic, see 513

.9   Basic secondary-school and college algebra

Including algebraic operations, e.g., addition, division, exponents, logarithms, approximation, ratio, combinations, permutations; progressions; theory of equations; matrices, determinants

513   Arithmetic

Including arithmetic combined with other branches of mathematics; arithmetic operations, e.g., addition, division, exponents, logarithms, approximation, ratio, combinations, permutations; progressions; numeration systems, e.g., binary, decimal

514   Topology

Including algebraic topology, analysis situs

Class topology combined with analysis in 515

515   Analysis

Including analysis and calculus combined with other branches of mathematics; sequences, series, equations, differential and integral calculus, calculus of finite differences, calculus of variations, vector and tensor analysis, functional analysis, functions of real and complex variables

Class here comprehensive works on theory of functions

Class engineering descriptive geometry [*formerly* 515] in 604.2

Class analysis combined with algebra, algebraic vector analysis, topological algebras in 512; differential geometry in 516; theory of a specific function or group of functions with the subject, e.g., applied numerical analysis 519.4

516   Geometry

Euclidean and non-Euclidean

Including plane and solid geometry, trigonometry; analytic geometries, e.g., algebraic, differential, integral geometry; projective and mathematical descriptive geometry

Class geometry combined with algebra in 512, with arithmetic in 513, with analysis in 515

> For topology, *see* 514

519   Probabilities and applied mathematics

Class here random processes

Class a specific application with the subject, e.g., game theory in gambling 795

.2   Probabilities

Mathematical theory of random phenomena (stochastic processes)

Including probabilistic processes, e.g., Markov processes; random walks (Monte Carlo), expectation, prediction

Class probabilities applied to statistical mathematics in 519.5

.3   Game theory

.4   Applied numerical analysis

Including computer mathematics, coding theory

Class information theory in 001.53, statistical mathematics in 519.5

.5   Statistical mathematics [*formerly also* 311]

Theory of sampling; measures of central tendency, e.g., median; measures of deviation; statistical inference, e.g., decision theory, expectation, prediction

.7   Programing

Single- and multistage, linear and nonlinear

.8   Special topics

> Queuing, inventory, storage, success runs, epidemics, fluctuations, quality control, other statistical adjustments

520   Astronomy and allied sciences

.1   Philosophy and theory

> Class theoretical astronomy in 521

.2   Miscellany

[.28]   Techniques, apparatus, equipment, materials

> Do not use; class in 522

521–525 Astronomy

Class comprehensive works in 520

For geodetic and positional astronomy, see 526

521   Theoretical astronomy and celestial mechanics

> Specific theories and their application to celestial bodies and kinds of bodies
>
> Including quasar theory, pulsar theory, universal gravitation, orbits
>
> Class celestial mechanics applied to description of specific celestial bodies and kinds of bodies in 523, theories of universe in 523.1, theory of earth in 525.01

522   Practical and spherical astronomy

> Observatories; telescopes and other astronomical instruments, e.g., heliographs, coronagraphs, heliostats; observational techniques, e.g., photography; corrections
>
> Including radio and radar astronomy [*both formerly* 523.01]
>
> Class applications to specific celestial bodies and phenomena in 523

523   Descriptive astronomy

> Including quasars, pulsars, zodiac
>
> Class here comprehensive works on specific celestial bodies, groupings, phenomena
>
> Class "earth" sciences of other worlds in 550
>
> *For theoretical astronomy, see* 521

.001   Philosophy and theory

> Class theoretical astronomy in 521

.002–.006   Standard subdivisions

> Notations from Table 1

.007   Study and teaching

.007 4   Museums and exhibits

            Class here planetariums [*formerly* 523.2]

.008–.009   Standard subdivisions

           Notations from Table 1

.01   **Astrophysics**

          Physics and chemistry of celestial bodies and phenomena

          Class radio and radar astronomy [*both formerly* 523.01] in 522

.1   **Universe (Cosmology)**

          Origin, development, structure, destiny of universe

          Including nebulas, interstellar matter, galaxies, e.g., Milky Way

          Class astrobiology [*formerly* 523.1] in 574.999

.101   Philosophy and theories

            Class specific theories in 523.1

.2   **Solar system**

          Structure, motion, physical properties

          Class planetariums [*formerly* 523.2] in 523.0074

          For specific parts of solar system, see 523.3–523.7

         523.3–523.7 Specific parts of solar system

          Physical properties and constitution, motion, orbits, eclipses, spectroscopy, constants, dimensions

          Class comprehensive works in 523.2

.3   **Moon**

          Including charts, photographs, tables

          Class physical features of moon in 919.9

.302 1   Tabulated and related materials

            Class tables in 523.3

.302 2   Illustrations and models

            Class charts and photographs in 523.3

[.39]   Charts, photographs, tables

          Number discontinued; class in 523.3

.4   Planets

       Including charts, photographs, tables

        For earth, see 525; satellites, 523.9

.402 1   Tabulated and related materials

         Class tables in 523.4

.402 2   Illustrations and models

         Class charts and photographs in 523.4

[.49]   Charts, photographs, tables

       Number discontinued; class in 523.4

.5   Meteors and zodiacal light

.6   Comets

       Including charts, photographs, tables

.602 1   Tabulated and related materials

         Class tables in 523.6

.602 2   Illustrations and models

         Class charts and photographs in 523.6

[.69]   Charts, photographs, tables

       Number discontinued; class in 523.6

.7   Sun

       Including charts, photographs

       Class heliographs, coronagraphs, heliostats in 522; sun tables in 525

.702 2   Illustrations and models

         Class charts and photographs in 523.7

[.79]   Charts and photographs

       Number discontinued; class in 523.7

.8   Stars

       Including binary, multiple, variable stars; clusters; charts, photographs, tables

       Class galaxies, e.g., Milky Way, in 523.1

        For sun, see 523.7

.802 1   Tabulated and related materials

         Class tables in 523.8

.802 2   Illustrations and models

         Class charts and photographs in 523.8

[.89]   Charts, photographs, tables

Number discontinued; class in 523.8

.9   Transits, satellites, occultations

For moon, see 523.3

525   Earth (Astronomical geography)

Constants, dimensions, orbit and motions, seasons, tides, astronomical twilight and twilight tables, sun tables; optical, thermal, radioactive properties

For geodesy, see 526

526   Mathematical geography

Including geodesy, geodetic and positional astronomy

Class here cartography (map-making)

For astronomical geography, see 525

.3   Geodetic surveying

Surveys in which curvature of earth is considered in measurement and computation

.8   Map drawing [*formerly* 744.4] and projections

Class map reading in 912

.9   Surveying

Boundary, topographic, hydrographic surveying (plane surveying)

Including aerial and terrestrial photogrammetry

Class engineering surveys in 622–628

For geodetic surveying, see 526.3

527   Celestial navigation

Determination of geographic position and direction from observation of celestial bodies

528   Nautical almanacs (Ephemerides).

Class tables of specific celestial bodies in 523

529   Time (Chronology)

Intervals of time, calendars, horology (finding and measuring time)

530 Physics

Class here matter and antimatter

Class astrophysics in 523.01; physical chemistry in 541; physics of specific elements, compounds, mixtures in 546

.1 Philosophy and theory

Including electromagnetic [*formerly* 537.1], relativity, statistical, kinetic, field, wave, measurement theories; quantum mechanics (quantum theory), mathematical physics

Class applications to specific states of matter in 530.4, electromagnetic spectrum in 539.2

[.11–.16] Specific theories

Numbers discontinued; class in 530.1

.4 States of matter

Plasma (ionized gas) and plasma physics [*both formerly* 537.1]; solid-, liquid-, gaseous-state physics

Including physical properties and behavior of matter as states: molecular, atomic, nuclear physics; sound and related vibrations, visible light, paraphotic phenomena, heat, electricity, electronics, magnetism, quantum mechanics

Class classical mechanics in 531–533

For crystallography, see 548

531 Mechanics

Statics (equilibrium and forces affecting it), dynamics (motion and forces affecting it), kinetics, kinematics

Including solid and particle mechanics, gravity, mass, energy; simple machines, e.g., levers; tables, review, exercise for solid mechanics

For universal gravitation, see 521; *mechanics of fluids,* 532

.021 Tabulated and related materials

Class tables for solid mechanics in 531

.076 Review and exercise

Class review and exercise for solid mechanics in 531

[.9] Tables, review, exercise for solid mechanics

Number discontinued; class in 531

532	Mechanics of fluids

Statics (equilibrium and forces affecting it), dynamics (motion and forces affecting it), kinetics, kinematics

Including mechanics of liquids (hydromechanics); tables, review, exercise for hydromechanics

For mechanics of gases, see 533

.021   Tabulated and related materials

Class tables for hydromechanics in 532

.076   Review and exercise

Class review and exercise for hydromechanics in 532

[.9]   Tables, review, exercise for hydromechanics

Number discontinued; class in 532

533   Mechanics of gases

Statics (equilibrium and forces affecting it), dynamics (motion and forces affecting it), kinetics, kinematics

Including vacuums, vacuum production, aeromechanics; tables, review, exercise for gases in general

.021   Tabulated and related materials

Class tables for gases in general in 533

.076   Review and exercise

Class review and exercise for gases in general in 533

[.6]   Aeromechanics

Number discontinued; class in 533

[.9]   Tables, review, exercise for gases in general

Number discontinued; class in 533

▶   534–538 Other branches of classical physics

Class comprehensive works in 530, properties of specific states of matter as states in 530.4

534   Sound and related vibrations

Including characteristics, e.g., frequency, pitch, noise; generation, propagation (transmission), measurement, analysis, synthesis of sound; tables, review, exercise

.021   Tabulated and related materials

Class tables in 534

[.076]	Review and exercise
	Do not use; class in 534
.5	Vibrations related to sound
	Subsonic and ultrasonic vibrations
[.9]	Tables, review, exercise
	Number discontinued; class in 534

535 Visible light (Optics) and paraphotic phenomena

Paraphotic: infrared and ultraviolet

Including microscopes [*formerly also* 578], other optical instruments; theories; physical and geometrical optics, optical and paraphotic spectroscopy; spectral regions, e.g., visible light; tables, review, exercise

Class here comprehensive works on spectroscopy

Class each kind of spectroscopy not provided for here with the subject, e.g., microwave spectroscopy 537.5; a specific application with the subject, e.g., qualitative spectroscopic analysis 544; optical instruments for a specific function with the subject, e.g., telescopes 522

.01	Philosophy and theory
	Class theories in 535
.02	Miscellany
.021	Tabulated and related materials
	Class tables in 535
.028	Techniques, apparatus, equipment, materials
	Class spectroscopy in 535
.07	Study and teaching
[.076]	Review and exercise
	Do not use; class in 535
.5	Beams and their modification
	Polarization and amplification
	Including amplification by stimulated emission of radiation (lasers)
.6	Color
[.9]	Tables, review, exercise
	Number discontinued; class in 535

536   Heat

Theories, transmission (heat transfer), heat effects, temperature, cryogenics, calorimetry, thermodynamics; change of state, e.g., solid to gas

Including tables, review, exercise

Class a specific aspect of cryogenics with the subject, e.g., conduction of electricity at low temperatures 537.6

.01   Philosophy and theory

Class theories in 536

.02   Miscellany

.021   Tabulated and related materials

Class tables in 536

.07   Study and teaching

[.076]   Review and exercise

Do not use; class in 536

[.9]   Tables, review, exercise

Number discontinued; class in 536

537   Electricity and electronics

Including tables, review, exercise

Class here electromagnetism

Class electromagnetic theory in 530.1

For magnetism, see 538

.01   Philosophy and theory

Class theories in 537.1

.02   Miscellany

.021   Tabulated and related materials

Class tables in 537

.07   Study and teaching

[.076]   Review and exercise

Do not use; class in 537

.1   Theories

Microwave circuit, waveguide, corpuscular theories

Class electromagnetic theory in 530.1, plasma and plasma physics in 530.4 [*all formerly* 537.1]

.2 Electrostatics

Charge and potentials, generators, dielectrics

.5 Electronics

Emission, behavior and effects of electrons in gas and vacuum tubes, photoelectric cells and similar mediums; spectroscopy, tubes, circuitry of radio waves, microwaves, X rays, gamma rays; electron and ion optics

Class microwave circuit and waveguide theories in 537.1

For semiconductors, see 537.6

.6 Electric currents (Electrodynamics) and thermoelectricity

Direct and alternating currents, semiconductors, conductivity

For dielectrics, see 537.2

[.9] Tables, review, exercise

Number discontinued; class in 537

538 Magnetism

Magnets, magnetic materials and phenomena, magnetohydrodynamics; geomagnetism and allied phenomena, e.g., auroras, Van Allen radiation belts

Including tables, review, exercise

.01 Philosophy and theory

Class electromagnetic theory in 530.1

.02 Miscellany

.021 Tabulated and related materials

Class tables in 538

.07 Study and teaching

[.076] Review and exercise

Do not use; class in 538

[.9] Tables, review, exercise

Number discontinued; class in 538

539   Modern physics

Molecular, atomic, nuclear physics

Including structure of matter; tables, review, exercise

Class here chemical physics

Class properties of specific states of matter as states in 530.4; molecular, atomic, nuclear physics of sound and related vibrations, of visible light and paraphotic phenomena, of heat, of electricity, of magnetism with the specific subject, e.g., auroras 538

For electronics, see 537.5

.01   Philosophy and theory

Class theories in 530.1

.02   Miscellany

.021   Tabulated and related materials

Class tables in 539

.07   Study and teaching

[.076]   Review and exercise

Do not use; class in 539

.2   Radiations (Radiant energy)

Including electromagnetic spectrum and radiations

Class a specific radiation or class of radiations with the subject, e.g., visible light 535

.7   Atomic and nuclear physics

Nuclear structure, reactions, interactions; nuclei and other particles; X, gamma, cosmic rays; detection and measurement of particles and radioactivity; particle acceleration; reactions emitting high energy

Including ionizing radiation

Class X-ray and gamma-ray electronics in 537.5, application of detection and measurement of particles and radioactivity to a specific subject with the subject, e.g., detection of uranium ores 622

[.75–.76]   Nuclear reactions

Numbers and their subdivisions discontinued; class in 539.7

[.9]   Tables, review, exercise

Number discontinued; class in 539

540 Chemistry and allied sciences

Class astrophysics in 523.01

.1 Philosophy and theory

Including ancient and medieval theories of chemistry, e.g., alchemy, phlogiston theory, philosopher's stone

Class theoretical chemistry in 541, analytical chemistry in 543–545

.2 Miscellany

.28 Materials

Class chemical apparatus and equipment in 542, analytical chemistry in 543–545

.7 Study and teaching

Class experimental research in 543–545

▶
541–547 Chemistry

Class comprehensive works in 540

▶
541–545 General chemistry

Inorganic and combined inorganic-organic chemistry

Class comprehensive works on general chemistry in 540, comprehensive works on inorganic chemistry in 546, organic chemistry in 547

541 Physical and theoretical chemistry

Molecular and atomic structure, stoichiometry, quantum chemistry, solutions, colloids, surface phenomena, chemical reactions and synthesis, radiochemistry (nuclear chemistry), thermodynamics; thermo-, photo-, electro-, magnetochemistry; periodic law

Class chemical physics in 539; physical and theoretical chemistry of specific elements, compounds, mixtures, groupings in 546; physical and theoretical organic chemistry in 547

542 Laboratories, apparatus, equipment

Class here general procedures, manipulation of equipment

Class a specific application with the subject, e.g., apparatus for volumetric analysis 545

▶   543–545 Analytical chemistry

Class here experimental research

Class comprehensive works in 543; analytical chemistry of specific elements, compounds, mixtures, groupings in 546; organic analytical chemistry in 547

543   General analysis

Reagents, sample preparation, instrumentation; instrumental methods, e.g., radiochemical analysis

For qualitative analysis, see 544; *quantitative analysis,* 545

544   Qualitative analysis

Systematic macro and semiquantitative methods and procedures for detecting and identifying constituents of a substance, e.g., spectrochemical (spectroscopic) analysis

545   Quantitative analysis

Determination of the amount of a constituent in a substance, e.g., by volumetric analysis

546   Inorganic chemistry

Chemistry of elements, of inorganic compounds and mixtures

Class here physical and theoretical chemistry, analytical chemistry, physics of specific elements, compounds, mixtures, groupings; comprehensive works on inorganic and organic chemistry of specific elements, compounds, mixtures, groupings

For organic chemistry, see 547

547   Organic chemistry

General, physical, theoretical, analytical chemistry of carbon compounds, e.g., vitamins, sugar, petroleum, rubber, dyes

For biochemistry, see 574.1

.01   Philosophy and theory

Class theoretical organic chemistry in 547

548   Crystallography

Geometrical, chemical, mathematical, physical, structural, optical crystallography; crystallization, crystal growth

549   Mineralogy

>   Occurrence, description, classification, identification of naturally-
>   occurring elements and compounds formed by inorganic
>   processes
>
>   Including determinative mineralogy
>
>   Class economic geology in 553
>
>>   *For crystallography, see 548*

.09   Historical and geographical treatment

>>   Class geographical distribution of minerals in 549.9

[.1–.7]   Determinative mineralogy and specific minerals

>   Numbers discontinued; class in 549

.9   Geographical distribution of minerals

>   Add "Areas" notation 1–9 from Table 2 to base number 549.9

550   Sciences of the earth and other worlds

>   Class here geology
>
>>   *For physical geography, see 910*

.9   Historical and geographical treatment

>   Class treatment by continent, country, locality, other worlds in 554–
>   559 (not 550.94–550.99)

551   Physical and dynamic geology

>   Geophysics and geochemistry of lithosphere, hydrosphere, atmosphere
>
>>   *For astronomical geography, see 525; geodesy, 526; mineralogy, 549;
>>   petrology, 552*

.1   Gross structure and properties of earth and other worlds

>   Structure and properties of interior and crust
>
>>   *For geomagnetism, see 538*

.2   Plutonic phenomena

>   Volcanoes, earthquakes, fumaroles, hot springs, geysers

.3   Surface and exogenous processes and their agents

>   Erosion, weathering, deposition, sedimentation, transport thru action
>   of ice, water, wind, frost
>
>   Including glaciology, geologic work of precipitation
>
>   Class here interdisciplinary works on ice
>
>   Class a specific aspect of ice with the subject, e.g., ice manufacture
>   621.5

.4   Geomorphology

Origin, development, transformations of topographic features, e.g., continents, islands, mountains, valleys, caves, plane and coastal regions

Including oceans and seas (oceanography); hydrology, e.g., lakes, waterfalls, subsurface waters

Class geologic work of water, land formations created and modified by specific exogenous agents, geomorphology of ice in 551.3; biological oceanography in 574.92

For hydrometeorology, see 551.5

.5   Meteorology

Composition of atmosphere, e.g., dust; regions of atmosphere, e.g., troposphere; mechanics of atmosphere, e.g., wind systems; thermodynamics; temperatures; radiations; atmospheric pressure; atmospheric formations, e.g., air fronts; atmospheric disturbances, e.g., hurricanes, tornadoes, thunder- and snowstorms, dust storms; atmospheric electricity, e.g., lightning; atmospheric optics, e.g., mirages, rainbows; hydrometeorology, e.g., humidity, fogs, mists, clouds, precipitation (rain, snow, hail)

Class auroras and magnetic phenomena in 538, geologic work of precipitation in 551.3

For climatology and weather, see 551.6

.6   Climatology and weather

Weather belts, forecasting, reports, artificial modification and control, microclimatology

Including paleoclimatology, use of weather satellites, weather lore

.609   Historical and geographical treatment

Class climate of specific areas in 551.6

.7   Historical geology (Stratigraphy)

For paleontology, see 560

.8   Structural geology (Tectonophysics)

Forms, positon, deformation of rocks, e.g., stratifications, joints, cleavages, synclines, antisynclines, faults, folds, veins, dikes, necks, bosses, laccoliths, sills, dips, outcrops, strikes

.9   Geochemistry

Class a specific material with the subject, e.g., composition of rocks 552

552   Rocks (Petrology)

Origin, properties, composition, analysis, structure

Including petrography, lithology

Class mineral content of rocks in 549, economic geology in 553

For geochemistry, see 551.9

553   Economic geology

Quantitative occurrence and distribution of geological materials of economic utility, e.g., coal, petroleum, metals, marbles, clays, salts, sulfur, soils, water, ice, gems, helium, limes

Class here interdisciplinary works on specific nonmetallic materials

Class a specific aspect of specific nonmetallic materials with the subject, e.g., prospecting 622; interdisciplinary works on ice in 551.3, on specific metals in 669

▶   **554–559 Regional geology**

Geology of specific continents, countries, localities; other worlds

Class comprehensive works in 550, a specific geological aspect of a region with the subject, e.g., geomorphology of England 551.40942

554   Geology of Europe

Add "Areas" notation 41–49 from Table 2 to base number 55, e.g., geology of England 554.2

555   Geology of Asia

Add "Areas" notation 51–59 from Table 2 to base number 55, e.g., geology of Japan 555.2

556   Geology of Africa

Add "Areas" notation 61–69 from Table 2 to base number 55, e.g., geology of South Africa 556.8

557   Geology of North America

Add "Areas" notation 71–79 from Table 2 to base number 55, e.g., geology of Ohio 557.71

558   Geology of South America

Add "Areas" notation 81–89 from Table 2 to base number 55, e.g., geology of Brazil 558.1

559   Geology of other parts of world and other worlds

Add "Areas" notation 93–99 from Table 2 to base number 55, e.g., geology of Australia 559.4, of moon 559.9

560   Paleontology   Paleozoology

Including stratigraphic paleontology, paleobotany, paleozoology

[.17]   Stratigraphic paleontology

Number discontinued; class in 560

.9   Historical and geographical treatment

Add to 560.9 the numbers following 574.9 in 574.909–574.99, e.g., marine paleontology 560.92

561   Paleobotany

Descriptive and taxonomic

Class stratigraphic paleobotany in 560

.09   Historical treatment

Class geographical treatment in 561

▶   562–569 Specific animals and groups of animals

Class here taxonomic paleozoology

Class comprehensive works in 560

562   Fossil invertebrates

For Protozoa, Parazoa, Metazoa, see 563; mollusks and mollusk-like animals, 564; other invertebrates, 565

563   Fossil Protozoa, Parazoa, Metazoa

Examples: unicellular animals, sponges, corals, starfishes

564   Fossil mollusks and mollusk-like animals

Examples: tooth shells, snails, slugs, whelks, sea hares, sea lemons, sea slugs, nautilus, lamp shells

565   Other fossil invertebrates

Examples: worms, barnacles, horseshoe crabs, millipedes, centipedes, insects

566   Fossil vertebrates (Fossil Chordata)

For Anamnia, see 567; Sauropsida, 568; mammals, 569

567   Fossil Anamnia

Cyclostomes, fishes, amphibians

568   Fossil Sauropsida

Reptiles, birds

Including dinosaurs

569   Fossil mammals

     For prehistoric man, see 573

570   Life sciences

     For paleontology, see 560

572   Human races

     Origin, distribution, physical characteristics of races

     Including causes of physical differences

     Class here ethnology

     Class primitive races [*formerly* 572] in 301.2

      For ethnopsychology, see 155.8

  .8   Specific races

     Add to 572.8 the numbers following 4 in 420–490, e.g., African races 572.896

  .9   Geographical distribution of races (Anthropogeography)

     Add "Areas" notation 1–9 from Table 2 to base number 572.9

     Class specific races in specific places in 572.8

573   Physical anthropology

     Including prehistoric man, environmental effects on physique, pigmentation, anthropometry

     Class here human biological ecology

     For human races, see 572

  .2   Organic evolution and genetics of man

     Including heredity, variation

574   Biology

     For botanical sciences, see 580; zoological sciences, 590; special biological fields and techniques, 575–579

  .09   Historical treatment

     Class historical treatment in specific areas in 574.9

.1   Physiology

> Circulation, respiration, nutrition, metabolism, secretion, excretion, reproduction, histogenesis (formation and differentiation of tissues), movements, control mechanisms, biophysics, biochemistry
>
> Including bioenergetics, bioluminescence, bioelectricity; proteins, carbohydrates, enzymes, vitamins, hormones as constituents of living matter
>
> Class here comprehensive works on physiology and anatomy
>
> Class microphysiology in 574.8
>
>> *For anatomy, see 574.4; development and maturation, 574.3*

.2   Pathology

> Anomalies, malformations, deformations, diseases
>
> Including immunity, pathogenicity [*both formerly 576*], degeneration, death [*both formerly 577*]
>
> Class histopathology, cell pathology in 574.8

.3   Development and maturation

> Including sex in nature [*formerly 577*], embryology, gametogenesis
>
>> *For histogenesis, see 574.1*

.4   Anatomy and morphology

> Class microanatomy in 574.8, anatomy of embryos in 574.3

.5   Ecology

> Interrelation of organisms to environment and to each other
>
> Including adaptations, migrations, parasitism

.6   Economic biology

> Organisms beneficial and deleterious to man's interests

.8   Tissue, cellular, molecular biology

> Including protoplasm, chromosomes, DNA, RNA; ultimate nature of living matter
>
>> *For histogenesis, see 574.1*

.9   Geographical treatment

.909   Zonal and physiographic treatment

> Class insular biology in 574.91, hydrographic biology in 574.92

.91   Insular biology

.92	Hydrographic biology

> Marine and fresh-water biology
>
> Class here plankton

[.929]	Fresh-water biology

> Number discontinued; class in 574.92

.93–.99	Treatment by specific continents, countries, localities, by extraterrestrial worlds

> Add "Areas" notation 3–9 from Table 2 to base number 574.9, e.g., astrobiology 574.999 [*formerly* 523.1]

─────────

▶ 575–579 Special biological fields and techniques

Class comprehensive works in 574

575 Organic evolution and genetics

> Organic evolution: origin of species thru historic descent with modification
>
> Including evolution thru sexual selection, evolutionary cycles, origin and evolution of sexes
>
> Class organic evolution and genetics of man in 573.2, of plants in 581, of animals in 591

.01	Theories

> Darwinian, neo-Darwinian, orthogenetic, mutation, Lamarckian, neo-Lamarckian theories

.1	Genetics

> Heredity and variation as factors in evolution
>
> *For variation, see* 575.2

.2	Variation

> Physiological and environmental aspects, hybrids, mutations, sports
>
> *For DNA, RNA, see* 574.8

576 Microbes

> Including ultramicrobes (rickettsiae, viruses)
>
> Class here microbiology
>
> Class immunity, pathogenicity [*both formerly* 576] in 574.2
>
> *For Thallophyta, see* 589; *Protozoa,* 593

[.1]	General principles

> Number discontinued; class in 576

577   General nature of life

Origin and beginnings of life, conditions needed for life, differences between living and nonliving substances

Class degeneration, death in 574.2, sex in nature in 574.3 [both formerly 577]

578   Microscopy in biology

Slide preparation, description and use of microscopes

Including photomicrography

Class microscopes in 535, comprehensive works on microscopy in 502.8 [both formerly 578]

579   Collection and preservation of biological specimens

Preparation and preservation of skeletons and total specimens, taxidermy, techniques of collecting and transporting

Class maintenance, display in museums [both formerly 579] in 069

580   Botanical sciences

For paleobotany, see 561

581   Botany

For specific plants and groups of plants, see 582–589

.09   Historical treatment

Class historical treatment in specific areas in 581.9

.1–.9   General principles

Add to 581 the numbers following 574 in 574.1–574.9, e.g., plant ecology 581.5, anatomy of leaves 581.4

▶   582–589 Specific plants and groups of plants

Class here taxonomic botany

Class comprehensive works in 581

582   Seed-bearing plants (Spermatophyta)

Including special groupings, e.g., trees, vines, flowering plants

Class here flowers, fruit, seeds

Class specific classes, orders, families, genera in 583–585

[.1]   Special groupings

Number and its subdivisions discontinued; class in 582

▶   583–584 Flowering plants (Angiospermae)

Class comprehensive works in 582

583   Dicotyledons

Example: rose family

584   Monocotyledons

Example: grasses

585   Naked-seed plants (Gymnospermae)

Example: conifers

586   Seedless plants (Cryptogamia)

For Pteridophyta, see 587; Bryophyta, 588; Thallophyta, 589

587   Vascular cryptogams (Pteridophyta)

Quillworts, ferns, club mosses, horsetail family

588   Bryophyta

Mosses, liverworts, hornworts

589   Thallophyta

Including lichens, fungi, molds, algae, diatoms, fission plants other than bacteria

Class here plant plankton

.9   Bacteria (Schizomycetes)

Class here bacteriology

590   **Zoological sciences**

For paleozoology, see 560

591   Zoology

For specific animals and groups of animals, see 592–599

.09   Historical treatment

Class historical treatment in specific areas in 591.9

.1–.9   General principles

Add to 591 the numbers following 574 in 574.1–574.9, e.g., animal physiology 591.1

Class physiological psychology in 156

▶   592–599 Specific animals and groups of animals

Class here taxonomic zoology

Class comprehensive works in 591

592   Invertebrates

Class here animal plankton

For Protozoa, Parazoa, Metazoa, see 593; mollusks and mollusk-like animals, 594; other invertebrates, 595

593   Protozoa, Parazoa, Metazoa

Examples: unicellular animals, sponges, corals, starfishes, hydras, medusas, jellyfishes, sea urchins, sea walnuts, comb jellies, sea cucumbers

594   Mollusks and mollusk-like animals

Examples: clams, mussels, oysters, shipworms, chitons, tooth shells, snails, slugs, whelks, octopuses, squids, devilfishes, moss animals, lamp shells

595   Other invertebrates

Including worms, cyclops, fish lice, barnacles, sand fleas, sow bugs, wood lice, sea mantles, squillas, sea onions, lobsters, crabs, shrimps, mites, ticks, spiders, harvestmen, scorpions, millipedes, centipedes

.7   Insects

Class here entomology

[.76–.79]   Specific orders of insects

Numbers discontinued; class in 595.7

596   Vertebrates (Chordata)

Including Tunicata (sea squirts and sea grapes)

For Anamnia, see 597; reptiles and birds, 598; mammals, 599

597   Anamnia

Cyclostomes, fishes, amphibians

Including caecilians, frogs, toads, salamanders, newts, mud puppies

Class here ichthyology

Class comprehensive works on amphibians and reptiles in 598.1

[.2–.5]   Specific kinds of Anamnia

Numbers discontinued; class in 597

598   Reptiles and birds

.1   Reptiles

Lizards, snakes, turtles, alligators

Class here herpetology

For amphibians, see 597

[.11–.14]   Specific kinds of reptiles

Numbers discontinued; class in 598.1

.2   Birds (Aves)

Including specific orders of birds [*formerly* 598.3–598.9]

Class here ornithology

[.29]   Geographical treatment

Number and its subdivisions discontinued; class in 598.2

[.3–.9]   Specific orders of birds

Class in 598.2

599   Mammals

Examples: spiny anteaters, platypuses, opossums, kangaroos, rodents, bats, whales, dolphins, porpoises, elephants, horses, rhinoceroses, pigs, hippopotamuses, ruminants, camels, carnivores, monkeys, apes, man

For physical anthropology, see 573; *medical sciences,* 610

[.1–.9]   Specific kinds of mammals

Numbers discontinued; class in 599

600 Technology (Applied sciences)

601 Philosophy and theory

602 Miscellany

> Class patents and inventions in 608

603 Dictionaries, encyclopedias, concordances

604 General technologies

.2 Technical drawing [*formerly* 744]

> Including engineering descriptive geometry [*formerly* 515]
>
> Class here engineering graphics
>
> *For architectural drawing, see 720.28; map drawing, 526.8*

.6 Waste technology

> Methods and equipment for salvaging and utilizing waste materials; products manufactured from waste materials [*formerly* 679]
>
> Class utilization of a specific waste material, manufacture of a specific product with the subject, e.g., scrap metals 669

.7 Hazardous materials technology

> Methods of extracting, manufacturing, processing, utilizing, handling, transporting, storing solids, liquids, gases of explosive, flammable, corrosive, radioactive, toxic, infectious nature
>
> Class technology of a specific material or situation with the subject, e.g., manufacture of explosives 662, public health aspects of fireworks 614.8

605 Serial publications

606 Organizations

607 Study and teaching

> Class here without further subdivision elements of study and teaching provided for in "Standard Subdivisions" notation 074–076 from Table 1

[.4–.9] In specific continents, countries, localities in modern world

> Numbers discontinued; class in 607

608   Collections, patents, inventions

>   Class history of inventions in 609 (not 608.09)

[.7]   Collected descriptions of inventions and their patents

>   Number discontinued; class in 608

609   Historical and geographical treatment

>   Class here history of inventions, industrial (technological) archeology

610   Medical sciences   Medicine

>   Class veterinary medicine in 636.089

[.23]   Medicine as a profession

>   Do not use; class in 610.69

.6   Organizations and personnel

.69   Medical personnel

>   Physicians, medical technicians and assistants, medical relationships
>
>   Class surgeons [*formerly* 610.69] in 617
>
>   Class nurses in 610.73, medical missionaries in 266, medical secretaries in 651, medical records librarians in 651.5; medical personnel, other than nurses, of a specific specialty with the subject, e.g., obstetricians 618.2; critical appraisal and description of work with the subject using "Standard Subdivisions" notation 092 from Table 1, e.g., heart surgeons 617.092

.7   Study, teaching, nursing practice

>   Class experimental medicine in 619

.73   Nursing

>   Duties and practices of professional and practical nurses, attendants, aides, orderlies, volunteers
>
>   Including specialized nursing, e.g., psychiatric nursing
>
>   *For home nursing, see* 649.8

611   Human anatomy, cytology, tissue biology

>   Including anatomic embryology
>
>   Class pathological anatomy [*formerly* 611] in 616.07, comprehensive works on human anatomy and physiology in 612

612   Human physiology

Functions, biophysics, biochemistry of human body

Including physiology of specific activities, e.g., work, sports

Class here comprehensive works on human anatomy and physiology, on human embryology

Class physiological psychology in 152, pathological physiology in 616.07

For human anatomy, cytology, tissue biology, anatomic embryology, see 611

.6   Reproduction, development, maturation

Class here interdisciplinary works on human sex

Class a specific aspect of sex with the subject, e.g., sex psychology 155.3

[.61–.67]   Specific topics

Numbers discontinued; class in 612.6

613   General and personal hygiene

Including inherited diseases, personal cleanliness, clothing as factors in health

For public health, see 614

.1   Hygiene in natural environments

Weather, climate, altitude, air, light, seasonal changes as factors in health

Including acclimation

Class air conditioning [*formerly* 613.1] in 613.5

▶   613.2–613.3 Factors in establishing and maintaining health

Class comprehensive works in 613

For air and light, see 613.1

.2   Dietetics

Place of specific foods and nutritive elements in promotion, restoration, maintenance of health

Including weight gaining and losing programs

For beverages, see 613.3

.3   Beverages

Including hot and cold beverages

For alcoholic beverages, see 613.8

[.4]   Personal cleanliness and clothing

> Number discontinued; class in 613

.5   Hygiene in artificial environments

> In homes and other enclosed spaces
>
> Including air conditioning [*formerly* 613.1]

.6   Special topics

> Industrial, military, camp, travel hygiene; self-defense; techniques of survival in accidents, disasters, other unfavorable circustances

.7   Physical fitness

> Exercise, posture, rest, sleep
>
> Including physical education, physical yoga, hygiene of athletes

.8   Addictions and health

> Use of narcotics, alcoholic beverages, tobacco; of amphetamine, ephedrine, other similar stimulants

.9   Birth control and sex hygiene

> Including eugenics, family planning, contraception

[.94–.95]   Eugenic practices and sex hygiene

> Numbers discontinued; class in 613.9

[.97]   Hygiene for specific age groups

> Number discontinued; class in 613

614   Public health

> Including forensic medicine, registration of births and deaths, reports of illness, premarital examination and certification, disposal of dead
>
> Class vital statistics in 312, licensure and registration of medical personnel in 351.8, medical and psychiatric social work in 362.1–362.4

.3   Adulteration and contamination control

> Inspection, certification, standardization, labeling, distribution, control of food, drugs, cosmetics, other commodities for human use to ensure purity, quality, safety

.4 **Incidence, distribution, control of disease**

> Control: immunization, quarantine, isolation, disinfection, fumigation, sterilization, control of nonhuman carriers of disease
>
> Contemporary and historical periods
>
> Including control of specific diseases [*formerly* 614.5], epidemiology, medical geography
>
> > For mental illness, see 614.5

.409 **Historical treatment**

> > Class treatment of incidence and distribution in specific places, history of epidemics in 614.4

.5 **Mental illness**

> Incidence, distribution, control
>
> Do not use standard subdivisions; class in 614.5
>
> Class control of other specific diseases [*formerly* 614.5] in 614.4

[.58] **Mental illness**

> Number discontinued; class in 614.5

.7 **Environmental sanitation and comfort**

> Sanitation in public buildings and assembly places, disposal of sewage and garbage; control of soil, water, air, noise pollution

.8 **Safety (Accidents and their prevention)**

> Water safety; safety in use of machinery and hazardous materials, e.g., explosives, fireworks; fire, industrial, domestic, travel safety; safety in athletics, sports, other recreational activities; safety and survival in natural disasters, e.g., hurricanes
>
> Including rescue operations, first aid
>
> Class safety engineering in 620.8; fire extinction technology in 628.9; safety equipment and engineering measures of a specific technology with the technology, e.g., space rescue operations 629.45

[.83–.85] **Specific kinds of accidents and their prevention**

> Numbers discontinued; class in 614.8

615   Pharmacology and therapeutics

Drugs (materia medica), pharmaceutical chemistry (manufacture, preparation, analysis of drugs), practical pharmacy (preparing prescriptions and dispensing drugs), pharmacodynamics (physiological and therapeutic action of drugs); methods of medication, e.g., oral; physical and other therapies, e.g., radium therapy; mental therapies, e.g., hypnotherapy

Including general therapeutic systems, e.g., homeopathy, chiropractic; primitive, ancient, medieval remedies; home remedies, folk medicine, patent medicine, faith healing

Class therapies applied to specific diseases or groups of diseases in 616–618

For first aid, see 614.8

.9   Poisons and poisoning (Toxicology)

Sources, composition, physiological effects, tests, detection, antidotes of poisons

616   Diseases

Causes (etiology), effects, diagnoses, prognoses, treatment

Class wounds and injuries, surgical treatment of diseases, diseases by body region, diseases of teeth, eyes, ears in 617; gynecological, obstetrical, pediatric, geriatric diseases in 618

For incidence, distribution, control of disease, see 614.4; general therapeutics, 615

.001–.008   Standard subdivisions

Notations from Table 1

.009   Historical and geographical treatment

Class case histories in 616

.01   Medical microbiology

Pathogenic microorganisms and their relation to disease

.07   Pathology

Causes, effects, symptoms, diagnoses, prognoses of pathological anatomy [*formerly also* 611] and physiology

For medical microbiology, see 616.01

.08   Psychosomatic medicine

▶

616.1–616.9 Specific diseases

Class comprehensive works in 616

▶

616.1–616.8 Diseases of specific systems and organs

Class comprehensive works in 616; tumors, cancers, tuberculosis of specific systems and organs in 616.9

.1   Diseases of cardiovascular system

Heart, blood vessels, blood

Including cardiology, hematology

Class cerebrovascular diseases in 616.8, bacterial blood diseases in 616.9

.2   Diseases of respiratory system

Nose, larynx, trachea, bronchi, lungs, pleura, mediastinum

Class here otorhinolaryngology, rhinology; comprehensive works on eye, ear, nose, throat; laryngology; asthma, hay fever

Class cardiac asthma in 616.1

For otology, see 617.8; ophthalmology, 617.7

.3   Diseases of digestive system

Mouth, throat, pharynx, esophagus, stomach, intestines, peritoneum, rectum, anus, pancreas, liver, gall bladder, bile duct

Including gastroenterology, proctology; nutritional and metabolic diseases, e.g., obesity

Class diabetes in 616.4

For laryngology, see 616.2; endocrinology, 616.4; dentistry, 617.6

.4   Diseases of blood-forming, lymphatic, endocrine systems

Spleen, bone marrow, lymphatic system, male breast, pancreatic internal secretion; thymus, thyroid, parathyroid, adrenal, pituitary, pineal glands

Including endocrinology

Class comprehensive works on diseases of breast [*formerly* 616.4] in 618.1

Class diseases of blood in 616.1; endocrinal obesity, nutritional and metabolic diseases in 616.3; diseases of urogenital system in 616.6; cretinism and myxedemism in 616.8

.5   Diseases of skin, hair, nails

         Including dermatology

         Class venereal diseases in 616.9

.6   Diseases of urogenital system

         Kidneys, ureters, bladder, urethra, prostate, penis, scrotum, testicles

         Including urology, nephrology

         Class venereal diseases in 616.9

         For gynecology, see 618.1

.7   Diseases of musculoskeletal system

         Bones, joints, muscles, tendons, fasciae, bursae, sheaths of tendons, connective tissue

         Class here rheumatology, comprehensive works on rheumatism

         Class rickets, gout in 616.3; rheumatic fever in 616.9

.8   Diseases of nervous system, mental and emotional disorders

         Diseases of nervous system: diseases of cranial and spinal nerves, e.g., sciatica; of autonomic system; cerebrovascular diseases, e.g., stroke; meningeal diseases; encephalitis, Parkinson's disease, multiple sclerosis, poliomyelitis, cerebral palsy, locomotor ataxia, epilepsy, chorea, hysterias, neurological speech disorders, migraine. Mental and emotional disorders: psychoneurotic speech disorders; disorders of personality and character, e.g., kleptomania, sexual aberrations; addictions, e.g., drug addiction, alcoholism; neuroses, e.g., phobias; psychoses, e.g., schizophrenia

         Including neurology, psychiatry; mental deficiency

         Do not use standard subdivisions; class in 616.8

         Class shingles in 616.5, psychosurgery in 617, puerperal psychoses in 618.2

[.85–.89]   Psychoneuroses and psychiatry

         Numbers discontinued; class in 616.8

.9 **Other diseases**

Communicable diseases, e.g., tuberculosis, rheumatic fever, leprosy; tumors, cancers; allergies; diseases due to climate and weather, to physical agents, e.g., motion, altitude, radiation sicknesses

Including medical parasitology, helminthology, climatology, meteorology; oncology; venereal, parasitic, bacterial blood diseases

Do not use standard subdivisions; class in 616.9

Class leukemias in 616.1, pulmonary tuberculosis in 616.2, parasitic skin diseases in 616.5, neurosyphilis in 616.8, injuries from radiation in 617; communicable diseases predominantly affecting a specific part of the body with the part affected, e.g., mumps 616.3; a specific allergy with the subject, e.g., hay fever, asthma 616.2

617 **Surgery and related topics**

Surgery: orthopedic, systemic, regional, plastic; reduction of fractures and dislocations, treatment of wounds and injuries

Including surgeons [*formerly* 610.69], anesthesiology; diagnosis and medical treatment of diseases by region

Class surgical treatment of tumors, cancers in 616.9; gynecological and obstetrical surgery in 618.1–618.2

.6 **Dentistry**

Dental diseases, orthodontics, pedodontics, extractions, cavities, prosthetic dentistry (dentures, crowns, bridges)

Including dental personnel other than nurses

.7 **Ophthalmology**

Pathology, medical and surgical treatment of ocular diseases; correction of refractive errors

Including optometry

.8 **Otology and audiology**

Pathology, medical and surgical treatment of diseases of the ear; correction of impaired hearing thru fitting and adjusting hearing devices

618   Other branches of medicine

.1   Gynecology

Diseases of ovaries, Fallopian tubes, uterus, cervix, vagina, vulva; periuterine diseases; disorders of menstruation, of menopause; sterility; diseases of breast

Class here comprehensive works on diseases of breast [*formerly* 616.4], on gynecology and obstetrics

Class tumors, cancer of genital tract in 616.9

For diseases of male breast, see 616.4; obstetrics, 618.2

.2   Obstetrics

Diseases and complications of pregnancy [*formerly* 618.3], normal labor (parturition) [*formerly* 618.4], complicated labor [*formerly* 618.5], normal puerperium [*formerly* 618.6], puerperal diseases [*formerly* 618.7], obstetrical surgery [*formerly* 618.8], e.g., caesarian section

[.3]   Diseases and complications of pregnancy

Class in 618.2

[.4]   Normal labor (Parturition)

Class in 618.2

[.5]   Complicated labor

Class in 618.2

[.6]   Normal puerperium

Class in 618.2

[.7]   Puerperal diseases

Class in 618.2

[.8]   Obstetrical surgery

Class in 618.2

.9   Pediatrics and geriatrics

Pediatrics: diseases (including specific diseases) of infants and children up to puberty. Geriatrics: diseases (including specific diseases) of the aged

Do not use standard subdivisions; class in 618.9

Class orthodontics and pedodontics in 617.6, pediatric and geriatric surgery in 617

[.92–.97] Pediatrics and geriatrics

Numbers discontinued; class in 618.9

619   Experimental medicine

> Study of pathology and treatment of diseases induced in laboratory animals
>
> Class experimental study of specific diseases in 616–618

620   Engineering and allied operations

> Including systems engineering
>
> Use 620.01–620.09 for standard subdivisions
>
> Class a specific application with the technology involved, e.g., principles of aerial flight 629.132, air-conditioning engineering 697.9
>
> *For chemical engineering, see 660.2*

.1   Engineering mechanics (Applied mechanics) and materials

> Applied statics and dynamics of solids, liquids, gases; engineering materials
>
> Class here comprehensive works on fluid-power technology
>
> Class specific fluid-power technologies in 621.1–621.2

.2   Sound and related vibrations

> Applied acoustics, ultrasonics, subsonics
>
> Including noise and counter measures
>
> Class electroacoustical devices in 621.382–621.389, comprehensive works on mechanical vibration in 620.3

.3   Mechanical vibration

> *For sound and related vibrations, see 620.2*

.8   Environmental engineering (Biotechnology)

> Engineering for human comfort, convenience, efficiency, health, safety

621   Applied physics

> Mechanical, electrical, electronic, electromagnetic, heat, light, nuclear engineering
>
> Class applied mechanics in 620.1; applied acoustics in 620.2; a specific application with the subject, e.g., military engineering 623

▶

> 621.1–621.2 Fluid-power technologies
>
> Class comprehensive works in 620.1

.1   Steam engineering

> Engines, boilers, steam generation and transmission, boiler-house practices
>
> Class locomotives in 625.2, tractors and rollers in 629.22 [*all formerly* 621.1]

.2   **Hydraulic-power technology**

> Former heading: Power derived from liquids
>
> Examples: waterwheels, hydraulic pumps, rams

.3   **Electrical, electronic, electromagnetic engineering**

.31   **Generation, modification, storage, transmission of electric power**

> Including transformers, condensers
>
> Class here electrical machinery

.312   **Generation, modification, storage**

> Former heading: Central stations
>
> Including mechanical generation, e.g., steam-powered, hydroelectric; nonmechanical generation (direct-energy conversion); emergency generating units
>
> Class applied electrochemistry in 621.35, thermoelectricity in 621.39
>
> > *For generating machinery and converters, see 621.313; solar batteries and cells, 621.47; nuclear generation of electric power, 621.48*

.313   **Generating machinery and converters**

> Direct-current, alternating-current, synchronous, asynchronous machinery; details and parts of generators
>
> Class here comprehensive works on generators and motors
>
> > *For electric motors, see 621.46*

.319   **Transmission (Distribution)**

> Systems, e.g., alternating-current; lines and circuitry (networks); equipment and components, e.g., cables

.32   **Illumination and lighting**

> Example: flood lighting
>
> Including historic forms of lighting, e.g., torches, candles, oil-burning devices, gas lighting
>
> Class laser technology [*formerly* 621.32] in 621.36
>
> > *For public lighting, see 628.9*

.33   **Traction**

> Electric-power transmission for railroads
>
> Including electrification of railroads

.35   **Applied electrochemistry**

> Primary and storage batteries, fuel cells

.36   Applied optics (Engineering optics) and paraphotic engineering

Paraphotic engineering: infrared and ultraviolet technology

Including laser technology [*formerly* 621.32]; radiography, technological infrared photography [*both formerly* 778.3], applied spectroscopy (industrial and engineering spectroscopy)

Class manufacture of optical instruments in 681

For illumination and lighting, see 621.32; laser communication devices, 621.389

.37   Electrical testing and measurement

Meters, instruments, measurement of electric and nonelectric quantities by electrical means

.38   Electronic and communication engineering

Class here relay and space communication

.381   Electronic engineering

Including microwave electronics, e.g., masers; x- and gamma-ray electronics; microelectronics (miniaturization and micro-miniaturization), e.g., printed circuits, electronic eavesdropping devices ("bugging" equipment)

For laser technology, see 621.36

.381 5   Short- and long-wave electronics

Including electronic and vacuum tubes, semiconductors, circuits

[.381 7]   Microelectronics (Miniaturization and microminiaturization)

Number discontinued; class in 621.381

.381 9   Special developments

Including computers

▶   621.382–621.389 Communication engineering

Electrical, electronic, other

Class comprehensive works in 621.38

.382   Wire telegraphy

Including specific instruments and apparatus of wire telegraphy [*formerly* 621.383], codes, systems, printing and writing telegraphy

[.383]	Specific instruments and apparatus of wire telegraphy

              Class in 621.382

.384   Radio and radar engineering

.384 1   Radio

Wave propagation and transmission; circuits; components and apparatus, e.g., crystal and transistorized receiving sets; communication systems, e.g., short- and long-wave; stations, e.g., regional broadcasting and amateur (ham) stations, walkie-talkies; manufacture and servicing of receiving sets; special developments, e.g., telecontrol and space communication, loran

For radiotelegraphy, see 621.3842; radiotelephony, 621.3845

[.384 19]   Special developments

              Number discontinued; class in 621.3841

.384 2   Radiotelegraphy

Systems, stations, types

Including specific instruments and apparatus of radiotelegraphy [*formerly* 621.3843], radio-facsimile

[.384 3]   Specific instruments and apparatus of radiotelegraphy

              Class in 621.3842

.384 5   Radiotelephony

Systems, stations, types

Including specific instruments and apparatus of radiotelephony [*formerly* 621.3846], citizen's band radio

[.384 6]   Specific instruments and apparatus of radiotelephony

              Class in 621.3845

.384 8   Radar

Systems, stations, scanning patterns; specific instruments and apparatus; special developments, e.g., racon, shoran

.385   Wire telephony

Intercommunication systems; stations; manual and automatic switchboard and trunking systems, e.g., direct-distant-dialing systems; private exchanges

Including wire telephone terminal equipment [*formerly* 621.386], e.g., public pay telephones; wire telephone transmission and nonterminal equipment [*formerly* 621.387], e.g., switchboards, long-distance systems, lines

[.386]   Wire telephone terminal equipment

                Class in 621.385

[.387]   Wire telephone transmission and nonterminal equipment

                Class in 621.385

.388   Television

                Black-and-white and color

                Including fundamentals, e.g., circuits; components and apparatus, e.g., cameras; systems, e.g., satellite; stations

[.388 1–.388 6]   Fundamentals, components, apparatus, stations

                Numbers discontinued; class in 621.388

.388 8   Manufacturing and servicing of receiving sets

.388 9   Special developments

                Example: space communication

.389   Sound recording and reproducing systems and other communication devices

                Including public-address systems; language translators; underwater devices, e.g., sonar; laser communication devices

.39   Other branches of electrical engineering

                Including thermoelectricity, rural and household electrification, conduction and induction heating, superconductivity

                Class electrification of railroads in 621.33

.4   Heat engineering and prime movers

                Including air motors, wind engines

                Class here engines, power plants, propulsion technology, turbines

                For steam engineering, see 621.1; hydraulic-power technology, 621.2; low-temperature technology, 621.5

.43   Internal-combustion engines and propulsion technology

                Gas-turbine, spark-ignition, jet, rocket, diesel, semidiesel engines

.46   Electric propulsion technology

                Electric, ion, plasma motors

.47   Solar-energy engineering

                Solar engines, batteries, cells, furnaces

.48   Nuclear engineering

Fission and fusion technology, their by-products (radioactive isotopes), treatment and disposal of radioactive waste

Including generation of thermal and electric power, nuclear reactors and power plants, nuclear propulsion technology

.5   Pneumatic, vacuum, low-temperature technology

Including air compression, refrigeration, ice manufacture, cryogenic technology (technology of extremely low temperatures)

For fans, blowers, pumps, see 621.6

[.55]   Vacuum technology

Number discontinued; class in 621.5

.6   Fans, blowers, pumps

Class hydraulic pumps in 621.2

.7   Factory operations engineering

Shop and assembly-line technology, mechanization and automation of factory operations

Including machine-shop practice, packaging technology

Class containers made of a specific material with the subject, e.g., paper containers 676

For tools and fabricating equipment, see 621.9

.8   Machine engineering

Theory, design, construction, installation, maintenance, repairs, testing of machinery, mechanical systems, related mechanisms

Examples: pulleys, power shovels, conveyors, cranes, derricks, elevators

Including machine parts, e.g., bearings, springs, gears, valves, pistons; fasteners, e.g., screws, nuts, bolts, nails; friction and its elimination, e.g., lubrication

.9   Tools and fabricating equipment

Design, construction, maintenance, repair, operations of machine, pneumatic, hand tools

Examples: planers, grindstones, saws, lathes, drills, screwdrivers, hammers, molds, dies (punches and matrixes), clamps, measuring tools

Including fastening and joining equipment

[.97]   Fastening and joining equipment

Number discontinued; class in 621.9

622   **Mining engineering and related operations**

Prospecting, surface and subsurface mining; mine environment technology, e.g., ventilation; mine transport systems, ore dressing (ore processing), mine health and safety

623   **Military and nautical engineering**

Planning, structural analysis and design, construction, operations, maintenance, repairs

Including fortifications (forts and fortresses), demolition operations, defense engineering

.4   **Ordnance**

Artillery, small arms, ammunition; delivery devices, e.g., bombs, missiles

Including ballistics and gunnery [*both formerly* 623.5], primitive weapons, e.g., bows and arrows; side arms, e.g., swords; mines; laser, thermal, ultrasonic weapons; nuclear, chemical, biological devices; nonexplosive agents, e.g., tear gas

For combat vehicles, see 623.74

[.5]   **Ballistics and gunnery**

Class in 623.4

.6   **Military transportation technology**

Roads, railroads and their rolling stock, bridges, tunnels; naval, air, space facilities

For vehicles, see 623.74

.7   **Other operations of military engineering**

Including topography, communication technology, health and electrical engineering, camouflage, concealment

.74   **Vehicles**

Combat and support aircraft, e.g., balloons, helicopters, bombers, fighters; motor land vehicles, e.g., jeeps, tanks; air-cushion vehicles; spacecraft

Class warships in 623.82

.8   **Nautical engineering and seamanship**

Including shipyards

.82   **Nautical craft**

Design, construction, maintenance, repairs of sailing craft, submersible craft, small and medium power-driven craft, merchant ships, warships and other government vessels, hand-propelled and towed craft, their models

Including parts and details of nautical craft [*all formerly* 623.84–623.87]

[.84–.87]   **Parts and details of nautical craft**

Class in 623.82

.88   **Seamanship**

Art and science of handling nautical craft

Including knotting and splicing ropes and cables, · rescue operations, wreckage studies

Class here interdisciplinary works on knotting and splicing

Class a specific application of knotting and splicing with the subject, e.g., knotting in camping 796.54

For navigation, see 623.89

.89   **Navigation**

Selection and determination of course thru piloting, dead reckoning, use of lighthouses, electronic and other aids

For celestal navigation, see 527

624   **Civil engineering**

Planning, structural analysis and design, construction, maintenance, repairs of tunnels, foundations, other supporting structures, e.g., retaining walls

Class here structural theory

Class roofs [*formerly* 624] in 690

Class specific branches of civil engineering in 625–629, military construction engineering in 623

For buildings, see 690

.2   **Bridges**

Planning, structural analysis and design, construction, maintenance, repairs

625   Engineering of railroads and roads

Planning, analysis, design, construction, maintenance, repairs

Class military transportation engineering in 623.6, tunnel engineering in 624, bridge engineering in 624.2

.1   Railroads

Surveying, design, maintenance, repairs; roadbeds; track and accessories, e.g., signals; railroad yards; model railroads and trains

Including monorailroads

Class electrification of railroads in 621.33

For railroad rolling stock, see 625.2

.2   Railroad rolling stock

Running gear, work cars, passenger cars, freight cars, accessory equipment, locomotives

Including steam locomotives [*formerly* 621.1]

Class models in 625.1

.7   Roads

Surveying, design, earthwork, maintenance, repairs, roadside areas, traffic

Including soil roads; traffic control equipment, protective roadside barriers

Class curbs in 625.8

For artificial road surfaces, see 625.8

.8   Artificial road surfaces

Design, construction, materials

Including sidewalks; auxiliary pavements, e.g., curbs, driveways

Class maintenance and repairs in 625.7

627   Hydraulic engineering

Planning, analysis, design, construction, maintenance, repairs of inland waterways, harbors, ports, roadsteads, dams and reservoirs, other measures for flood control, land and water reclamation

Including navigation aids, radar and drilling platforms

Class here water resource engineering

Class water supply engineering in 628.1

.7   Underwater operations

Diving, dredging, blasting, drilling for construction, salvage, research, maintenance

Class here interdisciplinary works on diving

For diving sports, see 797.2

628   Sanitary and municipal engineering

Planning, analysis, design, construction, maintenance, repairs

Including sewerage and sewage, public sanitation, sanitary engineering for rural and sparsely-populated areas

Class military health engineering in 623.7

For plumbing, see 696

.1   Water supply

Sources, storage, conservation, collection and distribution systems, analysis, treatment, pollution

Class engineering of dams and reservoirs for water supply in 627

.5   Pollution and industrial sanitation engineering

For treatment of radioactive wastes, see 621.48; water pollution, 628.1

.9   Fire-fighting and fire safety technology, and other branches

Including fire extinction methods, public lighting, public extermination of insects and rodents

Class forest-fire technology in 634.9

For fireproofing, see 693.8

629   Other branches of engineering

Planning, analysis, design, construction, operations, maintenance, repairs

.04   Transportation engineering

Technology of vehicles and other transportation equipment, of trafficways and other transportation facilities

Including health and safety engineering, navigation

Class military transportation engineering in 623.6; inland waterways, harbors, ports, roadsteads in 627

For celestial navigation, see 527; nautical engineering and seamanship, 623.8; engineering of railroads and roads, 625

.1   Aerospace engineering

Engineering and operation of flight vehicles

Including portable flight vehicles (units intended to be carried by a single person, e.g., on the back)

For ground-effect machines, see 629.3; astronautics, 629.4

.13   Aeronautics

.132   Principles of aerial flight

Aerostatics, aerodynamics, navigation, piloting, flight guides, wreckage studies, command systems for guided aircraft

.133   Aircraft

Lighter-than-air and heavier-than-air aircraft, their models

Class components and general techniques of specific aircraft types in 629.134

.134   Aircraft components and general techniques

Analysis, design, construction, tests, measurements, standards, maintenance, repairs

Including comfort and safety equipment, e.g., parachutes

For aircraft instrumentation and systems, see 629.135

.135   Aircraft instrumentation and systems

Instruments for navigation, flight operations, power-plant monitoring; electrical, electronic, other equipment

.136   Airports

Including heliports

.2   Motor land vehicles, and cycles

Including design and construction of vehicles; design, construction, maintenance, repairs of parts of vehicles; non-surface motor land vehicles, e.g., ocean-floor vehicles; vehicles for extraterrestrial surfaces, e.g., moon cars

.22   Types of vehicles

Passenger automobiles, trucks, tractors, trailers, cycles, racing cars, their models

Including steam tractors and rollers [*formerly* 621.1], three-wheel vehicles

.28   Tests, operation, maintenance, repairs

Including driving, garages, service stations

[.282–.284]   Operation (Driving), tests and related topics

Numbers discontinued; class in 629.28

.3   Air-cushion vehicles (Ground-effect machines, Hovercraft)

.4   Astronautics

Techniques of space flight, engineering of spacecraft and related equipment

.41   Space flight

Astromechanics, entry problems, space environments affecting flight, weightlessness and countermeasures

For unmanned flight, see 629.43; manned flight, 629.45

[.42]   Propulsion systems

Class in 629.47

.43   Unmanned flight

Including flight of artificial satellites

Class application of satellite flight to a specific purpose with the subject, e.g., use of satellites in weather forecasting 551.6

.44   Auxiliary spacecraft

Space stations and laboratories

.45   Manned flight

Including selection and training of astronauts; circumterrestrial, lunar, planetary flights; rescue operations

.46   Engineering of unmanned spacecraft

Example: artificial satellites

257

.47   Astronautical engineering

Analysis, design, construction, maintenance, repairs of spacecraft and their components

Including propulsion systems [*formerly* 629.42], e.g., rockets; communication and life-support systems; terrestrial facilities, e.g., launching pads

Class here comprehensive works on spacecraft engineering

For auxiliary spacecraft, see 629.44; engineering of unmanned spacecraft, 629.46

.8   Automatic control engineering

Open-loop and closed-loop (feedback) systems

Including automatons, e.g., robots; computer control

630   Agriculture and related technologies

.1   Philosophy and theory

Including scientific principles [*formerly* 630.21–630.29]

Class agricultural sociology in 301.34, agricultural civilization in 901.9 [*both formerly* 630.1]

.2   Miscellany

Class here without further subdivision miscellany provided for in "Standard Subdivisions" notation 021–025 from Table 1

Class techniques, apparatus, equipment, materials [*all formerly* 630.2] in 631

[.21–.29]   Scientific principles

Class in 630.1

631   General agricultural techniques, apparatus, equipment, materials [*all formerly also* 630.2]

Former heading: Farming

Class application to specific crops, products, groups of crops or products in 633–638; control methods for plant injuries, diseases, pests in 632

.2   Agricultural structures

Description, maintenance, use and place in agriculture of farmhouses, barns, granaries, silos, grain elevators, machine and equipment sheds, fences, walls, hedges, roads, bridges, dams

For greenhouses, see 631.3

.3   Agricultural tools, machinery, equipment

> Description and maintenance
>
> Including machine-shop practice, greenhouses
>
> Class uses in a specific operation with the operation, e.g., use in harvesting 631.5

.4   Soil and soil conservation (Soil science)

> Soil physics, chemistry, biology; soil erosion and its control
>
> *For soil improvement, see 631.6–631.8*

[.409]   Historical and geographical treatment

> Do not use; class in 631.4

.5   Cultivation and harvesting

▶   631.6–631.8 Soil improvement

> Class comprehensive works in 631.4

.6   Soil reclamation and drainage

> *For irrigation, see 631.7*

.7   Irrigation and and water conservation

.8   Fertilizers and soil conditioners

632   Plant injuries, diseases, pests

> Control methods, causes, characteristics, effects on crops
>
> Class injuries, diseases, pests of specific crops and groups of crops in 633–635

▶   633–635 Production of specific crops

> Class comprehensive works in 631

633   Field crops

> Large-scale production of crops, other than fruit, intended for agricultural purposes and industrial processing
>
> Including cereal grains, legumes and other forage crops; fiber crops, e.g., cotton; sugar and starch plants; alkaloidal crops, e.g., coffee; other plants grown for industrial processing, e.g., spices, flavorings
>
> Class garden crops in 635

634   Orchards, fruits, nuts, forestry

> Class melons, tomatoes, peanuts in 635

.9   Forestry

> Formation, maintenance, cultivation, exploitation of forests
>
> Including logging operations, primary forest products, e.g., logs, barks; forest-fire technology
>
> Class here comprehensive works on lumbering
>
> Class production of lumber and lumber products in 674

635   Garden crops (Horticulture)

> Market (truck) and home gardening
>
> Including vegetables, aromatic and sweet herbs, mushrooms, truffles

[.1–.6]   Vegetables

> Numbers discontinued; class in 635

.9   Flowers and ornamental plants (Floriculture)

[.902 8]   Technique, apparatus, equipment, materials

> Do not use; class in 635.9

[.93–.97]   Taxonomic and other groupings

> Numbers and their subdivisions discontinued; class in 635.9

636   Animal husbandry

> Production, maintenance, training of livestock and other domestic animals
>
> Use 636.001–636.009 for standard subdivisions
>
> Class culture of nondomesticated animals not provided for here in 639

.08   Production, maintenance, training

> Class here selection, breeding; production for specific purposes, e.g., fur; training for specific purposes, e.g., for pets

.089   Veterinary sciences

> Veterinary anatomy, physiology, hygiene, public health, pharmacology, diseases, therapeutics

.1   Equines

> Including horses, asses, mules, zebras

.2   Ruminants

> Including bovines (cattle, zebus, bison, antelopes, water buffaloes, eland, bongos, kudus, gazelles, musk-oxen), cervine animals (deer, elk, moose, reindeer, caribous, giraffes, okapis), camels, llamas, alpacas, vicuñas

> *For sheep and goats, see 636.3*

.3   Sheep and goats

.4   Swine

.5   Poultry

> Including chickens, turkeys, ducks, geese, pigeons, guinea fowl, peafowl, pheasants

[.59]   Other poultry

> Number discontinued; class in 636.5

.6   Birds other than poultry

> Plumage, song, ornamental birds

> *For peafowl, see 636.5*

.7   Dogs

[.72–.76]   Specific breeds

> Numbers discontinued; class in 636.7

.8   Cats

> Including nondomestic cats, e.g., lions

[.9]   Other warm-blooded animals

> Number discontinued; class in 636

637   Dairy and related technologies

> Milk, butter, cheese, egg production; manufacture of frozen desserts, e.g., ice cream, sherbets

638   Insect culture

> Culture of honeybees (apiculture), silkworms, other insects; production of honey and beeswax

> Class silk production in 677

639   Nondomesticated animals and plants

> Hunting, trapping, fishing, whaling, sealing; culture of invertebrates and cold-blooded vertebrates; conservation practices for animals and plants

> Class insect culture in 638, hunting and fishing as sport in 799.1–799.2

640   Home economics

>   Care of household, family, person
>
>   Class here household finances, household employees
>
>   Class personal hygiene in 613, personnel management of household employees in 658.3

.7   Study and teaching

.73   Consumer education

>   Including guides to quality and value in products and services
>
>   Class consumer education on a specific kind of product or service with the subject, e.g., cameras 771.3

641   Food and drink

>   *For food and meal service, see 642*

.1   Applied nutrition

>   Nutrient constituents in foods in relation to body needs
>
>   Class nutritive values of specific foods and foodstuffs in 641.3

.2   Alcoholic beverages [*formerly* 641.3]

>   Class here interdisciplinary works on alcoholic beverages
>
>   Class a specific aspect with the subject, e.g., manufacture (commercial preparation) 663, ethics 178

.3   Foods and foodstuffs

>   Class here interdisciplinary works on production, manufacture, preservation, preparation, use
>
>   Class alcoholic beverages [*formerly* 641.3] in 641.2
>
>   Class production in 630, manufacture (commercial preparation and preservation) in 663–664, home preservation and preparation in 641.4–641.8, customs in 394.1, supply in 338.1

▶   641.4–641.8 Preservation and preparation

>   Class comprehensive works in 641.3

.4   Preservation

>   Preliminary treatment, canning, drying and dehydrating, cold storage, deep freezing, brining, pickling, smoking, use of additives

.5   Cookery

Preparation of food with and without use of heat

Including cookery for specific meals, time- and money-saving cookery; cookery for one or two persons, for persons of specific ages; diet cookery, cookery for religious situations and occasions; quantity, institutional, outdoor cookery; cookery with specific appliances, utensils, fuels; cookery characteristic of specific geographical environments

For cookery of and with specific materials, see 641.6; specific cookery processes and techniques, 641.7; composite dishes, 641.8

.509   Historical and geographical treatment

Class cookery characteristic of specific geographical environments in 641.5

[.59]   Cookery characteristic of specific geographical environments

Number discontinued; class in 641.5

.6   Cookery of and with specific materials

Example: cookery with rice

Class composite dishes featuring specific materials in 641.8

.7   Specific cookery processes and techniques

Baking, roasting, boiling, simmering, stewing, broiling, grilling, barbecuing, frying, sautéing, braising

Including preparation of cold dishes

Class specific processes applied to specific materials in 641.6, to composite dishes in 641.8

.8   Composite dishes

Appetizers, savories, relishes, hors d'oeuvres, soups, sauces, salad dressings, breads, casserole dishes, pasta dishes, stews, meat and cheese pies, salads, sandwiches, preserves, candies, desserts, beverages

Including bartenders' manuals and recipes

642   Food and meal service

For home and family; for camp, picnic, travel; for public and private entertaining; in public eating places and institutions; table service, furnishings, decorations

Including catering

643 The home and its equipment

Selection, purchase, rental, location, orientation, arrangement

Including improvement and remodeling by members of household

Class appliances and installations for a specific purpose with the purpose, e.g., sewing machines 646.2

For household utilities, see 644; household furnishings, 645

644 Household utilities

Description, selection, operation, care of systems, appliances, fittings, fixtures, accessories for heating, lighting, ventilation, air conditioning, water supply

645 Household furnishings

Description, selection, installation by members of household, use, care, repair of rugs, carpeting, linoleum, tiles, wallpaper, paint, hangings, curtains, draperies, shades, blinds, accessories, furniture

Class design and decorative treatment of interior furnishings in 747

646 Sewing, clothing, personal grooming

Including clothing selection

.01–.09 Standard subdivisions of clothing

Notations from Table 1

.2 Sewing and related operations

For clothing construction, see 646.4

.4 Clothing construction

Patternmaking, cutting, sewing, fitting, remodeling

For construction of headgear, see 646.5

.5 Construction of headgear

.6 Cleaning and dyeing clothing

For laundering, see 648

.7 Personal grooming

Cleanliness; care of hair, nails, skin, lips, eyes; reducing, slenderizing, body-building

Including professional hairdressing, use of wigs

647 Public households

Apartments, flats, apartment hotels, tenements; hotels, motels, inns, hostels, clubs; trailer camps; eating and drinking places; institutions

Including employees

648   Household sanitation

> Processes, equipment, supplies for laundering, ironing, housecleaning, control and eradication of pests, storage

649   Child rearing and home nursing

> Including feeding, clothing, physical care, supervised activities, training in manners and habits of children; moral, religious, character training

[.1–.7]   Child rearing

> Numbers discontinued; class in 649

.8   Home nursing

> Care of sick and infirm

650   Managerial services   Business services

> Including success in business

651   Office services

> Office organization, operations, personnel
>
> Class here equipment, supplies
>
> Class specific elements of office management in 658; a specific type of equipment with its use, e.g., duplicating equipment 686
>
> > *For accounting, see 657*

.028   Techniques, apparatus, equipment, materials

> Class data processing in 651.8

.5   Records management

> Filing systems and procedures; storage, microreproduction and computerization of files
>
> Including medical records management [*formerly* 362.1–362.4]
>
> > *For filing in library and information science, see 025.3*

.7   Communication   Creation and transmission of records

> Written communication (correspondence, reports, minutes); oral communication (including use of telephone); internal communication, e.g., pneumatic conveyor systems, intercom systems
>
> Including handling of mail, dictation, use of dictating equipment
>
> Class records management in 651.5, managerial communication in 658.4
>
> > *For processes of written communication, see 652*

.8   **Data processing**

> Use in carrying out office functions
>
> Including nonmechanized, mechanized, automatic, electronic data processing
>
> Class comprehensive works on data processing in 001.6

652   **Processes of written communication**

> Including penmanship, cryptography
>
> Class calligraphy in 745.6
>
> *For shorthand, see 653*

.3   **Typewriting**

> Basic keyboard mastery; speed and accuracy tests and drills; typing for specific uses, e.g., medical typewriting

[.8]   **Cryptography**

> Number discontinued; class in 652

653   **Shorthand**

> General principles, use in dictation, transcription, speed, accuracy with machine and handwritten systems
>
> Including abbreviated longhand systems; shorthand for specific uses, e.g., for court reporting

[655]   **Printing and related activities**

> Class book arts [*formerly* 655] in 686, printing [*formerly* 655.1–655.3] in 686.2, publishing [*formerly* 655.4–655.5] in 070.5, bookbinding [*formerly* 655.7] in 686.3

657   **Accounting**

[.2–.8]   **Specific elements of accounting**

> Numbers discontinued; class in 657

658 General management (General administration)

> The science and art of conducting organized enterprises, projects, activities
>
> Planning, organizing, financing, staffing, directing, coordinating, reporting, other functions common to all types of enterprises
>
> Class here management of enterprises of specific sizes and scopes, e.g., small business; management of enterprises of specific forms, e.g., corporations, professional organizations; use of data processing in management
>
> Class sociology of management in 301; principles of management in 658.4; management of manufacturing activities in 658.5–658.7, of marketing in 658.8; use of data processing in office services in 651.8
>
> Except for management of manufacturing and of marketing, class management of activities peculiar to a specific kind of enterprise with the subject, e.g., scheduling of classes in schools 371.2
>
> > *For public administration, see 350*

.1 Organization and finance

> Initiation of enterprises; forms of ownership organization, e.g., partnerships, corporations; financial administration, reorganization, mergers, consolidations
>
> Former heading: Management by control of structure
>
> > *For accounting, see 657; internal organization, 658.4; credit management, 658.8*

.2 Management of plants

> Management of buildings, grounds, equipment, facilities
>
> Including location, layout

.3 Personnel management

> Procedures for hiring, developing, utilizing the capacities of employees
>
> Class here personnel management in specific kinds of enterprises and occupations; supervision
>
> Class industrial relations in 331
>
> > *For management of executive personnel, see 658.4*

.31 Elements of personnel administration

> Education [*formerly also* 658.38] and training, recruitment, selection, days and hours of work, leaves of absence, performance rating, promotion, demotion, placement, motivation, employer-employee relations, grievances and appeals, collective bargaining, separation from service
>
> > *For wage and salary administration, see 658.32; personnel health, safety, welfare, 658.38*

.32   Wage and salary administration

> Payroll administration, wage and salary scales; incentive payments, e.g., piece work, bonuses; fringe benefits, e.g., pensions

[.37]   Personnel management in specific kinds of enterprises and occupations

> Number discontinued; class in 658.3

.38   Personnel health, safety, welfare

> Class education [*formerly* 658.38] in 658.31

.4   Principles of management   Executive management

> Principles: planning, organizing, directing, coordinating, reporting, communication

> Including internal organization of enterprises, decision making, systems analysis, operations research, project management, management of executive personnel, social responsibility of management, managerial success, communication, business intelligence and security

> Class a specific activity of executive management not provided for here with the subject, e.g., management of production 658.5

[.42–.43]   Specific levels of executive management

> Numbers discontinued; class in 658.4

.5   Management of production

> Planning, programing, scheduling, methods, routing, operations, control of product quality, packaging, waste control and utilization, research and development

> Including standardization of equipment, procedures, products; work measurement and simplification; time, motion, fatigue studies

> Class here interdisciplinary works on packaging

> Class factory operations engineering, packaging technology in 621.7; management of marketing, use of packaging in sales promotion, market research on new products in 658.8; packaging for shipment in 658.7; management of transportation activities in 380.5

.7   Management of materials (Materials control)

> Procurement, receiving, materials handling (internal transportation), storage, inventory control, shipment

> Including packaging for shipment, procurement of office equipment and supplies

.8   Management of distribution (Marketing)

Sales management, sales promotion, market research and analysis, wholesale and retail marketing, credit management

Including use of packaging in sales promotion; consumer research; markets, fairs, auctions, vending machines

Class here marketing of specific kinds of goods and services

For advertising, see 659.1

[.83]   Market research and analysis

Number discontinued; class in 658.8

.85   Personal selling (Salesmanship)

Including personal selling of specific kinds of goods and services [*formerly* 658.89], retail salesmanship

[.86–.87]   Wholesale and retail marketing

Numbers discontinued; class in 658.8

[.88]   Credit management

Number discontinued; class in 658.8

[.89]   Personal selling of specific kinds of goods and services

Class in 658.85

659   Advertising and public relations

.1   Advertising

Policies, goals, organization, campaigns

Including exhibitions and shows; window, showcase, wall, counter displays; contests and lotteries

Class here advertising specific kinds of organizations, products, services

[.11]   Organization

Number discontinued; class in 659.1

.13   Advertising in printed and related media

Copywriting, art, layout, typography, color

Including direct advertising, e.g., circulars, letters, catalogs; outdoor advertising, e.g., billboards, electric signs; moving displays, e.g., posters on exteriors of moving vehicles

.14   Advertising by broadcast media

Radio and television

[.15–.17]   Miscellaneous methods of advertising

Numbers discontinued; class in 659.1

.2   **Public relations**

> Planned and sustained effort to establish and maintain mutual understanding between an organization and its public

> Including publicity

> *For advertising, see* 659.1

660   **Chemical and related technologies**

> Including industrial biology

> Use 660.01–660.09 for standard subdivisions

>> *For pharmaceutical chemistry, see* 615; *elastomers and elastomer products,* 678

.2   **Chemical engineering**

> Including applied physical chemistry

661   **Technology of industrial chemicals (heavy chemicals)**

> Acids, bases, salts, hydrocarbons, other organic chemicals

> Including sensitometry [*formerly* 771], cellulose, coal tar, ammonia, petroleum derivatives; special-purpose chemicals, e.g., photographic chemicals

> Class carbons in 662, industrial gases and gaseous elements in 665

>> *For plaster of Paris, see* 666; *glycerin,* 668

662   **Technology of explosives, fuels, related products**

> Including fireworks, propellants, detonators, matches; coal, coke, charcoal; nonfuel carbons, e.g., graphite, carbon black

> Class petroleum and gaseous fuels in 665

663   **Beverage technology**

> Manufacture (commercial preparation and preservation), packaging of alcoholic and nonalcoholic beverages

> Including potable water

> Class household preparation of beverages in 641.8, comprehensive works on processing food and beverages in 664

>> *For milk, see* 637

664   **Food technology**

> Manufacture (commercial preparation and preservation), packaging of edible products for human and animal consumption

> Including flavoring aids, e.g., table salt

> Class here comprehensive works on processing food and beverages

>> *For dairy and related technologies, see* 637; *honey,* 638; *household preservation and preparation,* 641.4–641.8; *beverage technology,* 663

665   **Technology of industrial oils, fats, waxes, gases**

> Nonvolatile, saponifying, lubricating oils, fats, waxes of organic and mineral origin; natural, derived, manufactured gases
>
> Including petroleum and petroleum products
>
> Class beeswax in 638; a specific use with the subject, e.g., heating buildings with industrial gases 697
>
> *For petroleum derivatives, ammonia, see 661*

666   **Ceramic and allied technologies**

> Glass, enameling and enamels, pottery; refractory materials, e.g., asbestos; structural clay products, e.g., bricks; synthetic and artificial minerals and stones; masonry adhesives, e.g., plaster of Paris

667   **Cleaning, color and related technologies**

> Cleaning and bleaching of textiles, furs, feathers, leathers; dyes, pigments, dyeing and printing, inks, paints; varnishes and allied products, e.g., lackers; coating and coatings
>
> Including sign painting
>
> Class a specific application of coating and coatings with the subject, e.g., painting automobiles 629.2
>
> *For carbon black, see 662*

668   **Technology of other organic products**

> Including soaps, detergents, wetting agents, glycerin, glues, crude gelatin, gums, resins, sealants, perfumes, cosmetics, fertilizers, soil conditioners, pesticides
>
> Class food gelatins in 664

.4   **Plastics**

> Class plastic fibers and fabrics in 677

[.402 8]   Techniques, apparatus, equipment, materials

> Do not use; class in 668.4

669   **Metallurgy**

> Including metallography, physical and chemical analysis of metals, formation of alloys
>
> Class here interdisciplinary works on metals
>
> Class a specific aspect of metals with the subject, e.g., mineralogy 549; fabrication of metals and manufacture of primary products in 671–673

[.1–.9]   Specific metals and their alloys, metallurgical furnaces, physical and chemical metallurgy

> Numbers discontinued; class in 669

670   Manufactures

> Planning, design, fabrication of products
>
> Class the arts in 700, manufacture based on chemical technologies in 660, other engineering products in 620
>
> *For miscellaneous manufactures, see 680*

671   Metal manufactures

> Fabrication of metals and manufacture of primary products
>
> Including electroforming of metals
>
> *For manufactures of specific metals, see 672–673*

.2   Foundry practice (Hot-working operations)

> Foundry equipment, patternmaking and moldmaking, melting, molding, casting

.3   Mechanical working and forming of metals

> Cold-working operations, rolling, forging, pressing, stamping, extruding, drawing, machining, grinding, heat treatment, hardening, powder metallurgical processes

.5   Joining and cutting of metals

> Welding, cutting, soldering, brazing, riveting

.7   Finishing and surface treatment of metals

> Buffing, polishing, coating
>
> Including cleaning

.8   Primary products

> Examples: strips, sheets, tubes, pipes, wires, cordage, cables, powder metal

---

▶   672–673 Manufactures of specific metals

> Class comprehensive works in 671

672   Ferrous metals manufactures

> Iron, steel, iron and steel alloys
>
> Add to 672 the numbers following 671 in 671.2–671.8, e.g., welding 672.5

673   Nonferrous metals manufactures

674   **Lumber, wood, cork technologies**

Production of rough and finished lumber; of veneers, plywood, wood laminates; of containers, e.g., barrels, crates; of products from wood waste and residues, e.g., excelsior; of minor products, e.g., spools, toothpicks; of cork and cork products; storage, seasoning, grading of lumber

Including comprehensive works on wood products

For pulp and paper technology, see 676; wooden furniture, 684.1

675   **Leather and fur technologies**

Tanning, dressing, finishing of natural leather; manufacture of imitation leathers, processing of natural furs, manufacture of imitation furs

For leather and fur goods, see 685

676   **Pulp and paper technology**

Materials, machinery, manufacturing processes, properties, tests, recovery of waste products

Including products molded from pulp, e.g., pulpboards, fiberboards; paperboard containers; by-products, e.g., turpentine

677   **Textiles**

Production of fibers, manufacture of fabrics and cordage

Including flat goods, e.g., carpets, rugs, blankets; unaltered vegetable fibers, e.g., rush, bamboo

Class dyeing and printing of textiles in 667

678   **Elastomers and elastomer products**

Natural and synthetic rubber and latexes

Including tires, overshoes, heels, rubber bands, sheeting, hose

Class elastic fiber textiles in 677

679   **Other products of specific materials**

Including ivory and feather products, brooms, brushes, mops, cigars, cigarettes

Class products manufactured from waste materials [*formerly* 679] in 604.6

680   Miscellaneous manufactures

> Planning, design, fabrication of final products

681   Precision instruments and other devices

> Instruments for measuring time, other testing and measuring instruments; calculating, counting, sorting machines and instruments (including slide rules); optical instruments, e.g., lenses, spectacles, telescopes, photographic equipment; printing, writing, duplicating machines and equipment; other scientific and technological instruments and machinery; musical instruments (including mechanical musical instruments)

> Including ancient and primitive instruments for measuring time, e.g., sundials

> Class electronic computers in 621.3819, film and other photographic supplies in 661, hand construction of musical instruments in 786–789, wooden pencils in 674

682   Small forge work (Blacksmithing)

> Horseshoeing, production of hand-forged tools and ironwork

683   Hardware

> Locksmithing, gunsmithing, manufacture of household appliances

> Class military small arms in 623.4; refrigerators and freezers in 621.5; heating, ventilating, air-conditioning equipment in 697

684   Furnishings and home workshops

> Class here woodworking, metalworking

.01–.09   Standard subdivisions

> Use of 684.08–684.09 for woodworking and metalworking is discontinued; class in 684

.1   Furniture

> Indoor and outdoor furniture of wood, metal, other materials; upholstered furniture

.3   Fabric furnishings

> Draperies, hangings, slipcovers, curtains

> *For carpets and rugs, see 677*

[.7]   Nonmotor land vehicles

> Class in 688.6

685   **Leather and fur goods, and related manufactures**

Saddlery and harness making, leather and fur clothing and accessories, footwear and related products, gloves and mittens (leather, fur, textile, other), luggage; camping equipment, e.g., tents, sleeping bags

Including skates, snowshoes, skis, stilts; orthopedic shoes, crutches, artificial legs

Class overshoes in 678

686   **Printing and related activities**

Including invention of printing

Class here book arts [*formerly* 655]

Class book illustration in 741.64

.2   **Printing** [*formerly* 655.1–655.3]

Typefounding, typecasting, typefaces, typesetting by hand and machine; presswork (impression from type, plates, planographic surfaces, stencils, by photomechanical techniques, e.g., photolithography)

Including printing special graphic materials, e.g., braille, maps, music

.209   Historical and geographical treatment

Class invention of printing in 686

.3   **Bookbinding** [*formerly* 655.7]

.4   **Photoduplication (Photocopying)** [*formerly* 778.1]

Microphotography [*formerly* 778.3], blueprinting [*formerly* 772], electrostatic processes (electrophotography), production of photostats

Including xerography

687   **Clothing**

Patternmaking, cutting, dressmaking, tailoring

Including production of items auxiliary to clothing construction (notions), e.g., buttons, needles, thread

For leather and fur clothing, footwear, gloves and mittens, see 685

688   **Other final products**

Including models, costume jewelry; smokers' supplies, e.g., pipes; accessories for personal grooming, e.g., razors, combs

Class models of a specific object with the subject, e.g., airplane models 629.133

For brushes, see 679; cosmetics, 668

.6   **Nonmotor land vehicles** [*formerly* 684.7]

Carriages, wagons, carts, wheelbarrows

For cycles, see 629.22

.7   Recreational equipment

Toys, equipment for games and sports

Class recreational equipment made of leather and fur, recreational footwear and handwear, camping equipment in 685

690   Buildings

Planning, analysis, engineering design, construction, maintenance, repairs, destruction of habitable structures and their utilities

Class here specific structural elements, e.g., roofs [*formerly* 624]; safety engineering, specific types of buildings

Class forts and fortresses in 623, home repairs by members of household in 643, interdisciplinary works on design and construction in 721

.1   Philosophy and theory

.2   Miscellany

.21   Tabulated and related materials

Class specifications in 692

.22   Illustrations and models

Class plans and drawings in 692

.3–.9   Standard subdivisions

Notations from Table 1

Use of 690.5–690.8 for specific types of buildings is discontinued; class in 690

691   Building materials

Selection, preservation, construction properties

Including plastics and their laminates, adhesives and sealants, insulating materials

692   Auxiliary construction practices

Plans, drawings, specifications; estimates of materials, time, labor; contracting

693   Construction in specific materials and for specific purposes

For selection, preservation, construction properties of building materials, see 691; wood construction, 694

▶   693.1–693.7 Construction in specific materials

Class comprehensive works in 693

For construction in other materials, see 693.9

.1   Natural stones

.2 Stabilized earth materials

> Bricks, adobe, pisé, cob, tapia, tabby
>
> *For hollow bricks, see 693.4*

.3 Tiles and terra cotta

> *For hollow tiles, see 693.4*

.4 Artificial stones and hollow blocks

> Concrete blocks, cinder blocks, hollow tiles and bricks

.5 Concrete

> *For concrete blocks, see 693.4*

.6 Plaster-, stucco-, lathwork

.7 Metals

.8 Resistant construction

> Fireproofing, insulation, soundproofing; pest-, shock-, lightning-resistant construction; water- and moistureproof construction

.9 Construction in other materials

> Ice, snow, glass; nonrigid materials, e.g., pneumatic construction
>
> Including prefabricated materials, sandwich panels
>
> Class materials prefabricated in a specific substance with the subject, e.g., precast concrete 693.5; sandwich panels in a specific substance with the subject, e.g., wood 694

694 Wood construction   Carpentry

> Including rough and finish carpentry
>
> Class roofing in 695

[.2–.6] Rough and finish carpentry

> Numbers discontinued; class in 694

695 Roofing and auxiliary structures

> Materials, installation, maintenance, repairs
>
> Including gutters, drainpipes, flashings

696 Utilities

> Design, installation, maintenance, repairs
>
> Including plumbing, pipe fitting, steam and gas fitting
>
> *For electrical engineering, see 621.3; heating, ventilating, air-conditioning engineering, 697*

697   Heating, ventilating, air-conditioning engineering

> Design, installation, maintenance, repair of systems, components, equipment
>
> Including local and central heating; heating with specific sources of energy, e.g., coal, solar and nuclear energy

[.1–.8]   Specific kinds of heating and heating equipment

> Numbers discontinued; class in 697

.9   Ventilation and air conditioning

698   Detail finishing

.1   Painting

> Exteriors, interiors
>
> Class sign painting in 667
>
> *For painting woodwork, see 698.3*

.2   Calcimining and whitewashing

.3   Finishing woodwork

> By staining, polishing, varnishing, lackering, painting

.5   Glazing and leading windows

.6   Paperhanging

.9   Floor coverings

> Measuring, cutting, laying rugs, carpeting, linoleum, tiles

700   The arts   Fine and decorative arts

Description, critical appraisal, techniques, apparatus, equipment, materials of the fine, decorative, literary, performing, recreational arts

For literature, see 800; book arts, 686

► ### 701–709 Generalities

Standard subdivisions and their extended meanings

Class comprehensive works in 700, generalities of individual artists in 709.2

701   Philosophy and theory

Including appreciative aspects (psychology, esthetics; theory, technique, history of criticism and appreciation); inherent features (composition, color, form, style, perspective, decorative values)

Class works of critical appraisal in 709

[.1–.9]   Specific aspects

Class techniques [*formerly* 701.8] in 702.8
Use of these numbers and their subdivisions for nature, character, research methodology is discontinued; class in 701

702   Miscellany

.8   Techniques [*formerly* 701.8], apparatus, equipment, materials

Including use of models

703   Dictionaries, encyclopedias, concordances

704   General special aspects

Including persons occupied with art

Class art dealers in 706, artists not limited by form in 709.2

.9   Iconography and collections of writings

.94   Iconography

Development, description, critical appraisal, collections of works

Including human figures and their parts, nature, still life, architectural subjects, abstractions, symbolism and allegory, mythology and legend

[.945–.947]   Abstractions, mythology, legend

Numbers discontinued; class in 704.94

.948   Religion and religious symbolism

> Class significance and purpose of art in religious worship in 246, 291.3, 292–299

705   Serial publications

706   Organizations

707   Study and teaching

[.4]   **Museums and exhibits**

> Do not use; class in 708

708   Galleries, museums, private collections, exhibits

> Including guidebooks and catalogs of specific collections
>
> Class art museum economy [*formerly* 708] in 069
>
> Class collections of writings in 704.9

[.1–.9]   **Geographical treatment**

> Numbers and their subdivisions discontinued; class in 708

709   Historical and geographical treatment

> Development, description, critical appraisal, collections of works

---

▶   709.01–709.04 Periods of development

> Class here schools and styles not limited by country or locality
>
> Class comprehensive works in 709

.01   Primitive peoples, and ancient times to 500 A.D.

.02   500–1500

> Class here early Christian, Byzantine, Romanesque, Gothic, Renaissance art
>
> Class Christian, Byzantine, Renaissance art of any other period with the period, e.g., earliest Christian art 709.01

.03   Modern period, 1500–

> Class here baroque, rococo, classical revival, romantic art
>
> *For 20th century, 1900–*   , *see* 709.04

.04   20th century, 1900–

> Class here modern art
>
> Class modern art of 19th century in 709.03

.1–.9   Geographical treatment

> Add "Areas" notation 1–9 from Table 2 to base number 709
>
> Class art of primitive peoples regardless of place in 709.01

710   **Civic and landscape art**

711   Area planning (Civic art)

> Design of physical environment for public welfare, convenience, pleasure on international, national, regional, local level
>
> Including social and economic factors affecting planning
>
> > *For landscape design, see 712*

712   Landscape design (Landscape architecture)

> Landscaping public, private, semiprivate, institutional parks and grounds
>
> > *For specific elements in landscape design, see 714–717; trafficways, 713; cemeteries, 718; natural landscapes, 719*

713   Landscape design of trafficways

▶   **714–717 Specific elements in landscape design**

> Class comprehensive works in 712

714   Water features

> Natural and artificial pools, fountains, cascades, streams

715   Woody plants

> Nonflowering and flowering trees, shrubs, vines
>
> Including topiary work
>
> Class comprehensive works on flowering plants in 716

716   Herbaceous plants

> Nonflowering and flowering
>
> Including ground cover
>
> Class here comprehensive works on flowering plants in landscape design
>
> > *For woody flowering plants, see 715*

717   Structures

> Relationship of buildings, terraces, fences, gates, steps, ornamental accessories to other elements of landscape design

718   Landscape design of cemeteries

719   Natural landscapes

> Including public parks and natural monuments, wildlife reserves, forest and water-supply reserves

720   Architecture

.28   Techniques, apparatus, equipment, materials

Including architectural drawing [*formerly* 744.4]

.9   Historical and geographical treatment

Class historical periods in 722–724

.91   Treatment by areas, regions, places in general

Add "Areas" notation 1 from Table 2 to base number 720.9, e.g., architecture in tropics 720.913

.92   Architects

Description and critical appraisal of work regardless of school or style

[.93]   In the ancient world

Do not use; class in 722

.94–.99   Treatment by continent, country, locality in modern world

Add "Areas" notation 4–9 from Table 2 to base number 720.9

Class Oriental schools and styles in 722 (not 720.95)

721   Architectural construction

Interdisciplinary works on design and construction of structures of specific shapes and materials; of structural elements, e.g., foundations, walls, columns, arches, roofs, floors, ceilings, doors, windows, stairs

Class architectural construction of specific types of structures in 725–728, structural engineering in 624

For engineering design and construction, see 690; design and decoration, 729

▶   722–724 Architectural schools and styles

Class comprehensive works, medieval and modern Western schools and styles limited to a specific country or locality in 720.9; architects of specific schools and styles not limited to a specific type of structure in 720.92; details of construction of specific schools and styles in 721; design and decoration of structures of specific schools and styles in 729; specific types of structures regardless of school or style in 725–728

722   Ancient and Oriental architecture

Ancient regardless of place, Oriental regardless of period

For Saracenic, see 723

723   Medieval architecture, ca. 300–1400

Early Christian, Byzantine, Saracenic (Muslim, Moorish, Mudejar),
Romanesque, Norman, Gothic architectures, not limited by
country or locality

724   Modern architecture, 1400–

Not limited by country or locality

Including Renaissance, Elizabethan, Jacobean, Queen Anne, Georgian,
colonial, baroque, rococo, Churrigueresque, classical revival, Gothic
revival, neoclassical, Romanesque revival architectures; eclecticism

.9   20th century

Including international style, functionalism

725–728 Specific types of structures

Development of architectural schools and styles, design, interdisciplinary works on design and construction

Class here specific structures

Class comprehensive works in 720, engineering design and construction of specific types of habitable structures in 690, structural
engineering in 624

725   Public structures

Not used primarily for religious, educational, research, residential
purposes

Government, military, commercial, transportation, storage, industrial,
welfare, health, recreational, prison, reformatory, exhibition, memorial
buildings; arches, gateways, walls, towers, bridges, tunnels, moats

Class memorial buildings for a specific purpose with the subject,
e.g., memorial library buildings 727

726   Buildings for religious purposes

Temples, shrines, mosques, minarets, synagogues, parish houses, baptis-
tries, churches, cathedrals, Sunday school buildings, monastic buildings,
mortuary chapels, tombs, parsonages, missions

727   Buildings for educational and research purposes

School, university, college, laboratory, botanical and zoological garden,
observatory, library, museum, art gallery, community center, learned
society buildings

728   **Residential buildings (Domestic architecture)**

Structures designed for permanent and temporary homes

Including low-cost housing, club houses, vacation cabins, houseboats, house trailers, gatehouses, farm buildings other than houses, domestic garages and conservatories

Class official residence buildings in 725, parsonages and episcopal palaces in 726, college dormitory buildings in 727

.3   **Urban types**

Row and duplex houses, separate houses of two or more stories, tenements, flats, apartments, apartment hotels

.5   **Hotels and motels**

For apartment hotels, see 728.3

.6   **Suburban and rural types**

Cottages, bungalows, ranch and split-level houses, farmhouses, solar houses

.8   **Large and elaborate private dwellings**

Castles, palaces, chateaux, mansions, manor houses, villas

729   **Design and decoration of structures and accessories**

Design in vertical and horizontal planes; design and decoration of structural elements, e.g., walls, columns, arches, roofs, floors, ceilings, doors, windows, stairs; decoration in specific mediums; built-in ecclesiastical furniture

Class design and decoration of specific types of structures in 725–728, interior decoration in 747

730   **Plastic arts   Sculpture**

.1   **Philosophy and theory**

Including appreciative aspects (psychology, esthetics; theory, technique, history of criticism and appreciation); inherent features (composition [*formerly* 731], color, form, style, decorative values)

Class works of critical appraisal in 730.9

.2   **Miscellany**

[.28]   **Techniques, apparatus, equipment, materials**

Do not use; class in 731

.9   Historical and geographical treatment

Class sculpture of primitive peoples regardless of time or place in 732, historical periods in 732–735

.91   Treatment by areas, regions, places in general

Add "Areas" notation 1 from Table 2 to base number 730.9, e.g., sculpture of Southern Hemisphere 730.9181

.92   Sculptors

Description and critical appraisal of work, collections of works regardless of process, representation, style, period, place

[.93]   In the ancient world

Do not use; class in 732–733

.94–.99   Treatment by continent, country, locality in modern world

Add "Areas" notation 4–9 from Table 2 to base number 730.9

Class Oriental schools and styles in 732 (not 730.95)

►   # 731–735 Sculpture

Fine art of producing figures and designs in relief or the round by fashioning in plastic and rigid materials

Class comprehensive works in 730

731   Processes and representations of sculpture

Including materials; universal styles, e.g., idealistic, naturalistic, realistic, grotesque; sculpture in relief, in the round; mobiles and stabiles; iconography

Class composition [*formerly* 731] in 730.1

Class processes and representations of individual sculptors in 730.92; processes and representations used in specific periods and by specific schools in 732–735

.3   Apparatus and equipment

Tools, machines, accessories

Class techniques employing specific apparatus and equipment in 731.4

.4   Techniques

Modeling, molding, casting, carving, firing and baking, restoration

[.5–.8]   Representations

Numbers discontinued; class in 731

► ## 732–735 Schools and styles of sculpture

Class comprehensive works, medieval and modern Western schools and styles limited to a specific country or locality in 730.9; sculptors of specific schools and styles in 730.92

For universal styles, see 731

732 Primitive, ancient, Oriental sculpture

Ancient regardless of place, Oriental regardless of period

For Greek, Etruscan, Roman sculpture, see 733

733 Greek, Etruscan, Roman sculpture

734 Medieval sculpture, ca. 500–1400

Early Christian, Byzantine, Romanesque, Gothic styles not limited by country or locality

735 Modern sculpture, 1400–

Not limited by country or locality

Including Renaissance, baroque, classical revival, romantic styles; abstractionism, geometric design, nonobjectivity

► ## 736–739 Other plastic arts

Processes and products

Class comprehensive works in 730, fine art of sculpture in 731–735, other plastic arts not provided for here in 745–749

736 Carving and carvings

In wood, stone, ivory, soap, other materials

Including paper cutting and folding, precious and semiprecious stones (glyptics), cameos, ornamental fans

737 Numismatics and sigillography

Including seals, stamps, signets, medals, talismans, amulets, counters, tokens

For paper money, see 769

.4 Coins

Including counterfeit coins

[.49] Of specific countries

Number discontinued; class in 737.4

738   Ceramic arts

For glass, see 748

[.028]   Techniques, apparatus, equipment, materials

Do not use; class in 738.1

.1   Techniques, apparatus, equipment, materials

Class techniques used in making specialized products in 738.4–738.8

▶

738.2–738.8 Products

Development, description, critical appraisal, collections of works

Class comprehensive works in 738

▶

738.2–738.3 Pottery

Class comprehensive works in 738; techniques, apparatus, equipment, materials in 738.1

.2   Porcelain (China)

.3   Earthenware and stoneware

▶

738.4–738.8 Specialized products and the techniques of making them

Class comprehensive works in 738

.4   Enameling and enamels

Including cloisonné

For jewelry, see 739.27

.5   Mosaic ornaments

.6   Ornamental bricks and tiles

.8   Other products

Lighting fixtures, candlesticks, stoves, braziers, figurines

739   Art metalwork

> Decorative metallic forms and their creation
>
> Including techniques, apparatus, equipment, materials for work in iron, copper, bronze, brass, tin, pewter, other base metals
>
> Class here decorative treatment
>
> *For numismatics, see 737*

.2   Work in precious metals

> Goldsmithing, silversmithing, platinumwork
> Class watch- and clockcases in precious metals in 739.3

.27   Jewelry

> *For mosaic ornaments, see 738.5; precious and semiprecious stones, 736*

.3   Watch- and clockcases

.7   Arms and armor

740   **Drawing, and decorative and minor arts**

[.1–.9]   Standard subdivisions of drawing and drawings

> Class in 741.01–741.09

741   Drawing and drawings

> Class calligraphy, artistic lettering [*both formerly 741*] in 745.6
>
> *For drawing and drawings by subject, see 743*

► 741.01–741.09 Generalities

> Standard subdivisions [*formerly also 740.1–740.9*] and their extended meanings
>
> Class comprehensive works in 741, generalities of individual artists in 741.092

.01   Philosophy and theory

> Including appreciative aspects (psychology, esthetics; theory, technique, history of criticism and appreciation); inherent features (composition [*formerly 741.4*], color, form, style, decorative values)
>
> Class works of critical appraisal in 741.09, perspective in 742

.02   Miscellany

[.028]   Techniques, apparatus, equipment, materials

> Do not use; class in 741.2

.03–.08	Standard subdivisions

> Notations from Table 1

.09	Historical and geographical treatment

> Class collections of drawings regardless of period or place in 741.9

.091	Treatment by areas, regions, places in general

> Add "Areas" notation 1 from Table 2 to base number 741.09,
> e.g., drawing in Communist countries 741.09171

.092	Artists

> Description and critical appraisal of work regardless of
> medium, process, application, subject, period, place

.093–.099	Treatment by continent, country, locality

> Add "Areas" notation 3–9 from Table 2 to base number 741.09

.2	Techniques [*formerly also* 741.4], apparatus, equipment, materials

> Charcoal, chalk, crayon, pencil, silverpoint, ink with pen or brush,
> scratchboard, airbrush drawing
>
> Class techniques, apparatus, equipment, materials used in special
> applications in 741.5–741.7; used in drawing specific subjects
> in 743; used by individual artists in 741.092
>
> *For perspective, see 742*

[.4]	Drawing processes

> Class composition in 741.01, techniques in 741.2

741.5–741.7 Special applications

Techniques, apparatus, equipment, materials, description, critical
appraisal, collections

Class comprehensive works in 741, description and critical appraisal
of individual artists regardless of application in 741.092

.5	Cartoons, caricatures, comics

> Including animated cartoons, cartoons with subordinate text
>
> Class cartoon films in 791.43

[.59]	Collections

> Number and its subdivisions discontinued; class in 741.5

.6	Illustration (Commercial art)

> Including match covers and labels

.64	Books and book jackets

> Class illumination of manuscripts and books in 745.6

.65	Magazines and newspapers
.67	Advertisements and posters

            Including fashion drawing

.68	Calendars, greeting and postal cards
.7	Silhouettes
.9	Collections of drawings

            Regardless of medium, process, period, place

            Class collections devoted to special applications in 741.5–741.7, to specific subjects in 743

742   Perspective

            Theory, principles, methods

            Class perspective in drawing specific subjects in 743, in special applications in 741.5–741.7

743   Drawing and drawings by subject

            Class individual artists regardless of subject in 741.092

            For fashion drawing, see 741.67

[744]   Technical drawing

            Class in 604.2

[.4]   Architectural and map drawing

            Class architectural drawing in 720.28, map drawing in 526.8

745   Decorative and minor arts

            Class here folk art

            Class interior decoration in 747, other decorative and minor arts in 736–739

.1	Antiques

            Class a specific kind of antique with the subject, e.g., brasses 739

.2	Industrial art and design

            Creative design of mass-produced commodities

.4	Pure and applied design and decoration

            Class design in a specific art form with the form, e.g., design in architecture 729

            For industrial design, see 745.2

[.409]	Historical and geographical treatment

            Do not use; class in 745.4

.5 Handicrafts

    Creative work done by hand with aid of simple tools or machines

    For decorative coloring, see 745.7; floral arts, 745.92

      745.51–745.57 In specific materials

   Class comprehensive works in 745.5, textile handicrafts in 746, glass handicrafts in 748

.51   In woods

    Examples: marquetry, inlay trim, ornamental woodwork

    For ornamental woodwork in furniture, see 749

.53   In leathers and furs

.54   In papers

    Examples: gift wrapping, use of end papers and wallpapers

    Class paper cutting and folding in 736

.55   In shells

.56   In metals

    Including wire

.57   In rubber and plastics

.59   Making specific objects

    Including handicrafts in composite materials, e.g., decorations for special occasions, artificial flowers, lampshades, candlesticks, toys

    Class arrangement of artificial flowers in 745.92

.6   Lettering, illumination, heraldic design

    Including calligraphy (elegant handwriting), artistic lettering [*both formerly* 741]

    Class development, description, critical appraisal of manuscripts in 091, of illustrated books in 096

.7   Decorative coloring

    Painting, lackering, japanning, stenciling, decalcomania, tolecraft

    For printing, painting, dyeing textiles, see 746.6

.8 Panoramas, cycloramas, dioramas

.9 Other decorative arts

.92   Floral arts

    Including flower arrangement: selection and arrangement of plant materials and appropriate accessories

746   Textile arts and handicrafts

Observe the following table of precedence, e.g., embroidering tapestry 746.3

     Products
        Laces and related fabrics
        Pictures, hangings, tapestries
        Rugs and carpets
        Other textile products
     Processes
        Spinning and weaving
        Needle- and handwork
        Beadwork
        Printing, painting, dyeing

.1   Spinning and weaving

For weaving unaltered vegetable fibers, see 746.4

.2   Laces and related fabrics

Needlepoint, bobbin, darned laces; passementerie

.3   Pictures, hangings, tapestries

[.309]   Historical and geographical treatment

Do not use; class in 746.3

.4   Needle- and handwork

Weaving, braiding, matting unaltered vegetable fibers, e.g., raffiawork, rushwork; knitting, crocheting, tatting, embroidery, patchwork, quilting

Including smocking, appliqué, couching, cutwork, needlepoint, crewelwork, drawn work, hardanger

.5   Beadwork

.6   Printing, painting, dyeing

Block and silk-screen printing, resist-dyeing, hand decoration, stenciling, batik

.7   Rugs and carpets

[.709]   Historical and geographical treatment

Do not use; class in 746.7

.9   Other textile products

Costume (including fashion design); interior furnishings (e.g., draperies, furniture covers, table linens, bedclothing, towels and toweling)

747   Interior decoration

> Design and decorative treatment of interior furnishings
>
> Including decoration of specific elements, e.g., ceilings, walls, doors, windows, floors; draperies, upholstery, carpets; decoration of specific rooms, for specific occasions
>
> > *For textile arts and handicrafts, see 746; furniture and accessories, 749*

[.09]   Historical and geographical treatment

> Do not use; class in 747

[.2]   Historical and geographical treatment

> Number and its subdivisions discontinued; class in 747

748   Glass

> Including methods of decoration, specific articles other than glassware

.2   Glassware

> Blown, pressed, molded, cast, decorated products other than stained glass

[.209]   Historical and geographical treatment

> Do not use; class in 748.2

.5   Stained, painted, leaded, mosaic glass

[.509]   Historical and geographical treatment

> Do not use; class in 748.5

749   Furniture and accessories

> Including built-in furniture, ornamental woodwork, heating and lighting fixtures, picture frames and shadow boxes
>
> > *For upholstery, see 747*

[.09]   Historical and geographical treatment

> Do not use; class in 749.2

.2   Historical and geographical treatment

> Class here antiques and reproductions, artists

[.201–.204]   Historical treatment

> Numbers discontinued; class in 749.2

[.21–.29]   Geographical treatment

> Numbers discontinued; class in 749.2

750   Painting and paintings

> Class painting in a specific decorative art with the subject, e.g., illumination of manuscripts and books 745.6

.1   Philosophy and theory

> Including appreciative aspects (psychology, esthetics; theory, technique, history of criticism and appreciation); inherent features (composition, form, style, perspective, decorative values)
>
> Class works of critical appraisal in 759, color in 752

.2   Miscellany

[.28]   Techniques, apparatus, equipment, materials

> Do not use; class in 751.2–751.6

[.9]   Historical and geographical treatment

> Do not use; class in 759

751   Processes and forms

> Class processes and forms of individual painters in 759.1–759.9

▶   751.2–751.6 Techniques, apparatus, equipment, materials

> Class comprehensive works in 751, color in 752

.2   Materials

> Surfaces, pigments, mediums, fixatives, coatings
>
> Class use of materials in specific techniques in 751.4

.3   Apparatus and equipment

> Models, tools, accessories
>
> Class use of apparatus and equipment in specific techniques in 751.4

.4   Techniques

> Painting with specific mediums
>
> Including collage, airbrush painting

.5   Reproduction and copying

> Including forgeries, alterations, expertizing, determination of authenticity
>
> *For print making and prints, see 760*

.6   Care, preservation, restoration

.7   Specific forms

Examples: easel paintings, murals, panoramas, theatrical scenery, miniatures

Class subjects in specific forms in 753–758; techniques, apparatus, equipment, materials employed in specific forms in 751.2–751.6

752   Color

753–758 Specific subjects (Iconography)

Development, description, critical appraisal, collections of works regardless of form

Class comprehensive works in 750; techniques, apparatus, equipment, materials regardless of subject in 751.2–751.6; individual painters regardless of subject in 759.1–759.9

753   Abstractions, symbolism, allegory, mythology, legend

For *religious symbolism, see* 755

754   Subjects of everyday life (Genre paintings)

755   Religion and religious symbolism

For *mythology, see* 753

756   Historical events

Examples: battles, coronations, disasters

757   Human figures and their parts

Not provided for in 753–756, 758

Class here portraits

758   Other subjects

Landscapes, still life, marine scenes, animal and plant life; industrial, technical, architectural subjects

759   Historical and geographical treatment

Development, description, critical appraisal, collections of works

759.01–759.06 Periods of development

Class here schools and styles not limited by country or locality

Class comprehensive works in 759

.01   Primitive peoples, and ancient times to 500 A.D.

.02   500–1400

     Including Romanesque, Gothic painting

     Class here early Christian, Byzantine painting

     Class Christian, Byzantine painting before 500 in 759.01

.03   1400–1600

     Class here Renaissance painting

     Class Renaissance painting before 1400 in 759.02

.04   1600–1800

     Including baroque, rococo painting

.05   19th century, 1800–1900

     Including classical revival, romanticism, naturalism, impressionism, luminism, pleinairism, neo-impressionism, pointillism, divisionism, postimpressionism

.06   20th century, 1900–

     Including expressionism, abstraction, nonobjective painting, cubism, Dadaism, surrealism, fauvism, futurism, intimism, neoplasticism

     Class here modern painting

     For 19th century, 1800–1900, see 759.05

759.1–759.9 Geographical treatment

Class here individual painters regardless of process, form, subject

Class comprehensive works in 759, paintings of primitive peoples regardless of place in 759.01

.1   North America

     Class painting and paintings of Middle America in 759.972

.11   Canada

.13   United States

     Including individual painters

     Class painting and paintings of specific states in 759.14–759.19

.14–.19   Specific states of United States

     Add to 759.1 the numbers following 7 in "Areas" notation 74–79 from Table 2, e.g., painting and paintings of California 759.194

     Class individual painters in 759.13, painting and paintings of Hawaii in 759.9969

.2–.8   Modern European countries

> Add to 759 the numbers following 4 in "Areas" notation 42–48 from Table 2, e.g., painting and paintings of France 759.4
>
> Class comprehensive works, painting and paintings of countries not provided for in "Areas" notation 42–48 in 759.94

.9   Other geographical areas

> Add "Areas" notation 1, 3–9 from Table 2 to base number 759.9, e.g., painting and paintings in Netherlands 759.9492, in Iran (Persia) 759.955, in Western Hemisphere 759.9181, Etruscan painting and paintings 759.937
>
> Do not use 759.92; class individual painters by country, e.g., Matisse 759.4

760   **Graphic arts   Print making and prints**

> Use 760.01–760.09 for standard subdivisions of graphic arts
>
> *For drawing and drawings, see 741; painting and paintings, 750; photography and photographs, 770; printing, 686.2*

▶   760.1–760.8 Generalities of print making and prints

> Standard subdivisions and their extended meanings
>
> Class comprehensive works in 760, generalities of individual print makers in 769

.1   Philosophy and theory of print making and prints

> Including appreciative aspects (psychology, esthetics; theory, technique, history of criticism and appreciation); inherent features (composition, color, form, style, perspective, decorative values)
>
> Class works of critical appraisal in 769

.2   Miscellany of print making and prints

[.28]   Techniques, apparatus, equipment, materials

> Do not use; class in 761–767

.3–.8   Standard subdivisions of print making and prints

> Notations from Table 1

[.9]   Historical and geographical treatment of print making and prints

> Do not use; class in 769

▶ ## 761–769 Print making and prints

Class comprehensive works in 760, commercial art in 741.6

▶ ## 761–767 Print making

Fine art of executing a printing block or plate representing a picture or design conceived by the print maker or copied from another artist's painting or drawing or from a photograph

Techniques, apparatus, equipment, materials

Class comprehensive works in 760; preservation in 769; techniques, apparatus, equipment, materials employed by individual print makers in 769

761   **Relief processes (Block printing)**

Printing from raised surfaces, e.g., wood, metal, linoleum blocks

763   **Lithographic (Planographic) processes**

Printing from flat surfaces, e.g., stone, aluminum, zinc

For chromolithography, see 764

764   **Serigraphy (Silk-screen printing) and chromolithography**

▶ ## 765–767 Intaglio processes

Printing from incised surfaces

Class comprehensive works in 765

765   **Metal engraving**

Including line, stipple, criblé engraving

Class here comprehensive works on metal relief and metal intaglio processes, on intaglio processes

For relief processes, see 761; mezzotinting and aquatinting, 766; etching and drypoint, 767

766   **Mezzotinting, aquatinting, related processes**

Including composite processes

767   **Etching and drypoint**

769   Prints

Description, critical appraisal, collections regardless of process

Including postage stamps (philately), paper money, other special forms; collecting, care, preservation

Class here print makers

[.09]   Historical and geographical treatment

Do not use; class in 769

770   **Photography and photographs**

.1   Philosophy and theory

Including inherent features (composition, color, form, style, perspective, decorative values)

.2   Miscellany

.28   Techniques

Camera use; preparation and preservation of negatives, positives, transparencies; reversing negatives, recovery of waste materials

Class apparatus, equipment, materials in 771

[.282–.284]   Specific techniques

Numbers discontinued; class in 770.28

771   Apparatus, equipment, materials

Including studios, laboratories, darkrooms, furniture, fittings, developing and printing apparatus, chemical materials

Class here interdisciplinary works on use and manufacture

Class sensitometry [*formerly* 771] in 661

Class apparatus, equipment, materials used in special processes in 772–774; in specific fields of photography in 778; manufacture of a specific kind of apparatus, equipment, materials with the subject, e.g., of cameras 681

.3   Cameras and accessories

––––––––––––

▶   772–774 Special processes

Techniques, apparatus, equipment, materials

Class comprehensive works in 770

For processing techniques in color photography, see 778.6; photomechanical printing techniques, 686.2

772   Metallic salt processes

Direct positive and printing-out, platinotype processes

Class blueprinting [*formerly* 772] in 686.4

773   Pigment processes of printing

Carbon, carbro, powder (dusting-on), imbibition, gum-bichromate, diazotype, photoceramic, photoenamel, oil processes

774   Holography

Photography by use of interference patterns produced by coherent light waves

778   Specific fields of photography

Techniques, apparatus, equipment, materials

Class here interdisciplinary works on use and manufacture of apparatus, equipment, materials

Class manufacture of a specific kind of apparatus, equipment, materials with the subject, e.g., of cameras 681

[.1]   Photoduplication (Photocopying)

Class in 686.4

.2   Photographic projection

Including filmstrips, filmslides

For stereoscopic projection, see 778.4; motion-picture projection, 778.5

.3   Scientific and technological applications

Photomicrography in black-and-white and color, telephotography; infrared, close-up, panoramic, aerial and space, ultra high-speed, flash-bulb photography

Class microphotography in 686.4; radiography, technological infrared photography in 621.36 [*all formerly* 778.3]

Class a specific application with the subject, e.g., use of photography in astronomy 522

For photogrammetry, see 526.9; motion-picture photomicrography, 778.5

.4   Stereoscopic photography and projection

Production of effects of binocular vision

Class stereoscopic motion-picture photography and projection in 778.5

.5   Motion pictures and television photography

Including motion-picture photography (cinematography), editing, projection, photomicrography; preservation and storage of motion-picture films; stereoscopic motion pictures

.59   Television photography

.6   Color photography and photography of colors

Orthochromatic and panchromatic photography, direct and indirect processing techniques in color photography

Class color motion-picture photography in 778.5, color photomicrography in 778.3

.7   Photography under specific conditions

Examples: outdoors, indoors, underwater, under extreme climatic conditions

Class flash-bulb, infrared photography in 778.3

.8   Trick photography

Examples: table-top photography; photography of specters, distortions, multiple images, silhouettes

.9   Photography of specific subjects

Class specific fields of photography regardless of subject in 778.2–778.8

779   Collections of photographs

780   Music

Including musicians, musicologists, amateurs in society

If desired, distinguish scores and parts by prefixing M to number for treatises, e.g., scores and parts for string instruments M787

Class description and critical appraisal of work of musicians not limited by form in 780.92

[.07]   Relation to society

Use of this number for musicians, musicologists, amateurs is discontinued; class in 780

Class official support and regulation of music [*both formerly* 780.07] in 350

.1   Philosophy and esthetics

Including appreciation, analytical guides, program notes, listening

Class "theory of music" in 781

[.15]   Criticism and appreciation

Number discontinued; class in 780.1

.2   Miscellany

[.28]   Techniques, apparatus, equipment materials

Do not use; class in 781

.7   Study, teaching, performances

.73   Performances

Concerts and recitals

.8   Collections and miniature scores

Miniature pocket scores regardless of medium or kind

781   General principles and considerations

Including mathematical, physical, physiological, psychological principles; musical sound, nomenclature and systems of terms, notation

Class here techniques, apparatus, equipment, materials; "theory of music"

Class principles and techniques of dramatic music in 782, of sacred music in 783, of music for specific mediums in 784–789

[.1–.2]   Preliminary principles

Numbers discontinued; class in 781

▶   781.3–781.4 Musical structure

Class comprehensive works in 781.3, musical structure in specific musical forms in 781.5

.3   Harmony

Class here comprehensive works on musical structure

For melody and counterpoint, see 781.4

.4   Melody and counterpoint

Including canon, fugue

.5   Musical forms

Examples: sonata, dance music, program music, jazz and related forms

For canon, fugue, see 781.4

.6   Composition and performance

.7   Music of ethnic and national orientation

Development, description, critical appraisal

Including folk music

Class geographical treatment of music in 780.91–780.99

.9   Other topics

Musical instruments, words to be sung or recited with music

(It is optional to class here bibliographies and catalogs of scores and parts; prefer 016.78)

782		Dramatic music and production of musical drama
	.1	Opera

            Grand, light, comic, satiric, chamber

                For operettas, see 782.8

	[.12–.15]	Librettos, stories, plots, analyses, scores and parts

            Numbers discontinued; class in 782.1

	.8	Theater music

            Operettas, musical comedies, revues, secular cantatas and oratorios, incidental dramatic music; film, radio, television music

	.9	Other forms of dramatic music

            Music for pantomimes, masks, pageants, ballets

783	Sacred music

            Music composed for public and private worship or dedicated to a religious purpose

            Class here music for specific religions and denominations

	.1	Instrumental music

            Treatises on instrumental music and instrumental accompaniment to vocal music

            Class scores and parts in 785–789

	.2	Liturgical and ritualistic music

            Including works combining texts (librettos) with scores

            Class texts used by a specific religion with the religion, e.g., liturgy and ritual of Christian church 264

	.3	Oratorios

            Including Passions

	.4	Nonliturgical choral pieces

            Anthems, motets, choruses, cantatas

                For oratorios, see 783.3

	.5	Nonliturgical chants

            Gregorian, Ambrosian, Anglican, Jewish chants

	.6	Songs

            Including carols

                For hymns, see 783.9

.7   Evangelistic music

> Treatises on mission, revival, Sunday school music
>
> Class scores and parts in 783.6, congregational singing in 783.9

.8   Choirs and vocal groups

> In churches and other local units of worship
>
> Including training, conducting
>
> Class scores and parts of music for choirs with the kind of music, e.g., anthems 783.4

.9   Hymns

> Songs for congregational singing
>
> Class texts used by a specific religion with the religion, e.g., texts of hymns for Christian denominations 264

▶   784–789 Individual mediums of musical expression

> Class here appreciation, composition, performance, concerts and recitals
>
> Observe the following table of precedence for works combining two or more mediums, e.g., voice and piano 784
> Voice
> String instruments
> Wind instruments
> Percussion instruments
> Accordion
> Organ
> Piano
>
> Class comprehensive works in 780, dramatic music for a specific medium in 782

784   Voice and vocal music

> With or without instrumental accompaniment
>
> Class here comprehensive works on or combining words and music (texts and scores)
>
> *For sacred music, see 783; words to be sung or recited with music, 781.9; music for orchestra with incidental vocal parts, 785.2*

[.1–.3]   Vocal music according to number of voices

> Numbers discontinued; class in 784

▶ 784.4–784.7 Vocal music according to origin, subject, special interest

Class comprehensive works in 784

.4 Folk songs

Class national airs, songs, hymns, and songs of specific ethnic and cultural groups in 784.7

.6 Songs for specific groups and on specific subjects

Topical songs; songs for home, community, students, children, societies, service clubs

.7 Other kinds of songs

National airs, songs, hymns; songs of specific ethnic and cultural groups

[.8] Collections of vocal music

Number discontinued; class in 784

.9 The voice

Training, performance, vocal ensemble

▶ 785–789 Instruments and instrumental music

Class comprehensive works in 780

For treatises on sacred instrumental music, see 783.1

785 Instrumental ensembles and their music

.06 Organizations

Examples: orchestras, bands, chamber music ensembles

.1 Symphonies and band music

Including overtures and suites for band

Class concertos for band in 785.6, dance music and jazz for band in 785.4

.2 Music for full, salon, string orchestra with incidental vocal parts

Class symphonies with vocal parts in 785.1

.3 Miscellaneous music for full, salon, string orchestra

Not provided for in 785.1–785.2, 785.4–785.8

Including serenades and other romantic music, symphonic poems and other program music, variations

.4   Music for small ensembles

> Examples: dance music, jazz, music for rhythm and percussion bands
>
> *For chamber music, see 785.7*

.5   Independent overtures for full, salon, string orchestra

.6   Concertos

> One or more solo instruments with orchestra or band
>
> Including concerti grossi
>
> Class music for organ, piano, orchestra in 786.5

.7   Chamber music

> Compositions for two or more different solo instruments
>
> Class music for organ and piano in 786.5

.8   Suites for full, salon, string orchestra

▶   786–789 Specific instruments and their music

> Class comprehensive works on instruments and their music in 780, on instruments in 781.9

786   Keyboard instruments and their music

> *For celesta, see 789*

.1   Keyboard string instruments [*formerly also* 786.2] and their music [*formerly also* 786.4]

> Piano, harpsichord, related instruments
>
> Including training and performance [*both formerly* 786.3]
>
> *For player pianos, see 789.7*

[.2]   Keyboard string instruments

> Class in 786.1

[.3]   Training and performance on keyboard string instruments

> Class in 786.1

[.4]   Music for keyboard string instruments

> Class in 786.1

.5   Organ [*formerly also* 786.6] and its music [*formerly also* 786.8]

> Including training and performance [*both formerly* 786.7]; music for organ and piano; for organ, piano, orchestra
>
> Class electronic organ, reed organ in 786.9

[.6]   Organ

   Class in 786.5

[.7]   Training in and performance on organ

   Class in 786.5

[.8]   Music for organ

   Class in 786.5

.9   Other keyboard instruments

   Electronic organ, reed organ (harmonium, melodeon, cabinet organ); accordion and concertina and their music

   Class training and performance in electronic and reed organ, their music in 786.5

787–789 Other instruments and their music

Class comprehensive works in 780, chamber music in 785.7

787   String instruments and their music

   Bowed and plectral instruments and their music, e.g., violin, viola, violoncello, double bass, viols, harp, guitar, mandolin, lute, banjo, zither, ukulele

788   Wind instruments and their music

   Brass and woodwind instruments and their music, e.g., trumpet, cornet, bugle, trombone, horns, flute, piccolo, fife, recorder, clarinet, saxophone, oboe, bassoon, bagpipe, harmonica (mouth organ)

789   Percussion, mechanical, electrical instruments

   Including membranophones, cymbals, triangle, bells, carillons, chimes, glockenspiel, marimba, xylophone, celesta, vibraphone

.7   Mechanical instruments and devices

   Including barrel organ, reproducing and player pianos and orchestrion

.8   Music box

.9   Electronic musical instruments and music recording

   (It is optional to class here catalogs and lists of music recordings; prefer 016.7899)

790   Recreational and performing arts

For music, see 780

.01   Philosophy and theory of recreation

> Including influence, psychological and other effects; effective use of leisure

[.013]   Value, influence, effect

> Number discontinued; class in 790.01

[.019]   Activities and programs for specific classes of people

> Class in 790.19

.02   Miscellany of recreation

[.023]   Hobbies

> Class in 790.13

.03–.09   Standard subdivisions of recreation

> Notations from Table 1

.1   Recreational activities

> Class standard subdivisions in 790.01–790.09, a specific activity with the subject, e.g., outdoor sports 796, piano playing 786.1, paper cutting and folding 736

.13   Activities generally engaged in by individuals

> Including collecting, play with mechanical and scientific toys, participation in contests; passive (spectator) activities, e.g., watching, listening, other sedentary activities

> Class here hobbies [*formerly* 790.023]

> Class a specific activity provided for elsewhere with the subject, e.g., puzzles 793.7

.15   Activities generally engaged in by groups

> Class a specific activity with the subject, e.g., baseball 796.357

.19   Activities and programs for specific classes of people [*formerly* 790.019]

> Including programs for families, children, senior citizens, invalids, persons with handicaps

> Class activities generally engaged in by individuals in 790.13, by groups other than families in 790.15

.2   The performing arts

> Class a specific art with the subject, e.g., motion pictures 791.43, symphony orchestra performance 785.06

791   **Public performances**

> Other than musical, sport and game performances
>
> *For magic, see 793.8; theatrical dancing, 793.3; stage presentations, 792*

.06   **Organizations**

> Including amusement parks

.1   **Traveling shows**

> Including medicine shows, minstrel shows and skits
>
> *For circuses, see 791.3*

.3   **Circuses**

.4   **Motion pictures, radio, television**

> Class texts of plays in 800

.43   **Motion pictures**

> (It is optional to class here bibliographies and catalogs of films; prefer 010)

.44   **Radio**

.45   **Television**

.5   **Miniature, toy, shadow theaters**

> Including puppetry
>
> Class texts of plays in 800

.6   **Pageantry**

> Examples: processions, festivals, illuminations, parades, floats for parades
>
> Class water pageantry in 797.2, circus parades in 791.3

.8   **Animal performances**

> Including bullfighting, rodeos, cockfighting
>
> Class circus animal performances in 791.3, equestrian sports and animal racing in 798

792   **Theater (Stage presentations)**

> Class texts of plays in 800
>
> *For miniature, toy, shadow theaters, see 791.5*

[.02]   **Miscellany**

> Do not use; class in 792

.09   Historical and geographical treatment

Class here description, critical appraisal of specific theaters and companies

Class description, critical appraisal of specific productions in 792.9

▶   792.1–792.8 Specific kinds of dramatic performance

Class comprehensive works in 792, specific productions of specific kinds in 792.9

.1   Tragedy and serious drama

Including historical, Passion, morality, miracle plays

.2   Comedy and melodrama

.3   Pantomime

.7   Vaudeville, music hall, variety, cabaret, night club presentations

.8   Ballet

Including dancing, choreography

.809   Historical and geographical treatment

Class specific performances in 792.8

[.82]   Ballet dancing

Number discontinued; class in 792.8

.9   Specific productions

Description, critical appraisal, production scripts (stage guides)

Class specific productions of specific ballets in 792.8

793   Indoor games and amusements

For indoor games of skill, see 794; *games of chance,* 795

.2   Parties and entertainments

Including charades, tableaux, children's and seasonal parties

.3   Dancing

Including folk and national dances, theatrical dancing, ballroom and square dancing, cotillions, germans, balls

For ballet dancing, see 792.8

[.33–.34]   Ballroom and square dancing

Numbers discontinued; class in 793.3

.4   Games of action

.5   Forfeit and trick games

.7   Games not characterized by action

> Including puzzles, puzzle games, mathematical games and recreations
>> *For charades, tableaux, see 793.2*

.73   Crossword puzzles

.8   Magic

> Scientific recreations, conjuring, juggling, ventriloquism
>> *For card tricks, see 795.4*

794   Indoor games of skill

> *For card games, see 795.4*

.1   Chess

> Including Chinese, Japanese, three-dimensional chess; automaton, mechanical, electronic chess players

[.12–.18]   Specific aspects

> Numbers discontinued; class in 794.1

.2   Checkers and similar games

.6   Bowling

.7   Ball games

> Including billiards, pool
>> *For bowling, see 794.6; athletic games, 796*

795   Games of chance

> Including dice games, wheel and top games, dominoes, mah-jongg, bingo
>
> Class here gambling and betting systems, probabilities of winning

.4   Card games

> Including card tricks

796   Athletic and outdoor sports and games

> *For aquatic and air sports, see 797; equestrian sports and animal racing, 798; fishing, hunting, shooting, 799*

.1   Miscellaneous games

> Singing and dancing games, leapfrog, hide and seek, puss in corner, prisoner's base, play with kites and similar toys
>> *For active games requiring equipment, see 796.2*

.2   Active games requiring equipment

> Including roller skating, quoits, horseshoes
>> *For ball games, see 796.3; play with kites, 796.1*

.3   **Ball games**

.31   **Ball thrown or hit by hand**

       Examples: handball, lawn bowling

.32   **Inflated ball thrown or hit by hand**

       Basketball, net ball, volleyball

.33   **Inflated ball driven by foot**

       American (U.S.), Canadian, Australian, association (soccer) football; rugby

       Including pushball

.34   **Racket games**

       Lawn tennis, court tennis, paddle tennis, table tennis, rackets and squash, badminton, lacrosse

.35   **Ball driven by club, mallet, bat**

       Including polo, croquet, field hockey

.352   **Golf**

.357   **Baseball**

       Including variants, e.g., softball, indoor baseball

[.357 2–.357 8]   **Specific aspects**

       Numbers discontinued; class in 796.357

.358   **Cricket**

.4   **Athletic exercises and gymnastics**

       Calisthenics; track and field athletics, jumping, vaulting, throwing, use of horizontal and parallel bars, trapeze work, rope climbing, wire walking, acrobatics, tumbling, trampolining, contortion

       Including Olympic games

       Class winter Olympic games [*formerly* 796.4] in 796.9

       Class games involving these activities in 796.1–796.3

.5   **Outdoor life**

       Including walking, mountaineering, spelunking, beach activities, dude ranching and farming

.54   **Camping**

       Including woodcraft, campfires

[.56]   **Dude ranching and farming**

       Number discontinued; class in 796.5

.6   Cycling

Use of wheeled vehicles driven by manpower

Including bicycle, soapbox racing

.7   Driving motor vehicles

For racing, for pleasure

Including trailer travel for pleasure

.8   Combat sports

Wrestling, boxing, fencing; jujitsus, e.g., judo, karate

Class combat with animals in 791.8

.9   Ice and snow sports

Ice skating, snowshoeing, skiing, tobogganing and coasting, curling, ice hockey, iceboating

Including winter Olympic games [*formerly* 796.4]

Class ice fishing in 799.1

797   Aquatic and air sports

For fishing, see 799.1

.1   Boating

Canoeing, rowboating, sailboating, motorboating, yachting, surf riding, water skiing, boat racing and regattas

.2   Swimming and diving

Including submarine swimming (skin diving, scuba diving), springboard and precision diving, water pageantry, water games

[.21–.24]   Swimming and diving

Numbers discontinued; class in 797.2

.5   Air sports

Aircraft racing, flying for pleasure, stunt flying, gliding and soaring, parachuting (skydiving)

798   Equestrian sports and animal racing

Horsemanship, horse racing, driving and coaching, racing other animals

799   Fishing, hunting, shooting

.1   Fishing

[.17]   Fishing for specific kinds of fish

Number discontinued; class in 799.1

.2   Hunting

Small and big game

Including falconry; selection, care, use of rifles, pistols, shotguns, bows and arrows, boomerangs, spears, other ballistic devices

[.209]   Historical and geographical treatment

Do not use; class in 799.2

[.24–.27]   Specific kinds of game

Numbers discontinued; class in 799.2

[.29]   Historical and geographical treatment

Number discontinued; class in 799.2

.3   Shooting other than game

With guns at stationary and moving targets, e.g., trapshooting, skeet shooting; with bows and arrows (archery)

Class selection, care, use of ballistic devices in 799.2

800 Literature (Belles-lettres)

Works of literature, works about literature

Observe the following table of precedence for works combining two or more literary forms, e.g., English poetic drama 822

> Drama
> Poetry
> Fiction
> Essays
> Speeches
> Letters
> Satire and humor
>> Class collections of satire and humor in several literary forms as satire and humor
>> If preferred, give precedence to satire and humor over all other forms
> Miscellaneous writings

Class folk literature in 398.2

801 Philosophy and theory

Including esthetics; theory, technique, history of literary criticism

802 Miscellany about literature

.8 Apparatus, equipment, materials

Class techniques in 808

803 Dictionaries, encyclopedias, concordances

805 Serial publications of and about literature

806 Organizations

807 Study and teaching

808 Rhetoric (Composition) and collections

Rhetoric: techniques of oral and written communication for clarity and esthetic pleasure

Including authorship and editorial techniques, e.g., preparation of manuscripts, writing for publication; professional, technical, expository writing on specific subjects; news, business, script writing; writing for chldren; plagiarism

(If preferred, class techniques of writing on a specific subject with the subject, using "Standard Subdivisions" notation 01 from Table 1, e.g., science writing 501)

[.02–.06] General composition

Numbers discontinued; class in 808

▶   808.1–808.7 Rhetoric (Composition) in specific literary forms

> Observe table of precedence under 800
>
> Class specific forms for children, comprehensive works in 808

.1   Rhetoric of poetry

.2   Rhetoric of drama

.3   Rhetoric of fiction

> Including short stories

[.31]   Short stories

> Number discontinued; class in 808.3

.4   Rhetoric of essays

.5   Rhetoric of speech

> Including public speaking (oratory), e.g., platform, radio, after-dinner speaking; recitation, e.g., storytelling; reading aloud; choral speaking
>
> Class here voice, expression, gesture
>
> *For preaching, see* 251

[.51]   Public speaking (Oratory)

> Number discontinued; class in 808.5

.53   Debating and public discussion

[.54–.55]   Recitation and choral speaking

> Numbers discontinued; class in 808.5

.56   Conversation

.59   Listening

.6   Rhetoric of letters

.7   Rhetoric of satire and humor

.8   **Collections from more than one literature**

Class here works giving equal attention to collections of literary texts and to history, description, critical appraisal of literature

Class more than one literature in the same language with literature of that language

For history, description, critical appraisal of more than one literature, see 809

►   808.81–808.88 Collections in specific forms

Observe table of precedence under 800

Class comprehensive works in 808.8

.81–.87   **Collections in specific literary forms**

Add to 808.8 the numbers following 808 in 808.1–808.7, e.g., collections of essays 808.84, of debates 808.853

.88   **Collections of miscellaneous writings**

Quotations, epigrams, diaries, journals, reminiscences, experimental and nonformalized works, prose literature

Class a specific identifiable form of prose literature with the form, e.g., essays 808.84

[.89]   **Collections for and by specific kinds of persons**

Number discontinued; class in 808.8

809   **History, description, critical appraisal of more than one literature**

Class theory, technique, history of literary criticism in 801, more than one literature in the same language with literature in that language

.1–.7   **Literature in specific forms**

Add to 809 the numbers following 808 in 808.1–808.7, e.g., history, description, critical appraisal of poetry 809.1

[.8–.9]   **Literature for and by specific kinds of persons, and literature displaying specific features**

Numbers discontinued; class in 809

▶   **810–890 Literatures of specific languages**

By language in which originally written

Class literature in a dialect with literature of the basic language

If preferred, class translations into a language locally emphasized, e.g., English, with the literature of that language

Under each literature identified by *, add to the designated base number the "Subdivisions of Individual Literatures" notation 01–809 from Table 3

Class comprehensive works in 800

810   *American literature in English

English-language literature of Western Hemisphere and Hawaii

Base number: 81

If desired, distinguish literatures of specific countries by initial letters, e.g., literature of Canada C810, of United States U810; or, if preferred, class literatures not requiring local emphasis in 819

Class comprehensive works on literature of English language in 820

811   American poetry

812   American drama

813   American fiction

814   American essays

815   American speeches

816   American letters

817   American satire and humor

818   American miscellany

819   Literatures not requiring local emphasis

> (It is optional to class here English-language literatures of specific American countries, e.g., libraries emphasizing United States literature may class here Canadian literature, and libraries emphasizing Canadian literature may class here United States literature. Prefer 810–818 for English-language literatures of all American countries, especially for works by and about individual authors)

* Add to base number as instructed under 810–890

820 **Literatures of *English and Anglo-Saxon languages**

> Base number for English: 82
>
> A special interpretation of the provisions of Table 3, "Subdivisions of Individual Literatures," for use with English appears below under 822
>
> If desired, distinguish English-language literatures of specific countries by initial letters, e.g., literature of England E820, of Ireland Ir820 (or of all British Isles B820), of Australia A820, of India In820; or, if preferred, class literatures not requiring local emphasis in 828.99
>
> *For American literature in English, see* 810

821 . English poetry

822 . English drama

  .3   William Shakespeare

823 English fiction

824 English essays

825 English speeches

826 English letters

827 English satire and humor

828 English miscellany

  .99   English-language literatures not requiring local emphasis

> (It is optional to class here English-language literatures of specific non-American countries, e.g., libraries emphasizing British literature may class here Australian, Anglo-Indian, other literatures, and libraries emphasizing Anglo-Indian literature may class here British literature. Prefer 820–828 for English-language literatures of all non-American countries, especially for works by and about individual authors)

829   Anglo-Saxon (Old English)

830 **Literatures of Germanic (Teutonic) languages   *German literature**

> Base number for German: 83
>
> *For literatures of English and Anglo-Saxon languages, see* 820

831 German poetry

832 German drama

833 German fiction

834 German essays

* Add to base number as instructed under 810–890

835	German speeches
836	German letters
837	German satire and humor
838	German miscellany
839	Literatures of other Germanic (Teutonic) languages

Including Yiddish [*formerly* 892.49]

.3	Dutch, Flemish, Afrikaans
.7	Swedish
.8	Danish and Norwegian

840   Literatures of *French, Provençal, Catalan languages

Base number for French: 84

Class here comprehensive works on literatures of Romance languages [*formerly also* 879.9]

> *For literatures of Italian, Romanian, Rhaeto-Romanic languages, see 850; of Spanish and Portuguese languages, 860*

841	French poetry
842	French drama
843	French fiction
844	French essays
845	French speeches
846	French letters
847	French satire and humor
848	French miscellany
849	Provençal and Catalan

850   Literatures of *Italian, Romanian, Rhaeto-Romanic languages

Base number for Italian: 85

851	Italian poetry
852	Italian drama
853	Italian fiction
854	Italian essays

* Add to base number as instructed under 810–890

855	Italian speeches
856	Italian letters
857	Italian satire and humor
858	Italian miscellany
859	Romanian and Rhaeto-Romanic

860   Literatures of *Spanish and Portuguese languages

Base number for Spanish: 86

861	Spanish poetry
862	Spanish drama
863	Spanish fiction
864	Spanish essays
865	Spanish speeches
866	Spanish letters
867	Spanish satire and humor
868	Spanish miscellany
869	*Portuguese

870   Literatures of Italic languages   *Latin literature

Base number for Latin: 87

Special interpretations of the provisions of Table 3, "Subdivisions of Individual Literatures," for use with Latin appear below under 871–874

For literatures of Romance languages, see 840

871   Latin poetry

For dramatic poetry, see 872; epic poetry, 873; lyric poetry, 874

872	Latin dramatic poetry and drama
873	Latin epic poetry and fiction
874	Latin lyric poetry
875	Latin speeches
876	Latin letters
877	Latin satire and humor
878	Latin miscellany

* Add to base number as instructed under 810–890

879　　　　Literatures of other Italic languages

　　　　　　Including Osco-Umbrian languages

　　　　　　Class Etruscan in 899

[.9]　　　　Literatures of Romance languages

　　　　　　Class in 840

880　　**Literatures of Hellenic languages　　*Classical Greek literature**

　　　　　　Class here comprehensive works on literatures of classical languages

　　　　　　Base number for classical Greek: 88

　　　　　　Special interpretations of the provisions of Table 3, "Subdivisions of Individual Literatures," for use with classical Greek appear below under 881–884

　　　　　　　For Latin literature, see 870

881　　　　Classical Greek poetry

　　　　　　　For dramatic poetry, see 882; epic poetry, 883; lyric poetry, 884

882　　　　Classical Greek dramatic poetry and drama

883　　　　Classical Greek epic poetry and fiction

884　　　　Classical Greek lyric poetry

885　　　　Classical Greek speeches

886　　　　Classical Greek letters

887　　　　Classical Greek satire and humor

888　　　　Classical Greek miscellany

889　　　　Modern Greek literature

　　　　　　Katharevusa and Demotic

890　　**Literatures of other languages**

891　　　　Literatures of east Indo-European and Celtic languages

　　　　　　Including Indic languages, e.g., Sanskrit, Panjabi, Hindi, Urdu, Bengali, Sinhalese, Romany (Gipsy); Iranian languages, e.g., Persian, Baltic languages, e.g., Lithuanian, Latvian (Lettish); Albanian, Armenian

[.1–.5]　　Specific languages

　　　　　　Numbers discontinued; class in 891

.6　　　　Celtic languages

　　　　　　Including Irish and Scottish Gaelic, Manx, Welsh (Cymric), Breton

* Add to base number as instructed under 810–890

.7 East Slavic languages   *Russian

> Including Ukrainian, Belorussian
>
> Base number for Russian: 891.7
>
> Class comprehensive works on Slavic languages in 891.8

[.79] Ukrainian and Belorussian

> Number discontinued; class in 891.7

.8 Slavic languages

> Including Common Slavic, Bulgarian, Macedonian, Serbo-Croatian, Slovenian, Polish, Czech, Slovak, Wendish, Polabian
>
> Class here Balto-Slavic languages
>
> Class East Slavic languages in 891.7, Baltic languages in 891

[.9] Baltic and other East Indo-European languages

> Number discontinued; class in 891

892 Literatures of Afro-Asiatic (Hamito-Semitic) languages

> Including Akkadian, Aramaic, Ethiopic, Samaritan, Arabic, Canaanite-Phoenician languages
>
> *For literatures of Hamitic and Chad languages, see 893*

.4 Hebrew

[.49] Yiddish

> Class in 839

893 Literatures of Hamitic and Chad languages

> Including Hausa [*formerly* 896], Old Egyptian, Coptic, Berber, Cushitic languages

894 Literatures of Ural-Altaic, Paleosiberian, Dravidian languages

> Altaic languages, e.g., Manchu, Mongolian, Turkish; Uralic languages, e.g., Samoyed, Hungarian, Finnish, Estonian, Lapp; Paleosiberian languages; Dravidian languages, e.g., Tamil, Malayalam, Kanarese, Telugu

895 Literatures of languages of East and Southeast Asia   Sino-Tibetan languages

> Including Tibeto-Burman, Burmese, Cambodian languages

.1 Chinese

.6 Japanese

* Add to base number as instructed under 810–890

.7   Korean

.9   Thai and Vietnamese (Annamese)

896   Literatures of African languages

Including Bantu, e.g., Swahili; Hottentot, Bushman, Ibo, Yoruba languages

Class Hausa [*formerly* 896] in 893

For Afro-Asiatic languages, see 892

897   Literatures of North American aboriginal languages

Class here comprehensive works on literatures of American aboriginal languages

For literatures of South American aboriginal languages, see 898

898   Literatures of South American aboriginal languages

899   Literatures of other languages

Including Negrito, Papuan, Malayan, Philippine, Polynesian, Melanesian, Micronesian, Australian, Basque, Elamitic, Etruscan, Sumerian, Caucasian languages; artificial languages, e.g., Esperanto

[.9]   Artificial languages

Number discontinued; class in 899

900 General geography and history and their auxiliaries

General history: narrative and analysis of events of the distant or immediate past in the life of mankind, not limited to a single discipline or subject

Class here military, diplomatic, political, economic, social, welfare aspects of specific wars

Class historical treatment of a specific subject with the subject, using "Standard Subdivisions" notation 09 from Table 1, e.g., pure sciences 509, economic events 330.9, purely political events 320.9, history of warfare 355.009; interdisciplinary works on geography and history of specific continents, countries, localities in 913–919

901 Philosophy and theory of general history

.9 Civilization

Man's spiritual, intellectual, material situation and change

Class here agricultural civilization [*formerly also* 630.1]

If preferred, class in 909

Class comprehensive works on ancient civilization to ca. 500 A.D. in 913; geographical treatment of civilization in 910, 913–919

.92 In the years 500–1500 .

.93 In the years 1500–1900

.94 In the years 1900–

902 Miscellany of general history

Including chronologies

903 Dictionaries, encyclopedias, concordances of general history

904 Collected accounts of specific events

Examples: earthquakes, volcanic eruptions, tidal waves, floods, storms, wars and battles, explosions, fires; mine, transportation, nuclear accidents

Including adventure

905 Serial publications on general history

906 Organizations of general history

907 Study and teaching of general history

908 Collections of general history

909 **General world history**

> Class here general history of specific racial, ethnic, national groups not limited by continent, country, locality, e.g., world history of Jews
>
> (It is optional to class here civilization; prefer 901.9)
>
> Class history of ancient world to ca. 500 A.D. in 930; history of specific continents, countries, localities in modern world in 940–990

.07 Ca. 500–1450/1500

> Including Crusades

.08 Modern history, 1450/1500–

> Class history of 1700–1799 in 909.7, of 1800– in 909.8

.7 1700–1799

.8 1800–

.81 1800–1899

.82 1900–1999

[.824–.826] Specific periods

> Numbers discontinued; class in 909.82

.83 2000–2099

910 **General geography   Travel**

> General geography: description and analysis by area of the earth's surface (physical geography) and man's civilization upon it, not limited to a single discipline or subject; also, by extension, description and analysis of the surfaces of and civilizations upon extraterrestrial worlds
>
> Including discovery and exploration
>
> Class geographical treatment of a specific subject with the subject, using "Standard Subdivisions" notation 09 from Table 1 unless otherwise instructed, e.g., geomorphology 551.409, social situation and conditions 309.1, the fine arts 709, religion 200.9; general history of civilization in 901.9

[.02–.09] Specific aspects of geography and travel

> Numbers discontinued; class in 910

.1 Philosophy and theory   •

> (It is optional to class here topical geography; prefer specific subject, e.g., economic geography 330.9. If option is chosen, add 001–899 to base number 910.1, e.g., economic geography 910.133)

.2 Miscellany

> Including world travel guides

.22 Illustrations and models

> Class charts and plans in 912

.4 Accounts of travel not limited geographically

Including trips around the world, ocean travel, seafaring life, shipwrecks, mutinies, buried treasure, pirates' expeditions

Class discovery and exploration in 910, scientific travels in 508.3

911 Historical geography

Growth and changes in political divisions

Class here historical atlases

912 Graphic representations of surface of earth and of extraterrestrial worlds

Atlases, maps, charts, plans

Including map making and reading

Class map projections in 526.8

[.1–.9] Specific subjects and places

Numbers discontinued; class in 912

▶ 913–919 Geography of and travel in specific continents, countries, localities, extraterrestrial worlds

Class here interdisciplinary works on geography and general history of specific continents, countries, localities; prehistoric and historic archeology (study of man's past civilizations thru discovery, collection, interpretation of his material remains); civilization of specific racial, ethnic, national groups in specific continents, countries, localities

If preferred, class in 930–990

Class comprehensive works; geography of and travel in more than one continent; geography of and travel in areas, regions, places not limited by continent, country, locality; civilization of specific racial, ethnic, national groups not limited by continent, country, locality, all in 910; general history of specific continents, countries, localities in 930–990; historical geography in 911; graphic representations in 912

913 Geography of and travel in ancient world

Class here prehistoric archeology

[.02–.04] Physical geography, civilization, travel

Numbers discontinued; class in 913

.3 Continents, countries, localities

> Add "Areas" notation 3 from Table 2 to base number 913, e.g., geography of ancient Greece 913.38

▶

914–919 Geography of and travel in specific continents, countries, localities in modern world; extraterrestrial worlds

Class here area studies; comprehensive works on ancient and modern geography of and travel in specific continents, countries, localities

Class comprehensive works in 910

For geography of and travel in ancient world, see 913

914 Geography of and travel in Europe

> Add "Areas" notation 41–49 from Table 2 to base number 91, e.g., Great Britain 914.2

915 Geography of and travel in Asia

> Add "Areas" notation 51–59 from Table 2 to base number 91, e.g., Japan 915.2

916 Geography of and travel in Africa

> Add "Areas" notation 61–69 from Table 2 to base number 91, e.g., Ethiopia 916.3

917 Geography of and travel in North America

> Add "Areas" notation 71–79 from Table 2 to base number 91, e.g., Ohio 917.71

918 Geography of and travel in South America

> Add "Areas" notation 81–89 from Table 2 to base number 91, e.g., Brazil 918.1

919 Geography of and travel in other parts of world and extraterrestrial worlds   Pacific Ocean islands (Oceania)

> Add "Areas" notation 93–99 from Table 2 to base number 91, e.g., Australia 919.4, moon (selenography) 919.9

920   Biography, genealogy, insignia

Class here autobiographies, diaries, reminiscences

There are three commonly accepted methods for classing biography. (1) Most general libraries using this edition will prefer to class all individual biography regardless of subject orientation in 92 or B (arranged alphabetically by biographee, and placed in sequence between 919 and 920), and all collected biography regardless of subject orientation in 920 without subdivision. (2) Some general libraries will prefer to class both individual and collected biography of persons associated with a specific subject in 920.1–928, e.g., biography of chemists 925. (3) Still other general libraries, and many specialized libraries, will prefer to class both individual and collected biography of persons associated with a specific subject with the subject, using "Standard Subdivisions" notation 092 from Table 1, e.g., biography of chemists 540.92; in any event, this is the preferred method for classing description and critical appraisal of a person's or several persons' work (as distinct from biography), e.g., criticism of the work in chemistry of Lavoisier 540.92

[.02–.09]   General collections of biography

Numbers discontinued; class in 920

▶   920.1–928 Biography of specific classes of persons

(Use of these numbers is optional; see treatment described at 920)

Class comprehensive works in 920

.1   *Bibliographers

.2   *Librarians and book collectors

.3   *Encyclopedists

.4   *Publishers and booksellers

.5   *Journalists and news commentators

.7   *Persons by sex

.71   *Men

.72   *Women

.9   *Persons associated with other subjects

Not provided for in 920.1–920.5, 921–928

921   *Philosophers and psychologists

922   *Religious leaders, thinkers, workers

Including collected biographies of communicants of specific religions and sects

* Use of this number is optional; see treatment described at 920

923   *Persons in social sciences

> Heads of state, nobility, public administrators, politicians, statesmen, military persons, philanthropists, social reformers, educators, explorers, geographers, pioneers, criminals; persons in economics (including labor leaders), law, commerce, communication, transportation

924   *Philologists and lexicographers

925   *Scientists

926   *Persons in technology

927   *Persons in arts and recreation

928   *Persons in literature

> Including historians, biographers

929   Genealogy, names, insignia

> Including family histories; genealogical sources, e.g., registers, wills, tax lists, census records, court records compiled for genealogical purposes; epitaphs

[.1–.3]   Genealogy

> Numbers discontinued; class in 929

.4   Personal names

> Including nicknames

[.5]   Epitaphs

> Number discontinued; class in 929

.6   Heraldry

> *For armorial bearings, see* 929.8

.7   Royal houses, peerage, gentry, secular orders of knighthood

> Including rank, precedence, titles of honor

.709   Historical and geographical treatment

> Class treatment by country in 929.7

.8   Armorial bearings and autographs

> Including coats of arms, crests, seals

.9   Flags

> National, state, provincial, ship, ownership flags
>
> Class military use in 355.1

* Use of this number is optional; see treatment described at 920

▶ ## 930–990 General history of specific continents, countries, localities

Class here general history of specific racial, ethnic, national groups in specific continents, countries, localities

(It is optional to class here general geography of and travel in specific continents, countries, localities, extraterrestrial worlds; prefer 913–919)

Add "Areas" notation 3–9 from Table 2 to base number 9, inserting a 0 if required to complete a three-digit number, e.g., general history of Europe 940, of British Isles 942; then, unless otherwise specified, add further as follows:

    001–008   Standard subdivisions
                    Notations from Table 1
    01–09   Historical periods
                    As shown in the schedules that follow

If no historical periods are shown, use 01–08 for standard subdivisions

These schedules enumerate in detail only those countries and localities denoted by three-digit class numbers or for which historical periods are indicated

Class comprehensive works in 909; history of areas, regions, places, racial groups, ethnic groups, national groups not limited by continent, country, locality in 909

930   *General history of ancient world to ca. 500 A.D.

931   *China to 420 A.D.

932   *Egypt to 640 A.D.

933   *Palestine to 70 A.D.

        Including Judea

934   *India to 647 A.D.

935   *Mesopotamia and Iranian Plateau to 642 A.D.

        Class central Asia in 939

936   *Europe north and west of Italian peninsula to 5th century A.D.

937   *Italian peninsula and adjacent territories to 476 A.D.

938   *Greece to 323 A.D.

939   *Other parts of ancient world to ca. 640 A.D.

* Add as instructed under 930–990

▶   **940–990 General history of modern world**

Class here comprehensive works on general history (ancient and modern) of specific continents, countries, localities

Class comprehensive works on more than one continent in 909

For general history of ancient world, see 930

940   *General history of Europe

From fall of Rome, 476, to present

.1   Middle Ages, 476–1453

Class Crusades in 909.07

.2   Modern period, 1453–

Including Napoleonic wars

For World War 1, see 940.3; 20th century, 1918–   , 940.5

.3   World War 1, 1914–1918

Social, political, economic, diplomatic, military history; causes, results

Including participation of specific countries and groups of countries

For military history, see 940.4

.4   Military history of World War 1 (Conduct of the war)

Including celebrations, commemorations, memorials, prisons, health, social services, secret service and spies, propaganda

.5   20th century, 1918–

.53   World War 2, 1939–1945

Social, political, economic, diplomatic, military history; causes, results

Including participation of specific countries and groups of countries

For military history, see 940.54

[.531–.539]   Specific topics

Numbers discontinued; class in 940.53

* Add as instructed under 930–990

.54   Military history of World War 2 (Conduct of the war)

> Including strategy, mobilization, racial minorities as troops, repressive measures and atrocities, military participation of specific countries; celebrations, commemorations, memorials, prisons, health, social services, secret service and spies, propaganda

[.541–.548]   Specific topics

> Numbers discontinued; class in 940.54

.55   Later 20th century, 1945–

941   *Scotland and Ireland

▶   941.01–941.08 Scotland since 410

> Class comprehensive works in 941

.01   Early history, 410–1057

.02   Efforts at control by England, 1057–1314

> Including Battle of Bannockburn, 1314

.03   Early period of independence, 1314–1424

.04   James 1–James 5, 1424–1542

.05   Reformation period, 1542–1603

.06   Personal union with England, 1603–1707

.07   18th century, 1707–1837

.08   19th–20th centuries, 1837–

.081   20th century, 1901–

.5   Ireland

.501–.508   Standard subdivisions

> Notations from Table 1

▶   941.51–941.59 Historical periods since 410

> Class comprehensive works in 941.5

.51   Early history, 410–1086

> Including Battle of Clontarf, 1014

.52   Disorder and English conquest, 1086–1171

.53   Under House of Plantagenet, 1171–1399

.54   Under Houses of Lancaster and York, 1399–1485

* Add as instructed under 930–990

.55	Under Tudors, 1485–1603
.56	Under Stuarts, 1603–1691
.57	18th century, 1691–1800
.58	19th century, 1801–1900
.59	20th century, 1900–

               Including Irish Free State, Eire

.6	*Ulster Northern Ireland
.609	Under Government of Ireland Act, 1920–

942   *British Isles   England

        Class here Great Britain, United Kingdom

        For Scotland and Ireland, see 941

.01	Early history, 410–1066
.02	Norman period, 1066–1154
.03	House of Plantagenet, 1154–1399
.04	Houses of Lancaster and York, 1399–1485
.05	Tudor period, 1485–1603
.06	Stuart period, 1603–1714
.07	House of Hanover, 1714–1837
.08	Victoria and House of Windsor, 1837–
.081	Victoria, 1837–1901
.082	20th century, 1901–

               Including reign of Edward 7, 1901–1910

                   For George 5, see 942.083; *period of World War 2,* 942.084; *later 20th century,* 942.085

.083	George 5, 1910–1936
.084	Period of World War 2, 1936–1945

               Reigns of Edward 8, 1936 and George 6, 1936–1952

.085	Later 20th century, 1945–

               Reign of Elizabeth 2, 1952

943   *Central Europe   Germany

.08	Germany since 1866
.085	Weimar Republic, 1918–1933

* Add as instructed under 930–990

.086   Third Reich, 1933–1945

.087   Later 20th century, 1945–

944   *France

.04   Revolution, 1789–1804

.05   First Empire, 1804–1815

             Class Napoleonic wars in 940.2

.06   Restoration, 1815–1848

.07   Second Republic and Second Empire, 1848–1870

.08   Third, Fourth, Fifth Republics, 1870–

.081   Third Republic, 1870–1945

.082   Fourth Republic, 1945–1958

.083   Fifth Republic, 1958–

945   *Italy

.09   Italy since 1870

.091   Fascist regime, 1918–1946

.092   Republic, 1946–

946   *Iberian Peninsula   Spain

.08   Spain since 1868

.081   Second Republic, 1931–1939

.082   Regime of Francisco Franco, 1939–

947   *Eastern Europe   Union of Soviet Socialist Republics (Soviet Union)

.08   Russia since 1855

.084   Communist regime, 1917–   (Union of Soviet Socialist Republics, 1923–   )

             Including revolutions of 1917

                 For later 20th century, see 947.085

.085   Later 20th century, 1953–

948   *Northern Europe   Scandinavia

949   *Other parts of Europe

* Add as instructed under 930–990

950 *General history of Asia   Orient   Far East

[.4]   20th century, 1905–

>   Number and its subdivisions discontinued; class in 950

951   *China and adjacent areas

▶   951.04–951.05 China since 1912

>   Class comprehensive works in 951

.04   Early 20th century, 1912–1949

.05   Period of People's Republic, 1949–

952   *Japan and adjacent islands

▶   952.03–952.04 Japan since 1868

>   Class comprehensive works in 952

.03   Re-establishment of imperial power, 1868–1945

.04   Postwar period, 1945–

953   *Arabian Peninsula and adjacent areas

954   *South Asia   India

.02   Asian dynasties and European penetration, 647–1774

.03   British rule, 1774–1947

.04   Independence and partition, 1947–

955   *Iran (Persia)

956   *Middle East (Near East)

957   *Siberia (Asiatic Russia)

958   *Central Asia

959   *Southeast Asia

.7   *Vietnam

.704   Independence, 1949–

>   Class here Vietnamese War, 1961–   (social, political, economic, diplomatic, military history)

* Add as instructed under 930–990

960   ***General history of Africa**

961   *North Africa

962   *Countries of the Nile   Egypt

963   *Ethiopia (Abyssinia)

964   *Northwest African coast and offshore islands

965   *Algeria

966   *West Africa and offshore islands

967   *Central Africa and offshore islands   East Africa

968   *South Africa   Republic of South Africa

    .02   Early history to 1488

    .03   Period of exploration and settlement, 1488–1814

    .04   19th century, 1814–1909

    .05   Union, 1909–1961

    .06   Republic, 1961–

969   South Indian Ocean islands

970   **General history of North America**

           Do not use standard subdivisions; class in 970

           Class Indians in 970.1

▶   970.01–970.05 Historical periods

                  Class comprehensive works in 970

    .01   Period of discovery and exploration to ca. 1600

                (Use of this number is optional; prefer 973.1)

    .02   1600–1700

    .03   1700–1800

    .04   1800–1900

    .05   1900–

    .051   To end of World War 1, 1900–1918

    .052   From end of World War 1 to end of World War 2, 1918–1945

    .053   Since World War 2, 1945–

* Add as instructed under 930–990

.1   Indians of North America

History and civilization in North America

Class world history of North American Indians in 909, history in a specific place outside North America with history of the place, civilization outside North America in 910

For specific tribes, see 970.3; Indians in specific places in North America, 970.4; government relations, 970.5

.3   Specific Indian tribes

Class government relations of specific Indian tribes in 970.5

.4   Indians in specific places in North America

Class specific tribes in specific places in North America in 970.3, government relations of Indians in specific places in North America in 970.5

.5   Government relations with Indians

History and policy

Class Indian wars of a specific place and period with history of the appropriate place and period, e.g., Black Hawk War 973.5; a specific aspect of government relations with the subject, e.g., social welfare services 362.8

971   *Canada

.01   Early history to 1763

(It is optional to class here War of the League of Augsburg (King William's War), War of the Spanish Succession (Queen Anne's War), War of the Austrian Succession (King George's War), Seven Years' War (French and Indian War); prefer 973.2)

.02   Early British rule, 1763–1791

.03   Period of separate colonies, 1791–1841

(It is optional to class here War of 1812; prefer 973.5)

.04   Growth of responsible government, 1841–1867

.05   Dominion of Canada during period 1867–1911

.06   20th century, 1911–

972   *Middle America   Mexico

.08   Mexico since 1867

* Add as instructed under 930–990

973 United States

Use 973.01–973.08 for standard subdivisions

For specific states, see 974–979

973.1–973.9 Historical periods

Class comprehensive works in 973

.1 Period of discovery and exploration to 1607

Class here period of discovery and exploration of America; if preferred, class in 970.01

Class period of discoveries and explorations in a specific country with history of the country

.2 Colonial period, 1607–1775

Class here King William's War, Queen Anne's War, King George's War, French and Indian War; if preferred, class in 971.01

Class local history in 974–975

.3 Revolution and confederation, 1775–1789

Social, political, economic, diplomatic, military history; causes, results

Including celebrations, commemorations, memorials, prisons, health, secret service and spies, propaganda

[.31–.38] Specific topics

Numbers discontinued; class in 973.3

.4 Constitutional period, 1789–1809

Administrations of George Washington, John Adams, Thomas Jefferson

.5 Early 19th century, 1809–1845

Administrations of James Madison, James Monroe, John Quincy Adams, Andrew Jackson, Martin Van Buren, William Henry Harrison, John Tyler

Including Black Hawk War, Seminole Wars

Class here War of 1812 (social, political, economic, diplomatic, military history); if preferred, class in 971.03

.6 Middle 19th century, 1845–1861

Administrations of James K. Polk, Zachary Taylor, Millard Fillmore, Franklin Pierce, James Buchanan

Class here Mexican War (social, political, economic, diplomatic, military history)

.7   Administration of Abraham Lincoln, 1861–1865 (Civil War)

> Social, political, economic, diplomatic, military history; causes, results
>
> Including celebrations, commemorations, memorials, prisons, health, social services, secret service and spies, propaganda
>
> *For period of reconstruction, see 973.8*

[.71–.78]   Specific topics

> Numbers discontinued; class in 973.7

.8   Later 19th century, 1865–1901 (Period of reconstruction)

> Administrations of Andrew Johnson, Ulysses S. Grant, Rutherford B. Hayes, James A. Garfield, Chester A. Arthur, Grover Cleveland, Benjamin Harrison, William McKinley
>
> Class here Spanish-American War (social, political, economic, diplomatic, military history)

.9   20th century, 1901–

.91   Early 20th century, 1901–1953

> Including administrations of Theodore Roosevelt, William Howard Taft, Woodrow Wilson, Warren G. Harding, Calvin Coolidge, Herbert C. Hoover

.917   Administration of Franklin D. Roosevelt, 1933–1945

.918   Administration of Harry S. Truman, 1945–1953

.92   Later 20th century, 1953–

.921   Administration of Dwight D. Eisenhower, 1953–1961

.922   Administration of John F. Kennedy, 1961–1963

.923   Administration of Lyndon B. Johnson, 1963–1969

.924   Administration of Richard M. Nixon, 1969–

►   974–979 Specific states of United States

> Class comprehensive works in 973
>
> *For Hawaii, see 996.9*

974   *Northeastern United States (New England and Middle Atlantic states)

975   *Southeastern United States (South Atlantic states)

976   *South central United States   Gulf Coast states

977   *North central United States   Lake states

* Add as instructed under 930–990

978　　*Western United States

　　　　　For Great Basin and Pacific Slope region of United States, see 979

979　　*Great Basin and Pacific Slope region of United States
　　　　Pacific Coast states

980　General history of South America

　　　　　Class here Latin America, Spanish America

　　　　　Do not use standard subdivisions; class in 980

　　　　　Class Indians in 980.1–980.5

　.1–.5　　Indians of South America

　　　　　　Add to 980 the numbers following 970 in 970.1–970.5, e.g.,
　　　　　　specific tribes 980.3

981　　*Brazil

982　　*Argentina

983　　*Chile

984　　*Bolivia

985　　*Peru

986　　*Northwestern South America and Panama

987　　*Venezuela

988　　*Guianas

989　　*Other parts of South America

**990　*General history of other parts of world　　Pacific Ocean
　　　islands (Oceania)**

993　　*New Zealand and Melanesia

　.1　　　*New Zealand

　.101　　　Early history to 1840

　　　　　　Including Maori history

　.102　　　Colonial period, 1840–1908

　.103　　　Dominion status, 1908–

994　　*Australia

　.01　　　Early history to 1788

* Add as instructed under 930–990

.02	Settlement and growth, 1788–1851
.03	Colonial administration, 1851–1901
.04	Early 20th century, 1901–1945

Class here comprehensive works on 20th century

For postwar period and Menzies administration, see 994.05; later 20th century, 994.06

.05	Postwar period and Menzies administration, 1945–1965
.06	Later 20th century, 1965–
995	*New Guinea (Papua)
996	*Other parts of Pacific Polynesia
.9	*Hawaii
997	*Atlantic Ocean islands
998	*Arctic islands and Antarctica

* Add as instructed under 930–990

Relative Index

Use of the Index

Full instructions on use of the index may be found in the Introduction, section 3.6.

Alphabeting is word by word. A hyphenated word is filed as one word.

Abbreviations are filed as if spelled out; their meanings are identified in the table immediately following this page.

Boldface: Entries and numbers in **boldface** type are subdivided in the schedules or tables, either by specification or by a note advising the classifier to add.

Grouping of digits: Digits are printed in groups of three purely for ease in reading and copying. The spaces are not part of the numbers, and the groups are not related to those shown in DDC numbers on Library of Congress cataloging records.

Tables: A number preceded by "*s.s.–*" may be found in Table 1, by "*area–*" in Table 2, by "*lit. sub.–*" in Table 3, by "*lang. sub.–*" in Table 4. Such numbers are never used alone.

Abbreviations Used in the Index

Abbreviations are alphabeted letter by letter.

admin.	administration(s)	geog.	geographical, geography
adv.	advertisement(s), advertising	geog. subd.	geographical subdivisions
agric.	agricultural, agriculture	geol.	geological, geology
anal.	analysis, analytic(al)	govt.	government(s), governmental
anc. hist.	ancient history	hist.	historical, history
&	and	hist. subd.	historical subdivisions
anthr.	anthropological, anthropology	home econ.	home economics
appl(s).	application(s), applied	illus.	illustration(s)
arch.	architectural, architecture	ind.	industrial, industries, industry
bact.	bacteria, bacteriological, bacteriology	indiv.	individual
		inorg. chem.	inorganic chemistry
biog.	biographical, biography	inst.	institution(s), institutional
biol.	biological, biology	instr.	instrument(s), instrumental
bldg(s).	building(s)	int.	interior, internal
bus.	business(es)	int. dec.	interior decoration
bus. tech.	business technology	internat.	international
Can.	Canada	isl(s).	island(s)
chem.	chemical, chemistry	jur.	jurisdiction(s)
chem. tech.	chemical technology	*lang. sub.–*	*language subdivision* [Table 4]
clim.	climate(s), climatological, climatology	lang(s).	language(s)
		ling.	lingual, linguistics
coll(s).	collected, collecting, collection(s)	lit.	literary, literature(s)
		lit. sub.–	*literature subdivision* [Table 3]
comm.	commerce, commercial	math.	mathematical, mathematics
commun.	communication(s)	meas.	measures
comp.	comparative	mech.	mechanical, mechanics
condit.	condition(s)	mech. eng.	mechanical engineering
cpd(s).	compound(s)	med.	medical, medicine
crit.	criticism	med. sci.	medical science
crys.	crystal(s), crystallography	medv. hist.	medieval history
dec.	decoration(s), decorative	met.	meteorological, meteorology
dept(s).	department(s)	mf.	manufacture(s), manufacturing
desc.	description, descriptive	mil.	military
econ.	economic(s)	mil. sci.	military science
econ. geol.	economic geology	min.	mineral(s), mineralogical, mineralogy
ed.	education(al)		
elect.	electric(al), electricity	misc.	miscellaneous, miscellany
Eng.	England	mod. hist.	modern history
eng.	engineering, engineers	mt(s).	mountain(s)
equip.	equipment	nat.	national, natural
exp.	experiment(s), experimental	org. chem.	organic chemistry
gen.	general	O.T.	Old Testament
gen. wks.	general works	paleob.	paleobotany

345

paleon.	paleontology	res.	reservoir
paleoz.	paleozoology	*s.a.*	*see also*
path.	pathological, pathology	sci.	science(s), scientific
perf.	performance	Scot.	Scotland
pers.	personnel	sep.	separate, separation(s)
pharm.	pharmacological, pharmacology	soc.	social, socialization, sociology
phil.	philosophical, philosophy	spec.	specific
phys.	physiological, physiology	*s.s.–*	*standard subdivision*
pol.	political, politics	St.	Saint
pol. sci.	political, politics	subj.	subject(s)
prac.	practical, practice	sys.	system(s), systematic(s)
proc.	procedure, process(es), processing	tech.	technical, technique, technological, technology
prod.	producing, production, products	Ter.	Territory
		transp.	transport, transportation
prof.	profession(s), professional	trmt.	treatment
psych.	psychological, psychology	U.S.	United States
pub.	public	USSR	Union of Soviet Socialist Republics
qual.	qualitative, quality		
quan.	quantitative, quantity	vet.	veterinary
rec.	recreation(al)	vet. sci.	veterinary science
reg.	regulation(s), regulatory	vs.	versus
rel.	religion(s)	zool.	zoological, zoology

Relative Index

A

ABM 623.4
ADP *see* Data processing
ALGOL *see* Data processing
Abacuses
 arithmetic 513.028
Abandoned children
 soc. services 362.7
Abbey
 buildings
  architecture 726
 establishments *see* Religious
  congregations
Abbott
 John J. C. Can. hist. 971.05
Abbreviations 410
 spec. langs.
  desc. & anal. *lang. sub.*–1
  dictionaries *lang. sub.*–3
  usage *lang. sub.*–8
 spec. subj. *s.s.*–01
Abdias
 Bible 224
Abduction *see* Criminal offenses
Aberdeen Scot. *area*–412
Ability
 psychology 153.9
Abnormal
 anatomy
  biology *see* Pathological
   anatomy biology
  med. sci. *see* Pathology
   med. sci.
 children *see* Exceptional children
 psychology 157
  children 155.4
 sexual relations *see* Sexual
  aberrations
Abolition
 pol. sci. 326
 U.S. hist. 973.7
Aboriginal *see* Primitive
Abortion
 criminal *see* Criminal offenses
 ethics 179
 surgical 618.2
Abrasive materials 553
Abscesses
 medicine 616.5

Absences
 employment *see* Leaves
  (absence)
 mil. offense 355.1
 school discipline *see* Teachers
  & Teaching
Absentee ownership
 land. econ. 333.4
Absolute
 monarchies 321.6
 temperature *see* Low
  temperatures
Absolution Christian rel.
 doctrines 234
 rites 265
Abstinence
 ethics 178
Abstract algebra 512
Abstracting documentation 029.4
Abstractions
 art representation 704.94
Abstracts
 information retrieval 025.5
  mechanized 029.7
 of title law 346.43
Abuse
 of legal process 346.3
 of power
  central govts. 351.9
Abused children
 soc. services 362.7
Abutments *see* Columnar
  structures
Abyssinia *see* Ethiopia
Abyssinian Church 281
Academic
 costumes
  education 378
 degrees 378
 freedom 371.1
  universities & colleges 378.1
 year 371.2
  higher ed. 378.1
Academies (organizations) *see*
  Organizations
Academies (schools) *see* Secondary
  schools
Acadia Colony
 Can. hist. 971.6

Africa	*area*–6	Agricultural (continued)	
African		banks	
languages		economics	332.3
linguistics	496	botany	630.1
literatures	896	chemistry	630.1
Afrikaans		**civilization**	**901.9**
language		classes *see* Social classes	
linguistics	439.3	climatology	630.1
literature	839.3	cooperatives econ.	334
Afro-Asiatic languages		credit econ.	332.7
linguistics	**492**	economics	338.1
literatures	**892**	equipment	
After-dinner		mf. tech.	681
speaking	808.5	use	631.3
speeches *see* Speeches		industries	
Agave fibers		govt. control	351.8
agriculture	633	management	658
Age qualifications suffrage		prod. econ.	338.1
pol. sci.	324	instruments *see* Agricultural	
Aged people		equipment	
institutions for		insurance	368.1
law	344.3	land	
soc. services	362.6	economics	333.7
labor econ.	331.3	machinery *see* Agricultural	
law	346.1	equipment	
libraries for	027.62	meteorology	630.1
med. sci.		pests	632
geriatrics	618.9	physics	630.1
hygiene	613	prices	338.1
Christian personal rel.	248	schools	630.7
psychology	155.67	sociology	301.34
sociology	301.43	tools *see* Agricultural equipment	
soc. insurance	368.4	zoology	630.1
soc. services	362.6	**Agriculture**	**630**
s.a. Adults; Men; Women; *also*		departments	
spec. kinds e.g. Sick		U.S. govts.	
people		federal	353.81
Agency law	346.2	**states**	**353.9**
Aggeus		production *see* Agricultural	
Bible	224	industries	
Aggregates		regulation	
pol. sci.	323.1	law	343.7
sociology	**301.4**	Agronomy *see* Agriculture	
Aging		Ainu *see* Paleosiberian	
biology	574.3	Air	
animals	591.3	bases	358.4
plants	581.3	combat *see* Air warfare	
med. sci.	612	compression *see* Pneumatic	
Agnosticism		conditioning *see* Air-conditioning	
Christian church hist.	273	currents	
nat. rel.	211	meteorology	551.5
philosophy	149	forces	
Agrarian reform *see spec. subj. e.g.*		law	343.1
Agricultural land		mil. sci.	358.4
Agricultural		*s.a.* Air-force	
areas		freight *see* Freight transportation	
civic art	711	hygiene of	613.1
sociology	301.34	mechanics *see* Mechanics	
bacteriology	630.1	navigation	629.132

Ascension	
Christian doctrines	232.9
Asceticism	
Christian rel. experience	248
Ash Wednesday *see* Lent	
Asia	*area*–5
Asia Minor	*area*–561
ancient	*area*–392
Asparagus	
agriculture	635
Asphalts	
bituminous materials *see*	
Bituminous materials	
petroleum products	665
pitch	553
waxes	665
Asphyxiation	
prevention *see* Safety	
surgical trmt.	617
Assamese language	
linguistics	491
literature	891
Assassination *see* Criminal offenses	
Assault & battery	
crimes *see* Criminal offenses	
torts	346.3
Assaying	
metallurgy	669
pharmaceutical chem.	615
Assemblies	
pol. sci.	328
sociology	301.18
Assembling products	
factory eng.	621.7
prod. management	658.5
Assembly	
civil right pol. sci.	323.4
Assembly-line processes *see*	
Assembling products	
Asses	
animal husbandry	636.1
Assimilation	
physiology	612
Association	366
civil right pol. sci.	323.4
football	
sports	796.334
psychology	
ideation	153.2
learning	153.1
Associations	366
religion *see* Ecclesiastical theology	
sociology	301.18
other aspects see Organizations	
Assumption of Mary	
Christian doctrines	232.91
Assurance *see* Insurance	

Assyrian	
Empire Mesopotamia hist.	935
s.a. East Semitic	
Assyro-Babylonian *see* Afro-Asiatic	
Astatine *see* Nonmetallic elements	
Asteroids *see* Planets	
Asthma	616.2
Astrobiology	
& religion nat. rel.	215
gen. wks.	574.999
animals	591.999
plants	581.999
Astrodynamics *see* Celestial	
mechanics	
Astrology	
occultism	133.5
Astromechanics *see* Celestial	
mechanics	
Astronautics	**629.4**
Astronavigation	527
Astronomical	
geography	525
twilight earth astronomy	525
Astronomy	**520**
& religion nat. rel.	215
Astrophysics	523.01
Asylum	
internat. law	341.48
pol. sci.	323.6
Asylums *see* Welfare	
Atheism	211
Athletic sports	
recreation	**796**
Atlantic	
Coastal Plain U.S.	*area*–75
Ocean	
biology *see* Hydrographic	
biology	
islands	*area*–97
oceanography	551.4
regional subj. trmt.	*area*–163
Provinces Canada	*area*–715
regional subj. trmt.	*area*–182
Atlantis	
folk lit.	398.2
Atlases	
geography	912
history	911
library trmt.	025.17
Atmosphere	
physical geol.	551.5
regional subj. trmt.	*area*–161
Atmospheric entry	
manned space flight	629.45
Atolls *see* Islands	
Atomic	
astrophysics	523.01
bombs	
mil. eng.	623.4

Atomic (continued)	
physics	539.7
structure	
matter	
astrophysics	523.01
physics	539
theoretical chem.	541
s.a. Nuclear	
Atoms *see* Atomic	
Atonement	
of Jesus Christ	
Christian doctrines	232
Attachment	
law	347.7
Attack operations	
mil. sci.	355.4
Attention	
psychology	
learning	153.1
perception	153.7
Attitudes	
psychology	152.4
students	371.8
Attorneys *see* Lawyers	
Auckland Isls.	*area*–931
Auction	
catalogs	
articles	*s.s.*–021
books	017–019
spec. subj.	**016**
Audiences	
mass communication	301.16
soc. psych.	301.18
Audio records	
communication	001.54
Audiology	
med. sci.	617.8
psychology	152.1
Audiovisual	
materials	
ed. use	371.33
library trmt.	025.17
management use	658.4
records	
communication	001.54
Auditing	
accounting records	657
pub. admin.	
central govts.	351.7
local govts.	352
Audition *see* Audiology	
Auditorium bldgs.	
architecture	725
Auditory	
materials *see* Audiovisual	
materials	
memory	
psychology	153.1
perception	
psychology	152.1

Aureomycin *see* Antibiotics	
Auroras	
geomagnetism	538
meteorology	551.5
Australia	*area*–94
Australian	
aboriginal languages	
linguistics	499
literatures	899
Capital Ter.	*area*–947
football	796.336
Austria	*area*–436
Austrian Succession War	940.2
Austroasiatic languages	
linguistics	495
literatures	895
Austronesian languages	
linguistics	499
literatures	899
Author catalogs books	018
Authoritarian states	
pol sci.	321.9
Authority	
Christian ecclesiastical theology	262
ethical systems	
Christian religion	241
philosophy	171
sociology	301.15
Authorized version	
Bible	220.5
Authorship techniques	808
Autobiography	**920**
Autographs	929.8
Automatic	
control *see* Automation	
data proc. *see* Data processing	
movements	
psychology	152.3
Automation	
engineering	629.8
factory eng.	621.7
postal commun.	383
prod. econ.	
secondary ind.	338.4
sociology	301.24
Automatons	
chess players rec.	794.1
Automobile	
driving *see* Driving motor vehicles	
racing sports	796.7
Automobiles	
commerce	388.34
engineering	**629.2**
influence on crime	364.2
law	343.9
sports	796.7
Automotive *see* Automobile; *also*	
Automobiles	

Avalanches	
disasters	
history	904
relief soc. welfare	361.5
geology	551.3
Ave Maria	
private prayers	242
Aves *see* Birds	
Avestan language	
linguistics	491
literature	891
Aviation	
fuels	
chem. tech.	665
insurance	368
medicine	616.9
meteorology	629.132
psychology	155.9
technology	**629.13**
Aviculture	636.5–.6
Avocados	
agriculture	634
Awards	
research	001.4
other spec. fields	*s.s.*–07
Axis Powers	
World War 2 hist.	940.53
Axles	
mech. eng. *see* Bearings	
mechanics	531
Ayr Scot.	*area*–414
Azerbaijan	*area*–55
Iran	*area*–55
USSR	*area*–47
Azerbaijani *see* Turkic	
Azores	*area*–469

B

Babies *see* Children	
Babism	
religion	297
Baby sitters' handbooks	649
Babylonian Empire Mesopotamia	
hist.	935
Bacillary diseases	616.9
Backgammon	
recreation	795
Backward *see* Mentally deficient	
Bacteria *see* Bacteriology	
Bacterial diseases	
med. sci.	616.9
Bactericides	
agric. use	632
production	668
Bacteriological warfare *see*	
Biological warfare	

Bacteriology	589.9
medical	616.01
s.a. Microbiology	
Bactria	*area*–39
Badminton	
sports	796.34
Bagpipes	
musical art	788
Baguios	
meteorology	551.5
Bahai faith	
religion	297
Bahama Isls.	*area*–729
Bahrein	*area*–53
Bail	
criminal law	345.7
Bakery goods	
home proc.	641.8
Baking	
cookery tech.	641.7
Balance	
of payments	
internat. banking	332.1
internat. comm.	382.1
of power internat. rel.	327
of trade internat. comm.	382.1
Baldness	616.5
Bali	*area*–598
Balinese *see* Javanese	
Balkan	
Peninsula	***area*–496**
Wars hist.	949.6
Ball	
bearings *see* Bearings	
games	
indoor	794.7
outdoor & gen.	**796.3**
Ballads	
literature *see* Poetry	
music	781.5
voice	784
Ballet	
music	782.9
stage performance	792.8
Ballistics	
gen. wks. *see* Mechanics	
mil. eng.	623.4
Balloons	
aircraft *see* Aircraft	
Ballots pol. sci.	324
Balls (rec. equip.)	
manufacturing	688.7
recreation	
athletic *see spec. games*	
indoor	794.7
Baltic	
languages	
linguistics	491
literature	891
Sea *see* Atlantic Ocean	

Bastardy *see* Illegitimacy
Basutoland — area–68
Bath mitzvahs
  etiquette — 395
  Jewish rites — 296.4
  soc. customs — 392
Bathing
  hygiene — 613.4
Bathing-beaches *see* Beaches
Bathrooms
  furnishings — 645
  household management — 643
  plumbing — 696
  residential int. dec. — 747
Baths
  hygiene — 613.4
Battalions
  mil. organization — 355.3
Batteries (electric)
  elect. eng. — 621.35
  s.a. spec. uses
Batteries (military)
  mil. organization — 358
Battery *see* Assault & battery
Battle tactics *see* Tactics mil. sci.
Battles
  history — 904
  mil. analysis — 355.4
Battleships *see* Vessels (nautical)
Bazooka rockets — 623.4
Bazookas — 623.4
Beaches
  civic planning — 711
  landscape arch. — 714
  reclamation eng. — 627
Beadwork
  dec. arts — 746.5
Beams (structural element)
  structural eng. — 624
Beards *see* Hairdressing
Bearings
  gen. machine eng. — 621.82
  internal combustion engines
    automobiles
      tech. & mf. — 629.2
Bears
  animal husbandry — 639
Beatitudes
  Gospels — **226**
Beatniks
  sociology — 301.44
    sex behavior — 301.41
Beauty
  personal *see* Personal appearance
  shops
    pub. health — 614.7
    technology — 646.7
Bechuanaland — area–68

Bedclothing
  domestic mf. — 646.2
  textile arts — 746.9
Bedford Eng. — area–425
Bedrooms
  furnishings — 645
  household management — 643
  int. dec. — 747
Beds (furniture)
  dec. arts — 749
  mf. tech. — 684.1
Bedspreads *see* Bedclothing
Beef *see* Meats
Beers *see* Alcoholic beverages
Bees *see* Insects
Beeswax
  prod. tech. — 638
Beets
  agriculture
    field crops — 633
    garden crops — 635
    sugar crops — 633
Behavior
  animals
    ecology — 591.5
    psychology — 156
  ed. psych. — 370.15
  gen. psych. — **150**
  soc. psych. — **301.1**
Behavioral sciences — **300**
Being
  metaphysics — **111**
Belgian Congo — area–675
Belgium — area–493
Belief
  epistemology — 121
Beliefs
  sociology — 301.2
    soc. change — 301.24
    soc. psych. — 301.15
Belize — area–728 2
Belles-lettres *see* Literature
Belligerency
  law of war — 341.6
Bells
  elect. commun. eng. — 621.389
  musical art — 789.5
Belorussia — area–476
Belorussian language
  linguistics — 491.7
  literature — 891.7
Belts
  clothing *see* Clothing
  machine eng.
    conveyors — 621.8
    power transmission — 621.8
Beltways *see* Roads
Bends (curves)
  liquid flow *see* Mechanics

Bends (disease)	616.9	Bibliographical centers	
Benefit societies		services	021.6
economic	334	**Bibliographies**	**010**
s.a. Insurance		documentation use	029.7
Benevolent societies *see* Benefit		reference use	025.5
societies		Bicameral legislatures	
Bengal		pol. sci.	328
East Pakistan	*area*–549	Bicycles *see* Cycles (vehicles)	
India	*area*–54	Biennials	
Bengali language		floriculture	635.9
linguistics	491	Big	
literature	891	bang theory cosmogony	523.1
Bennett		business	
Richard Bedford Can. hist.	971.06	management	658
Benue-Niger *see* African		prod econ.	338.6
Benzenes		Sioux River	*area*–783
fuel		Bigamy	
chem. tech.	662	criminology *see* Criminal	
org. chem.	547	offenses	
Berber languages		*other aspects see* Polygamy	
linguistics	493	Bihari language	
literatures	893	linguistics	491
Bergsonism		literature	891
philosophy	143	Biliary tract	
Berkelium *see* Metals		diseases	616.3
Berkshire Eng.	*area*–422	Billiards	
Bermuda	*area*–729 9	recreation	794.7
Berries		Bills (proposed laws)	
agriculture	634	pol. sci.	328
Berwick Scot.	*area*–414	Bills of exchange	
Beryllium *see* Metals		law	346.7
Bessarabia	*area*–47	Binding books *see* Bookbinding	
Beta particles		Binoculars	
physics	539.7	manufacturing	681
Bethrothals		Bioastronautics biophysics	
etiquette	395	gen. wks.	574.1
Betting		animals	591.1
ethics	175	plants	581.1
horse racing	798	*s.a. spec. organisms*	
systems		med. sci.	612
recreation	795	Biochemistry	
Beverages		gen. wks.	574.1
gen. wks.	641.3	animals	591.1
alcoholic	641.2	plants	581.1
hygiene	613.3	med. sci.	612
inspection pub. health	614.3	animals	636.08
manufacturing	663	Bioclimatology *see* Ecology	
preparation		Bioecology *see* Ecology	
home econ.	641.8	Biogeochemistry *see* Ecology	
Bhutan	*area*–549	**Biogeography**	**574.9**
Biafra	*area*–669 4	**animals**	**591.9**
Bible	**220**	**plants**	**581.9**
Biblical		**Biographies**	**920**
characters & events		Biological	
art representation		**determinism soc.**	**301**
arts	704.948	devices	
Christian rel.	247	mil. ammunition	623.4
Greek language	487	drives psych.	152.5
		forces mil. sci.	358

Biological (continued)	
resources	
conservation tech.	639
utilization econ.	333.9
sciences	**570**
specimens	
preservation	579
warfare	
defense against	
mil. eng.	623.3
mil. sci.	358
Biology	**574**
& religion	
nat. rel.	215
Bionics cybernetics	001.53
Bionomics *see* Ecology	
Biophysics	
gen. wks.	574.1
animals	591.1
plants	581.1
med. sci.	612
animals	636.08
Biotechnology	620.8
Birds	
agric. pests	632
animal husbandry	**636.5–.6**
cruelty to	
ethics	179
disease carriers	
pub. health	614.4
hunting	
commercial	639
sports	799.2
paleozoology	568
zoology	598.2
s.a. Wildlife	
Birth	
control	
law	344.7
sociology	301.32
s.a. Contraception	
customs	392
etiquette	395
defects	
gen. med.	616
Births	
obstetrics	618.2
statistics	312
Bishops (clergy) *see* Clergy	
Bismarck Archipelago	*area*–93
Bismuth *see* Metals	
Bison	
animal husbandry	636.2
Bituminous	
coal *see* Coals	
materials	
eng. materials	620.1
road eng.	625.8

Black	
art *see* Magic	
death	
Europe hist.	940.1
medical aspects *see*	
Bubonic plague	
Hawk War U.S. hist.	973.5
magic *see* Magic	
Muslims	
religion	297
people *see* Minority groups;	
also African	
Sea *see* Atlantic Ocean	
Black-eyed peas	
agriculture	635
Blackheads	616.5
Blacklisting	
labor econ.	331.89
Blackmail *see* Criminal offenses	
Blacks (Negroes) *see* Negroes	
Blacksmithing	682
Bladder (urinary)	
diseases	616.6
Blankets *see* Textiles; *also*	
Bedclothing	
Blasphemy	
ethics	179
religion	
Christianity	241
comp. rel.	291.5
Blasting	
foundation eng.	624
underwater eng.	627.7
Blast-resistant construction	
buildings	693.8
Bleaching	
technology	667
Blessings at meals *see* Private	
worship	
Blighted areas	
civic art	711
Blimps *see* Aircraft	
Blind people	
education	371.9
library services	027.6
soc. services	362.4
Blindness	
ophthalmology	617.7
soc. path.	362.4
s.a. Blind people	
Block	
diagraming *see* Programing	
printing	
graphic arts *see* Relief (art)	
printing graphic arts	
textiles *see* Printing processes	
textiles	

Bukovina	*area*–498
Romania	*area*–498
Ukraine	*area*–47
Bulbs (lamps) *see* Lighting	
Bulgaria	*area*–497 7
Bulgarian language	
linguistics	491.8
literature	891.8
Bull	
Moose Party U.S.	
history	973.91
pol. sci.	329
Run Battles	
U.S. hist.	973.7
Bullets *see* Ammunition	
Bullfights	
ethics	175
performing arts	791.8
Bunker Hill Battle	
U.S. hist.	973.3
Bureaucracy	
pub. admin.	
central govts.	351.04
sociology	301.18
Burglary *see* Criminal offenses	
Burial of dead	
customs	393
pub. health	614
Buried treasure	
travel	910.4
Burlap *see* Textiles	
Burma	*area*–591
Burmese language	
linguistics	495
literature	895
Burns	
surgery	617
Burundi	*area*–675
Bus transportation	
commerce	388.3
govt. control	351.8
law	343.9
Buses	
commerce	388.34
engineering	629.22
Business	
arithmetic	513
cycles	
economics	338.5
enterprises	
& state pol. sci.	322
law	346.6
management	**650**
prod. econ.	338.7
spec. subj.	*s.s.*–06
ethics	174
etiquette	395
forecasting	
economics	338.5

Business (continued)	
insurance	368.8
machines	
manufacturing	681
use	651.8
management	**658**
schools	
secondary ed.	373.2
taxes	
law	343.4
pub. finance econ.	336.2
s.a. Commercial	
Bute Scot.	*area*–413
Butter	
manufacture	637
Buttons	
comm. mf.	687
Buyers' guides	
home econ.	640.73
Buying *see* Procurement	
Buzz groups & sessions *see*	
Discussion	
Byelorussian *see* Belorussian	
By-products	
foods	664
s.a. Wastes	
Byzantine	
art	709.02
design & dec.	745.4
s.a. spec. art forms	
Empire hist.	949.5
law	340.5
Byzantium	*area*–39

C

CARE	
soc. welfare	361
CENTO *see* Mutual defense &	
security	
COBOL *see* Data processing	
Cabala	
Judaistic sources	296.1
Calabistic traditions	
occultism	135.4
Cabbages	
agriculture	635
Cabinda	*area*–67
Cabinet	
systems	
pol. sci.	321.8
pub. admin.	351.04
Cabinets (furniture) *see* Furniture	
Cabinets (govt. agencies) *see*	
Cabinet systems	
Cable commun. systems	
commerce	384.6
govt. control	351.8

Canes (sticks)
  dress customs   391
Canes (sugar)
  agriculture   633
  other aspects see Sugars
Canine police services *see* Crime
        prevention
Canines *see* Dogs
Cannibalism
  soc. customs   394
Canning foods
  commercial   664
  domestic   641.4
Cannons
  art metalwork   739.7
  mil. eng.   623.4
Canoeing
  sports   797.1
Canoes *see* Vessels (nautical)
Canon law *see* Religious law
Canonization
  Christian doctrines   235
Cantatas
  sacred   783.4
  secular   782.8
Canticle of Canticles
  Bible   223
Canute
  Eng. hist.   942.01
Canyons *see* Depressions
        (geomorphology)
Capital
  financial econ.   332
  gains taxes
    law   343.4
    pub. finance   336.2
  management financial management 658.1
  punishment
    ethics   179
    penology   364.6
Capitalism
  economics   330.12
Capitalization (linguistics)   411
  spec. langs.
    desc. & anal.   *lang. sub.*–1
    usage   **lang. sub.–8**
Capitols
  architecture   725
Caps *see* Clothing
Capstans
  machine eng.   621.8
Carbines
  art metalwork   739.7
  mil. eng.   623.4
Carbohydrates
  appl. nutrition
    home econ.   641.1
  org. chem.   547

Carbon
  dioxide
    chem. tech.   665
  other aspects see Nonmetallic
        elements
Card
  catalogs *see* Library catalogs
  games recreation   795.4
  tricks recreation   795.4
Cardinals (clergy) *see* Clergy
Cardiology
  med. sci.   616.1
Cardiovascular system
  diseases   616.1
    surgery   617
Cargo
  insurance   368.2
  transportation *see* Freight
        transportation
Cargo-handling equipment
  port eng.   627
Caribbean
  islands   *area*–729
  Sea *see* Atlantic Ocean
Caribbees   *area*–729
Caribous
  animal husbandry   636.2
Caricatures *see* Cartoons
Carillons
  musical art   789
Carlow Ireland   *area*–418
Carnivores
  animal husbandry   636
  paleozoology   569
  zoology   599
Carolingian dynasty
  France hist.   944
  Ger. hist.   943
Carols
  sacred music   783.6
Carpentry
  bldg. construction   694
  shipbuilding   623.82
Carpeting *see* Floor coverings
Carpets *see* Rugs
Carriers
  pneumatic eng.   621.5
Carrots
  agriculture
    field crops   633
    garden crops   635
Cars *see* Automobiles
Cartels
  prod. econ.   338.8
Carthage ancient   *area*–39
Cartography   **526**
  mil. eng.   623.7
Cartomancy
  parapsychology   133.3

Chemistry	**540**
& religion	
nat. rel.	215
applied	**660**
astronomy	523.01
cells *see* Physiology cells	
soil sci.	631.4
s.a. Chemical; *also spec. fields*	
e.g. Geochemistry	
Cherries	
agriculture	634
Cheshire Eng.	*area*–427
Chess	
recreation	794.1
Chests (furniture) *see* Furniture	
Chicken pox	
gen. med.	**616.914**
Chickens *see* Poultry	
Chicory	
agriculture	
field crops	633
garden crops	635
Chief executives	658.4
law	342.6
pub. admin.	350.04
Child	
care	
home econ.	649
development	
human phys.	612
guidance clinics	
soc. services	362.7
labor *see* Children's labor	
offenders *see* Juvenile	
delinquents	
psychology	155.4
welfare *see* Young people soc.	
services	
s.a. Children	
Childbirth	
obstetrics	618.2
Children	
criminal offenders *see* Juvenile	
delinquents	
cruelty to	
ethics	179
psychology	155.4
rearing of	
customs	392
home econ.	649
sociology	301.43
other aspects see Young people;	
also Persons	
s.a. Child; *also* Boys; *also* Girls	
Children's	
books	
bibliography	028.52

Children's (continued)	
clothing	
child care home econ.	649
other aspects see Clothing	
diseases	
gen. med.	618.9
garments *see* Children's clothing	
labor	
economics	331.3
labor law *see* Labor law	
libraries	027.62
parties	793.2
Chile	*area*–83
Chilean literature	**860**
Chimes	
musical art	789
Chimneys	
bldg. heating	697
other aspects see Roofs	
China	*area*–51
ancient	*area*–31
Chinaware	
table setting	642
other aspects see Porcelain	
Chinese	
chess	
recreation	794.1
language	
linguistics	495.1
literature	895.1
Chirognomy palmistry	133.6
Chiromancy palmistry	133.6
Chiropody	
med. sci.	617
Chiropractic	
therapeutics	615
Chivalry	
soc. customs	394
Chlorine *see* Nonmetallic elements	
Chlorophyta	
botany	589
Chocolate	
agriculture	633
beverage *see* Cocoa	
foods	641.3
cookery	641.6
Choice	
freedom *see* Freedom of choice	
mathematics	511
psychology	153.8
Choirs	
sacred music	783.8
Choking *see* Asphyxiation	
Choleras	
gen. med.	616.9
Cholesterol	
blood chem.	612
org. chem.	547

Cinematography	778.5
Ciphers (cryptography)	652
Circassian *see* Caucasic	
Circulation	
library services	025.6
Circulation (biology)	
pathology	
gen. wks.	574.2
animals	591.2
plants	581.2
med. sci.	616.1
physiology	
gen. wks.	574.1
animals	591.1
plants	581.1
med. sci.	612
Circumcision	
Jewish rites	296.4
soc. customs	392
surgery	617
Circumnavigational travel	910.4
Circumstantial evidence	
crime detection	364.12
law	347.6
criminal	345.64
Circumterrestrial flights	
astronautics	629.45
Circuses	
performing arts	791.3
Cirrhosis	
gen. med.	616.3
Cities	
local govt. admin.	352
soc. planning	309.2
sociology	301.34
s.a. City	
Citizens & state	
pol. sci.	**323**
Citizenship	
ethics	172
law	
international	341.48
municipal	342.8
pol. sci.	323.6
suffrage qualification	324
Citrus fruits	
agriculture	634
City	
buildings	
architecture	725
managers	
local govt. admin.	352
planning	
civic art	711
law	346.44
states	
pol. sci.	321
s.a. Urban; *also* Cities	

Civic	
art	711
duties ethics	172
Civics	320.4
elementary ed.	372.8
Civil	
architecture *see* Public structures	
defense	363.3
law	
international	341.72
municipal	344.5
pub. admin.	
central govts.	351.7
engineering	624
mil. eng.	623
government *see* Government	
law systems	340.5
liberty *see* Civil rights	
procedure *see* Legal procedure	
rights	
law	
international	341.48
municipal	342.8
pol. sci.	**323.4**
service	
administration	
central govts.	351.1
law	342.6
war	
citizenship ethics	172
internat. law	341.6
wars	
ethics	172
history	904
U.S.	973.7
societies	369
s.a. hist. of other spec.	
countries	
Civilization	
hist. & crit.	
areal & group trmt.	910
spec. countries	**913–919**
gen. trmt.	910
ancient	**913**
soc. trmt.	**309.1**
other aspects see Geography	
sociology	**301.2**
Civil-military relations	
pol. sci.	321.5
pub. admin.	
central govts.	351.8
Clackmannan Scot.	*area*–413
Clairaudience	
parapsychology	133.8
Clairvoyance	
parapsychology	133.8
Clamps	
tech. & mf.	621.9
Clare Co. Ireland	*area*–419

Coals	553
mining	622
processing	662
Coast	
artillery	
armed forces	358
guard	
mil. sci.	359.9
Ranges	*area*–795
Coatings	
manufacturing	667
painting material	
arts	751.2
Coats *see* Clothing	
Cobalt *see* Metals	
Cobol *see* Data processing	
Cockfighting	
ethics	175
performing arts	791.8
Cocks (mechanical) *see* Mechanics	
Cocktails *see* Alcoholic beverages	
Cocoa	
agriculture	633
beverage	
comm. proc.	663
cookery	641.8
Coconut oil	
comm. proc.	665
Coconuts	
agriculture	
fiber crops	633
food crops	634
Codes	
of conduct	
Christian moral theology	241.5
other rel. see Moral theology	
of law *see* Legal codes	
Coding	
data processing *see* Data	
processing	
documentation	**029**
Coeducation	376
Coercion	
soc. accommodation	301.6
soc. control	301.15
Coffee	
agriculture	633
hygiene	613.3
Cognac *see* Alcoholic beverages	
Cognition	
psychology	153.4
Cogs *see* Mechanics	
Coinage	
law	343.3
monetary policy *see* Monetary	
policy	
Coins	
numismatics	737.4
Coir textiles *see* Textiles	

Coke	
manufacturing	662
Cola	
agriculture	633
Colchis ancient	*area*–39
Cold	
beverages	
hygiene	613.3
climates	
hygiene	613.1
fronts	
meteorology	551.5
s.a. Cryogenics	
Coldness *see* Low temperatures	
Colds (disease)	616.2
Colitis	616.3
Collagen diseases	616.7
Collecting	
museology	069
recreation	790.13
spec. objects	*s.s.*–075
Collections	
museology	069
spec. objects	*s.s.*–075
texts *see* Anthologies	
Collective	
bargaining	
labor econ.	331.8
labor law *see* Labor law	
personnel admin.	658.31
pub. admin.	
central govts.	351.1
security	
internat. relations	327
Collectivism	
economics	**335**
pol. ideology	320.5
College & university *see* University	
& college	
College of Cardinals *see* Clergy	
Colleges & universities *see*	
Universities & colleges	
Colloidal fuels	
manufacturing	662
Colloids	
physical chem.	541
applied	660.2
organic	547
Colloquialisms	417
spec. langs.	*lang. sub.*–7
Colognes *see* Perfumes	
Colombia	*area*–861
Colombian literature	**860**
Colonial	
administration	
pol. sci.	325
Dames	369
period	
U.S. hist.	973.2
Wars society	369

Commercial (continued)		Communist	
policy	380.1	bloc	
domestic comm.	381	regional subj. trmt.	*area*–171
internat. comm.	382	international organizations	
revenues		pol. sci.	329
pub. finance	336.1	parties	
s.a. Business		pol. sci.	329
Commission government		states	
local admin.	352	pol. sci.	321.9
Commissioned officers		Communities	
armed forces	355.3	ecology *see* Ecology	
Committees		psych. influences	155.9
legislative bodies		sociology	301.34
pol. sci.	328	Community	
sociology	301.18	centers	
Common		adult ed.	374.2
cold		chests	
gen. med.	616.2	soc. welfare	361.8
land		property law	346.4
economics	333.2	songs	784.6
law systems	340.5	Companies	
Common-law marriage		firms *see* Corporations	
law	346.1	mil. organization	355.3
Commonwealth		Comparative	
Eng. hist.	942.06	psychology	156
Communal land		**religion**	**291**
economics	333.2	Compends	*s.s.*–02
Communes		Compensation	
local govt. admin.	352	income distribution	
Communicable diseases	616.9	macroeconomics	339.2
pub. health	614.4	**labor econ.**	**331.21**
Communication	001.54	personnel admin.	658.32
animal ecology	591.5	pub. admin.	
engineering	**621.38**	central govts.	351.1
military	623.7	Complex variable functions	
facilities		mathematics	515
commerce	380.3	Complexes	
forces		depth psych.	154.2
mil. sci.	358	Composing machines	
management use	658.4	manufacturing	681
office services	651.7	Composite foods	
services		cookery	641.8
commerce	380.3	Composition (arts)	701
sociology	301.14	*s.a. spec. art forms*	
spec. subj.	*s.s.*–01	Composition (music)	781.6
Communications		*s.a. spec. mediums*	
law		Composition (printing)	686.2
international	341.7	Composition (writing)	
municipal	343.9	appl. ling.	418
satellites		**spec. langs.**	**lang. sub.–8**
commerce		**rhetoric**	**808**
radio	384.54	Compounds	
television	384.55	chemistry	546
eng. aspects	629.46	**technology**	**660**
Communion		Comprehension *see* Perception	
sacrament *see* Holy communion		Compressed-air transmission	
Communism		technology	621.5
econ. ideology	**335.4**	Compressible flow *see* Mechanics	
pol. ideology	320.5	Compression sickness	616.9

Cryogenics	
technology	621.5
other aspects see Low	
temperatures	
Cryptogams	
botany	586
paleobotany	561
other aspects see Plants	
Cryptography	
mil. sci.	358
technique	652
verbal commun.	001.54
Crystal	
gazing	
parapsychology	133.3
use	
table setting	642
Crystallographic mineralogy	549
Crystallography	548
Cuba	*area*–729 1
Cuban literature	**860**
Cubism	
painting arts	759.06
Cucumbers	
agriculture	635.6
Cultural	
anthropology	**301.2**
exchanges	
law	
international	341.7
municipal	344.7
processes	
sociology	**301.2**
Culture *see* Civilization	
Cumberland Eng.	*area*–428
Cumbrae Isls. Scot.	*area*–413
Cuneiform inscriptions	417
Cuprammonium textiles *see*	
Textiles	
Cups *see* Containers	
Curaçao isl.	*area*–729
Curates *see* Clergy	
Curiosities	001.9
Curium *see* Metals	
Curling (sport)	796.9
Currants	
agriculture	634.7
Currency *see* Paper money	
Curriculums	375
elementary ed.	372.1
exceptional students	371.9
govt. supervision	379
higher ed.	378.1
secondary ed.	373.1
spec. subj.	*s.s.*–07
Curtains	
domestic mf.	646.2
textile arts	746.9
window furnishings	645

Cushitic languages	
linguistics	493
literatures	893
Customs (social)	**390**
Customs (tariffs)	
internat. comm.	382.7
law	
international	341.7
municipal	343.4
pub. finance	336.2
Cutlery	
cleaning	648
table setting	642
Cuts	
wounds	
surgical trmt.	617
Cutting-tools	
tech. & mf.	621.9
Cybernetics	001.53
Cycles (vehicles)	
commerce	388.34
engineering	
gen. tech. & mf.	629.22
maintenance	629.28
Cyclic compounds	
org. chem.	547
Cycling	
sports	796.6
Cyclopedias *see* Encyclopedias	
Cyclostomes *see* Anamnia	
Cymbals	
musical art	789
Cymric *see* Welsh	
Cynic philosophy	183
Cyprus	*area*–564
ancient	*area*–392
Cyrenaic philosophy	183
Cyrenaica	*area*–61
ancient	*area*–39
Cyrillic alphabet	
linguistics	411
Cytology	
gen.wks.	574.8
animals	591.8
plants	581.8
med. sci.	611
Czech language	
linguistics	491.8
literature	891.8
Czechoslovakia	*area*–437

D

DDT *see* Insecticides	
DNA *see* Nucleus cells cytology	
Dactylology	419
Dadaism	
painting arts	759.06
Dahana	*area*–53

Decoration		Democratic	
arts	745.4	Party	
Decorative		U.S.	
arts	**745**	history	973
values		pol. sci.	329.3
arts	701	socialism	
Deductive reasoning		economics	335.5
logic	162	pol. ideology	320.5
psychology	153.4	states	
Deers		pol. sci.	321.8
animal husbandry	636.2	pure	321.4
Defense (legal)		Democritean philosophy	182
criminal law	345.7	Demography *see* Populations	
Defense (military)		Demolition	
law	343.1	mil. eng.	623
operations		mil. sci.	358
mil. eng.	623	Demonology	
mil. sci.	355.4	occultism	133.4
air forces	358.4	Demons *see* Devils	
land forces	355.4	Denbigh Wales	*area*–429
naval forces	359.4	Dendrology	582
pub. admin.		Denial	
activities	351.8	epistemology	121
departments	351.04	Denmark	*area*–489
U.S. govt.	353.6	Denominations	
Deficiency diseases		**Christianity**	**280**
gen. med.	616.3	Judaism	296.8
Deflation		Dentinal materials prod.	
economics	332.4	manufacturing	679
Degeneration		Dentistry	617.6
biology *see* Pathological		Deposits	
Degrees academic	**378**	pub. revenues	336.1
Dehumidification		Depressions (economics)	338.5
air-conditioning *see* Air-		Depressions (geomorphology)	551.4
conditioning		regional subj. trmt.	*area*–14
Dehydrating		**Depth psych.**	**154**
foods	641.4	Derby Eng.	*area*–425
commercial	664	Derivation (linguistics) *see*	
Deism		Etymology	
nat. rel.	211	Dermatology	616.5
Deities		Derry Ireland	*area*–416
rel. worship		Descriptive	
comp. rel.	291.2	**astronomy**	**523**
Delaware	*area*–751	cataloging	025.3
Deleterious organisms		geometry	
econ. biol.	574.6	abstract	516
animals	591.6	**government**	**320.4**
plants	581.6	**pub. admin.**	**350**
Delinquent children		research	001.4
education	371.9	Desegregation *see* Social classes	
psychology	155.4	Deserts	
s.a. Juvenile delinquents		regional subj. trmt.	*area*–15
Delusions	001.9	Design	
Dementia praecox *see*		arts	745.4
Schizophrenia		elementary ed.	372.5
Demobilization		metaphysics *see* Teleology	
mil. resources	355.2	operations research *see* Operations	
		research	
		Desks *see* Furniture	

Drafts *see* Commercial paper
Drainage
  agric. soil reclamation — 631.6
  land reclamation eng. — 627
  mining eng. — 622
  road eng. — 625.7
Drama
  elementary ed. — 372.6
  gen. wks.
    collections — 808.82
    crit. theory — 801
    hist. & crit. — 809.2
    rhetoric — 808.2
  spec. lits. — *lit. sub.*–2
  stage presentation *see* Theater
Dramatic
  music — **782**
  programs
    radio performances — 791.44
    television performances — 791.45
Draperies
  int. dec. — 747
  manufacturing — 684.3
  textile arts — 746.9
  window furnishings home econ. — 645
Dravidian languages
  linguistics — 494
  literatures — 894
Drawing
  arts — **740**
    elementary ed. — 372.5
  maps — 526.8
  technical — 604.2
Drawings
  arts — **740**
  bldg. construction — 692
Drawn work
  textile arts — 746.4
Dreams
  occultism — **135**
  psychology — 154.6
Dress *see* Clothing
Dressmaking
  comm. mf. — 687
  home econ. — 646.4
Driftwood
  dec. arrangements — 745.92
Drink — **641**
Drinking
  ethics — 178
  soc. customs — 394.1
Drinks *see* Beverages
Drives (psychology) *see* Motivation
Driving
  horses
    sports — 798
  motor vehicles
    sports — 796.7
    technology — 629.28

Dropouts
  education — 371.2
Droughts
  plant injuries
    agriculture — 632
Drowning *see* Asphyxiation
Drugs — 615
  control
    pub. health — 614.3
    soc. services — 363.4
  pharmacology — 615
  s.a. Narcotics
Druidism
  religion — 299
Drumbeats *see* Nonverbal language
Drums
  musical art — 789
Drunkenness
  criminal offense *see* Criminal
    offenses
  s.a. Alcoholism
Druzes — 297
Dry
  cleaning
    home econ. — 646.6
    technology — 667
  farming — 631.5
  ice
    chem. tech. — 665
    refrigeration — 621.5
Drying foods — 641.4
  commercial — 664
Drypoint
  graphic arts — 767
Dualism
  nat. rel. — 212
  philosophy — 147
  Hindu — 181
Dublin Ireland — *area*–418
Ducks *see* Poultry
Ductless glands
  diseases — 616.4
Dude ranching & farming
  sports — 796.5
Dueling
  ethics — 179
  soc. customs — 394
Dulcimers
  musical art — 787
Dumfries Scot. — *area*–414
Dunbarton Scot. — *area*–413
Dunkards — 286
Dunkers — 286
Duplicating-machines
  manufacturing — 681
Duplicating-techniques
  photoduplication — 686.4
  printing — 686.2

Ecology	
life sci.	574.5
animals	591.5
man	573
plants	581.5
sociology	301.31
Economic	
biology	574.6
animals	591.6
plants	581.6
botany	581.6
conditions	**330.9**
fluctuations	338.5
geography	**330.91–.99**
geology	553
growth	
macroeconomics	339.5
history	**330.9**
institutions	
sociology	301.5
planning	**338.9**
rent land econ.	333
resources	
mil. sci.	355.2
rights	
pol. sci.	323.4
situation	**330.9**
stabilization	
macroeconomics	339.5
zoology	591.6
Economics	**330**
Ecuador	*area*–866
Ecuadorean literature	**860**
Ecumenical	
councils	
Christian church hist.	
Middle Ages	270.2
modern period	270.8
Christian ecclesiology	262
movement	
Christian church hist.	270.8
Ecumenicalism	
ecclesiology	262
Eczema	
gen. med.	616.5
Edinburgh Scot.	*area*–414
Editing	808
journalism	070.4
Education	**370**
depts. pub. admin.	
central govts.	351
U.S. govt.	353.84
local govts.	352
govt. control	**379**
law	344.7
guidance	371.4
institutions	
libraries for	**027.7–.8**
sociology	301.5

Education (continued)	
programs	
radio performances	791.44
television performances	791.45
psychology	370.15
services	
library econ.	025.5
museology	069
sociology	370.19
Edward	
reign Eng. hist.	
1–3	942.03
4–5	942.04
6	942.05
7	942.082
8	942.084
Confessor	942.01
Effect	
metaphysics	122
Efficiency	
employees	
personnel admin.	658.31
pub. admin.	351.1
engineering for	620.8
prod. econ.	338
primary ind.	
agriculture	338.1
mineral ind.	338.2
other	338.3
secondary ind.	338.4
communication	380.3
transportation	380.5
Eggs	
prod. tech.	637
Egoism	
ethical systems	171
Egypt	*area*–62
ancient	*area*–32
Egyptian languages	
linguistics	493
literatures	893
Eighteenth century	
civilization	901.93
history	909.7
Eighth century	
civilization	901.92
history	909.07
Einsteinium *see* Metals	
Eire	*area*–415
Eisenhower	
Dwight D. admin. U.S. hist.	973.921
Elands	
animal husbandry	636.2
Elasticity	
earth's crust	551.1
eng. materials	620.1
solid dynamics *see* Mechanics	

Fluids	
mechanics *see* Mechanics	
s.a. Gases; *also* Liquids	
Fluorine *see* Nonmetallic elements	
Fluoroscopic examinations	
med. sci.	616.07
dentistry	617.6
surgery	617
Flutes	
musical art	788
Flying	
saucers	001.9
techniques	
aeronautical eng.	629.132
sports	797.5
Fogs	
meteorology	551.5
Folds	
structural geol.	551.8
Folk	
arts	**745**
beliefs	398
literature	398.2
music	
music theory	781.7
songs	
music	784.4
Folklore	**398**
Folkways	
sociology	301.2
Food	
poisons	
toxicology	615.9
services	642
supply	
mil. admin.	355.6
prod. econ.	338.1
Foods	641.3
inspection pub. health	614.3
soc. customs	394.1
technology	
agriculture	**630**
chem. tech.	664
home econ.	**641**
Foot warfare & forces	356
Football	**796.33**
Footings	
arch. construction	721
Footwear	
manufacturing	685
other aspects see Clothing	
Forage crops	
agriculture	633
Force	
metaphysics	118
Forces	
mechanics *see* Mechanics	

Forecasting	
business	338.5
weather	551.6
Foreign	
affairs	
pub. admin.	
activities	351.8
departments	351.04
U.S. Govt.	353.1
other aspects see International relations	
exchange	
economics	332.4
groups *see* Minority groups	
investments	
economics	332.6
legions	
mil. organization	355.3
s.a. International	
Foremanship *see* Supervision	
personnel admin.	
Forensic	
medicine	614
psychiatry	614
psychology	
law	347.6
criminal	345.6
Foreordination	
Christian rel. doctrines	234
Forest fires	
technology	634.9
Forestry	634.9
Forfar Scot.	*area*–413
Forgeries	
books	098
financial instruments	
economics	332.9
paintings	751.5
other aspects see Criminal offenses	
Forgetting	
psychology	153.1
Forging metals	
arts	
decorative	739
fine	731.4
blacksmithing	682
mf. tech.	671.3
ferrous metals	672.3
Forgiveness	
Christian doctrines	234
Form letters	
office use	651.7
Form (concept)	
arts	701
metaphysics	117
Formosa	*area*–51
Forms	
sculpture	731

Formulas	*s.s.*–021
Fortifications	
mil. eng.	623
Fortran *see* Data processing	
Fortresses	
architecture	725
mil. eng.	623
Fortunetelling	
parapsychology	133.3
Forums *see* Public discussions	
Fossils *see* Paleontology	
Foster homes	
child welfare	362.7
Foundation eng.	624
Foundations (organizations)	
law	346.6
welfare	361.7
Foundations (supports)	
arch. construction	721
Foundry practice	
metal prod.	
manufacturing	671.2
ferrous metals	672.2
Fountains	
landscape design	714
Fourierism	
socialist school	335
Fourteenth century	
civilization	901.92
history	909.07
Fourth	
dimension	
physics	530.1
Republic	
France hist.	944.082
Fowl *see spec. kinds e.g.* Chickens	
Fractures	
bones	
first aid	614.8
surgery	617
France	*area*–44
Franchises	
pub. revenues	
economics	336.1
Francium *see* Metals	
Franco-German War	
history	943.08
Franklin	
state	
Tenn. hist.	976.8
Franz Josef Land RSFSR	*area*–985
Fraternal insurance	368.3
Fraternities	
education	371.8
Frauds	
criminology *see* Criminal offenses	
occultism	133

Free	
markets	
price determination	338.5
Methodist Church of North	
America	287
ports	
transportation	387.1
thought	
nat. rel.	211
trade	
internat. comm.	382.7
will	
soteriology	
Christianity	234
Freedom	
law *see* Civil rights law	
metaphysics	123
of choice	
rel. doctrines	
Christianity	233
nat. rel.	216
s.a. Free will	
of conscience	
civil right	323.44
of contract	
civil right	323.4
of press	
civil right	323.44
of religion	
civil right	323.44
of speech	
civil right	323.44
Free-enterprise economy	330.12
Freemasonry	366
Freeways *see* Roads	
Freewill Baptists	286
Freezers	
low-temperature eng.	621.5
Freezing foods	
commercial	664
domestic	641.4
Freight	
airplanes *see* Aircraft	
cars railroad rolling stock	
commerce	385
engineering	625.2
transportation	
commerce	380.5
air	387.7
inland-waterway	386
maritime	387.5
rail	385
truck & bus	388.3
local	388.4
govt. control	
central govts.	351.8

French	
& Indian war	
U.S. hist.	973.2
s.a. Seven Years' War	
Guiana	*area*–88
horns	
musical art	788
Indochina	
history	959.7
s.a.	*area*–597
language	
linguistics	**440**
literature	**840**
Revolution	
history	944.04
Somaliland	*area*–67
Fresh-water biology	574.92
animals	591.92
plants	581.92
Freudian systems	
psychology	150.19
Friction *see* Mechanics	
Friendly	
Islands	*area*–96
societies	
economics	334
Friends	
psych. influences	155.9
relationships with	
appl. psych.	158
Friends (religious society)	289.6
Friendship	
ethics	177
Friends-of-the-library groups	021.7
Frigid Zones	
climate	551.6
diseases *see* Environmental	
diseases	
earth astronomy	525
regional subj. trmt.	*area*–11
Frisian language	
linguistics	439
literature	839
Frost	
geol. agent	551.3
meteorology	551.5
Frozen desserts	
prod. tech.	637
Fruits	
agriculture	634
art representation *see* Still life	
foods	641.3
cookery	641.6
paleobotany	561
plant anatomy	582
preservation	
commercial	664
domestic	641.4

Frustrations	
popular psych.	131
Fuel	
cells	
appl. electrochem.	621.35
oils	
chem. tech.	665
Fuels	
bldg. heating	697
cookery	641.5
heat eng.	621.4
internal combustion engines	
automobiles	629.2
manufacturing	662
metallurgical furnaces	669
Fumigants	
agric. use	632
manufacturing	668
Fumigation	
disease control	
pub. health	614.4
pest control	
agriculture	632
Functional analysis	515
Functions (mathematics)	511
theory	515
Fund raising	
soc. welfare	361.7
Fundamental education	370.19
Funerals	
customs	393
dress	391
etiquette	395
flower arrangements	745.92
Fungi	
botany	589
paleobotany	561
Fungicides	
agric. use	632
production	668
Fungus diseases	
med. sci.	616.9
plant husbandry	632
Fur goods	
manufacturing	685
Furnaces	
heat eng.	621.4
heating equip.	
buildings	697
Furnishings	
Christian rel. significance	247
domestic customs	392
home econ.	645
cleaning	648
library bldgs.	022
manufacturing	684
museum bldgs.	069

Furniture	
dec. arts	**749**
home econ.	645
library bldgs.	022
manufacturing	684.1
museum bldgs.	069
office services	651
Furs	
processing	675
Fusion	
effect of heat	
physics	536
nuclear physics	539.7
reactors	
nuclear eng.	621.48
technology *see* Nuclear	
engineering	
Future	
interests	
property law	346.4
state of man *see* Eschatology	

G

GNP	
macroeconomics	339.3
GOP *see* Republican Party	
Gables *see* Roofs	
Gabon	*area*–67
Gadolinium *see* Metals	
Gaelic	
Irish *see* Irish Gaelic	
Scottish *see* Scottish Gaelic	
Gaetulia	*area*–39
Galápagos Isls.	*area*–866
Galatia	*area*–392
Galatians	
Bible	227
Galaxies	
astronomy	
description	523.1
theory	521
Galician language	
linguistics	469.7
literature	**869**
Gall bladder diseases	
gen. med.	616.3
Galleries	
arts	708
Gallium *see* Metals	
Galloway Scot.	*area*–414
Galls	
plant injuries	
agriculture	632
botany	581.2
Gallstones	616.3
Galway Ireland	*area*–417
Gambia	*area*–66
Gambier Isls.	*area*–96

Gambling	
criminology *see* Criminal offenses	
ethics	175
pub. control	363.4
systems	
recreation	795
Gambling-business	
ethics	174
Game refuges	
land econ.	333.9
Games	
camp sports	796.54
child care	
home econ.	649
ethics	175
indoor	**793**
management use	658.4
of chance	
recreation	**795**
of skill	
indoor	**794**
outdoor	**796**
soc. customs	394
Gametogenesis	
life sci.	574.3
animals	591.3
plants	581.3
Gamma rays	
physics	539.7
Gamma-ray	
electronics	
physics	537.5
technology	621.381
photography	621.36
spectroscopy *see* Spectroscopy	
spec. kinds x- & gamma-ray	
electronics	
Gangs	
sociology	301.18
Gangsterism	
soc. path.	364.1
Gaols *see* Penal institutions	
Garages	
automobiles	629.28
Garbage	
disposal *see* Wastes control &	
utilization	
fertilizers	
agric. use	631.8
gen. wks. *see* Refuse	
Garden	
crops	
horticulture	635
furnishings	
home econ.	645
furniture *see* Outdoor furniture	
Gardening	
horticulture	**635**
landscape design	712

Geometry	516		Gifts		
of numbers	512		libraries	021.8	
Geomorphology	551.4		acquisition	025.2	
Geonavigation	623.89		pub. revenues	336.1	
Geophysics	**551**		Gilbert Isls.	*area*–96	
Geopolitics			Gins *see* Alcoholic beverages		
pol. sci.	320.1		Gipsy language *see* Dard languages		
internat. relations	327		Giraffes		
George			animal husbandry	636.2	
reign Eng. hist.			Girl Scouts	369.463	
1–4	942.07		Girls		
5	942.083		**societies**	**369.46**	
6	942.084		*other aspects see* Children		
Georgia			Glaciology	551.3	
Soviet Republic	*area*–47		Glamorgan Wales	*area*–429	
state	*area*–758		Glasgow Scot.	*area*–414	
Geriatrics	618.9		Glass		
Germ cells *see* Gametogenesis			bldg. construction	693.9	
German			**dec. arts**	**748**	
Democratic Republic	*area*–43		eng. materials	620.1	
language			manufacturing	666	
linguistics	**430**		Glassware		
literature	**830**		table setting home econ.	642	
Germanic			Glaucoma	617.7	
languages			Glazing windows	698.5	
linguistics	**430**		Gliders *see* Aircraft		
literatures	**830**		Gliding		
regions			sports	797.5	
ancient	*area*–363		Globes *see* Maps		
religion	293		Glockenspiels		
Germanium *see* Metals			musical art	789	
Germany	*area*–43		Glottis		
Germs *see* Microbiology			diseases	616.2	
Gerontology			Gloucester Eng.	*area*–424	
physical	612		Gloves *see* Handwear		
social *see* Social gerontology			Glues *see* Adhesives		
Gerrymandering			Gluttony		
legislative bodies	328		**Christian rel.**	**241**	
Gestalt psychology	150.19		ethics	178	
Gettysburg Battle			Glycerin		
U.S. Civil War hist.	973.7		manufacturing	668	
Geysers			Glyptics		
geology	551.2		dec. arts	736	
Ghana	*area*–667		Gnosticism		
Ghosts			heresies		
folk lit.			Christian church hist.	273	
texts & lit. crit.	398.2		Goat-hair textiles *see* Textiles		
occultism	133.1		Goats		
Giants (supernatural)			animal husbandry	636.3	
folk lit.			Gobi Desert	*area*–51	
texts & lit. crit.	398.2		God		
Gibraltar	*area*–46		rel. doctrines		
Gifted			Christianity	231	
children			comp. rel.	291.2	
psychology	155.4		Judaism	296.3	
students			nat. rel.	211	
education	371.9		Gods & goddesses		
			rel. worship		
			comp. rel.	291.2	

Goiter		Government (continued)	
gen. med.	616.4	liability	
Gold (metal) *see* Metals		law	
Gold Coast		international	341.26
history	966.7	municipal	342.8
Golden Rule		pub. admin.	
Christian moral theology	241.5	central govts.	351.9
Goldsmithing		libraries	027.5
arts		for spec. groups	027.6
decorative	739.2	malfunctioning	
mf. tech.	673	central govts.	351.9
Golf		service	
sports	796.352	pub. admin.	
Gonorrhea		central govts.	351.1–.3
gen. med.	616.9	workers *see* Civil service	
Goodness		*s.a.* Public	
freedom of choice		Governmental *see* Government	
Christian doctrines	233	Governments	
metaphysics	111.8	**pol. sci.**	**320.3–.4**
of God		soc. theology	
rel. doctrines		Christianity	261.7
Christianity	231	comp. rel.	291.1
nat. rel.	214	Governors (executives)	
Goose *see* Poultry		pub. admin.	351.04
Gooseberries		**spec. jur.**	**353–354**
agriculture	634	U.S.	353.9
other aspects see Fruits		**spec. states**	**353.94–.99**
Gorges *see* Depressions		Grace	
(geomorphology)		at meals *see* Private worship	
Gospels		Christian doctrines	234
Bible	226	Grade schools	372.1
pseudepigrapha	229	Grades (levels)	
Gossip		military	355.3
ethics	177	religions *see* Governing leaders	
Gothic art	709.02	ecclesiology	
s.a. spec. art forms		Grades (ratings)	
Gout		education	371.2
gen. med.	616.3	Graft *see* Criminal offenses	
Governing		Grain elevators	
boards		agriculture	631.2
libraries	021.8	Grains	
management	658.4	agriculture	633
leaders		Grammar (linguistics)	415
ecclesiology		spec. langs.	
Christianity	262	nonstandard forms	*lang. sub.*–7
comp. rel.	291.6	standard forms	
Judaism	296.6	desc. & anal.	*lang. sub.*–5
Government		**usage**	***lang. sub.*–8**
buildings		**study & teaching**	**415.07**
architecture	725	elementary ed.	372.6
corporations		Grampian Mts. Scot.	*area*–412
law	346.6	Gran Chaco	*area*–82
pub. admin.		Grand	
central govts.	351.04	Army of the Republic	369
local govts.	**352**	juries	
employees *see* Civil service		proceedings	
grants		criminal law	345.7
prod. econ.	**338.9**	opera *see* Opera	
		Granites *see* Stone	

Grant			Greek (continued)	
Ulysses S. admin. U.S. hist.	973.8		Orthodox Church	281.9
Grants			philosophy	
prod. econ.	**338.9**		ancient	182–185
Grapes			modern	199
agriculture	634		religion	292
Graphic arts	**760**		sculpture	733
Graphs			Greek-letter societies	
mathematics	511		education	371.8
spec. subj.	*s.s.*–021		Greenland	*area*–98
statistical method	001.4		Gregorian chants	783.5
spec. subj.	*s.s.*–01		Grievances	
Grasses			labor econ.	331.88
agriculture	633		personnel admin.	658.31
botany	584		public	351.1
Graveyards *see* Cemeteries			Grooming personal	646.7
Gravitation			Gross	
celestial mech. *see* Celestial			nat. prod.	
mechanics			macroeconomics	339.3
physics	531		structure	
liquids	532		earth	551.1
solids	531		Ground	
Gravity			cover	
determinations			landscape design	716
geodesy	526		**forces mil. sci.**	**355**
mechanics *see* Mechanics			**operations mil. sci.**	**355**
Great			transportation	
Barrier Reef Australia	*area*–943		**commerce**	**388**
Basin states U.S.	***area*–79**		**warfare mil. sci.**	**355**
Britain *see* British Isles			waters	553
circle course			econ. geol.	553
celestial navigation	527		extraction	622
Lakes	***area*–77**		geomorphology	551.4
Canada	*area*–713		hydraulic eng.	627
U.S.	***area*–77**		utilization	
Northern War	947		land econ.	333.9
Plains	***area*–78**		Ground-effect machines *see*	
schism			Air-cushion vehicles	
Christian church hist.	270.3		Grounds	
War (1914–1918)			functional use	
history	940.3		libraries	022
Greater Antilles	*area*–729 1–729 5		local Christian churches	254
Greco-Turkish War	949.5		schools	371.6
Greece	*area*–495		landscape design	712
ancient	*area*–38		Group	
Greediness			behavior	
ethics	178		**sociology**	**301.1**
Greek			education	
architecture	722		adult ed.	374.2
islands	***area*–499**		guidance	
ancient	*area*–391		education	371.4
languages			insurance	368.3
classical			work	
linguistics	**480**		soc. welfare	361.4
literature	**880**		Groups	
modern			algebra	512
linguistics	489		personal	
literature	889		soc. psych.	301.18
postclassical				
linguistics	487			

Handball		Harmonicas (mouth organs)	
sports	796.31	musical art	788
Handbooks	s.s.–02	Harmonies	
Handcrafts *see* Handicrafts		Gospels	226
Handedness		Harmoniums	
psychology	152.3	musical art	786.9
Hand-forged tools		Harmony	
technology	682	music theory	781.3
Handicapped		Harps	
children		musical art	787
psychology	155.4	Harpsichords	
people		musical art	786.1
mental *see* Mentally deficient		Harrison	
people		administrations U.S. hist.	
physical		Benjamin	973.8
soc. services	362.4	William H.	973.5
workers		Harvesting crops	
labor econ.	331.5	agriculture	631.5
labor law *see* Labor law		Hastings	
Handicaps		battle Eng. hist.	942.02
soc. path.	362.4	Hats *see* Headgear	
Handicrafts		Hausa language	
arts	**745.5**	linguistics	493
elementary ed.	372.5	literature	893
Handkerchiefs		Hawaii	*area*–969
comm. mf.	687	Hay fever	
domestic mf.	646.4	gen. med.	616.2
soc. customs	391	Hayes	
Hands		Rutherford B. admin. U.S. hist.	973.8
diseases & surgery	617	Hayti	*area*–729 4
divinatory reading	133.6	Hazardous materials	
Handwear		safety	
comm. mf.	685	pub. health	614.8
other aspects see Clothing		technology	604.7
Handwork		Head	
textile arts	746.4	physical anthropometry	573
Handwriting	652	surgery	617
analysis		Headaches	
crime detection	364.12	symptoms	616.07
popular psych.	137	Headgear	
elementary ed.	372.6	comm. mf.	687
Hangings		domestic mf.	646.5
domestic mf.	646.2	soc. customs	391
home econ.	645	Health	
int. dec.	747	buildings	
textile arts	746.3	architecture	725
Hanover		departments	
House Eng. hist.	942.07	pub. admin.	
Hansen's disease	616.9	central govts.	351.04
Hants Co. Eng.	*area*–422	U.S. govt.	353.84
Happiness		engineering	
popular psych.	131	gen. wks.	620.8
Hara-kiri *see* Suicide		sanitation *see* Sanitary	
Harding		engineering	
Warren G. admin. U.S. hist.	973.91	insurance	368.3
Hardware		soc. security	368.4
manufacturing	683	services	362.1–.4
Hares		mil. sci.	355.3
animal husbandry	636	schools	371.7

Hi-fi	
tech. & mf.	621.389
High	
blood pressure	616.1
schools *see* Secondary schools	
seas	
internat. law	341.42
temperatures	
physics	536
Higher	
criticism	
Bible	220.6
education	**378**
law	344.7
High-fidelity systems	
tech. & mf.	621.389
Highway transp. *see* Vehicular	
transp.	
Highways *see* Roads	
Hiking	
sports	796.5
Hill climbing	
sports	796.5
Hills *see* Elevations (physiography)	
Himalayas	**area–54**
Hindi language	
linguistics	491
literature	891
Hindu Kush	*area*–581
Hinduism	
philosophy	181
regions	*area*–176
religion	294.5
Hinges	
manufacturing	683
Hippies	
sociology	301.44
Hippocratic oath	
medical ethics	174
Hire-purchase	
law	346.7
Hispaniola	*area*–729 3
Histology	
life sci.	574.8
animals	591.8
plants	581.8
Historical	
books (O.T.)	222
pseudepigrapha	229
events	
art representation	704.94
painting	756
geography	**911**
geology	551.7
periods	
gen. hist.	**909**
spec. areas	**930–990**
spec. subj.	*s.s.*–09

Historical (continued)	
research	001.4
spec. subj.	*s.s.*–07
treatment	
spec. subj.	**s.s.–09**
Historiography	907.2
History	**900**
appls. to spec. subj.	**s.s.–09**
gen. wks.	
ancient	**930**
general	
spec. places	**940–990**
world	**909**
medieval	909.07
spec. centuries	909
s.a. spec. places	
modern	909.08
spec. centuries	**909**
s.a. spec. places	
study & teaching	**907**
curriculums	375
elementary ed.	372.8
Hoarding	
macroeconomics	339.4
Hoaxes	001.9
books hist. & crit.	098
Hobbies	
recreation	790.13
spec. subj.	*s.s.*–023
Hockey	
sports	
field	796.35
ice	796.9
Hogs	
animal husbandry	636.4
Hokan-Siouan *see* American	
aboriginal	
Holding-companies	
prod. econ.	338.8
Holidays	
labor econ. *see* Leaves (absence)	
soc. customs	394.2
s.a. Holy days	
Holiness	
Christian doctrines	234
Holland	*area*–492
Holmium *see* Metals	
Holography	774
Holy	
Bible	**220**
Communion *see* Sacraments	
days	
observance	
Christianity	263
Judaism	296.4
soc. customs	394.2
s.a. Holidays	
Family	
Christian doctrines	232.9

Knowledge	001
classification	112
metaphysics	121
sociology	301.2
Koine	487
Kongo *see* Congo	
Koran	297
Korea	*area*–519
Korean language	
linguistics	495.7
literature	895.7
Krypton *see* Nonmetallic elements	
Ku-Klux Klan	322
Kurdish language	
linguistics	491
literature	891
Kurdistan	*area*–56
Kurile Isls.	*area*–57
Kuwait	*area*–53
Kwa *see* African	
Kwajalein	*area*–968

L

LSD *see* Hallucinogenic drugs	
Labor	
conditions	331.2
disputes *see* Collective bargaining	
economics	**331**
govt. control	
central govts.	351.8
departments	351.04
U.S. govt.	353.83
law	
international	341.7
municipal	344.1
movements	
pol. sci.	322
parties	**329.9**
relations	**331**
theory of value	
Marxist econ.	335.4
unions	331.88
Labor (childbirth)	
obstetrics	618.2
Laboratories	
chemistry	542
other spec. subj.	
apparatus & tech.	*s.s.*–028
research	*s.s.*–07
Laboratory method	
education	371.3
Laboring classes	
soc. welfare	362.8
sociology	301.44
Labrador	*area*–719

Lackering	
dec. arts	745.7
furniture arts	749
woodwork bldgs.	698.3
Lackers	
manufacturing	667
Lacquering *see* Lackering	
Lacrosse (game)	
sports	796.34
Lactation	
diseases	
obstetrics	618.2
Ladin *see* Rhaeto-Romanic	
Ladino *see* Judeo-Spanish	
Lagomorphs	
animal husbandry	636
Lahnda language	
linguistics	491
literature	891
Laissez-faire econ. theory	330.15
Laity	
church govt.	
Christianity	262
comp. rel.	291.6
Judaism	296.6
pastoral duties	
Christianity	253.5–.7
Lake	
District Eng.	*area*–428
states U.S.	*area*–77
transportation	
commerce	386
govt. control	351.8
s.a. spec. lakes e.g. Erie Lake	
Lakes	
geomorphology	551.4
govt. control	
law	346.44
hydraulic eng.	627
internat. law	341.42
regional subj. trmt.	*area*–16
utilization	
economics	333 9
Lamé *see* Textiles	
Lamentations	
Bible	224
Laminates	
wood	
mf. tech.	674
Lanark Scot.	*area*–414
Lancashire Eng.	*area*–427
Lancaster	
House of	
Eng. hist.	942.04
Land	
descriptions	
law	346.43
drainage	
engineering *see* Drainage	
geology	551.3

Land (continued)	
economics	**333**
forces	
mil. sci.	**355**
forms	
geomorphology	551.4
subj. trmt.	*area*–14
operations	
mil. sci.	**355**
reclamation	
engineering	627
reform	
law	346.44
regions subj. trmt.	*area*–14
titles	
law	346.43
use surveys	631.4
utilization econ.	333.7
warfare	**355**
law of war	341.6
s.a. Real property	
Landlord-tenant relations	
land econ.	333.5
Landscape	
architecture	712
art	712
design	712
Landscapes	
art representation	704.94
painting	758
Landsmaal *see* Norwegian	
Language	**400**
communication	001.54
disorders	
abnormal psych.	157
gen. med.	616.8
regions subj. trmt.	*area*–17
sociology	301.2
Languages	**400**
study & teaching	**407**
curriculums	375
elementary ed.	372.6
Langue d'oc (dialect)	447
Lanthanide series metals *see*	
Metals	
Lanthanum *see* Metals	
Lao language	
linguistics	495
literature	895
Laoighis Ireland	*area*–418
Laos	*area*–594
Laotian *see* Lao	
Lapidary work	
glyptics	736
Lapland	*area*–471
Lapp language	
linguistics	494
literature	894
Larceny *see* Criminal offenses	

Laryngitis	616.2
Laryngology	
med. sci.	616.2
Larynx	
diseases	
gen. med.	616.2
Laser	
commun. devices	621.389
weapons	
mil. eng.	623.4
Lasers	
engineering	621.36
physics	535.5
Last	
judgment	
Christianity	236
Supper	
Christian doctrines	232.9
things *see* Eschatology	
Latches	
mf. tech.	683
Latexes	
manufacturing	678
Lathes	
tech. & mf.	621.9
Latin	
America	*area*–8
language	
linguistics	**470**
literature	**870**
Latinian languages	
linguistics	479
literatures	879
Latitude	
celestial navigation	527
geodetic astronomy	526
Latter-Day Saints church	289.3
Latvia	*area*–47
Latvian language	
linguistics	491
literature	891
Laundering	
home econ.	648
technology	667
Laurentian Plateau	*area*–714
Laurier	
Wilfred admin. Can. hist.	971.05
Law	**340**
armed forces	355.1
enforcement	
crime prevention	364.4
law	345.5
police services	363.2
libraries	026
of religion *see* Religious law	
Lawn	
bowling	
sports	796.31
tennis	
sports	796.34

Lawns	
landscape design	716
Lawrencium *see* Metals	
Laws	
enactment	
pol. sci.	328
moral theology *see* Moral	
theology	
texts	348
Laying on of hands	
Christian rel. rites	265
Layoffs of employees	
personnel admin.	
discipline	658.31
gen. wks.	658.31
pub. admin.	
central govts.	351.1
union control	
labor econ.	331.88
Layouts	
plant management	658.2
Laziness	179
Lead *see* Metals	
Leadership	
appl. psych.	158
sociology	301.15
Leading windows	698.5
League of Nations	
internat. law	341.22
Leapfrog recreation	796.1
Learners *see* Students	
Learning	001.2
ed. psych.	370.15
psychology	153.1
Leases	
real property	
economics	333.5
law	346.43
Leasing	
personal property	
law	346.47
Leather goods	
manufacturing	685
Leathers	
arts	745.53
manufacturing	675
Leave periods	
labor law *see* Labor law	
Leaves (absence)	
armed forces	355.1
labor econ.	331.2
personnel admin.	658.31
pub. admin.	
central govts.	351.1
Leaves (plants)	
plant anatomy	581.4
Lebanon	area–569 2
Lecture method	
education	371.39

Lectures	
gen. colls. *see* Anthologies	
library services	025.5
museum services	069
Leeward Isls. West Indies	area–729
Legal	
administration	
management	658.1
aid	
law	345
soc. services	362.5
codes	
law	348
Roman Catholic rel. law	262.9
counseling	
soc. welfare	361.3
procedure	
Christian rel. law	262.9
internat. law	341.5
municipal law	**347**
criminal	345.5
systems	340.5
Legends	
art representation	704.94
folklore	398.2
religion *see* Religious	
mythology	
Legislation	
pol. sci.	**328**
Legislative	
bodies	
pol. sci.	**328**
branch of govt.	
law	342.5
powers & privileges	
law	342.5
pol. sci.	328
procedure	
law	342.5
Legislators	
law	342.5
pol. sci.	328
Legislatures	
pol. sci.	**328**
Legitimation	
law	346.1
Legs	
diseases & surgery	617
Legumes	
agriculture	635
Leicester Eng.	area–425
Leinster Ireland	area–418
Leisure	
rec. arts	790.01
Leitrim Ireland	area–417
Leix Ireland	area–418
Lemons	
agriculture	634

Light (radiation)		Line-&-staff organization	
engineering	621.36	armed forces	355.3
mil. eng.	623	management	658.4
hygiene	613.1	Linear	
physics	**535**	motion *see* Mechanics	
other aspects see Radiations		programing	
Lighter-than-air aircraft *see*		mathematics	519.7
Aircraft		Linen textiles *see* Textiles	
Lighthouses		Lingerie *see* Clothing	
hydraulic eng.	627	Linguistic analysis	
navigation	623.89	philosophy	149
Lighting		**Linguistics**	**410**
arch. design	729	**spec. langs.**	**420–490**
domestic customs	392	Linlithgow Scot.	*area*–414
engineering	621.32	Linoleum *see* Floor coverings	
int. dec.	747	Linoleum-block printing	
library bldgs.	022	graphic arts	
museum bldgs.	069	processes	761
plant management	658.2	products	769
work environment		Lions	
personnel admin.	658.38	animal husbandry	636.8
pub. admin.	351.1	Lions' clubs	369.5
Lighting-equipment		Lip reading	
household management	644	study & teaching	371.91
Lighting-fixtures		Lipids	
ceramic arts	738.8	org. chem.	547
furniture arts	749	Liqueurs *see* Alcoholic beverages	
Lightning		Liquids	
meteorology	551.5	chemistry	541
Lima beans		applied	660
agriculture	635	engineering	
Limbo Christian doctrines	236	mechanics	620.1
Limerick Ireland	*area*–419	sound transmission	620.2
Limes (cements)		physics	
technology	666	heat expansion & contraction	536
Limes (fruit)		mechanics	532
agriculture	634	sound transmission	534
Limitation of actions		specific heats	536
law	347.5	state of matter	530.4
criminal	345.5	Liquor traffic	
Limited		pub. control	363.4
editions		pub. admin.	
hist. & crit.	094	central govts.	351.7
government		Liquors *see* Alcoholic beverages	
pol. ideology	320.5	Listening	001.54
monarchies		appl. ling.	418
pol. sci.	321.8	spec. langs.	*lang. sub.*–83
partnerships *see* Partnerships		communication	001.54
Limnology	551.4	elementary ed.	372.6
Lincoln		music	780
Abraham admin. U.S. hist.	973.7	psychology	153.7
Lincolnshire Eng.	*area*–425	recreation	790.13
Line		rhetoric	808.59
engraving		Lists	*s.s.*–021
graphic arts		Literary	
processes	765	arts *see* Literature	
products	769	composition *see* Composition	
Islands	*area*–96	(writing)	

Malta	area–458
ancient	area–37
Maltese language	
linguistics	492
literature	892
Mammals	
agric. pests	632
animal husbandry	636.9
conservation tech.	639
drawing tech.	743
hunting	
commercial	639
sports	799.2
paleozoology	569
zoology	599
Mammary glands	
diseases	618.1
Man	
anthropology *see* Anthropology	
metaphysics	128
rel. doctrines	
Christianity	233
comp. rel.	291.2
Judaism	296.3
nat. rel.	218
zoology	599.9
Man (isle)	area–428
Management	**658**
pub. admin.	**350**
armed forces	355.6
sociology	**301**
Managerial	
sciences	**650**
success	658.4
Manchester Eng.	area–427
Manchuria	area–51
Mandated states	
pol. sci.	321
Mandates	
internat. law	341.2
Mande *see* African	
Mandingo *see* African	
Mandolins	
musical art	787
Maneuvers	
mil. sci.	355.5
naval forces	359.5
Manganese *see* Metals	
Manic-depressive psychoses	
gen. med.	616.8
psychology	157
Manitoba	area–712 7
Man-made fibers	
textiles *see* Textiles	
Manned space flight	629.45
Manners (customs) *see* Social	
customs	
Manners (etiquette) *see* Etiquette	

Manpower	
labor econ.	331.1
mil. resources	355.2
procurement	
mil. law	343.1
Mansions	
architecture	728.8
Manslaughter *see* Criminal offenses	
Manual	
alphabet	
language	419
arts	
elementary ed.	372.5
training *see* Vocational education	
Manuals	s.s.–02
Manufactures	
marketing *see* Marketing	
prod. econ.	338.4
technology	**670**
Manufacturing firms	338.7
cooperatives	334
management	658
Manuscripts	
hist. & crit.	091
library trmt.	025.17
cataloging	025.3
preparation	
rhetoric	808
Manx language	
linguistics	491.6
literature	891.6
Maori *see* Polynesian	
Maps	
geography	912
library trmt.	025.17
cataloging	025.3
making *see* Cartography	
mathematical geography	526.8
Maracas	
musical art	789
Marathi language	
linguistics	491
literature	891
Marbles *see* Stones	
Marches	
band music	785.1
musical form	
piano music	786.1
Marching bands	785.06
Mardi gras	
recreation	791.6
soc. customs	394.2
Margiana ancient	area–39
Marginal utility school econ.	330.15
Marianas Isls.	area–96
Marijuana *see* Narcotics	
Marimbas	
musical art	789

Marinas
  port eng. 627
Marine
  biology *see* Hydrographic biology
  engineering & engines 623.8
  scenes
    art representation 704.94
     painting 758
  transportation
    commerce 387.1–.5
    govt. control
      central govts. 351.8
    law
      international 341.42
      municipal 343.9
  waters
    geol. agent 551.3
  s.a. Nautical
Mariology
  Christian doctrines 232.91
Marionettes
  handicrafts 745.59
  mf. tech. 688.7
  performing arts 791.5
Marital
  property
    law **346.4**
  sex relations
    sociology 301.41
  s.a. Marriage
Maritime
  law
    international 341.42
    municipal 343.9
  Provinces Can. *area*–715
  s.a. Marine
Mark
  Bible 226
Marketing
  commerce 380.1
  law 343.8
  management **658.8**
  technology **658.8**
Marks (ratings)
  education 371.2
Marmara Sea *see* Atlantic Ocean
Marquesas Isls. *area*–96
Marquetry
  furniture arts 749
  wood handicrafts 745.51
Marriage
  counseling
    soc. welfare 362.8
  customs 392
  law 346.1
  sociology 301.42
  s.a. Matrimony; *also* Marital
Marshals
  law 347.1

Marshes
  drainage *see* Drainage
Marsupials *see* Mammals
Martial law 342.6
Martinique *area*–729
Martyrs
  Christian church hist. 272
Marxian socialism
  economics **335.4**
  pol. ideology 320.5
Marxism *see* Marxian socialism
Marxist *see* Marxian
Mary
  mother of Jesus
    Christian doctrines 232.91
    private prayers to 242
  queen of Eng.
    1
      history 942.05
      persecutions
        Christian church hist. 272
    2 942.06
Maryland *area*–752
Mascarene Isls. *area*–69
Mascots
  occultism 133.4
Masers
  microwave electronics 621.381
Mashonaland *area*–689
Masochism *see* Sexual aberrations
Masonry
  adhesives
    bldg. materials 691
    eng. materials 620.1
    manufacturing 666
  materials
    engineering 620.1
  organization **366**
Mass communication
  sociology 301.16
Mass (religion)
  Christian liturgical music 783.2
  Christian liturgy 264
Mass (substance)
  measurements 389
  physics mech. *see* Mechanics
Massachusetts *area*–744
Massage
  personal care 646.7
  therapeutics 615
Mass-energy
  conservation
    physics 531
  equivalence
    relativity theory 530.1
Master-servant relationships
  law 346.2

Mastoid processes	
diseases	
gen. med.	617.8
Masturbation *see* Sexual aberrations	
Matabeleland	*area*–689
Matches	
manufacturing	662
Mate selection *see* Courtship	
Materia medica *see* Drugs	
Material remains *see* Archeology	
Materialism	
doctrinal controversies	
Christian church hist.	273
philosophy	146
Materials	
buildings	691
engineering	620.1
foundation eng.	624
management	658.7
science	620.1
Materials-handling equip.	
machine eng.	621.8
Materiel	
armed forces	355.8
Maternity	
homes	
soc. services	362.1
hospitals	
soc. services	362.1
insurance	
soc. security	368.4
Mathematical	
crystallography	548
games	793.7
geography	**526**
logic	511
models	
mathematics	511
operations research *see*	
Operations research	
physics	530.1
techniques	
management use	658.4
Mathematics	**510**
Matriarchal state	
pol. sci.	321.1
Matriculation	
schools	**371.2**
Matrimony	
Christian doctrines	234
rel. rites	
Christianity	265
Judaism	296.4
Matter	
chemistry *see* Chemistry	
metaphysics	117
physics *see* Physics	
states *see* States of matter	

Matter (continued)	
structure	
astrophysics	523
physics	539
Matthew	
Bible	226
Mattresses *see* Beds (furniture)	
Maturation *see* Development	
(biology)	
Mauretania	
ancient country	*area*–39
Mauritania	*area*–66
Mauritius	*area*–69
Maxims	
folk lit.	398.9
Mayo Ireland	*area*–417
Mazdaism *see* Zoroastrianism	
Meals	
cookery	641.5
soc. customs	394.1
Measles	
gen. med.	616.9
Measurement	
education	371.2
elect. eng.	621.37
engineering	620
time	529
Measurement-theory	
physics	530.1
Measuring-instruments	
manufacturing	681
Measuring-tools	
tech. & mf.	621.9
Meath Ireland	*area*–418
Meats	641.3
diets	
hygiene	613.2
foods	641.3
cookery	641.6
preservation	
commercial	664
domestic	641.4
processing	664
Mechanical	
drawing	604.2
engineering	**621**
generation elect. power	621.312
musical instruments	
musical art	789.7
power *see* Power	
vibrations	
engineering	620.3
wave theory of light	
physics	535
Mechanics	531
air	533
applied	620.1
astronautics	629.41
astronomy	521

Melons	
agriculture	635
Membership	
local Christian parishes	254
s.a.	*s.s.*–06
Membranophones	
musical art	789
Memoirs	**920**
Memorial bldgs.	
architecture	725
Memory processes	
ed. psych.	370.15
psychology	153.1
Men	
art representation	704.94
drawing tech.	743
painting	757
biography	**920**
sociology	301.41
other aspects see Adults	
Mendelevium *see* Metals	
Mendelian laws	575.1
man	573.2
Mending	
books	025.7
clothing	646.2
Meningitis	616.8
Mennonite churches	289.7
Menopause disorders	
gynecology	618.1
Menstruation	
disorders	
gynecology	618.1
Mensuration	389
Mental	
capacity popular psych.	139
deficiency	
gen. med.	616.8
psychology	157
soc. path.	362.3
s.a. Mentally deficient	
diseases *see* Mental illness	
health	
law	344.4
school programs	371.7
s.a. Mental pub. health	
hospitals	
soc. services	362.2
hygiene *see* Mental health	
illness	
cause of crime	364.2
pub. health	614.5
soc. path.	362.2
s.a. Mentally ill people	
pub. health	614.5
retardation *see* Mental deficiency	

Mentally	
deficient	
people	
psychology *see* Abnormal	
psychology	
soc. services	362.3
students	
education	371.9
handicapped *see* Mentally	
deficient	
ill people	
criminology	364.3
penal institutions	365
soc. services	362.2
retarded *see* Mentally deficient	
Menticide	
psychology	153.8
Menus	
meal planning	642
Merchant	
marine *see* Marine transportation	
ships *see* Vessels (nautical)	
Mercury (element) *see* Metals	
Mercy	
killing	
ethics	174
quality	179
Mergers	
banks econ.	332.1
management	658.1
transp. ind.	
commerce	380.5
govt. control	
central govts.	351.8
Merit	
Christian doctrines	234
system *see* Civil service	
Mescal *see* Alcoholic beverages	
Mesons	
physics	539.7
Mesopotamia Iraq	*area*–567
ancient	*area*–35
Messiahs	
Christianity	232
comp. rel.	291.6
Messianism	
Judaistic doctrines	296.3
Metabolism	
diseases	616.3
Metal	
engraving	
intaglio	765
relief	761
textiles *see* Textiles	
Metallography	669
Metallurgy	669

Mogul Empire		Monasticism *see* Religious	
India hist.	954.02	congregations	
Mohammed the Prophet		Monetary policy	
Islam	297	economics	332.4
Mohammedan *see* Islamic		central banking	332.1
Mohorovicic discontinuity		macroeconomics	339.5
geophysics	551.1	Money	
Moldavia	*area*–498	economics	332.4
Romania	*area*–498	issuance	
USSR	*area*–47	pub. admin.	351.8
Molding		law	
sculpture	731.4	international	341.7
Molding-equipment		municipal	343.3
tech. & mf.	621.9	Money-orders	
Moldmaking		economics	332.7
metal prod. tech.	671.2	law	346.7
ferrous metals	672.2	Mongol Empire hist.	950
Molecular		Mongolia	*area*–51
biology	574.8	Mongolian People's Republic	*area*–51
animals	591.8	Mongolic languages	
plants	581.8	linguistics	494
mixtures		literatures	894
metals *see* Metals		Mongolism	
physics	539	gen. med.	616.8
structure		psychology	157
chemistry	541	Monism	
organic	547	philosophy	147
physics	539	Mon-Khmer languages	
Molecules	539	linguistics	495.9
chemistry *see* Molecular		literatures	895.9
structure chemistry		Monmouthshire	*area*–424
physics	539	Monocotyledons	
Molinism		botany	584
doctrinal controversies		paleobotany	561
Christian church hist.	273	Monocycles *see* Cycles (vehicles)	
Molinists		Monogamy	
persecutions		sociology	301.42
Christian church hist.	272	Monologs	
Molluscoidea		drama *see* Drama	
paleozoology	564	recitations *see* Speeches	
zoology	594	Monophysite churches	281
Mollusks		Monopoly	
agric. pests	632	law	
conservation tech.	639	international	341.75
culture	639	municipal	343.7
drawing tech.	743	prod. econ.	338.8
fisheries	639	Monotheism	
paleozoology	564	comp. rel.	291.1
zoology	594	nat. rel.	212
Moluccas	*area*–598	Monroe	
Molybdenum *see* Metals		James admin. U.S. hist.	973.5
Monaco	*area*–44	Montana	*area*–786
Monaghan Ireland	*area*–416	Montenegro	*area*–497
Monarchs *see* Royalty		Montserrat	*area*–729 7
Monastic		Moods	
buildings		psychology	152.4
architecture	726	Moon	
life		astronomy	
Christianity	248	description	523.3
orders *see* Religious congregations		theory	521
schools ed.	377	*s.a.* Lunar	

Mountain	
climbing	
sports	796.5
troops armed forces	356
warfare	
mil. sci.	355.4
Mountaineering	796.5
Mountains *see* Elevations	
(physiography)	
Mounted forces	
mil. sci.	357
Mourning	
soc. customs	393
Mouth	
diseases	
gen. med.	616.3
Mouth organs	
musical art	788
Movements	
biology	
med. sci.	616.7
physiology	
gen. wks.	574.1
animals	591.1
plants	581.1
med. sci.	612
perception	
intellectual	153.7
visual	152.1
psychology	152.3
Moving pictures *see* Motion	
pictures	
Mozambique	*area*–67
Muhammad the Prophet	
Islam	297
Muhammadan *see* Islamic	
Mules (animals)	
animal husbandry	636.1
Mules (footwear) *see* Footwear	
Mules (machines)	
textile tech.	677
Multiple	
dwelling bldgs.	
architecture	728.3
sclerosis	
gen. med.	616.8
Multiplication	512.9
algebra	512.9
arithmetic	513
Mu-mesons	
physics	539.7
Mumps	
gen. med.	616.3
Munda languages	
linguistics	495.9
literatures	895.9

Municipal	
engineering	628
incorporation	
local govt.	352
s.a. Local; *also* Government	
Municipal (domestic) law	**342–348**
Municipalities	
local govt.	352
Munitions *see* Ordnance	
Munster Ireland	*area*–419
Muntz metal *see* Metals	
Muons	
physics	539.7
Murder *see* Criminal offenses	
Muscat & Oman	*area*–53
Muscles	
diseases	
gen. med.	616.7
drawing arts	743
Muscular dystrophy	
gen. med.	616.7
Musculoskeletal system	
diseases	
gen. med.	616.7
Museology	**069**
Museum	
buildings	
architecture	727
catalogs & guidebooks	*s.s.*–074
Museums	
law	344.9
museology	**069**
spec. subj.	*s.s.*–074
Mushrooms	
agriculture	635
Music	**780**
bldgs. for	
architecture	725
govt. control	
central govts.	351.8
libraries	**026**
study & teaching	**780.7**
curriculums	375
elementary ed.	372.8
Music hall	
stage performance	792.7
Musical	
comedies	782.8
drama	**782**
instruments	
manufacturing	681
music theory	781.9
s.a. spec. instruments	
scores *see* Scores (music)	
shows	782.8
Mutinies	
travel	910.4

Natural (continued)	
products	
org. chem.	547
religion	**210**
resources	
economics	**333**
rights	
pol. sci.	323.4
scenes	
art representation	704.94
sciences	500.1
selection	
evolution theory	575
sociology	301
theology	**210**
Naturalism	
philosophy	146
Naturalization	
pol. sci.	323.6
Nature	
rel. worship	
comp. rel.	291.2
study	
elementary ed.	372.3
Nauru	*area*–96
Nautical	
almanacs	528
engineering	**623.8**
s.a. Marine	
Naval	
architecture	623.82
artillery	
mil. eng.	623.4
forces	
mil. sci.	**359**
medicine	616.9
operations *see spec. wars*	
schools	373.2
govt. supervision & support	**379**
science	359
ships *see* Vessels (nautical)	
warfare	
law of war	341.6
mil. sci.	**359**
s.a. Military; *also* Nautical	
Navigation	
aids	
commerce	
inland waterways	386
maritime transp.	387.1
hydraulic eng.	627
technology	629.04
aeronautics	629.132
manned space flight	629.45
seamanship	623.89
Nazarene Church	289.9
Nazism *see* Fascism	
Neanderthal man	573
Near East *see* Middle East	

Nearsightedness	617.7
Nebraska	*area*–782
Nebulas	
astronomy	
extragalactic *see* Galaxies	
galactic	
description	523.1
theory	521
Necessity	
metaphysics	123
Necks (structural geol.)	551.8
Neckwear *see* Clothing	
Needlework	
textile arts	746.4
s.a. Sewing	
Negligence	
law	346.3
Negotiable instruments	
law	346.7
Negotiation	
internat. law	341.5
Negrito languages	
linguistics	499
literatures	899
Negro	
Baptist churches	286
Methodist churches	287
Negroes	
gen. hist.	**909**
s.a. Minority groups; *also* African	
Nehemiah	
Bible	222
Neoclassical architecture	724
Neodymium *see* Metals	
Neo-Kantianism	
philosophy	142
Neomechanism	
philosophy	146
Neon	
lighting eng.	621.32
other aspects see Nonmetallic elements	
Neonates	
pediatrics	618.9
Neoplasms	
gen. med.	616.9
Neoplatonic philosophy	141
ancient school	186
Neoplatonists	
Christian apologetics vs.	239
Neorealism	
philosophy	149
Nepal	*area*–549
Nepali language	
linguistics	491
literature	891
Nephrology	
med. sci.	616.6

Ocean	
basins	
regional subj. trmt.	*area*–182
travel	910.4
waters *see* Sea waters	
Oceania	*area*–9
Oceanic languages	
Austronesian *see* Austronesian	
languages	
nonaustronesian	
linguistics	499
literatures	899
Oceanography	551.4
Oceans	
biology *see* Hydrographic biology	
econ. utilization	333.9
geomorphology	551.4
regional subj. trmt.	*area*–162–167
Odor	
control foods	
comm. proc.	664
perception	152.1
Offaly Ireland	*area*–418
Offenders	
criminal law	345
criminology	364.3
welfare services	364.6
Offenses	
criminal *see* Criminal offenses	
mil. law	355.1
Offensive arms	
art metalwork	739.7
customs	399
Office	
buildings	
architecture	725
holding	
pol. right	323.5
personnel	
personnel admin.	658.3
services	651
Officers	
mil. units	355.3
Official	
ceremonies & observances	
soc. customs	394
residence bldgs.	
architecture	725
Offset printing *see* Planographic	
printing	
Ohio	
River	*area*–769
state	*area*–771
Valley	*area*–77
Oil processes	
photographic printing	773

Oils	
eng. materials	620.1
food proc.	664
industrial	
manufacturing	665
Okinawa	*area*–52
Oklahoma	*area*–766
Old	
age	
insurance	368.4
sociology *see* Social gerontology	
s.a. Aged people	
Catholic Church	284
English *see* Anglo-Saxon	
German Baptist Brethren	286
Icelandic language	439
Northwest U.S.	*area*–77
people *see* Aged people	
School Baptists	286
Southwest U.S.	*area*–76
Testament	
Bible	221
liturgy	264
Old-age & survivors' insurance *see*	
Social insurance	
Olfactory perception	
psychology	152.1
Oligarchies	
pol. sci.	321.5
Olives	
agriculture	634
Olympic games	
sports	796.4
winter	796.9
Oman	*area*–53
Ombudsman system	
law	342.6
legislative bodies	328
pub. admin.	351.9
Omens *see* Divination	
Oncology	
med. sci.	616.9
Onions	
agriculture	635
Ontario	
Lake	.*area*–747
Canada	*area*–713
province	*area*–713
Ontogeny *see* Development	
(biology)	
Ontology	111
Opera	
buildings	
architecture	725
music	782.1
Operation studies	
prod. management	658.5

Operations			Orchard grasses	
mathematics	511		agriculture	633
prod. management	658.5		Orchards	
research	001.4		agriculture	634
management use	658.4		Orchestras	785.06
spec. appls.	*s.s.*–01		Orchestrions	
surgery	**617**		musical art	789.7
Operettas	782.8		Order work	
Ophicleides			library econ.	025.2
musical art	788		Ordnance	
Ophthalmology			law of war	341.6
med. sci.	617.7		mil. eng.	623.4
Opinion			mil. sci.	355.8
formation			testing	
soc. psych.	301.15		internat. law	341.73
journalism	070.4		Oregon	*area*–795
Optical			Ores	
communication	621.38		dressing	
crystallography	548		mining eng.	622
properties			Organic	
earth astronomy	525		chemicals	
eng. materials	620.1		manufacturing	661
minerals	549		chemistry	547
representations			drugs	
sound			pharmacology	615
engineering	620.2		evolution *see* Evolution life sci.	
physics	534		poisons	
scanning devices			toxicology	615.9
electronic eng.	621.381 9		psychoses	
spectroscopy			abnormal psych.	157
physics	535		medicine	616.8
Optics			Organization	
gen. wks. *see* Light (radiation)			of management	
Optimism			internal	658.4
philosophy	149		ownership	658.1
Optometry	617.7		of meetings	
Oral			law	346.6
communication	001.54		**Organizations**	**060**
linguistics *see* Languages			fraternal	366
rhetoric	**808.5**		law	
contraceptives	613.9		international	341.7
hygiene			municipal	346.6
med. sci.	617.6		prod. econ.	338.7
medication			sociology	301.18
therapeutics	615		spec. subj.	*s.s.*–06
surgery	617.5		Organs (anatomy)	
Oranges (fruit)			transplants	
agriculture	634		med. ethics	174
Oratorios			med. sci.	617
sacred	783.3		Organs (music)	
secular	782.8		musical art	786.5
Oratory	808.5		**Orient**	*area*–5
texts *see* Speeches			Oriental	
Orbits			architecture	722
astronomy			**churches**	**281**
description *see spec. celestial bodies*			law	340.5
			Orientation	
theory	521		employees	
space flight	629.41		personnel admin.	658.31
			pub. admin.	
			central govt.	351.1

Panorama paintings		Parades	
arts	751.7	circuses	791.3
Panoramas		performing arts	791.6
dec. arts	745.8	soc. customs	394
Panpsychism		Paradoxes	
philosophy	141	logic	165
Pan-Slavism		Paraguay	area–892
pol. ideology	320.5	Paraguayan	
Pantelleria	area–458	**literature**	**860**
Pantheism		War hist.	989.2
comp. rel.	291.1	Paralysis	
nat. rel.	212	manifestation of disease	616
philosophy	147	Paranoia	
Pantomime		gen. med.	616.8
nonverbal commun. *see*		psychology	157
Nonverbal language		Paraphotic	
Pantomimes		engineering	621.36
music	782.9	mil. eng.	623
stage performance	792.3	phenomena	
Papal		physics	535
administration	262	**Parapsychology**	**133**
schism church hist.	270.5	Parasitic diseases	
States	area–45	gen. med.	616.9
Paper		skin diseases	616.5
chromatography		Paratroops	
qual. anal. chem.	544	armed forces	356
cutting & folding		Pardons	
dec. arts	736	criminal law	345.7
handicrafts	745.54	penology	364.6
money		Parent-child relationships	
arts	769	law	346.1
economics	332.4	Parenthood	
printing	686.2	customs	392
textiles *see* Textiles		Parish welfare work	361.7
Paperboard		Parishes	
eng. materials	620.1	Christian ecclesiology	262
s.a. Containers		**local Christian church**	**254**
Paperhanging		Park structures	
bldg. details	698.6	architecture	725
int. dec.	747	Parking facilities	
Papers		civic art	711
eng. materials	620.1	urban transp.	
manufacturing	676	commerce	388.4
Paphlagonia	area–392	Parks	
Papiamento language		civic art	711
linguistics	467	govt. control	
literature	**860**	law	346.44
Papier-mâché		land utilization	
manufacturing	676	economics	333.7
sculpture material	731	landscape design	712
Papua	area–95	pub. works	363.5
Papuan languages		pub. admin.	
linguistics	499	central govts.	351.8
literatures	899	wildlife conservation tech.	639
Parables		Parkways *see* Roads	
Gospels	226	Parliamentary	
Parachute troops		procedures & rules	060.4
armed forces	356	legislatures	328

Poisons	
ammunition	
mil. eng.	623.4
toxicology	615.9
Poker (game)	
recreation	795.4
Polabian language	
linguistics	491.8
literature	891.8
Poland	area–438
Polar *see* Arctic	
Polaris missiles	
mil. eng.	623.4
Polarization	
light	
physics	535.5
sound	
physics	534
Polemics	
Christian doctrinal theology	239
Police	
buildings	
architecture	725
patrols *see* Crime prevention	
services	363.2
crime prevention	364.4
law	344.5
pub. admin.	
central govts.	351.7
local govts.	352
Policy making	
executive management	658.4
Poliomyelitis	
gen. med.	616.8
Polish language	
linguistics	491.8
literature	891.8
Polishes	
manufacturing	667
Polishing	
housecleaning	648
metal prod.	671.7
ferrous metals	672.7
woodwork bldgs.	698.3
Politeness	
ethics	177
etiquette	395
Political	
action groups	
pol. sci.	322
campaigns	
pol. sci.	329
conditions	
pol. sci.	**320.9**
divisions	
historical geog.	911
groups	
status in law	342.8
Political (continued)	
ideologies	
pol. sci.	320.5
institutions	
sociology	301.5
machines	
pol. sci.	329
parties	
pol. sci.	329
status in law	342.8
prisons	
penology	365
refugees	
pol. sci.	325
relationships	
ethics	172
rights	
law	342.7
pol. sci.	323.5
sabotage *see* Criminal offenses	
science	**320**
unions	
regional subj. trmt.	area–171
Politics	
ethics	172
Polk	
James K. admin. U.S. hist.	973.6
Poll taxes	
pub. finance	336.2
suffrage pol. sci.	324
Pollen	
paleobotany	561
plant anatomy	582
Pollution	
control	
law	
international	341.7
municipal	344.4
pub. admin.	
central govts.	351.8
local govts	352
economics	333.7–.9
human ecology	301.31
pub. health	614.7
water supply	363.6
water-supply eng.	628.1
Polo	
sports	796.35
Polonium *see* Metals	
Poltergeists	
occultism	133.1
Polyamides	
textiles *see* Textiles	
Polyandry *see* Polygamy	
Polyfluoro hydrocarbons	
textiles *see* Textiles	
Polygamy	
customs	392
sociology	301.42

Profits		Propaganda (continued)	
income distribution		services	
macroeconomics	339.2	armed forces *see* Psychological	
management	658.1	warfare	
prod. econ.	338.5	soc. psych.	301.15
Prognoses		Propagation	
med. sci.	616.07	biology *see* Reproduction	
Program		Properties	
languages *see* Data processing		earth	551.1
music		minerals	549
band music	785.1	*s.a. other spec. subj.*	
music theory	781.5	Property	
orchestra music	785.3	damage insurance	368.1
Programed instruction		law	
education	371.39	**private**	**346.4**
spec. subj.	*s.s.–07*	public	343.2
Programing		rights	
computers *see* Data processing		civil right	323.4
mathematics	519.7	theory	
operations research *see*		economics	330.1
Operations research		Prophetic	
prod. management	658.5	books (O.T.)	224
Prohibited books		message	
hist. & crit.	**098**	Bible	220.1
Project method		Prophets (religious leaders)	
education	371.3	Biblical biog. & crit.	221.9
Projectiles		comp. rel.	291.6
mil. eng.	623.4	Prophets (scriptures)	
solid dynamics *see* Mechanics		pseudepigrapha	229
Projection		*s.a. Prophetic books*	
photography *see* Photographic		Proportional	
projection		representation	
Projections		legislative bodies	328
maps	526.8	taxation	
tech. drawing	604.2	pub. finance	336.2
Promethium *see* Metals		Proprietary libraries	027
Promotion		Proprietorships	
armed forces	355.1	management	658
education	371.2	prod. econ.	338.7
employees		Proprioceptive perceptions	
personnel admin.	658.31	psychology	152.1
pub. admin.		Propulsion systems *see* Power plants	
central govts.	351.1	Prose	
labor rights		language *see* Languages	
economics	331.2	literature	
labor law *see* Labor law		gen. colls.	808.88
Pronouns *see* Words		spec. lits.	*lit. sub.–808*
Pronunciation		spec. periods	*lit. sub.–8*
linguistics	414	Prosecution procedure	
spec. langs.		criminal law	345.7
nonstandard forms	*lang. sub.–7*	Prosody	
standard forms		linguistics	416
desc. & anal.	*lang. sub.–1*	spec. langs.	
usage	*lang. sub.–81*	nonstandard forms	*lang. sub.–7*
vocal music	784.9	standard forms	*lang. sub.–6*
Propaganda		rhetoric	808.1
activities		Prospecting	
internat. relations	327	mining eng.	622
		Prospectuses	*s.s.–02*

Prostate	
diseases	
gen. wks.	616.6
neoplasms	616.9
geriatrics	618.9
Prostitution	
criminology *see* Criminal	
offenses	
ethics	176
pub. control	363.4
pub. admin.	
central govts.	351.7
soc. law	344.5
sociology	301.41
Protactinium *see* Metals	
Protective	
coatings *see* Coatings	
construction	
mil. eng.	623
structures	
port eng.	627
railroad eng.	625.1
tariffs	
internat. comm.	382.7
Protectorates	
internat. law	341.2
Proteins	
appl. nutrition	641
biochemistry *see* Biochemistry	
org. chem.	547
Protest groups	
pol. sci.	322
Protestant	
art	
rel. significance	246
converts	
rel. experience	248
Episcopal Church	283
Protestantism	
Christian churches	280
s.a. spec. denominations	
Protocols	
internat. law	341
Protons	
physics	539.7
Protoplasm	
cytology	574.8
animals	591.8
plants	581.8
Protozoa	
paleozoology	563
zoology	593
Protozoan diseases	
gen. med.	616.9
s.a. Medical protozoology	
Provençal language	
linguistics	449
literature	849
Provence	*area*–44

Proverbs	
folk lit.	398.9
Proverbs (O.T.)	
Bible	223
Providence	
island	*area*–694
of God	
rel. doctrines	
Christianity	231
nat. rel.	214
Prussia	***area*–43**
Psalms	
Bible	223
Psalteries	
musical art	787
Psalters	
liturgy	264
Pseudepigrapha	
Bible	229
Pseudonymous works	
bibliographies	014
spec. subj.	016
Pseudopsychology	131
Psychedelic drugs *see*	
Hallucinogenic drugs	
Psychiatric	
hospitals & sanitariums	
law	344.3
soc. services	362.2
soc. work	362.2
Psychiatry	
med. sci.	616.8
Psychical research	**133**
Psychoanalysis	
psychiatry	616.8
Psychoanalytic systems	
psychology	150.19
Psychodiagnoses	
clinical psych.	157
Psychokinesis	
parapsychology	133.8
Psycholinguistics	401
Psychological warfare	
activities	
internat. relations	327
s.a. spec. wars	
services	
armed forces	355.3
Psychology	**150**
appls. to spec. subj.	*s.s.*–019
of ed.	370.15
Psychoneuroses	
abnormal psych.	157
Psychoneurotic speech disorders	
gen. med.	616.8
psychology	157
Psychopathic personality	
gen. med.	616.8
psychology	157

Public (continued)
  streets
    land econ.   333.1
    other aspects see Roads
  structures
    architecture   725
    pub. works
      pub. admin.
        central govts.   351.8
        soc. services   363.5
  transportation
    automobiles
      commerce   388.34
      engineering   629.22
        maintenance & operation   629.28
  utilities
    law   343.9
    pub. admin.
      central govts.   351.8
      soc. services   363.6
    welfare work   361.6
      pub. admin.   351.8
  workers *see* Civil service
  works   363.5
    govt. control
      central govts.   351.8
    law   344.6
  worship
    Christianity   264
    comp. rel.   291.3
    Judaism   296.4
    nat. rel.   217
Public-address systems
  tech. & mf.   621.389
Publication
  civil right
    pol. sci.   323.44
Public-health offenses *see*
    Criminal offenses
Publicity
  technology   659.2
Publics
  sociology   301.18
Public-service workers *see* Civil
    service
Publishing   070.5
  library econ.   025.1
  museology   069
Puerperal diseases
  obstetrics   618.2
Puerto Rican literature   **860**
Puerto Rico   *area*–729 5
Pulleys
  mechanics   531
Pulmonary tuberculosis
  gen. med.   616.2
Pulp
  manufacturing   676

Pulsars
  astronomy
    description   523
    theory   521
Pulse
  circuits
    radio-wave electronics   621.381 5
  modulators
    electronic circuits
      radio-wave electronics   621.381 5
Pumpkins
  agriculture   635
Pumps
  engineering   621.6
  hydraulic-power tech.   621.2
Punched cards
  computer tech.   621.381 9
  electronic data proc. *see*
      Data processing
Punches (beverages) *see*
    Beverages
Punches (molds)
  tech. & mf.   621.9
Punching-tools
  tech. & mf.   621.9
Punctuation
  linguistics   **410**
  spec. langs.
    desc. & anal.   *lang. sub.*–1
    usage   *lang. sub.*–**8**
Punishments
  armed forces   355.1
  criminal law   345.7
  education   371.5
  penology   364.6
Puppetry
  performing arts   791.5
Puppets
  handicrafts   745.59
  mf. tech.   688.7
Purchasing *see* Procurement
Purgatory
  Christian doctrines   236
Purim
  customs   394.2
  Judaism   296.4
Puritanism
  Christian rel.   285
Purpose
  metaphysics *see* Teleology
Purses
  manufacturing   685
Pursuit
  forces
    air warfare   358.4
    police services   363.2
Pushball
  sports   796
Pushto *see* Pashto

Radiation	
devices	
mil. eng.	623.4
sicknesses	
gen. med.	616.9
injuries	617
therapy	615
Radiations	539.2
genetics	575.1
animals	591.1
man	573.2
plants	581.1
medicine	
effects *see* Radiation sicknesses	
therapeutic use	615
meteorology	551.5
particles *see* Particles (matter)	
physics	539.2
Radio	**384.5**
astronomy	522
broadcasting *see* Radio-communication	
communication *see* Radio-communication	
ed. use	371.33
eng. & mf.	621.384 1
military	623.7
nautical	623.82
manufacture *see* Radio eng. & mf.	
music	782.8
performing arts	791.44
ethics	175
sociology	301.16
work	
local Christian parishes	254.3
Radioactivity	
physics	539.7
Radiobroadcasting *see* Radio-communication	
Radiochemistry	541
applied	660.2
organic	547
Radiocommunication	**384.5**
govt. control	
central govts.	351.8
Radiocontrol	
engineering	621.384 1
Radiography	
engineering	621.36
Radioisotopes	
technology	621.48
Radiotelegraphy	
commerce	384.5
govt. control	
central govts.	351.8
technology	621.384 2
military	623.7
nautical	623.82

Radiotelephony	
commerce	384.5
govt. control	
central govts.	351.8
technology	621.384 5
military	623.7
nautical	623.82
Radio-wave electronics	
engineering	621.381 5
physics	537.5
Radishes	
agriculture	635
Radium	
therapy	615
other aspects see Metals	
Radon *see* Rare gases	
Raeto-Romanic *see* Rhaeto-Romanic	
Raffia	
agriculture	633
Rage	
psychology	152.4
Rail	
fastenings	
railroad eng.	625.1
transportation	
law	343.9
local	343.9
services	
gen. wks.	
commerce	385
govt. control	351.8
local systems	
commerce	388.4
govt. control	
central govts.	351.8
local govts.	352
Railroad cars	
engineering	625.2
transportation *see* Rail transportation	
Railroading	625.2
Railroads	
electrification	621.33
engineering	625.1
military	623.6
Rails	
metal prod. *see* Primary metal products	
railroad eng.	625.1
Railway *see* Railroad	
Rain	
meteorology	551.5
Raised characters	
printing	686.2
Raised-character books	
library trmt.	025.17
cataloging	025.3

Reaming-tools	
tech. & mf.	621.9
Reasoning	
depth psych.	154.2
ed. psych.	370.15
gen. psych.	153.4
logic	**160**
Rebellion *see* Criminal offenses	
Recall	
information theory	001.53
memory	
psychology	153.1
pol. sci.	324
Receiverships	
law	346.7
Recessions	
economics	338.5
Recidivists	
criminology	364.3
Recipes	
cookery	641.5
Recitation	
education	371.3
rhetoric	808.5
Recitations *see* Speeches	
Reclamation	
engineering	627
soil sci.	631.6
Recognition	
memory	
psychology	153.1
of states & govts.	
internat. law	341.26
Reconnaissance tactics	
mil. sci.	355.4
Reconstruction	
mil. sci.	355.02
U.S. hist.	973.8
World War 1 hist.	940.3
World War 2 hist.	940.53
Recorders (wind instrument)	
musical art	788
Recording	
accounting	657
museology	069
music	789.9
Recordings	
communication	001.54
commercial	384
ed. use	371.33
library trmt.	025.17
cataloging	025.3
music	789.9
tech. & mf.	621.389
Records	
communication	001.54
management	
office services	651.5
pub. admin.	351.7

Records (discs) *see* Recordings	
Recreation	**790**
buildings	
architecture	725
ethics	175
influence on crime	364.2
law	344.9
parochial work	
Christianity	259
Recreational	
arts	**790**
equipment	
manufacturing	688.7
facilities	
pub. works	363.5
institutions	
sociology	301.5
reading	
library sci.	028
services	
armed forces	355.3
libraries	025.5
museums	069
Rectors *see* Clergy	
Rectum	
diseases	
gen. med.	616.3
Red	
Cross	
nursing	610.73
soc. welfare	361.7
Sea *see* Indian Ocean	
Redeemer	
God	
Christian doctrines	231
Redemption	
Christian doctrines	234
Reducing	
personal care	646.7
Reductionism psych.	150.19
Reed	
instruments	
musical art	788
organs	
musical art	786.9
Refereeing *see spec. sports*	
Reference	
libraries public	**027.4**
services library econ.	025.5
sources library sci.	028.7
works	
bibliographies	011
spec. kinds	**012–016**
use	028.7
Referendum	
pol. sci.	328
Reflective thought	
psychology	153.4

Religions in society *see* Society
    soc. theology
Religious
  architecture *see* Religious-purpose
      buildings
  art *see* Religion art
      representation
  associations

Christianity	267
comp. rel.	291.6
Judaism	296.6

  attitudes
    doctrines *see* Doctrinal
      theology
    secular matters *see* Social
      theology
  beliefs *see* Doctrinal theology
  calendar *see* Church year

conditions	**200.9**

  conflict

sociology	301.6

  congregations

Buddhism	294.3
Christianity	255
church hist.	271
ecclesiology	262
comp. rel.	291.6

    s.a. Religious (members of
      orders)
  culture groups *see* Religious
      groups
  discipline *see* Religious law
  education *see* Religious
      instruction
  experience

Christianity	248
comp. rel.	291.4
Judaism	296.7

  freedom

civil right	323.44

  groups
    & state

pol. sci.	322
legal status	342.8
libraries for	027.6

  holidays *see* Holy days

institutions soc.	301.5

  instruction
    ecclesiastical theology

Christianity	268
comp. rel.	291.7
Judaism	296.6
gen. ed.	377
law	344.7

  law

Christianity	262.9
comp. rel.	291.8
Judaism	296.1

Religious (continued)
  liberty

civil right	323.44

  life *see* Religious (members
      of orders)
  minorities
    discrimination *see* Discrimi-
      natory practices

sociology	301.452

  music *see* Sacred music

mythology	200.4
Christianity	204
classical rel.	292
comp. rel.	291.1
Germanic rel.	293

  observances
    private *see* Private worship
    public *see* Public worship
  orders *see* Religious congregations
  practices
    personal *see* Personal religion
    private *see* Private worship
    public *see* Public worship
  qualifications

suffrage	324

  services (worship) *see* Public
      worship
  supremacy *see* Theocracy
  symbolism

art representation	704.948
painting	755

  training *see* Religious
      instruction
  wars
    history *see hist. of spec. places*
    religion

comp. rel.	291.7
Islam	297

  worship
    private *see* Private worship
    public *see* Public worship
Religious (members of orders)
  Christianity

meditations	242
personal rel.	248
prayers	242
retreats	269
sermons for	252
comp. rel.	291.6

  s.a. Religious congregations
Religious-purpose bldgs.

architecture	726
Christian rel. significance	246

Remains
  archeology *see* Archeology
Remedies

law	347.7
medicine	615

Resins		Retail	
eng. materials	620.1	cooperatives	
manufacturing	668	economics	334
org. chem.	547	credit	
Resistance		marketing management	658.8
elect. measurement	621.37	marketing	658.8
electrodynamics	537.6	Retaining walls	
Resistance-furnaces		structural eng.	624
elect. eng.	621.39	Retarded *see* Mentally deficient	
Resistant construction		Retirement	
buildings	693.8	armed forces	355.1
shipbuilding	623.82	employees	
Respiration		personnel admin.	658.31
physiology		pub. admin.	
biology	574.1	central govts.	351.1
animals	591.1	psychology	155.67
plants	581.1	sociology	301.43
med. sci.	612	*s.a.* Aged people	
Respiratory system		Retreats	
diseases		Christian practices	269
gen. med.	616.2	mil. tactics	355.4
tuberculosis	616.9	Retrieval of information	025.5
pulmonary	616.2	mechanized	029.7
Responsibility *see* Accountability		Réunion isl.	*area*–69
Responsive readings		Revelation (scriptures)	
Christian pub. worship	264	Bible	228
Rest		Revelation of God	
homes		Christian doctrines	231
soc. services	362.1	Revenue	
hygiene	613.7	law	343.3
periods		pub. finance	336
labor econ.	331.2	tariffs	
rooms *see* Comfort stations		internat. comm.	382.7
Restaurant buildings		Reveries	
architecture	725	psychology	154.3
Restaurants		Review	
cookery	641.5	study & teaching	*s.s.*–076
food services	642	Revivals	
Restitution		Christian rel. practices	269
law of war	341.6	Revolutionary groups	
Restoration		pol. sci.	322
Eng. hist.	942.06	Revolutions	
France hist.	944.06	sociology	301.6
of paintings	751.6	Revolvers *see* Pistols	
of sculpture	731.4	Revues	782.8
of wooden furniture	684.1	Rhaeto-Romanic languages	
Restraint of trade		linguistics	459
law		literatures	859
international	341.7	Rhenium *see* Metals	
municipal	343.7	**Rhetoric**	**808**
Restrictive influences		Rheumatic	
psychology	155.9	fever	
Resurrection		gen. med.	616.9
of dead		pediatrics	618.9
Christian doctrines	236	heart diseases	
of Jesus Christ	**232**	gen. med.	616.1
		Rheumatism	
		gen. med.	616.7

Romances *see* Fiction	
Romania	area–498
Romanian language	
linguistics	459
literature	859
Romans (scriptures)	
Bible	227
Romansh *see* Rhaeto-Romanic	
Romanticism	
philosophy	141
Romany language *see* Dard languages	
Rome Italy	area–45
ancient	area–37
Roofing	
bldg. construction	695
Roofs	
architectural	
construction	721
design & decoration	729
Roosevelt	
Franklin D. admin.	
U.S. hist.	973.917
Theodore admin.	
U.S. hist.	973.91
Root crops	
agriculture	633
Rope climbing	
sports	796.4
Ropes	
eng. materials	620.1
knotting & splicing	623.88
power transmission	
machine eng.	621.8
textiles *see* Textiles	
Rorschach tests	
indiv. psych.	155.2
Rosary	
private prayers	242
Roscommon Co. Ireland	area–417
Rose family	
botany	583
Roses Wars	
Eng. hist.	942.04
Rosh Hashanah	
customs	394.2
Judaism	296.4
Rosicrucian mysteries	
occultism	135.4
Ross & Cromarty Scot.	area–411
Rotary	
clubs	369.5
fans, blowers, pumps	
engineering	621.6
Rotation	
mechanics *see* Mechanics	
Rotational flow *see* Mechanics	
Rough carpentry	
bldg. construction	694
Roumania	area–498

Roumanian *see* Romanian	
Round-table discussions *see* Public	
discussions	
Routing & routes	
postal commun.	383
prod. management *see* Processes	
control	
transp. services	
commerce	380.5
air	387.7
bus	388.3
local	388.4
inland waterway	386
marine	387.5
rail	385
truck	388.3
local	388.4
govt. control	
central govts.	351.8
local govts.	352
Roxburgh Scot.	area–414
Royal	
houses	
genealogy	929.7
office Jesus Christ	
Christian doctrines	232
Royalty	
customs	**390**
sociology	301.44
Ruanda-Urundi	area–67
Rub' al Khali	area–53
Rubber	
agriculture	633
eng. materials	620.1
handicrafts	745.57
manufacturing	678
Rubella	616.9
Rubeola	616.9
Rubidium *see* Metals	
Rubies *see* Gems	
Rugby football	
sports	796.333
Rugs	
fabrics *see* Textiles	
int. dec.	747
textile arts	746.7
Rule of law	340.1
Rules of the road	
maritime law	
international	341.42
municipal	343.9
Rumania	area–498
Rumanian *see* Romanian	
Ruminants	
animal husbandry	636.2
Running	
sports	
horses	798
men	796.4

Sahara Desert	*area*–**66**
Saint	
Barthélemy isl.	*area*–729
Christopher isl.	*area*–729
Eustatius isl.	*area*–729
Helena isl.	*area*–97
Kitts isl.	*area*–729
Laurent	
Louis S. admin.	
Can. hist.	971.06
Lucia isl.	*area*–729
Martin isl.	*area*–729
Paul isl.	*area*–69
Pierre isl.	*area*–718
Vincent isl.	*area*–729
Saints	
art representation	704.948
Christian doctrines	235
Saipan	*area*–96
Sakhalin	*area*–57
Salad	
dressings	
cookery	641.8
processing	664
greens	
agriculture	635
Salads	
cookery	641.8
Salaries *see* Compensation	
Sales	
law	346.7
management	658.8
Salesmanship	658.85
Saline	
water conversion	
water-supply eng.	628.1
waters	553
extraction	622
Salts	553
chem. tech.	661
food mf.	664
metals *see* Metals	
Salvador	*area*–728 4
Salvadoran literature	**860**
Salvage operations	
maritime transp.	387.5
underwater eng.	627.7
Salvation	
Christian doctrines	234
Salvation Army	267
Samaritan language	
linguistics	492
literature	892
Samarium *see* Metals	
Samnium	*area*–37
Samoa	*area*–96
Samoyedic languages	
linguistics	494
literatures	894

Samuel	
Bible	222
San Marino principality	*area*–45
Sanatoriums *see* Sanitariums	
Sanctification	
Christian doctrines	234
Sanctions	
internat. law	341.5
Sandblasts	
pneumatic eng.	621.5
Sands	553
mining	622
Sandwiches	
cookery	641.8
Sanitarium bldgs.	
architecture	725
Sanitariums	
law	344.3
soc. services	362.1
govt. control	
central govts.	351.8
Sanitary engineering	**628**
military	623.7
Sanitation	
domestic customs	392
home econ.	648
law	344.4
plant management	658.2
pub. health	614.7
Sanskrit language	
linguistics	491
literature	891
Sapphires *see* Gems	
Saps	
forest prod.	
prod. tech.	634.9
Sarawak Malaysia	*area*–595
Sarcomas	
medicine	616.9
Sardinia	*area*–459
ancient	*area*–37
Sark	*area*–423
Saskatchewan	*area*–712 4
Sassanian Empire hist.	935
Satan	
Christian doctrines	235
Satanism	
occultism	133.4
Satellite communication	621.38
Satellites	
artificial *see* Artificial satellites	
astronomy	
description	523.9
theory	521
Satellites (states)	
internat. law	341.2

Sciences	**500**
& religion	
nat. rel.	**215**
appls. to spec. subj.	*s.s.*–01
documentation	029
govt. control	
central govts.	351.8
law	344.9
libraries	026
museums	
desc. & colls.	507.4
museology	069
sociology	301.2
social change	301.24
study & teaching	**507**
curriculums	375
elementary ed.	372.3
Scientific	
evidence	
law	347.6
criminal	345.6
recreations	793.8
relations	
internat. law	341.7
Scores (music)	780.8
library trmt.	025.17
cataloging	025.3
Scotland	*area*–41
Scottish	
Gaelic language	
linguistics	491.6
literature	891.6
Highlands	*area*–411
Scouring compounds	
chem. tech.	668
Scouting	
military	355.4
movement *see spec. kinds e.g.*	
Boy Scouts	
Scrap metals	669
Screens	
dec. arts	749
ecclesiastical furniture	
built-in arch. decoration	729
library bldgs.	022
museum bldgs.	069
Screw	
mechanics	531
Screw-cutting tools	
tech. & mf.	621.9
Screwdrivers	
tech. & mf.	621.9
Screws	
machine eng.	621.8
Scripture readings	
Christian pub. worship	264
Scriptures *see* Sacred books	
Sculptural schools & styles	732–735

Sculpture	**730**
Christian rel. significance	247
Sculpturing	
elementary ed.	372.5
Scurvy	
gen. med.	616.3
Scythia	*area*–39
Sea	
basins	
regional subj. trmt.	*area*–182
forces mil. sci.	**359**
warfare	359
waters	
internat. law	341.448
oceanography	551.460 1
Seafaring life	910.4
Sealants	
bldg. materials	691
eng. materials	620.1
manufacturing	668
Sealing (fastening) devices	
machine eng.	621.8
Sealing (hunting) industries	639
Seals (devices)	
genealogy	929.8
numismatics	737
Seamanship	623.88
Seaplanes *see* Aircraft	
Seaports	
commerce	387.1
govt. control	
central govts.	351.8
law	
international	341.42
municipal	343.9
Search	
& seizure	
crime detection	364.12
criminal law	345.5
of information	025.5
mechanized	029.7
Seas	
geomorphology	551.4
regional subj. trmt.	*area*–162–167
utilization	
economics	333.9
Seasickness	
gen. med.	616.9
Seasons	
earth astronomy	525
Seats	
ecclesiastical furniture	
built-in arch. decoration	729
Second International	
pol. sci.	329
Secondary	
consciousness	
psychology	154.3
education	**373**

Separation	
domestic	
ethics	173
law	346.1
of powers	
constitutional law	342.4
pub. admin.	351.04
Septicemia	
gen. med.	**616.9**
obstetrics	618.2
Sequential machines	
automation eng.	629.8
Serbia	*area*–497
Serbo-Croatian language	
linguistics	491.8
literature	891.8
Serfs	
sociology	301.44
Serials	
library trmt.	025.17
cataloging	025.3
publications	**050**
spec. subj.	*s.s.*–05
Serigraphy	
graphic arts	
processes	764
products	769
Sermons	
Christian worship	264
texts Christian	252
s.a. Preaching	
Serpents (reptiles) *see* Reptiles	
Serums	
pharmacology	615
Service	
clubs	369.5
marks	*s.s.*–02
of process	
law *see* Pretrial procedure	
law	
stations	
automobiles	629.28
Services	
religion *see* Public worship	
Serving	
table service	
home econ.	642
Servitudes	
law	
international	341.4
municipal	346.43
Servomechanisms	
automation eng.	629.8
Seven Years' War	
Europe hist.	940.2
Seventeenth century	
civilization	901.93
history	909.08

Seventh		
century		
civilization		901.92
history		909.07
Day		
Christian observance		263
Severance pay		
wage & salary admin. *see*		
Compensation personnel		
admin.		
Severnaya Zemlya RSFSR	*area*–98	
Sewage		
disposal *see* Wastes control &		
utilization		
pollution		
water-supply eng.		628.1
trmt. & disposal		
engineering		628
military		623.7
Sewerage eng.		628
Sewing		
elementary ed.		372.5
home econ.		646.2
clothing construction		646.4
Sex		612
cells *see* Gametogenesis		
customs		392
development		
life sci.		574.3
animals		591.3
plants		581.3
deviation *see* Sexual aberrations		
differentiation		
life sci.		574.3
animals		591.3
plants		581.3
hormones *see* Hormones		
human phys.		612
hygiene		613.9
manuals		301.41
offenses *see* Criminal offenses		
psychology		155.3
s.a. Sexual		
Sexes		
sociology		301.41
Sexual		
aberrations		
criminology *see* Criminal		
offenses		
gen. med.		616.8
psychology		157
sociology		301.41
behavior		
sociology		301.41
ethics		176
selection		
evolution		575
animals		591.3
plants		581.3
s.a. Sex		

Siege warfare	
mil. sci.	355.4
Sierra	
Leone	*area*–66
Nevada Calif.	*area*–794
Sign language	
manual alphabet	419
s.a. Nonverbal language	
Signals	
commun. eng.	621.38
other aspects see Nonverbal	
language	
Signets	
numismatics	737
Sikhism	
philosophy	181
religion	294.6
Sikkim	*area*–549
Silesia	*area*–438
Silhouettes	
drawing	741.7
photography	778.8
Silicon *see* Nonmetallic elements	
Silicones	
plastics *see* Plastics	
Silk textiles *see* Textiles	
Silk-screen printing	
graphic arts *see* Serigraphy	
Silkworms	
culture	638
Silver *see* Metals	
Silversmithing	
arts	739.2
mf. tech.	673
Silverware	
table setting	642
Silviculture	634.9
Simple machines	
mechanics	531
Sin	
Christian doctrines	233
s.a. Sins	
Sinai Peninsula	*area*–53
ancient	*area*–394 8
Sindhi language	
linguistics	491
literature	891
Singapore	*area*–595
Singhalese *see* Sinhalese	
Singing	
music *see* Vocal music	
pub. worship *see* Sacred music	
Christian religion	
Single-tax theory	
economics	330.15
Sinhalese language	
linguistics	491
literature	891
Sino-Japanese War	952.03

Sino-Tibetan languages	
linguistics	**495**
literature	**895**
Sins	
Christian moral theology	241
s.a. Sin	
Sinuses	
diseases	616.2
Sirenia *see* Mammals	
Sisterhoods *see* Religious	
congregations	
Sites	
library bldgs.	022
museum bldgs.	069
Six Days' War 1967	956
Sixteenth century	
civilization	901.93
history	909.08
Sixth century	
civilization	901.92
history	909.07
Size standards	
metrology	389
prod. management	658.5
Skates (footwear)	
mf. tech.	685
Skating	
sports	
ice	796.9
roller	796.2
Skeptic philosophy	
ancient	186
Skepticism	
nat. rel.	211
philosophy	149
Skiing	
sports	796.9
water	797.1
Skilled workers *see* Laboring	
classes	
Skin	
diseases	
surgery	617
personal care	646.7
Skin-diving	
sports	797.2
Skull	
diseases	
surgery	617
fractures	617
Skydiving	
sports	797.5
Skylights *see* Roofs	
Skyscrapers	
architecture	725
Slander	
criminology *see* Criminal offenses	
ethics	177
torts law	346.3

Social (continued)

law

international	341.7
municipal	**344**
maladjustments	**362**

organizations *see* Nonprofit
  organizations

pathology	**362**
planning	309.2
problems	362
psychology	**301.1**
reform	301.24

relations

ethics	177
sciences	**300**
security insurance	368.4
services	**360**
stratification	301.44–.45
structure	**301.4**

studies

elementary ed.	372.8

theology

Christianity	**261**
comp. rel.	291.1
Judaism	296.3

welfare *see* Welfare

Socialism

economics	**335**
pol. ideology	320.5

Socialist

communities econ.	335

Party

  U.S.

history	**973.9**
pol. sci.	329

other countries

history *see* hist. *of spec.*
  countries

pol. sci.	**329.9**

Socialization

sociology	301.15

Societies *see* Associations

Society

Islands	*area*–96
of Friends	289.6

soc. theology

Christianity	261.1
comp. rel.	291.1

s.a. Social

Socinianism	288

Socioeconomic problems

soc. theology

Christianity	261.8
comp. rel.	291.1
Sociology	**301**
Socotra	*area*–67
Socratic philosophy	183

Sodas

chem. tech.	661

Sodium *see* Metals

Sodomy *see* Sexual aberrations

Soft drinks *see* Beverages

Softball

sports	796.357
Sogdiana	*area*–39

Soil

biology	631.4

conditioners

production	668
use agric.	631.8

conservation

agriculture	631.4

improvement

agriculture	631.6–.8

pollution

pub. health	614.7
sanitary eng.	628.5
science	631.4

Soils

agriculture	631.4
eng. materials	620.1
foundation eng.	624
railroads	625.1
roads	625.7
regional subj. trmt.	*area*–14
Sokotra	*area*–67

Solar

cells & batteries

tech. & mf.	621.47
day	529

engines

tech. & mf.	621.47

furnaces

tech. & mf.	621.47

heating

buildings	697

houses

architecture	728.6

system

astronomy

description	523.2
theory	521
regional subj. trmt.	*area*–99

s.a. Sun

Solar-energy eng.	621.47

Soldiers

parochial work with

Christianity	259

s.a. Military

Solidification

effect of heat

physics	536
technology	621.5

Solids

chemistry	541
applied	**660**
eng. mech.	620.1

physics

mechanics	531
state of matter	530.41

Space (continued)	
forces	
mil. sci.	358
influences	
psychology	155.9
internat. law	341.4
medicine	616.9
photography	778.3
physiology *see* Bioastronautics	
probes astronautics	629.43
projectiles in	
solid dynamics	531
psychology	155.9
regional subj. trmt.	*area*–19
rights	
land econ.	333.3
sciences	500.5
stations astronautics	629.44
suits	
spacecraft eng.	629.47
transportation	
commerce	387.8
govt. control	
central govts.	351.8
law	
international	341.4
municipal	343.9
safety	
pub. health	614.8
utilization	
economics	333.9
warfare	
mil. sci.	358
Space (abstraction)	
metaphysics	114
nat. rel.	215
Space (area)	
chemistry *see* Stereochemistry	
heaters	
bldg. heating	697
Spacecraft	
engineering	
gen. wks.	629.47
unmanned	629.46
use	
manned flight	629.45
unmanned flight	629.43
influences	
psychology	155.9
Spaces	516
geometry	516
topology	514
Space-time *see* Relativity theories	
Spain	*area*–46
Spanish	
America	***area*–8**
American literature	**860**
Guinea	*area*–67

Spanish (continued)	
language	
linguistics	**460**
literature	**860**
Sahara	*area*–64
Succession War	
Europe hist.	940.2
West Africa	*area*–64
Spanish-American War	
U.S. hist.	973.8
Spanish-Moroccan War	
history	964
Spark-ignition engines	
tech. & mf.	621.43
land vehicles	629.2
marine vehicles	623.82
Sparta	
ancient	*area*–38
Spatial	
atomic arrangements	
theoretical chem.	541
organic	547
molecular arrangements *see*	
Stereochemistry	
perception	
psychology	
intellectual	153.7
visual	152.1
Speaking	
appl. ling.	418
spec. langs.	*lang. sub.*–83
communication	001.54
rhetoric	**808.5**
Speaking in tongues	
Christianity	
doctrines	234
rel. experience	248
Special	
education	371.9
libraries	026
buildings	
architecture	727
materials	
library trmt.	025.17
cataloging	025.3
services	
armed forces	355.3
Specific gravity *see* Mechanics	
Spectacles *see* Eyeglasses	
Spectral	
regions radiations	
chemistry	541
engineering	621.36
physics	535
Spectrography	621.36

Springs (water)	
geomorphology	551
Sprinting	
sports	796.4
Spur gears *see* Mechanics	
Spurious knowledge	001.9
Square books	
hist. & crit.	099
Squash	
sports	796.34
Squashes	
agriculture	635
Stabiles	
sculpture	**731**
Stabilized earth materials	
bldg. construction	693.2
Stadiums	
architecture	725
sports	796.4
Stafford Eng.	*area*–424
Staffs	
libraries	023
museums	069
Stage presentations *see* Theater	
Stained glass	
arts	748.5
Stammering *see* Psychoneurotic	
speech disorders	
Stamps	
engraved	
numismatics	737
postage *see* Postage stamps	
Standard	
of living	
macroeconomics	339.4
time	529
Standardization	
metrology	389
prod. management	658.5
Standards	
govt. control	
central govts.	351.8
law	343.7
Starch plants	
agriculture	633
Starches	
food	
processing	664
Stars	
astronomy	
description	523.8
theory	521
State	
departments	
U.S. govt.	353.1
s.a. Foreign affairs	
finance	
economics	**336**

State (continued)	
governments	
U.S.	**353.9**
other	**354**
libraries *see* Government libraries	
planning	
civic art	711
soc. sci.	309.2
socialism	
economics	335.5
Stateless persons	
internat. law	341.48
pol. sci.	323.6
States (political body)	
internat. law	341.26
pol. sci.	320.1
States of matter	
chemistry	541
applied	**660**
physics	**530.4**
mechanics	531–533
States of the Church	*area*–45
Statics *see* Mechanics	
Statistical	
mathematics	519.5
mechanics	530.1
method	001.4
spec. appls.	*s.s.*–01
theories	
physics	530.1
Statistics	**310**
mathematics	519.5
populations	312
other spec. subj.	*s.s.*–021
Statuary	
arts	**731**
Statute of limitations *see* Limitation	
of actions	
Statutes	
law	348
Steam	
engineering	621.1
generation	
electrodynamic eng.	621.312
heating	
buildings	697
locomotives	
commerce	385
engineering	625.2
pipes	
buildings	696
Steel *see* Metals	
Steeplechasing	
horses sports	798
Stenciling	
dec. arts	745.7
Stencils	
mech. printing tech.	686.2
Stenography	653

Surveys	
desc. research	001.4
land econ.	333.3
scientific	508.3
Survival	
hygiene	613
mil. sci.	355.5
Sussex Eng.	*area*–422
Sutherland Scot.	*area*–411
Suttee	
death customs	393
Svalbard	*area*–98
Swahili language	
linguistics	496
literature	896
Swamps	
drainage *see* Drainage	
Swans	
animal husbandry	636.6
Swanskin fabrics *see* Textiles	
Swaziland	*area*–68
Swearing	
soc. customs	394
Sweden	*area*–485
Swedenborgianism	289.4
Swedish language	
linguistics	439.7
literature	839.7
Sweeping	
housecleaning	648
streets	628
Sweet	
clovers	
agriculture	633
corn	
agriculture	635
other aspects see Vegetables	
potatoes	
agriculture	
field crops	633
garden crops	635
Swimming	
pools	
pub. health	614.7
safety	614.8
sports	797.2
Swindles *see* Criminal offenses	
Swine	
animal husbandry	636.4
Swing	
music	781.5
Swiss literature	
French	**840**
German	**830**
Italian	**850**
Switzerland	*area*–494
Syllogisms	
logic	166

Symbioses	
ecology *see* Synecology life sci.	
Symbolic	
divination	
parapsychology	133.3
logic	511
Symbolism	
art representation	704.94
Symbols	
art representation	704.94
rel. significance	
Christianity	246
Judaism	296.4
spec. subj.	*s.s.*–01
other aspects see Nonverbal language	
Symmetry	
arts *see* Composition (arts)	
Symphonies	
orchestra music	785.1
Symptomatology	
med. sci.	616.07
Synagogues	
Judaistic organizations	296.6
Synclines	
structural geol.	551.8
Syncretism	
philosophy	148
Syndicalism	
economics	335
Synecology	
life sci.	574.5
animals	591.5
plants	581.5
Synods	
Christian ecclesiology	262
Synonyms	**410**
spec. langs.	
nonstandard forms	*lang. sub.*–7
standard forms	
dictionaries	*lang. sub.*–3
usage	***lang. sub.*–8**
spec. subj.	*s.s.*–01
Synopses	*s.s.*–02
Syntax (linguistics) *see* Grammar (linguistics)	
Synthetic	
drugs	
pharmacology	615
fuels	
manufacturing	662
minerals	
manufacturing	666
organic chemicals	
chem. tech.	661
perfumes	
chem. tech.	668
poisons	
toxicology	615.9

Taxes (continued)			Telecommunication	
law	343.4		**commerce**	**384**
macroeconomics	339.5		govt. control	
pub. admin.			central govts.	351.8
central govts.	351.7		law	
pub. finance	336.2		international	341.7
Taxicabs *see* Automobiles			municipal	343.9
Taxidermy	579		**technology**	**621.38**
Taxonomic			Telecontrol	
botany	**582–589**		engineering	620
paleobotany	561		Telegraphy	
paleozoology	562–569		commerce	384.1
zoology	**592–599**		govt. control	
Taylor			central govts.	351.8
Zachary admin.			wire	
U.S. hist.	973.6		commun. eng.	621.382
Tea plant			military	623.7
agriculture	633		wireless *see* Radiotelegraphy	
Tea (beverage)			Telemetry	
comm. proc.	663		technology	621.37
hygiene	613.3		Teleology	
Tea (meal)			metaphysics	124
soc. customs	394.1		**nat. rel.**	**210**
Teachers & teaching	371.1		Telepathy	
govt. supervision	379		parapsychology	133.8
law	344.7		Telephones	
spec. subj.	**s.s.–07**		use in offices	651.7
elementary ed.	372.3–.8		Telephoning	
Teaching-machines			etiquette	395
education	371.39		Telephony	
Teaching-methods	**371.3**		commerce	384.6
Christian rel. instruction	268		govt. control	
special ed.	371.9		central govts.	351.8
Team teaching	371.1		wire	
Technetium *see* Metals			commun. eng.	621.385
Technical			military	623.7
assistance			nautical	623.82
internat. law	341.7		wireless *see* Radiotelephony	
chemistry	**660**		Telescopes	
drawing	· 604.2		astronomy	522
education *see* Vocational			mf. tech.	681
education			Teletype *see* Telegraphy	
forces			Television	384.55
land warfare	358		broadcasting *see* Television	
naval warfare	359.9		communication	
processes			cameras	
library econ.	025		engineering	621.388
Techniques	s.s.–028		communication	384.55
Technology	**600**		govt. control	
appls. to spec. subj.	s.s.–028		central govts.	351.8
documentation	029		drama *see* Drama	
libraries	026		ed. use	371.33
museums			**eng. & mf.**	**621.388**
desc. & colls.	607		military	623.7
museology	· 069		nautical	623.82
sociology	301.2		ethics	175
Teeth			manufacture *see* Television	
diseases			eng. & mf.	
dentistry	617.6		music	782.8
Telautography *see* Telegraphy				

Trousers *see* Clothing	
Troy ancient	area–392
Truancy	
law	344.7
Trucial States	area–53
Truck	
gardening	635
transportation	
commerce	388.3
local	388.4
govt. control	
central govts.	351.8
local govts.	352
law	343.9
Trucks	
commerce	388.34
engineering	629.22
maintenance & operation	629.28
Trudeau	
Pierre Elliott admin.	
Can. hist.	971.064 4
Truffles	
agriculture	635
Truk	area–96
Truman	
Harry S. admin.	
U.S. hist.	973.918
Trumpets	
musical art	788
Trunks (luggage)	
manufacturing	685
Trust	
companies	
banking	332.2
Ter. of the Pacific Isls.	area–96
Trustees	
libraries	021.8
universities & colleges	378.1
Trusteeships	
internat. law	341.2
Trusts (organizations)	
management	**658**
prod. econ.	338.8
Truth	
metaphysics	111.8
Truthfulness	
ethics	177
Tuamotu Isls.	area–96
Tubas	
musical art	788
Tube railroads *see* Underground	
railroads	
Tuber crops	
agriculture	633
Tuberculosis	
gen. med.	616.9
pulmonary	616.2
Tubes	
metal prod. *see* Primary metal	
products	

Tubing	
rubber	
manufacturing	678
Tubuai Isls.	area–96
Tudors	
Eng. hist.	942.05
Tularemia	
gen. med.	616.9
Tumbling	
sports	796.4
Tumors	
gen. med.	616.9
Tungsten *see* Metals	
Tungusic languages	
linguistics	494
literatures	894
Tunisia	area–61
Tunnels	
architecture	725
commerce	
highway transp.	388.1
rail transp.	385.3
structural eng.	624
military	623.6
underground mining	622
Tupper	
Charles admin.	
Can. hist.	971.05
Turbine steam engines	
stationary	
tech. & mf.	621.1
other kinds see Steam locomotives	
Turbines	
tech. & mf.	621.4
hydraulic power	621.2
Turbulent flow *see* Mechanics	
Turkestan	area–58
Turkey	area–561
Turkeys *see* Poultry	
Turkic languages	
linguistics	494
literatures	894
Turkish *see* Turkic	
Turkmenistan	area–58
Turning tools	
tech. & mf.	621.9
Turnips	
agriculture	
field crops	633
garden crops	635
Turpentines	
manufacturing	665
Tweeddale Scot.	area–414
Twelfth century	
civilization	901.92
history	909.07
Twentieth century	
civilization	901.94
history	909.82

United (continued)
  charities
    soc. welfare   361.8
  Church of Canada   287
  Church of Christ   285
  Evangelical Lutheran Church   284
  Kingdom   *area*–42
  Lutheran Church in America   284
  Methodist Church   287
  Nations (mil. alliance)
    World War 2 hist.   940.53
  Nations (world community)
    finance econ.   336
    internat. law   341.23
  Presbyterian Church   285
  States   *area*–73
    governments
      pub. admin.   **353**
Unity
  Christian church   262
  metaphysics   111.8
  School of Christianity   289.9
Universal
  gravitation *see* Celestial
    mechanics
  history   **909**
  joints
    machine eng.   621.8
  languages   401
  mil. training & service   355.2
Universalist Church   289.1
Universe
  astronomy
    description   523.1
    theory   521
  origin *see* Cosmogony
Universities & colleges   378.1
  spec. subj.   *s.s.*–07
University & college
  buildings
    architecture   727
  libraries   **027.7**
    buildings
      architecture   727
      functional planning   022
Unjust enrichment
  law   346.2
Unlawful assembly *see* Criminal
  offenses
Unmanned
  space flight
    technology   629.43
  spacecraft eng.
    technology   629.46
Unmarried mothers
  soc. services to   362.8
Unskilled workers
  labor econ.   331.7

Untouchables
  sociology   301.44
Upholstery *see* Furniture
Upper
  atmosphere
    meteorology   551.5
  Canada
    history   971.302
    s.a.   *area*–713
  extremities
    diseases & surgery   617
  Guinea   *area*–66
  Volta   *area*–66
Ural-Altaic languages
  linguistics   494
  literatures   894
Uranium *see* Metals
Urban
  areas
    civic art   711
    regional subj. trmt.   *area*–173
  communities
    sociology   301.34
  lands
    economics
      conservation & use   333.7
  transportation
    commerce   388.4
    govt. control
      central govts.   351.8
      local govts.   352
    law   343.9
  s.a. City
Urdu language
  linguistics   491
  literature   891
Uremia
  gen. med.   616.6
Urine
  diseases
    gen. med.   616.6
Urogenital system
  diseases
    gen. med.   616.6
Urology
  med. sci.   616.6
Uruguay   *area*–895
Uruguayan literature   **860**
Usury
  economics   332.8
Utah   *area*–792
Uterus
  diseases   618.1
Utilitarianism
  ethical systems   171
  philosophy   144

Veins	
diseases	
gen. med.	616.1
Vellum books	
hist. & crit.	096
Velocity	
of flow *see* Mechanics	
of light	
physics	535
of sound	
engineering	620.2
physics	534
Vending machines	
automation eng.	629.8
food services	642
retail marketing	658.8
Venereal diseases	
gen. med.	616.9
Venezuela	*area*–87
Venezuelan literature	**860**
Ventilation	
bldg. construction	697.9
library bldgs.	
relation to function	022
plant management	658.2
sewers	628
Ventilation-equipment	
household management	644
Ventriloquism	
recreation	793.8
Verbal communication	001.54
Verbs *see* Words	
Verdicts	
law	347.7
criminal	345.7
Vermiform appendix	
diseases	
surgery	617
Vermont	*area*–743
Verses *see* Poetry	
Versification *see* Prosody	
Vertebrates	
agric. pests	632
paleozoology	566
zoology	596
Vertical-lift aircraft *see* Aircraft	
Vessels (containers) *see* Containers	
Vessels (nautical)	
commerce	
gen. wks.	
inland-waterway	386
marine	387.2
govt. control	
central govts.	351.8
law	
international	341.42
municipal	343.9
engineering	623.82

Veterans	
benefits & rights	
mil. sci.	355.1
law	343.1
preference	
personnel admin.	
central govts.	351.1
Veterinary sciences	636.089
Vibrations	
solid dynamics	
engineering	620.3
physics	531
Vices	
ethics	
philosophy	179
religion	
Christianity	241
comp. rel.	291.5
Judaism	296.3
Victims of crime	
welfare services	362.8
Victoria	
queen reign	
Eng. hist.	942.081
state Australia	*area*–945
Vicuña wool *see* Textiles	
Vicuñas	
animal husbandry	636.2
Videotapes *see* Television	
Vietnam	*area*–597
Vietnamese	
language	
linguistics	495.9
literature	895.9
War	959.704
Village planning	
civic art	711
Villas	
architecture	728.8
Vines	
botany	582
floriculture	635.9
landscape design	715
Vinyls	
plastics *see* Plastics	
textiles *see* Textiles	
Violas	
musical art	787
Violence	
prevention	
pub. admin.	
central govts.	351.7
soc. services	363.3
sociology	301.6
Violent crimes *see* Criminal offenses	
Violins	
musical art	787
Violoncellos	
musical art	787

Voting	
pol. sci.	324
Vowels *see* Notations languages	
Voyages *see* Travel	
Vulgarisms *see* Slang	
Vulva	
diseases	618.1

W

Wages *see* Compensation	
Wagons	
manufacturing	688.6
Wake Isl.	*area*–96
Waldenses	
persecutions	
Christian church hist.	272
Waldensian churches	284
Waldensianism	
heresies	
Christian church hist.	273
Wales	*area*–429
Walking	
recreation	796.5
Walkways *see* Roads	
Wallpaper	
handicrafts	745.54
home econ.	645
mf. tech.	676
Walls	
of bldgs.	
architectural	
construction	721
design & decoration	729
cleaning	648
int. dec.	747
structures	
architecture	725
Walvis Bay South Africa	*area*–68
War	
crimes *see* Criminal offenses	
customs	399
dances	399
ethics	172
of 1812	
Canada hist.	971.03
U.S. hist.	973.5
of the Pacific	
history	983
powers	
legislative bodies	
pol. sci.	**328**
relief	
soc. welfare	361.5
risk insurance	368.1
risk life insurance	368.3
veterans *see* Veterans	
Warehouse bldgs.	
architecture	725

Warfare	
mil. sci.	355.02
technology	**623**
Warning systems	
civil defense	363.3
commun. services	384
Wars	
history	**900**
internat. law	341.6
mil. sci.	355.02
sociology	301.6
Warsaw Pact *see* Mutual defense	
& security	
Warships *see* Vessels (nautical)	
Warwick Eng.	*area*–424
Washing	
clothing	
home econ.	648
housecleaning	**648.5**
Washing-machines	
mf. tech.	683
Washington	
city D.C.	*area*–753
George admin.	
U.S. hist.	973.4
state	*area*–797
Wastes	
control & utilization	
prod. management	658.5
pub. health	614.7
technology	604.6
s.a. Refuse	
Watchcases	
art metalwork	739.3
Watches	
mf. tech.	681
time measurement	529
Watchworks	
mf. tech.	681
Water	553
appl. nutrition	641.1
bodies	
geomorphology	551.4
hydrodynamic eng.	627
chemistry	
inorganic	546
technology	661
conservation	
agriculture	631.7
consumption	
land econ.	333.9
diversion	
hydraulic eng.	627
econ. geol.	553
eng. materials	620.1
extraction	622
features	
landscape design	714

Welfare (continued)
economics   330.15
law   344.3
services
  gen. wks.
    methods   361
    penal institutions   365
    spec. groups   362
  govt. control
    central govts.   351.8
    local govts.   352
  law   344.3
state
  economics   330.12
Welsh language
  linguistics   491.6
  literature   891.6
Wendish language
  linguistics   491.8
  literature   891.8
Wesleyan Methodist Church   287
West
  Africa   *area*–66
  Indian literature
    English   810
    French   840
    Spanish   860
  Indies   *area*–729
  Irian   *area*–95
  Lothian Scot.   *area*–414
  Pakistan   *area*–549
  U.S.   *area*–78
  Virginia   *area*–754
West-Atlantic languages *see*
        African languages
Western
  Australia   *area*–941
  bloc
    regional subj. trmt.   *area*–171
  Europe   *area*–4
    ancient   *area*–36
  Hemisphere   *area*–181
    regional organizations internat.
    law   341.24
  states U.S.   *area*–78
Westland N.Z.   *area*–931 5
Westmeath Ireland   *area*–418
Westmorland Eng.   *area*–428
Wexford Co. Ireland   *area*–418
Whaling industries   639
Wheat
  agriculture   633
Wheel
  & axle
    mechanics   531
  games
    recreation   795

Whig Party
  U.S.
    history   973.5–.6
    pol. sci.   329.4
  other countries   329.9
Whiskies *see* Alcoholic beverages
Whist
  recreation   795.4
Whistling   784.9
White
  Russia   *area*–47
  Russian *see* Belorussian
  slave traffic *see* Criminal offenses
White-collar classes
  sociology   301.44
Whittling wood *see* Wood
        sculpture
Wholesale marketing
  management   658.8
Whooping cough
  gen. med.   616.2
Wickerwork plants
  agriculture   633
Wicklow Ireland   *area*–418
Widowed persons
  psychology   155.6
  sexual behavior   301.41
Wight Isle Eng.   *area*–422
Wigs
  manufacturing   679
  personal care   646.7
  soc. customs   391
Wigtown Scot.   *area*–414
Wildlife
  conservation tech.   639
  habitats & refuges
    land econ.   333.9
  reserves
    conservation tech.   639
    economics   333.9
    landscape design   719
Will
  psychology   153.8
William
  reign Eng. hist.
    1–2   942.02
    3   942.06
    4   942.07
Willow fibers
  agriculture   633
Wills
  genealogy   929
  law   346.5
Wilson
  Woodrow admin.
    U.S. hist.   973.91
Wiltshire Eng.   *area*–423
Winches
  machine eng.   621.8

Obsolescent Schedules

As noted at their respective points in the schedules, the developments for 340 Law and 510 Mathematics are completely new, tho built on the same base numbers as in the past. The obsolescent schedules that follow present the provisions of Abridged edition 9 for these two disciplines, but according to the editorial rules established for Edition 10. They do not supply any new provisions, and are printed here for the convenience of librarians and scholars who cannot immediately reclassify their collections. They will not appear in any later edition.

As noted in section 5.4 of the Introduction, classifiers are urged to reclassify their collections in law and mathematics according to the new phoenix schedules. So that this task may be somewhat simplified, the two obsolescent schedules are followed by tables of concordance showing the correct class numbers from Editions 9 and 10 for a substantial list of legal and mathematical topics.

340　Law

Principles and regulations emanating from government and applicable to the people, in the form of legislation, custom, policies recognized and kept in force by judicial decision

Including library laws, Sunday laws, wage laws, price control legislation, administrative law, correctional courts, school laws and regulations, legal status of woman, laws and regulations of public health, copyright, patents, trademarks, building laws and codes

If preferred, class law of a specific subject with the subject using "Standard Subdivisions" notation 026 from Table 1

341　International law (Law of nations)

Laws, procedures, institutions that govern public relations between sovereign states, private relations between their citizens, in peace and war; international cooperation and international responsibility of states

Including jurisdiction on land and sea, in air and space

.1　Cooperation to promote peace and order

For pacific settlement of disputes, see 341.6

[.106]　Organizations

Do not use; class specific organizations in 341.12–341.18

▶   341.12–341.18 Specific organizations

Class comprehensive works in 341.1

.12	League of Nations
.13	United Nations
.132	Charter
.133	General Assembly and general committees
.135	Security Council and its committees
.137	Secretariat

         Executive office, departments, personnel

.139	Relationship to specific countries and regions

         Add "Areas" notation 1–9 from Table 2 to base number 341.139

.18	Regional associations
.2	Treaties

         Process of treaty making, texts of treaties

.3	Law of war

         Law of land, sea, air warfare

.4	Criminal law

         Including law of extraterritorial crime, trials of war criminals

         For extraterritoriality, see 341.7

.5	Special topics

         Including commercial law, law of outer space, private international law

         For law of war, see 341.3

.6	Pacific settlement of disputes

         Negotiation, good offices, conciliation and commissions of inquiry, outlawry of war, arbitration and mediation, compulsive measures short of war; armaments reduction, limitation, control

.7	Diplomacy

         Laws, rules, customs governing conduct of official relations between governments

         Including capitulations, extraterritoriality, diplomatic privileges and immunities, protocol

.8	Consular systems

▶ ## 342–349 Municipal (Internal) law

Class comprehensive works in 340

342 ## Constitutional law

Fundamental law of states

Add "Areas" notation 1–9 from Table 2 to base number 342

343 ## Criminal law

Including punishments, specific kinds of offenses

.09 ### Historical and geographical treatment

Class here penal codes, reports, procedure, trials, evidence, handbooks and outlines

Add "Areas" notation 1–9 from Table 2 to base number 343.09

344 ## Martial law

Military authority to carry on government functions in times of war or emergency

▶ ## 345–346 United States and British statutes and cases

Session laws and statutes at large, codes and revised statutes, law digests, reports, digests of cases

If preferred, class in 349

345 ## United States

346 ## British

United Kingdom and all parts of Commonwealth

347 ## Private law and judicial system

Including common law, law of persons, property, equity (chancery)

.01–.09 ### Standard subdivisions of private law

▶ ## 347.4–347.7 Private law

Class comprehensive works in 347

.4 ### Contract and quasi contract

.5 ### Tort, negligence, damage

.6 ### Domestic relations and succession

.7 ### Commercial law

Including agency law, maritime law

.9   Judicial systems

Procedure, trials, rules

Class criminal system in 343, administrative system in 340

.909   Historical and geographical treatment

Class historical and geographical treatment of courts in 347.99

.99   Historical and geographical treatment of courts

Organization, jurisdiction, history, procedure, trials, rules

Class here specific courts and court systems

Add "Areas" notation 1–9 from Table 2 to base number 347.99

349   Statutes and cases other than United States and British

(It is optional to class here United States and British statutes and cases; prefer 345–346)

Add "Areas" notation 1–9 from Table 2 to base number 349

510   Mathematics

Use 510.01–510.09 for standard subdivisions

.78   Computation instruments and machines

Mathematical principles of mechanical, electromechanical, electronic calculating devices

Including analog instruments and digital machines

511   Arithmetic

.02   Miscellany

Class business arithmetic in 511.8

.021   Tabulated and related materials

Class tables in 511.9

.07   Study and teaching

.076   Review and exercise

Class problems in 511.9

.8   Business arithmetic

Including mensuration, mercantile rules, calculation of interest

.9   Problems and tables

512   Algebra

.021   Tabulated and related materials

Class tables in 512.9

.076   Review and exercise

Class problems in 512.9

.9   Problems and tables

513–516 Geometries

Class comprehensive works in 513

513   **Synthetic geometry**

      Class here comprehensive works on geometries

       For trigonometry, see 514; *descriptive geometry,* 515; *analytic (coordinate) geometry,* 516

.076   Review and exercise

       Class problems in 513.9

.9   Problems

514   **Trigonometry**

.076   Review and exercise

       Class problems in 514.9

.9   Problems

515   **Descriptive geometry**

516   **Analytic (Coordinate) geometry**

.076   Review and exercise

       Class problems in 516.9

.9   Problems

517   **Calculus**

.076   Review and exercise

       Class problems in 517.9

.9   Problems

519   **Probabilities and statistical calculations**

Tables of Concordance

Law

	Edition 9	*Edition 10*
Agency	347.7	346.2
Air warfare	341.3	341.6
Appellate procedure	347.9	347.8
Arbitration (internat. law)	341.6	341.5
Bail	343.09	345.7
Chancery	347	347
Civil war (internat. law)	341.3	341.6
Codes	345–346, 349	348
Commercial law		
international	341.5	341.7
municipal	347.7	346.7
Common law	347	340.5
Conflict of laws (domestic)	342	342.4
Conflict of laws (internat. law)	341.5	340.9
Constitutional law	342	342
Consular systems	341.8	341.3
Contract	347.4	346.2
Court rules		
civil	347.9	347.5
criminal	343.09	345.5
Criminal jurisdiction (internat. law)	341.4	341.48
Criminal law		
international	341.4	341.77
municipal	343	345
Criminal procedure	343.09	345.5–345.8
Damage	347.5	346.3
Digests of laws and cases	345–346, 349	348
Diplomacy	341.7	341.3
Disarmament	341.6	341.73
Domestic relations	347.6	346.1
Equity	347	340.5
procedure in equity	347.9	347
Evidence		
civil procedure	347.9	347.6
criminal procedure	343.09	345.6
Extradition (internat. law)	341.4	341.48

	Edition 9	Edition 10
Forms	347.9	347.5
Inheritance	347.6	346.5
International law	341	341
Judicial system	347.9	347.1
Jurisdiction of courts	347.99	347.1
League of Nations	341.12	341.22
Maritime law		
international	341.5	341.42
municipal	347.7	343.9
Martial law	344	342.6
Mediation (internat. law)	341.6	341.5
Municipal law	342–349	342–348
Negligence	347.5	346.3
Neutrality	341.3	341.6
Occupation (internat. law)	341.3	341.6
Offenses (criminal law)	343	345
Peaceful settlement of disputes		
(internat. law)	341.6	341.5
Personal property	347	346.47
Persons	347	346
Prisoners of war	341.3	341.6
Private law	347	346
Probate law	347.6	346.5
Procedure		
civil	347.9	347.5–.8
criminal	343.09	345.5–.8
Punishments	343	345.7
Quasi contract	347.4	346.2
Real property	347	346.43
Regional associations (internat. law)	341.18	341.24
Reports of cases	345–346, 349	348
Roman codes of law	349.37	348
Sale	347.4	346.7
Sanctions	341.6	341.5
Sea warfare	341.3	341.6
Space law (internat. law)	341.5	341.4
law of war	341.5	341.6
Statutes & cases	345–346, 349	348
Succession	347.6	346.5
Torts	347.5	346.3
Treaties	341.2	341.3
peace treaties	341.2	341.6
source of law	341.2	341.1
texts	341.2	341

	Edition 9	*Edition 10*
Trials		
civil	347.9	347.7
criminal	343.09	345.7
United Nations	341.13	341.23
War, law of	341.3	341.6
War criminals (internat. law)	341.4	341.6

Mathematics

	Edition 9	*Edition 10*
Abstract algebra	512	512
Algebraic geometry	516	516
Algebraic operations	512	512.9
Analysis (Calculus)	517	515
Analytic geometry	516	516
Arithmetic	511	513
Boolean algebra	512	511
Business arithmetic	511.8	513
Calculus	517	515
Computer mathematics	517	519.4
Decision theory (Statistics)	519	519.5
Descriptive geometry (Mathematical)	515	516
Determinants	512	512.9
Equation theory (Algebra)	512	512.9
Euclidean geometry	513	516
Functional analysis	517	515
Game theory	512	519.3
Geometries	513–516	516
Graph theory	510	511
Groups	512	512
Linear algebras	512	512.5
Logarithms (Algebra)	512	512.9
Logarithms (Arithmetic)	511	513
Matrices	512	512.9
Non-Euclidean geometries	513	516
Number theory	512	512
Numeration systems	511	513
Numerical analysis	517	511
applied	517	519.4
Permutations (Algebra)	512	512.9
Permutations (Arithmetic)	511	513
Probabilities	519	519.2
Programing	519	519.7

	Edition 9	*Edition 10*
Progressions (Algebra)	512	512.9
Progressions (Arithmetic)	511	513
Projective geometry	516	516
Quality control	519	519.8
Queuing	519	519.8
Rings (Algebra)	512	512
Sequences	517	515
Series	517	515
Sets	512	511
Statistical mathematics	519	519.5
Stochastic processes	519	519.2
Tensor algebra	512	512.5
Tensor analysis	516	515 .
Topology	513	514
Trigonometry	514	516
Vector algebra	512	512
Vector analysis	516	515